Proof of
Vedic Culture's
Global Existence

By
Stephen Knapp

Find out more about
The World Relief Network
Stephen Knapp and his books at:
http://www.Stephen-Knapp.com

Dedicated to all who are searching
for the real answers to
historical and spiritual truth

Cover photo: The great temple of Lord Dwarakadish (Krishna) at Dwaraka, India. This holy site dates back at least 5,000 years. Much of the present temple, as seen here, was built in the 16th century, but parts of the sanctuary walls date back to the 12th century. However, the main sanctum is said to date back at least 2500 years or earlier. This is an example of how the Vedic culture is the oldest living tradition in the world today. Photo taken by Stephen Knapp.

ISBN: 0-9617410-6-6
Library of Congress Catalogue Card Number: 98-061104

PUBLISHED BY

PROVIDING KNOWLEDGE
OF
REALITY DISTINGUISHED FROM ILLUSION
FOR THE WELFARE OF ALL

The World Relief Network
P. O. Box 15082
Detroit, MI 48215
U.S.A.

Other books by the author:
  The Secret Teachings of the Vedas
  The Universal Path to Enlightenment
  The Vedic Prophecies: A New Look into the Future
  Toward World Peace: Seeing the Unity Between Us All
  Facing Death: Welcoming the Afterlife
  How the Universe was Created and Our Purpose In It

Contents

PREFACE

History is like a puzzle, when you put enough pieces together it provides a key to unlocking the truth of our past, where we came from, and who and what we really are. The main purpose of this book is to help restore world unity by taking another look at global history. It will provide proof that the world once had a single culture that expanded and diffused from a particular region. As we uncover ancient history, we find that we often have to re-evaluate theories that were once, or still are, accepted to be factual. When we find out-of-the-mainstream information that provides contradictory evidence for what many people think to be true, we have to think again about what has really happened in this world and where we really stand, and what is the reality and purpose of this planet.

This book provides some amazing if not startling historical evidence that reveals the prominence of the age old Vedic culture. It is not an attempt simply to glorify one culture over another, nor is it merely a chore in academic research. It is an honest attempt to allow humanity to understand its real roots, before the world came to be so divided by factions and divisions. This historical evidence provides a means by which the world and its leaders can find a way back to the peaceful unity that can exist in the pristine way of Vedic life, which is meant for the peaceful coexistence and spiritual progress of everyone.

What we will be doing in this volume is looking at the origin of the world through the ancient Sanskrit language and literature, and the culture that came from it, and the reasoning that numerous scholars have presented. Why? Because abundant evidence of Vedic culture and the Sanskrit language exists all over the world, which proves its once global influence and pervasiveness. In light of this, then no matter whether we are presently Christians, Muslims, Jews, or whatever, our ancient forefathers were once members of a global Vedic brotherhood, all speaking Sanskrit. People have forgotten their common Vedic heritage, which was originally established by the Supreme Being after the creation of the cosmos. Therefore, the divisions of the world divided by language or scripture, and sects of Muslims against Christians, or Arabs against Jews, is a great tragedy of the world. It is only due to a lack of historical understanding and the forgetfulness of our great past. This is what we are going to uncover in this volume.

Rather than trying to manipulate or misuse history to promote divisiveness and mutual animosity, true history can promote better social relations. This volume will show how the deliberate manipulation and misinterpretation of history has caused humanity to not only forget its Vedic roots, but also how some cultures and religions have destroyed historical evidence to attempt to establish its own false superiority.

Any religion should be established on Universal Spiritual Truths. A Universal Truth is applicable in any religion, in any culture, in any time in history. Unfortunately, many religions and their histories have been manipulated in a way to help establish their own superiority over all others. Thus, they have become polluted with stories that are not factual, and sayings not always based on Universal Truths. Thus, they are not religions that can bring humanity to the highest levels of spiritual understanding because they cannot deliver unadulterated spiritual knowledge, or Universal Truth. This is why we will study the oldest living culture in the world, the Vedic Aryan culture, the roots of which can be found in many areas of this planet, but are still practiced in India and wherever groups of sincere followers exist.

The importance of studying the ancient Vedic culture is explained by many scholars. For example, in his *Discourse on Sanskrit and Its Literature*, given at the College of France, Professor Bournouf states, "We will study India with its philosophy and its myths, its literature, its laws and its language. Nay it is more than India, it is a page of the origin of the world that we will attempt to decipher."

In *History of Ancient Sanskrit Literature* (page 557), Max Mueller observed, "In the *Rig-veda* we shall have before us more real antiquity than in all the inscriptions of Egypt or Ninevah. . . the *Veda* is the oldest book in existence. . ."

In the same book (page 63) Max Mueller also noted, "The *Veda* has a two-fold interest: It belongs to the history of the world and to the history of India. In the history of the world the *Veda* fills a gap which no literary work in any other language could fill. It carries us back to times of which we have no records anywhere."

Max Mueller further remarked in his *India--What It Can Teach Us* (Page 21), "Historical records (of the Hindus) extend in some respects so far beyond all records and have been preserved to us in such perfect and legible documents, that we can learn from them lessons which we can learn nowhere else and supply missing links."

In this same line of thinking, Mr. Thornton, in his book *History of British India*, observed, "The Hindus are indisputably entitled to rank among the most ancient of existing nations, as well as among those most early and most rapidly civilized. . . ere yet the Pyramids looked down upon the Valley of the Nile. . . when Greece and Italy, these cradles of modern civilization, housed only the tenants of the wilderness, India was the seat of wealth and grandeur."

The well-known German philosopher Augustus Schlegel in his book, *Wisdom of the Ancient Indians*, noted in regard to the divine origin of Vedic civilization, "It cannot be denied that the early Indians possessed a knowledge of the God. All their writings are replete with sentiments and expressions, noble, clear, severely grand, as deeply conceived in any human language in which men have spoken of their God. . ."

On a more personal note, another famous German thinker, Schopenhaur, remarked in his book, *The Upanishads, Introduction* (page 61): "In the whole world there is no study so beneficial and so elevating as that of the *Upanishads*. It has been the solace of my life (and) it will be the solace of my death."

The famous English woman philosopher Dr. Annie Besant also had much praise for India, as written in the cover notes from the book, *Hindus, Life-Line of India*, by G. M. Jagtiani. Her words put great emphasis on the value of India, its history, the Vedic culture, and its importance to the world. She says: "After a study of some forty years and more of the great religions of the world, I find none so perfect, none so scientific, none so philosophic, and none so spiritual as the great religion known by the name of Hinduism. The more you know it, the more you will love it; the more you try to understand it, the more deeply you will value it. Make no mistake; without Hinduism, India has no future. Hinduism is the soil into which India's roots are struck, and torn of that she will inevitably wither, as a tree torn out from its place. Many are the religions and many are the races flourishing in India, but none of them stretches back into the far dawn of her past, nor are they necessary for her endurance as a nation. Everyone might pass away as they came and India would still remain. But let Hinduism vanish and what is she? A geographical expression of the past, a dim memory of a perished glory, her literature, her art, her monuments, all have Hindudom written across them. And if Hindus do not maintain Hinduism, who shall save it? If India's own children do not cling to her faith, who shall guard it? India alone can save India, and India and Hinduism are one."

All of these quotations show the value that great thinkers have placed on India and its Vedic Aryan culture. The Vedic culture, as well as the ancient history of the world, is preserved in the Vedic Sanskrit literature. This does not mean the *Samhitas* of the *Vedas* alone, such as the *Rig*, *Sama*, *Atharva* and *Yajur Vedas*, but it means all literature that contains and upholds the Vedic tradition and culture, which includes the *Upanishads*, the *Puranas*, the *Ramayana*, the *Mahabharata*, and the *Bhagavad-gita*. These contain the mysteries of the origin of the world and its ancient history.

It does not matter whether everyone is fully convinced of what we present here, but the overall evidence is hard to deny. The object is that by seeing our commonalities we may help to widely open the doors for further understanding and our peaceful coexistence. From that point, what we do with this information is up to us. We can work in cooperation and work out our differences. Or we can act like none of this information has any bearing on us today and live in the illusion that whatever history we uncover from 2500 years ago and beyond has no meaning. Then not only will we continue with our superficial differences, but more of such variations and factions will spring up. Most of these are a modern creation in the sense that they have only come about within the past 1400, 2000, and 2500 years with the advent of the Muslim, Christian, or Buddhist religions. This will only bring more discord and dis-harmony between us in this world. Is that what we want? I don't think so. So let us be serious about looking at our common cultural heritage as explained in the pages that follow.

THIS BOOK IS GREAT FOOD FOR THOUGHT
AT THE VERY LEAST

In writing this volume, a few of the chapters in this book are based on the research that I have done over the years and presented in a couple of my previous books, but herein they have been greatly expanded with much new and different information which adds to the presentation. I did this in order to make this book as complete as possible for covering this particular subject.

A great number of books were researched to present the information in this volume. One book that provided great assistance is *World-Wide Hindu Culture and Vaishnava Bhakti*, by Dr. S. Venu Gopalacharya. I use quotes from his book in several chapters. I also thank him for the great research he has done in this field, as well as for giving me permission to quote from his work.

I would also like to thank Mr. Purushottam Nagesh Oak for giving me permission to quote from his research. I have referred to the portions of his work that fits into the premise of this book and is worth considering, and what concurs with the previous research that I have done. He has investigated this topic for many years, and has allowed me to gather and summarize some of the most important points and evidence found in his books, which include *World Vedic Heritage, Some Blunders of Indian Historical Research*, and *Some Missing Chapters of World History*.

At the very least, all of the many quotes from scholars and researchers on this topic provides for some great food for thought, whether it is fully accepted by others or not. It is natural that various scholars and the readers of this book may have different opinions and will arrive at various conclusions, but the research that is presented herein can certainly add to the appreciation into the insights of others.

Furthermore, when numerous authorities and investigators draw similar conclusions, the more weight these concurring opinions carry. When enough scholars and researchers agree on the ancient and modern evidence that points to the widespread connection with the Vedic culture, then it is hard simply to sweep it away without proper consideration. So I do not say that all of the information in this book should be taken without question, but all of the corroborating findings by the various scholars and great thinkers that are mentioned in this book provide for some fairly strong evidence, if not outright proof, of the consistency in the conclusions. The outcome being that Vedic culture in India was once a global influence and the prime source of advanced, organized, and civilized society.

We should not forget that this topic of the Vedic Aryans and its culture is an ongoing study that will continue for many generations to come. So the conclusions will also continue to be adjusted as newer forms of evidence are uncovered. As more evidence comes forth, it will only further prove what we are presenting.

This volume is a beginning and a primer for those interested in understanding the real history of the world before the practice of manipulating historical facts by some of the more modern religions became in vogue. No one should be afraid to look at the real original culture that inhabited the planet thousands of years ago. I am sure many people would like to know this information, but many people may also be fearful of it if it contradicts what they have believed for much of their life. However, changes in our understanding of history are happening all the time, whether we like it or not. Not only is it being discovered that civilized man lived many thousands of years earlier than we once thought, but also society was much more advanced than we knew. It may not have been such a dark and evil or godless civilization thousands of years ago before it was "saved" by Christianity or Islam, as some people like to believe. It may have been far more organized and peaceful, with a much more insightful means of knowing who we are and what is God than many of us care to admit. It is time to push aside whatever prejudices we may have and get to the core of the truth. As we proceed we will recognize the fact that our present society is certainly not the apex of civilization.

ABOUT THE NAME "HINDU"

Before we get started, I did want to say something about the use of the words "Hindu" and "Hinduism." The fact is that true "Hinduism" is based on Vedic knowledge, which is related to our spiritual identity. Such an identity is beyond any temporary names as Christian, Muslim, Buddhist, or even Hindu. After all, God never describes Himself as belonging to any such category, saying that He is only a Christian God, or a Muslim God, or a Hindu God. That is why some of the greatest spiritual masters from India have avoided identifying themselves only as Hindus. The Vedic path is eternal, and therefore beyond all such temporary designations. So am I calling the name "Hindu" a temporary designation?

We must remember that the term "hindu" is not even Sanskrit. It is not found in any of the Vedic literature. So how can such a name truly represent the Vedic path or culture? And without the Vedic literature, there is no basis for "Hinduism." We must also remember that the name "hindu" was first developed by the invading Muslims from such places as Afghanistan and Persia. The name was used to describe the inhabitants from the tract of land in the northwestern provinces of India where the Sindhu River (the modern Indus) is located. Because the Sanskrit sound of "S" converts to "H" in the Parsee language, the Muslims pronounced the Sindhu as "hindu," even though the people of the area did not use the name "hindu" themselves. This word was used by foreigners to identify the people and the religion of those who lived in that area. Otherwise, the word has no meaning except for those who use it out of convenience. This is what the British did with the effect of focusing on the differences between the Muslims and the people who became known as "Hindus." This was done with the rather successful intention of creating friction among the people of India. This was in accord with their divide and rule policy to make it easier for their continued dominion over the country.

Therefore, the name "hindu" started simply as a bodily and regional designation. It is merely a continuation of a Muslim term that originated only within the last 1300 years. In this way, we can understand that it is not a valid Sanskrit term, nor does it have anything to do with the Vedic culture or the Vedic spiritual path.

Unfortunately, the word "hindu" was gradually adopted by everyone, even the Indians, and is presently applied in a very general way, so much so, in fact, that now "Hinduism" is often used to describe anything from religious activities to even Indian social or nationalistic events. Some of these so-called "Hindu" events are not endorsed in the Vedic literature, and, therefore, must be considered non-Vedic. Thus, not just anyone can call themselves a "Hindu" and still be considered a follower of the Vedic path.

The Vedic spiritual path is called *sanatana-dharma*, which means the eternal, unchanging occupation of the soul in its relation to the Supreme Being. Following the principles of *sanatana-dharma* can bring us to the pure state of regaining our forgotten relationship with the Supreme Lord. This is the goal of Vedic knowledge. Thus, the knowledge of the *Vedas* and all Vedic literature, such as Lord Krishna's message in *Bhagavad-gita*, as well as the teachings of the *Upanishads* and *Puranas*, are not limited to only "Hindus," but are actually meant for the whole world. It is also the fully developed spiritual philosophy that fills whatever gaps may be left by the teachings of other less philosophically developed religions. Direct knowledge of the soul is a "universal spiritual truth" which can be applied by all people, in any part of the world, in any time in history, and in any religion. It is eternal. Therefore, being an eternal spiritual truth, it is beyond all time and worldly designations. Knowledge of the soul is the essence of Vedic wisdom and is more than what the name "Hindu" implies, especially after understanding from where the name comes. Even if the time arrives in this deteriorating age of Kali-yuga after many millennia when Christianity, Islam, Buddhism, and even Hinduism (as we call it today) may disappear from the face of the earth, there will still be the Vedic teachings that remain as a spiritual and universal truth, even if such truths may be forgotten and must be re-established again in this world by Lord Krishna Himself. I doubt then that He will use the name "Hindu." He certainly said nothing of the sort when He last spoke *Bhagavad-gita*.

Thus, although I do not feel that "Hindu" is a proper term to represent the Vedic Aryan culture or spiritual path, I do use the word from time to time in this book to mean the same thing since it is already so much a part of everyone's vocabulary.

INTRODUCTION

WHAT IS THE VEDIC ARYAN CULTURE?

It is often considered that the Vedic Aryans are a race of people. *Aryan* actually means a standard of living, an ideal. It was the Sanskrit speaking people of thousands of years ago that gave the word *arya* to signify a gentleman, an ideal person, someone on the path of purity. It was a term meant for those who were on the cutting edge of social evolution. Another way of interpreting the word *aryan* is that *ar* also means white or clear. *Ya* refers to God. *Ya* also refers to Yadu, or Krishna. Thus, *aryan* means those who have, or are developing, a clear path or a clear consciousness toward God.

In this way, we can understand that Aryanism, or Vedic culture, is a way of life. It is not a race of people or a sectarian creed or religion. It belongs to no particular country or race. It is a path that upholds a code of conduct which values peace and happiness and justice for all. Thus, it is a path open for all who want to be trained to be happy with simple living and high thinking, while engaged in proper conduct, a moral life, and selfless service to humanity. Therefore, anyone who wants to live in such a manner may be called an Aryan, a member of the Vedic culture, no matter from which race or country a person may come.

So what does it mean to follow this Vedic Aryan path? It generally means to learn the ways of a spiritually progressed person. This includes understanding one's spiritual identity, knowing that he or she is not the body but is spirit soul, that there is *karma* for one's actions, and rebirth in another life after death. Thus, everyone will automatically reap the reward or punishment for his own good or evil thoughts, words, and deeds. By having a solid understanding of such spiritual knowledge, there is automatically a respect for all others regardless of race, sex, or species. This brings a moral and peaceful social behavior in everybody toward everyone. By having respect for everyone's spiritual identity, this also brings an innate happiness in us all. We can understand that we are only visiting this planet for a short time, and that we are all in this together. In other words, my contribution to your well-being, especially spiritual well-being, will be an automatic contribution to my own existence. In this way, society at large is in a state of constant improvement. That is the goal of the Vedic Aryan way of life.

1

Not everyone, however, wants to reach this stage of life or follow this path. That is why the Vedic system installs rules for moral behavior and regulatory sacraments and practices beginning from the prenatal stage all the way through death. Of course, many of these moralistic rules are also quite common in other forms of religion and behavior. However, anybody who is unwilling to follow such rules for a balanced moral standard is dubbed a non-Aryan. Such a person is not on the spiritual path of life, regardless of what other standards or principles of etiquette he may follow. So a person who lacks spiritual tendencies and acts on the bodily platform of life, willing to do whatever he likes, or who thinks he is a white body, or a black body, or from this country or that, and who holds loyalty only to that conception and shows it by criticizing everyone who is not like him, is a non-Aryan. He may hold love for his family and those who are like him, but makes no elevating contribution to the rest of society. Furthermore, he often instills into his children the same prejudice that he carries, thus perpetuating this view and the misunderstandings of life that he has. In this way, we can see the need to return to the Vedic standards of life through authentic spiritual education.

Therefore, the Sanskrit word *Aryan* means a way of life that aims at the elevation of everyone in society to a higher level of consciousness. It means to assist ourselves through a disciplined and godly life to understand the purpose of our existence as well as to become a spiritually realized person. It also means that we help every other individual soul because by helping others we help ourselves. That itself is a natural state of being when we can perceive God as the Supersoul, Paramatma, within everyone. All of this is encouraged by, and increases, a natural faith in an all-pervading Supreme Being. Such faith and focus on the Supreme Being can elevate us to return to our real spiritual home after death, which is one of the most important goals of the Vedic lifestyle.

CHAPTER ONE

Vedic Culture Since the Time of Creation

In this chapter we will show how the Vedic knowledge was given to humanity by the Supreme Being and has been available since the beginning of creation. Although while speaking of the creation, we must understand that there is not, nor can there be, any record of when the spiritual living beings first wanted to enter the material elements to experience life in the material creation. However, at some point there were those spiritual beings who felt they wanted to live separate from the Supreme Being and His spiritual domain. So in order to accommodate them, the Supreme Being manifests the material creation into which enter those materially attracted living beings. And some of those are us.

The Vedic literature explains that the material creation is only a small portion of the Supreme's energy, and only about 10% of all living beings exist within the confines of this material creation. The other 90% of all living beings are eternally liberated in the spiritual realm. So we can get an idea of how small this cosmic creation is, and how few of us there are in it, although it appears to be so vast and populated by innumerable living beings. Our existence in this cosmic creation continues as long as our materialistic consciousness is not spiritualized.

We must understand that the real world is the spiritual world, from where we all originate. Within the spiritual sky, the material world manifests like a cloud in the corner of it. It is said that the cloud of the material world is but a perverted reflection of the real spiritual world. Everything that you find in this material world is also in the spiritual realm, except everything there is in its pure state of being.

For example, it is explained that the spiritual world is also filled with planets, but those planets are spiritually self-effulgent, eternal, and millions of times larger than any one of the material universes. The residents of those planets have eternal, blissful, spiritual bodies that are full in the six opulences of beauty, strength, knowledge, wealth, fame, and detachment. The spiritual world is a place of ever-increasing joy. There one finds complete freedom from all pains and suffering, and the atmosphere is unlimitedly full of ever-expanding beauty, joy, happiness, knowledge, and eternal, loving relationships. In this way, the needs of the soul for complete freedom and unbounded happiness are found in that spiritual atmosphere. Such existence is beyond the imagination of our limited mind. It cannot be analyzed merely by the materialistic forms of logic. We cannot fathom it unless our mind becomes spiritualized. Only then are we able to have some little comprehension of what the spiritual world is like. The duty of any intelligent person, therefore, is to wake up to understanding the spiritual reality. And this spiritual reality can be experienced right here and now, in this world, in this body by the perfected practice of a spiritual lifestyle. This is one of the goals within the Vedic Aryan lifestyle.

The Vedic texts teach that the Supreme Personality, the master of all living entities, exists in the spiritual world prior to the material creation as one without a second, along with all the other purified beings who live in that eternal spiritual realm. However, the materially conditioned souls who had not regained their spiritual consciousness from the last material creation lie dormant, along with the material energy, within the body of the Supreme. At some point, however, the Lord, without all of His separated parts and parcels, feels somewhat incomplete and again manifests His material energy to allow the dormant souls to become active again.

This Supreme Being has unlimited potencies, out of which willpower, the power of knowledge, and the creative energy are topmost. There is no possibility of material creation without thinking, feeling, willing, knowledge, and activity. The combination of knowledge and action of the Supreme Will is what brings about the cosmic manifestation.

This process begins when Krishna expands Himself into Balarama, who is recognized as Krishna's brother. Lord Balarama is the predominator of the creative energy and is the origin of all the material universes. Material nature itself cannot create anything. It is inert. It must be guided or manipulated by a higher authority, just as clay is formed into a pot by a pot-maker. In this way, the material energy is organized and produces the cosmic creation by the power of the Supreme in the form of Lord Balarama.

Though the Lord resides in the spiritual world, the form of the Lord that descends into the material world to create is called an incarnation. The first such incarnation is Maha-Vishnu, the master of eternal time, space, cause and effects, mind, elements, and all living beings. From Maha-Vishnu comes the unlimited expanse of water called the Causal Ocean in which He lies down accompanied by all the ingredients of material creation, or *maya*. This Causal Ocean, otherwise called the Viraja River, is the border between the spiritual and material worlds. The material energy is kept within the boundary of the Viraja River and cannot go beyond.

Within this Causal Ocean, Maha-Vishnu enters *yoga-nidra*, a divine sleep. In this *yoga-nidra*, the Lord appears to dream and the dream manifests as the creation, maintenance, and annihilation of the cosmic manifestation. Therefore, this world is nothing more than the cosmic dream of the Supreme Personality.

In the beginning there is neither day nor night, nor sky, nor earth, nor darkness, nor light, nor any other things. There was only the Supreme Spirit and the unmanifest material energy. This material energy, *maya*, the limited potency, having manifested from the spiritual power of the Supreme, is the efficient cause of the material creation and is also the total material ingredients in its nonmanifest form. This material nature, being lifeless, can do nothing until empowered by the Supreme, which takes place when Maha-Vishnu glances upon the material energy. This glance impregnates the material nature with the souls of the innumerable living entities who had been lying dormant within the body of the Supreme. Consciousness is thus created and *maya* becomes agitated into activity. In this way, the Supreme is the original seed or father of all existence.

Then, influenced by the interactions of the time factor, the total ingredients of matter, called the *mahat-tattva*, become manifest and gradually the creation takes place by the progressive development of the various elements, such as air, water, fire, earth, etc. Subsequently, the material elements differentiate themselves into many different forms that will be the physical compositions of the various species of the innumerable living entities who appear within the material atmosphere. In this way, the cause of the conditioned soul's material body and senses is the material nature which is directed by the Supreme.

The Supreme Being then creates all the universes by combining the different ingredients with the material elements. These combined material elements take shape in the form of the unlimited universes within the cosmic creation. The universes all begin to take the form of unintelligent eggs with a shell made up of layers of water, air, fire, sky, ego, and *mahat-tattva*, surrounded by the *pradhana*, or the unmanifest material energy in the form of the Causal Ocean. Each universe is considered like an atomic particle floating in air as it emanates from the pores and exhalations of the gigantic Maha-Vishnu. All these universes are created by Maha-Vishnu when He exhales. At the end of creation when He inhales they return to His body. Thus, the cosmic worlds remain alive for the duration of one breath of Maha-Vishnu, but there is no limit to His breathing. So the material manifestation continues until the Supreme finally withdraws all of His material energy into Himself.

After the creation of the universes, Maha-Vishnu expands Himself into unlimited forms, as Garbhodakashayi Vishnu. He then enters each universe, all of which contain nothing but darkness. From Garbhodakashayi Vishnu's body an expanse of water, called the Garbhodaka Ocean, is formed that fills almost half of the universe. He lies down on that ocean and again falls into a mystic slumber. When the subtle subject matter of creation is agitated by the mode of passion, known as the universal desire for activity, the secondary process of creation is ready to begin. Then the total form of all fruitive activities and living entities pierces through Sri Vishnu's abdomen and takes the form of a lotus flower. This lotus expands and grows up to the top of the universe and becomes the topmost heavenly planet of the self-born Lord Brahma, the personality of Vedic wisdom and most advanced living entity within the material world. It is he who later engineers the secondary stage of creation. The stem of the lotus is the fourteen levels of planetary systems that fill the universe. These are the dwelling places for the various living entities. Also, from Garbhodakashayi Vishnu comes the unlimited number of expansions known as Ksirodakashayi Vishnu. This form of Vishnu becomes the Supersoul within every living entity.

After qualifying himself through penance, Lord Brahma, through his mystic potency, creates all the various forms of life that inhabit the different planetary systems. Such forms include the fish and other aquatics, then trees, plants, creepers, flowers, and vegetation. Then the insects are manifest. Then there are the animals such as the cows, lambs, camels, horses, dogs, tigers, elephants, and so on. Then the birds and finally the human beings, along with the astral beings, such as the demigods, the Gandharvas and Apsaras, or angels, the Siddhas, the ghostly beings, the superhuman beings, and so on. Thus, as the Supreme Personality manifests His various energies throughout the cosmic creation, all the living entities are enlivened into different activities, just as one is engaged in his work after awakening from a long sleep.

After the universe has been created, it will continue to exist for one lifetime of Brahma. Lord Brahma lives for one hundred years. One day of Brahma is equivalent to 4,320,000,000 of our years on earth. Brahma's night is equally as long and there are 360 of such days and nights in one year of Brahma. Each day of Brahma is divided into one thousand cycles of four *yugas*, namely Satya-yuga, Treta-yuga, Dvapara-yuga, and finally the Kali-yuga, which is the *yuga* we are presently experiencing. Satya-yuga lasts 1,728,000 years, Treta-yuga lasts 1,296,000 years, Dvapara-yuga lasts 864,000 years, and Kali-yuga lasts 432,000 years, of which 5,000 have now already passed. At the end of Kali-yuga, the age of Satya-yuga starts again and the *yugas* continue through another cycle. One thousand such cycles consist of one day of Brahma.

When the Supreme Being creates this world, He does not let us enter this world without the means of getting out. So throughout these cycles of *yugas* there are various processes of spiritual-realization that are recommended for the spiritual upliftment of society. This is all explained within Vedic knowledge. There are also various incarnations of the Supreme who appear in this creation to maintain the world and guide society. Each incarnation is described in the Vedic scripture with explanations of their appearance, nature, and activities. Their activities are described in the Vedic texts. This is how you can recognize a real incarnation of the Supreme. No imposter can authorize himself as an incarnation by Vedic evidence. (All of this information on the Vedic version of the creation is much more elaborately explained in one of my previous books, called *How the Universe was Created and Our Purpose In It*.)

When the Supreme Being creates this world, He also sets up society and gives the proper means for the advancement of humanity. Within that earliest of cultures, known as the Vedic civilization, there is one God, one religion or path to spiritual perfection, and one language. Originally the knowledge the Supreme gives to humanity is the Vedic knowledge. This Vedic knowledge was first spoken in the Sanskrit language by the Supreme Being to Brahma, the first created living being in the universe. The *Srimad-Bhagavatam* (Canto Twelve, Chapter Six) relates how Brahma qualified himself by his austerity to perceive the nonmaterial vibration of *om* (*omkara*), the subtle form of the *Vedas*. This is the seed of all Vedic hymns from which Brahma created all the sounds of the alphabet, Sanskrit. From this he produced the four *Vedas*, the *Rig*, *Yajur*, *Sama*, and *Atharva*. Brahma taught these to his sons, who were great sages and who imparted this knowledge to others. However, as stated in the *Bhagavatam* (12.13.10), before the process of creation began, the Supreme Being enlightened Lord Brahma by first revealing the full *Srimad-Bhagavatam* (*Bhagavat Purana*) to him while Brahma was sitting in meditation on the lotus flower, frightened by material existence. Only then did he realize his duty and purpose in the process of universal creation. Thus, we can understand that Vedic knowledge was available from the very beginning of time.

Although this is the Vedic version, some readers may dispute the idea of using the Vedic literature to confirm that it happened this way. However, we have to understand that this is the purpose of the Vedic knowledge and literature, to inform us of what is beyond our experience and sense perception. Furthermore, there have been many powerful sages and spiritual masters who have also confirmed the authority of the Vedic version, and who, in their own meditations and by following the Vedic process, have experienced the truth of what the Vedic knowledge explains. Thus, it behooves us to follow in their footsteps to accept the authority of Vedic knowledge. Furthermore, this is the descending process of knowledge which comes down to us from previous authorities who have also been qualified and experienced to explain the truth.

In the *Bhagavad-gita* (4.1) Sri Krishna explains that He also instructed this Vedic knowledge of *Bhagavad-gita* to Vivasvan, the controlling deity of the sun, who then instructed it to Manu, the father of mankind. The life span of the current Manu is said to last some 305,300,000 years, of which 120,400,000 have passed. So from this perspective, a rough estimate is that the *Bhagavad-gita* was first spoken in the early part of the last 120,400,000 years.

Furthermore, Manu in turn instructed it to his son and disciple, King Iksvaku. It is calculated that this knowledge of *Bhagavad-gita* was spoken by Manu to Iksvaku nearly 2,005,000 years ago, at the beginning of Treta-yuga. This is figured by calculating the 5,000 years of Kali-yuga that we have gone through so far, then 800,000 years of Dvapara-yuga, and 1,200,000 years of Treta-yuga, which equals 2,005,000 years ago. Iksvaku was king of the earth planet at that time, and forefather of the Raghu (also called Solar) dynasty in which Lord Ramachandra later appeared. This is an indication of how old is the Vedic culture. From the time of Iksvaku, this Vedic knowledge had been passed down through the ages amongst the learned sages for the welfare of all humanity.

However, if this knowledge breaks down or fades away or disappears, the Supreme Being descends in one of His incarnations to reestablish that knowledge. This has already happened once. Over the years this knowledge did fade away, which is why Lord Krishna again spoke the *Bhagavad-gita* to Arjuna 5,000 years ago on the battlefield of Kuruksetra, India. Without the direction of the Supreme in delivering this Vedic science of yoga and spiritual knowledge within human society in this material creation, there is no way we could ever have it. That is why there are various incarnations and messengers of the Supreme to keep and preserve this spiritual information. Otherwise, mankind would not be able to reach a state of purification to again leave this material world and return to the spiritual domain. Because this Vedic knowledge was spoken and delivered to this world by the Supreme Being, it is considered superhuman knowledge. Therefore, this Vedic knowledge is always present somewhere in the universe at all times. It is the highest knowledge in regard to the spiritual position of the living beings, and is the original culture of the world.

THE DIVINITY OF SANSKRIT

As stated above, originally the Supreme Being gives Vedic knowledge to humanity, which is first spoken in the Sanskrit language to Brahma. Thus, according to the Vedic references, the creation is based on one God, one form of knowledge, and one language. That knowledge existed long before it was ever compiled in writing. It was revealed through Lord Brahma to the sages and then to the people of the world through an oral tradition. Later it was compiled into the written form by Srila Vyasadeva, the incarnation of the Supreme Being Himself. The many branches of Vedic scripture are all in Sanskrit, having remained in the same form for thousands of years.

The last of the Vedic scriptures compiled by Srila Vyasadeva was the *Srimad-Bhagavatam*. Although some scholars feel that apparent different styles of writing in the texts indicate earlier or later versions, this is not an accurate assessment. They had always been perfect in grammar ever since they were first revealed. Sanskrit has remained without any change of inflection for thousands of years, which happens to all other languages of the world. No one as yet, even in the past 3,000 years, has been able to produce a more sophisticated language or a more perfect grammar than Sanskrit.

Even the oldest of languages, such as Latin and Greek, had few words in their most primitive stages. English also had only 3,000 words in its first dictionary in 1604. So this is evident of slow development, and not like Sanskrit. It has been mere gossip and speculation by some scholars to think that there was a "parent" language that gave rise to Sanskrit, Greek, and Latin. No such prior existing "Indo-European Language" has been found. All such "Indo-European" languages are but fragments or dialects of what was the original Sanskrit language.

Furthermore, all such "Indo-European people" are but members of the once global Vedic Aryan culture. This is why so many common customs, rituals, and philosophies are found throughout the world that resemble the Vedic culture in various ways. This is also why there are so many similarities between Sanskrit and other languages around the world.

This gives rise to the understanding that Sanskrit was not a man-made language, but originated in Divinity as did Vedic knowledge. There never was a pre-Vedic or pre-Aryan period as mundane scholars may try to present. Everything we have now, and what we see from the past that appears to be pre-Vedic, are but breakdowns, remnants, offshoots, and new interpretations or perverted reflections of the original Vedic knowledge and culture.

Sanskrit is a Divine language, the parent of all other languages. Similarly, the Vedic literature are Divine scriptures meant for the assistance and advancement of all living beings. Likewise with the Vedic Aryan culture. It has existed from before the time of universal creation in the spiritual realm. It has been given to the world and is existing during the creation. And it will continue to exist after the annihilation of this cosmic creation. This is the spiritual nature of the Sanskrit language and Vedic knowledge. It exists as a frequency through which pure spiritual knowledge travels into and through the material creation, yet retains its natural existence beyond it. In other words, it reveals the nature of the Absolute Truth, and the Absolute Truth exists within it, with or without any material cosmic manifestation. As the consciousness of people reach the frequency level of the Vedic knowledge, as has been the experience of great sages who are on this spiritual path, the insights and understanding that Vedic literature offers will become self-evident.

CHAPTER TWO

The History and Traditional Source of the Vedas

Continuing from the previous chapter, I will now present additional details about the formation of the Vedic literature and culture which will answer such questions as: How were the *Vedas* established? What were their origins? What is their history? How were they divided, and why does it seem that there are different spiritual paths from which to choose within the Vedic literature?

First of all, there are two ways to answer these questions: One is to consider the theories presented by some of the contemporary scholars and historians in regard to when the *Vedas* appeared, and the second way is to consider the traditional account as presented in the Vedic literature itself.

Many historians have held the idea that it was the Aryans who invaded India in the second millennium B.C. and were the founders of the Indian culture and Vedic traditions. They said that the Aryans came from somewhere near the southern part of Russia and brought their Vedic rituals and customs with them.

This theory, however, does not hold as much weight as it used to among modern historians for various reasons. For example, the culture of the Indus Valley, where the Aryans are said to have invaded, flourished between 3500 and 2500 B.C. The two main cities were Harappa and Mohenjo-Daro. Many finds have come from the archeological excavations from Harappa which give evidence to suggest that many aspects of later Vedic culture were already a part of the early Indus Valley society. Some of the findings include images of yogis sitting in meditation, as well as many figures of a god similar to Lord Shiva. Evidence has also been found to suggest that temple worship played a major role in daily life, which is what the *Vedas* prescribe as the process for attaining the greatest amount of spiritual advancement for people of that time. Evidence also shows that fire worship played an important role, and fire was a representation of Vishnu. Traditionally constructed fire altars have been found that were made according to the descriptions in the ancient *Brahmana* texts.

Another point is that the Indus Valley enveloped a vast area and the cultural traits of that society continued to survive for a long time, so how could the pre-Aryan language of the Indus valley people, which is not known today, die out without leaving any trace of its existence? Maybe there actually was not any pre-Aryan language. And if not, if this is where the Aryan invaders were supposed to have appeared when they brought their Vedic culture with them, it must be concluded that there really was not any Aryan invasion, not at least the way some scholars seem to think. It is more likely that the Vedic Aryans were already there.

Furthermore, most scholars agree that the earliest Vedic hymns seem to belong to a pre-1500 B.C. date. Some researchers, however, feel that parts of the *Rig-veda* date back to several thousand years earlier than 1500 B.C. This means it was not necessarily invaders who had brought Vedic culture with them since at least the oldest Vedic books, if not most of them, had already been in existence by the time any invaders were supposed to have arrived.

Let us consider another point using nothing more than our common sense. It is generally accepted that Lord Buddha appeared about 2,500 years ago. (However, some scholars have calculated that the birth of Buddha was around 1887 B.C. We will discuss this further in a later appendix.) The point is that we know Lord Buddha preached against the *Vedas*. So, the *Vedas* had to have been existing at that time, otherwise how could he have preached against them? In fact, the reason why he did not accept the *Vedas* was because many of the leading Vedic followers were no longer truly following them but were abusing them. Any student of history knows that abuse of something takes place after there is a flourishing. So, if the deterioration reached such an extreme 2,500 years ago that people embraced Buddha's teachings, then clearly such gradual degeneration had been going on for many hundreds of years. Since the *Vedas* were a highly developed form of philosophy, this would indicate that they must have been in existence and quite widespread several thousand years before that. Therefore, we can easily understand how old the *Vedas* must be.

Furthermore, let us not forget that it was the British Sanskritists and educators in India, during the 1700 and 1800's, who first portrayed Vedic literature and culture as something barbaric, inferior, and recent. They formed estimated dates on when the different Vedic books were written according to such things as the contents of the books and style of writing, although this has never been dependable. However, it should be pointed out that even the Vedic tradition describes that after the Vedic knowledge was divided and the different volumes were written, they were handed down to sages who became expert in the content of that portion of Vedic knowledge. They continued to hand it down to others who formed sub-branches of it. Thus, it may look as if portions of Vedic literature show their gradual evolution as if they had been developed and influenced by many authors over a long period of time, but, actually, that is not the case.

We also have to remember that for many years the Vedic literature was written on palm leaves and would have to be copied when they wore out or when other copies were wanted. Down through the years, as other copies were repeatedly made, certain conventional modifications of the script would have taken place, making some scholars think their origin was more recent. However, in the case of the *Bhagavat Purana*, the Sanskrit text still contains the archaic form of writing, verifying its antiquity. Nonetheless, the English scholars said the author of that *Purana* must have purposely used the archaic script to make people think it was older than it was. The fact that the English proposed this sort of theory in an attempt to disqualify its ancient origins simply shows how biased they were against the antiquity and authority of the Vedic literature.

This cultural prejudice was the result of deliberate undermining with the disguised intention of asserting the superiority of their own Christian-based values and outlook, as well as the perpetuation of colonial rule. This intention actually played a prominent role in the reason why they wanted the Sanskrit texts translated into English and to have their Christian scripture translated into Sanskrit. Many of the notable professors at the time had the audacity to consider themselves to be better authorities on their questionable translations of the *Vedas* than the Indian scholars. Thus, estimating the dates of the *Vedas* was common.

Mr. P. N. Oak mentions on page 83 of his *World Vedic Heritage* the futility of trying to establish the age of the *Vedas* by their language. "Trying to determine the age of the *Vedas* from their language is highly unjustified when it is realized that even in physical sciences date-estimates of different scientists are at great variance from one another. Thus, for instance, according to various geologists 20,000 to 80,000 years have elapsed since the close of the last glacial epoch. Yet another scientist, Avinash Chandra Das, has presented two different estimates in two editions of the same book. In one edition he asserts that the territory of Rajasthan was under the sea 60,000 years ago while in another he says it was only 27,000 years ago. Considering such uncertainties even in physical sciences, a philological dating of the *Vedas* does not deserve any serious consideration. Moreover, it must be realized that Vedic language being neither mundane nor human, measuring its antiquity by human philological conjectures is highly improper.

"Summarizing some representative estimates of the date of the *Vedas*, a Vedic scholar, the late Balasaheb Hardas of Nagpur, pointed out in a public lecture series in the 1950's in Pune that Pundit Patankar of Rajapur believed the *Vedas* to be 21,000 years ancient on the basis of astronomy. Another scholar, Mr. Lele, put the figure at 40,000 years. Pundit Sudhakar Dwivedi estimates the *Vedas* to be 54,000 years ancient. Pundit Krishnashastri Godbole added another 18,000 years to that figure. Another scholar, Pundit Dinanath Chulet believed the age of the *Vedas* to be 150,000 years. Yet another scholar, Swami Dayanand Saraswati, founder of the Arya Samaj organization, basing his calculations on the Yuga computation of the Vedic almanac, concluded that the *Vedas* were obtained over 1960 million years ago.

"All the spiraling speculations mentioned above seem to confirm the traditional view that the *Vedas* were conferred on humanity by Divinity at the start of the universe. And that was millions and millions of years ago. Readers who shudder to think in terms of millions of years of antiquity may, perhaps, at the very least, concede that the *Vedas* are of immeasurable antiquity."

In any case, the attempt to belittle the Vedic literature by some of the English scholars made only a minor impact. In fact, by translating such texts, many of the notable writers and poets in the West were allowed to see what lofty wisdom the Vedic literature held and were indeed very impressed and influenced by them.

So, where did the *Vedas* come from? Though modern historians may offer their many changing theories about how the *Vedas* were compiled and where they originated, we can see that this is their attempt to find an oversimplified key to understanding Vedic thought, or to even discredit the value of the *Vedas*. However, they must admit that they are still unsure of their theories and lack detailed evidence for many of their opinions. In fact, most historians today feel that any accurately recorded history only goes back to around 600 B.C., 2500 years ago, and prior to this period all events and stories related in the scriptures are simply imaginary myths and legends. This reflects an extremely narrow-minded way of looking at things. Many Vedic authorities and self-realized sages in the past have accepted the stories, as found in the *Mahabharata* and *Puranas*, to be factual, and have also attained lofty states of consciousness by following the Vedic instructions for spiritual perfection. So the best way to understand the history of how the *Vedas* were formed is to simply let the Vedic literature speak for itself.

* * *

According to Vedic tradition, when the Supreme Lord created this material world, His transcendental energy pervaded every corner of it. This spiritual energy was the pure frequency vibration, *shabda-brahma*, in which the Supreme Himself can be found. This pure sound vibration is manifested as the *om mantra*, comprised in English of the letters "A," "U," and "M." The spiritually elevated Gosvamis of Vrindavana have explained that the letter "A" refers to the Supreme Person, Bhagavan Krishna, who is the master of all living entities of the material and spiritual planets and is the source from which everything emanates. The letter "U" indicates the energy of the Supreme, and "M" indicates the innumerable living entities. Therefore, *omkara* (*om* or AUM) is the resting place of everything, or, in other words, all potencies are invested within this holy vibration. As further explained in the *Chaitanya-caritamrta*:

"The Vedic sound vibration *omkara*, the principal word in the Vedic literature, is the basis of all Vedic vibrations. Therefore one should accept *omkara* as the sound representation of the Supreme Personality of Godhead and the reservoir of the cosmic manifestation." (*Cc.Adi-lila*, 7.128)

Krishna also explains: "I am the father of this universe, the mother, the support and the grandsire. I am the object of knowledge, the purifier and the syllable *om*. I am also the *Rig-veda*, *Sama-veda* and the *Yajur-veda*." (*Bg*.9.17)

Further confirmation is in the *Yajur-veda*, (31.7): "From that Absolute God unto Whom people make every kind of sacrifice, were created the *Rig-veda*, the *Sama-veda*. From Him were created the *Atharva-veda* and also the *Yajur-veda*."

These verses indicate that the pure Absolute Truth and the pure spiritual sound vibration are nondifferent and that the *Vedas* are the expansions of that Absolute Truth. By understanding Vedic knowledge, one can understand the Absolute. Therefore, the end result of all spiritual realizations, based on the authority of the Vedic literature, is to understand that Supreme Personality.

It is said that originally the *pranava* or *om mantra* expanded into the sacred *gayatri mantra* (*om bhur bhuvah svah tat savitur varenyam bhargo devasya dimahi dhiyo yo nah pracodayat*). The *gayatri* was then expanded into the following four central verses of the *Srimad-Bhagavatam*, called *Chatuh-sloki*:

"Prior to this cosmic creation, only I exist, and nothing else, either gross, subtle, or primordial. After creation, only I exist in everything, and after annihilation, only I remain eternally.

"What appears to be truth without Me is certainly My illusory energy, for nothing can exist without Me. It is like a reflection of real light in the shadows, for in the light there are neither shadows nor reflections.

"As the material elements enter the bodies of all living beings and yet remain outside them all, I exist within all material creations and yet am not within them.

"A person interested in transcendental knowledge must therefore always directly and indirectly inquire about it to know the all-pervading truth." (*Bhag*.2.9.33-36)

These *Catuh-sloki* verses were taught by the Supreme Lord Vishnu to Brahma at the time of creation, and all other Vedic literature was expanded from them. The *Bhagavatam* (*Bhagavat Purana*) is considered to be the complete expansion of these four verses.

From this we can now begin to see how incorrect the assumption is of some scholars who think the Vedic literature was written by ordinary men over a length of time, which displays the gradual evolutionary changes in man's religious thinking. The fact of the matter is that Vedic knowledge was given by the Supreme in order for us to understand this world, who we are, our relationship with the Absolute Reality, and how to work according to that relationship. Sri Krishna says in the *Bhagavatam*: "As the unlimited, unchanging and omnipotent Personality of Godhead dwelling within all living beings, I personally establish the Vedic sound vibration in the form of *omkara* within all living entities. It is thus perceived subtly, just like a single strand of fiber on a lotus stalk." (*Bhag*.11.21.37)

What this means is that since we are all spiritual in nature, our constitutional position is to be full of eternal knowledge and bliss. The purpose of the Vedic literature is to reawaken that knowledge within us. Our spiritual position is of a very subtle nature and we cannot force our entry into the understanding of this knowledge simply by the deliberate manipulation of intelligence or logic. As pointed out earlier, one must practice the Vedic system to get the full results. By this process, one develops the power to perceive that which exists on the spiritual platform. Otherwise, how can one become qualified for understanding the higher principles of spiritual self-realization?

The next few verses clearly indicate that the *shabda-brahma*, spiritual sound vibration, exists in the Absolute Truth before creation, during the creation, and after the annihilation of this material world. Therefore, the source for all kinds of knowledge stems back to the Vedic literature.

"Just as a spider brings forth from its heart its web and emits it through its mouth, the Supreme Personality of Godhead manifests Himself as the reverberating primeval vital air, comprising all sacred Vedic meters and full of transcendental pleasure. Thus, the Lord, from the ethereal sky of His heart, creates the great and limitless Vedic sound by the agency of His mind, which conceives of variegated sounds such as the *sparsas* (Sanskrit consonants). The Vedic sound branches out in thousands of directions, adorned with the different letters expanded from the syllable *om*: the consonants, vowels, sibilants, and semivowels. The *Veda* is elaborated by many verbal varieties, expressed in different meters, each having four more syllables than the previous one. Ultimately, the Lord again withdraws His manifestation of Vedic sound within Himself." (*Bhag.*11.21.38-40)

Since the *Vedas* are a manifestation of the Absolute Truth and exist eternally, the *Manu-samhita* (the first law book for human civilization) explains that all other doctrines or philosophies not based on Vedic knowledge are impermanent. They exist for short times in history while they undergo constant transformations because of mankind's ever-changing attitudes of likes and dislikes. We can especially see this happening today in many religions where people want changes to be made in the basic precepts. If such a thing goes on, then eventually all that is left as the years go by is simply a watered down hodgepodge with no potency. Therefore, the *Manu-samhita* says: "All those traditions (*Smriti*) and all those despicable systems of philosophy, which are not based on the *Veda*, produce no reward after death; for they are declared to be founded on darkness. All those doctrines differing from the *Veda*, which spring up and (soon) perish, are worthless and false, because they are of modern date." (*The Laws of Manu*, Chapter 12, verses 95-96)

"Of modern date" means that it is recent, emerging within the last several hundred or few thousand years, or arising from someone's imagination who gives something completely new or makes up a doctrine that combines a number of different traditions. Thus, it is a philosophy of questionable benefit for the people in general. It is what is called a cheating process, though it may be in the name of religion. It may have some flowery language and basic wisdom in its scripture, but it is nothing that will give people tangible results on the spiritual level. At best, all you will have is a group of people, whether a small community or several nations, who are temporarily united in their blind faith and who work together for a cause which produces no truly beneficial outcome.

THE COMPILING OF THE VEDIC LITERATURE

If the *Vedas* are eternal and were manifest from the Supreme, then how were they first compiled into written form? I will now explain this more elaborately than in the previous chapter. After the creation of the universal elements, Brahma was born from Lord Vishnu, the incarnation of God who directly manifests the material ingredients. Brahma is the first living entity in the universe and helps engineer the part of the creation which includes all the different forms of humans, vegetation, insects, aquatics, planetary systems, etc.

When Brahma was first generated, he was not sure what this material world was or who he was. There was no one else to enlighten him; so he thought about it for a long time and tried to search out the cause of his existence but came to no conclusion. This is the same result that people will come to if they try to understand this universe simply by observing things through their senses. By analyzing the world with the mind and senses, they are bound to make many mistakes in their perception of things. Even with instruments like telescopes or microscopes, mistakes will be there because such machines are simply extensions of the same faulty senses. Therefore, retiring from his searching and mental speculation, Brahma engaged in deep meditation by controlling the mind and concentrating on the Supreme Cause.

By Brahma's meditation and practice of penance for many years, the Supreme Lord Vishnu became satisfied with him and from within Brahma's heart there awakened all transcendental knowledge and creative power. From his spiritual realizations, Brahma manifested the *gayatri mantra*. He also manifested the four primary *Vedas*. This is confirmed in the *Vishnu Purana* as well as the *Vayu, Linga, Kurma, Padma, Markandaya*, and *Bhagavat Puranas*.

Lord Vishnu taught this Vedic knowledge to Brahma and Brahma in turn taught this knowledge to other great sages who became manifest, including Narada Muni who also taught it to others. This is where the oral tradition began, and how the Vedic knowledge was spoken from one person to another for thousands of years before it was written and compiled into the original *samhitas*. The *Vedas* were taught to the great saints and mystics who had such mental capabilities that they could memorize anything by hearing it once. This should not be considered too unusual because even today there are those who have memorized large amounts of scripture. For thousands of years the *Vedas* were carefully handed down in this way. This is further elaborated in the *Bhagavatam*.

"Out of the aforesaid (AUM or *om mantra*) the almighty Brahma (the creator born from Lord Vishnu) evolved the alphabet, comprising *Antahsthas* (semi-vowels), *Usmas* (aspirants), *Swaras* (vowels), *Sparsas* (sibilants) and the short, long, and prolated measures of sound. With this alphabet Brahma gave expression through his mouth to the four *Vedas* along with the *om* and *Vyahritis* (mystical names of the three planetary systems, *Bhuh, Bhuvah* and *Svaha*) with the intention of pointing out the duties of the four priests (officiating at a sacrifice, namely *Adhwaryu, Udgata, Hota,* and *Brahmana*). He then taught them to his (mind born) sons (Marichi and others) who were *brahmana* sages and expert in reciting the *Vedas*. The latter in their turn proved to be the promulgators of righteousness and taught the *Vedas* to their sons (Kasyapa and others). Received from generation to generation in the course of the four *yugas* by the pupils of the various sages--pupils who observed the vow of (lifelong) celibacy [in order to retain the *Vedas* in their memory]--the *Vedas* were later divided by great seers at the end of the Dvapara age [just before the deteriorating age of Kali-yuga]. Perceiving the men to be short-lived, deficient in energy and dull-witted due to the action of time (in the form of unrighteousness prevailing in it) the *brahmana* seers rearranged the *Vedas* as directed by the immortal Lord residing in their heart.

"Descended from the sage Parasara through (his wife) Satyavati in the form of Vedavyasa (Vyasadeva) as prayed to by Brahma, Lord Shiva, and other guardians of the spheres for the vindication of righteousness, the almighty Lord, the life-giver of the universe, divided the *Veda* into four parts. Picking out and classifying in four (distinct) groups the multitudes of *mantras* belonging to the categories of *Rig, Atharva, Yajus,* and *Sama,* as various kinds of gems are assorted into so many groups, the sage Vyasadeva compiled four *samhitas* or collections of those *mantras*." (*Bhag.*12.6.42-50)

This is the basic story of how the *Vedas* appeared and were then divided. However, *Srimad-Bhagavatam* also explains: "In Satya-yuga, the first millennium, all the Vedic *mantras* were included in one *mantra--pranava* (*om*), the root of all Vedic *mantras*. In other words, the *Atharva-veda* [some say the *Yajur-veda*] alone was the source of all Vedic knowledge. The Supreme Personality of Godhead Narayana [an expansion of Krishna] was the only worshipable Deity; there was no recommendation for worship of the demigods. Fire was one only, and the only order of life in human society was known as *hamsa* [the swanlike sages who were all spiritually self-realized]." (*Bhag.*9.14.48)

This indicates that originally there was no need for expanding the Vedic literature because everyone was self-realized. In Satya-yuga, the age of purity and peace, everyone knew the ultimate goal of life and they were not confused about this as people are today. There was only one *Veda* (which was unwritten until Vyasadeva compiled the Vedic literature at the end of the Dvapara-yuga), one *mantra*, one process of spiritual self-realization, and one form of worship. But as time passed and unrighteousness began to spread, things changed and there was a need for further elaboration of Vedic knowledge. Other processes of self-realization were then presented to accommodate the various levels of consciousness of the people. Thus, the primary purpose of the *Vedas*, which was the worship of the Supreme Lord for material liberation, changed and began focusing on the worship of demigods for the attainment of various material rewards through the performance of detailed rituals, as can especially be seen from the verses in the *Rig* and *Sama Vedas*.

To explain further, in Satya-yuga, which lasts 1,728,000 years, people live a very long time and the process for self-realization is meditating on Narayana. In the next age, Treta-yuga, which lasts 1,296,000 years, the spiritual tendency of the people declined by twenty-five percent, and the process for self-realization was the performance of ritualistic sacrifice, which the early *Vedas* fully describe. In the next age, Dvapara-yuga, which lasts 864,000 years, people engaged in opulent temple worship as the prescribed process for spiritual self-realization, but the religious inclination of people again declined by another twenty-five percent. In the present age of Kali-yuga, which lasts 432,000 years and started 5,000 years ago, people are all short-lived and exhibit almost no interest in self-realization or spiritual topics. For this reason, the *Vedas* were expanded and put into written form so that less intelligent people could more easily understand them. This is confirmed in the *Bhagavatam* in its description of the different incarnations of God who appear in this world:

"Thereafter, in the seventeenth incarnation of Godhead, Sri Vyasadeva appeared in the womb of Satyavati through Parasara Muni, and he divided the one *Veda* into several branches and subbranches, seeing that the people in general were less intelligent." (*Bhag.*1.3.21)

Here we also find that Vyasadeva was in fact an incarnation of the Supreme who appeared with the purpose of establishing the Vedic knowledge in writing. The *Vedas* had previously been passed down through an oral tradition, but now there was a need for them to be written. How exactly Vyasadeva divided the *Vedas* is nicely told in *Srimad-Bhagavatam* in the following story:

"Once upon a time he (Vyasadeva), as the sun rose, took his morning ablution in the waters of the Sarasvati and sat alone to concentrate. The great sage saw anomalies in the duties of the millennium. This happens on the earth in different ages, due to the unseen forces in the course of time. The great sage, who was fully equipped with knowledge, could see, through his transcendental vision, the deterioration of everything material, due to the influence of the age [of Kali]. He could see also that the faithless people in general would be reduced in duration of life and would be impatient due to lack of goodness. Thus he contemplated for the welfare of men in all statuses of life." (*Bhag.*1.4.15-18)

Srila Vyasadeva could see that in the future men would be very short-lived, quarrelsome, impatient, easily angered, and their memory would be very inefficient. So, there was now the need to put the Vedic sound vibration into writing. Otherwise, people would never be able to remember it as they had in the past, not to mention trying to study and understand it.

"He (Vyasadeva) saw that the sacrifices mentioned in the *Vedas* were means by which people's occupations could be purified. And to simplify the process he divided the one *Veda* into four, in order to expand them among men. The four divisions of the original sources of knowledge (the *Vedas*) were made separately. But the historical facts and authentic stories mentioned in the *Puranas* are called the fifth *Veda*." (*Bhag.*1.4.19-20)

How the one *Veda* was divided into four is explained more fully in the following quote from the *Vishnu Purana*: "There was but one *Yajur-veda*; but dividing this into four parts, Vyasa instituted the sacrificial rites that are administered by four kinds of priests: in which it was the duty of the *Adhvaryu* (priest) to recite the prayers (*Yajus*) (or direct the ceremony); of the *Hotri* (priest) to chant other hymns (*Sama*); and of the *Brahmana* (priest) to pronounce the formula called *Atharva*. Then the Muni, having collected together the hymns called *Richas*, compiled the *Rig-veda*; with the prayers and directions termed *Yajushas* he formed the *Yajur-veda*; with those called *Sama*, *Sama-veda*; and with the *Atharvas* he composed the rules of all ceremonies suited to kings, and the function of the *Brahmana* agreeably to practice." (*Vishnu Purana*, Book Three, Chapter Four)

In this way, the one *Veda* was divided into the *Rig-veda*, the *Yajur-veda*, the *Sama-veda*, and the *Atharva-veda*. What follows in the *Vishnu Purana* is a detailed description of how these four *Vedas* were handed down from spiritual master to disciple through many generations and how many different branches of Vedic knowledge were formed. To keep the length of this chapter from getting unnecessarily long, we will use the considerably shorter account as given in the *Bhagavat Purana*:

"After the *Vedas* were divided into four divisions, Paila Rishi became the professor of the *Rig-veda*, Jaimini the professor of the *Sama-veda*, and Vaisampayana alone became glorified by the *Yajur-veda*. The Sumantu Muni Angira, who was very devotedly engaged, was entrusted with *Atharva-veda*. And my (Suta Gosvami's) father, Romaharsana, was entrusted with historical records [the *Puranas*]. All these learned scholars, in their turn, rendered their entrusted *Vedas* unto their many disciples, grand-disciples, and great grand-disciples, and thus the respective branches of the followers of the *Vedas* came into being. Thus, the great sage Vyasadeva, who is very kind to the ignorant masses, edited the *Vedas* so they might be assimilated by less intellectual men.

"Out of compassion, the great sage thought it was wise that this would enable men to achieve the ultimate goal of life. Thus, he compiled the great historical narration called the *Mahabharata* for women, laborers, and friends of the twice-born (unqualified *brahmanas*). O twice-born *brahmana*, still his mind was not satisfied, although he engaged himself in working for the total welfare of all people. Thus, the sage, being dissatisfied at heart, at once began to reflect, because he knew the essence of religion, and he said within himself: 'I have, under strict disciplinary vows, unpretentiously worshiped the *Vedas*, the spiritual master, and the altar of sacrifice. I have also abided by the rulings and have shown the import of disciplic succession through the explanation of the *Mahabharata*, by which even women, laymen, and others can see the path of religion. I am feeling incomplete, though I myself am fully equipped with everything required by the *Vedas*. This may be because I did not specifically point out the devotional service of the Lord, which is dear both to perfect beings and to the infallible Lord.'" (*Bhag.*11.4.21-31)

Even though Vyasadeva had worked for the welfare of all by writing the Vedic literature, still he felt dissatisfied. This is a great lesson. Naturally, we all desire freedom from the problems that material life causes us, but only by engaging in direct spiritual activities does the spiritual living entity, the soul within these temporary material bodies, begin to feel any real relief or happiness. How to do this by engaging in service or *bhakti-yoga* to the Supreme Being is what the *Vedas* are meant to establish, and because this had not yet been prominently presented in the literature Vyasadeva had written, such as the four *Vedas*, the *Upanishads*, and *Vedanta-sutras*, he was still feeling dissatisfied. Now he was trying to understand the cause of his dissatisfaction.

In all the literature compiled by Vyasadeva, there were many descriptions of the temporary universe, prayers to the demigods, the process for attaining material necessities, information about the soul, the Brahman, the Supersoul, and the process of yoga for attaining spiritual realizations. There was also information about the Supreme Lord Bhagavan, Krishna. But the detailed descriptions of God, His form, His incarnations, His names, activities, potencies, and energies, and how He is the source of everything, including the ever-increasing spiritual bliss which we are always seeking, had not yet been fully described.

While questioning his unexpected dissatisfaction, Vyasadeva was at that very moment greeted by the sage Narada Muni, who had just arrived at Vyasadeva's cottage. Acting as Vyasadeva's spiritual master, as described in *Srimad-Bhagavatam* (Canto One, Chapters Five and Six), Narada Muni instructed him in the cause of his problem. He said that Vyasa had not actually broadcast the sublime and spotless glories of the Supreme Personality. Therefore, Narada Muni encouraged Vyasadeva to write and describe the eternal spiritual truths in a more direct manner:

"O Vyasadeva, your vision is completely perfect. Your good fame is spotless. You are firm in vow and satisfied in truthfulness. And thus you can think of the pastimes of the Lord in trance for the liberation of the people in general from all material bondage. The Supreme Lord is unlimited. Only a very expert personality retired from the activities of material happiness, deserves to understand this knowledge of spiritual values. Therefore, those who are not so well situated, due to material attachment, should be shown the way of transcendental realization, by Your Goodness, through descriptions of the transcendental activities of the Supreme Lord. Persons who are actually intelligent and philosophically inclined should endeavor only for that purposeful end which is [spiritual and] not obtainable even by wandering from the topmost planet down to the lowest.

"The Supreme Lord is Himself this cosmos, and still He is aloof from it. From Him only has this cosmic manifestation emanated, in Him it rests, and unto Him it enters after annihilation. Your good self knows all about this. You yourself can know the Supersoul Personality of Godhead because you are present as the plenary portion of the Lord. Although you are birthless, you have appeared on this earth for the well-being of all people. Please, therefore, describe the transcendental pastimes of the Supreme Personality of Godhead, Sri Krishna, more vividly."

After Narada Muni took leave of Vyasadeva, Vyasa, in his own *ashrama*, on the bank of the River Sarasvati, sat down to meditate. He fixed his mind, perfectly engaging it by linking it in devotional service (*bhakti-yoga*) without any tinge of materialism, and thus he saw the Absolute Personality of Godhead along with His external energy, which was under full control. Then the learned Vyasadeva compiled the topmost fruit of the tree of Vedic knowledge, the *Srimad-Bhagavatam* [*Bhagavat Purana*], which is in relation to the Supreme Truth, as well as being Vyasadeva's own commentary on all the other Vedic writings. Thus, the *Srimad-Bhagavatam* is the ultimate conclusion of all Vedic knowledge.

In this way, the different levels of Vedic literature, all in Sanskrit, came into being and spread throughout the world. This includes the four primary *Vedas*, namely the *Rig*, *Yajur*, *Sama*, and *Atharva-vedas*, the *Upanishads*, the *Vedanta-sutras*, the *Mahabharata*, the *Puranas*, and finally, as related in the above story, the *Bhagavat Purana*. Within this literature and their many supplementary books on health, architecture, music, etc., are contained the essential teachings of spirit, the material sciences, and the processes for attaining transcendental realizations. This is explained further in my book titled *The Universal Path to Enlightenment*.

CHAPTER THREE

Rediscovering the Advancements of Vedic Science

Not only do the ancient Vedic texts contain a high level of philosophical and spiritual knowledge, but they also hold information on advanced levels of material science. So this chapter will present a list of the many topics contained in Vedic science and the ideas and knowledge that were known many hundreds and thousands of years ago. We must also recognize that without these developments that originated in Vedic civilization in the many fields that will be described, this world and our society certainly would not be what it is today. Thus, we owe much to the advanced nature of the Vedic wisdom.

The Vedic literature includes such works as the *Ayur-veda*, the original science of holistic medicine as taught by Lord Dhanvantari; *Dhanur-veda*, the military science as taught by Bhrigu; *Gandharva-veda*, which is on the arts of music, dance, drama, etc., by Bharata Muni; *Artha-sastram*, the science of government and economic development; *Sthapatya-veda*, science of architecture; and *Manu-samhita*, the Vedic lawbook.

There are also the *Shulba Sutras*, which contains the Vedic system of mathematics. The *Shulbasutras* are the earliest forms of mathematical knowledge, and certainly the earliest for any religious purpose. They basically appear as a supplement to the ritual (*Shrauta*) aspect of the *Kalpasutras*, which show the earliest forms of algebra. They essentially contain the mathematical formulas for the design of various altars for the Vedic rituals of worship. Each *Shrautasutra* had its own *Shulbasutra*, so there were probably several such texts long ago, though only seven *Shulbasutras* are known today. Among these the Baudhayana, Apastamba (both of which belong to the *Taittiriya Samhita* or *Black Yajur-veda*), and Katyayana (which belongs to the *Vajasaneya* or *White Yajur-veda*) are the most important, while the Manava, Maitrayana, the Varaha, and the Vidula are less significant.

The date of the *Shulbasutras*, after comparing the Baudhayana, Apastamba and Katyayana *Shulbas* with the ancient mathematics of ancient Egypt and Babylonia, as described by N. S. Rajaram in *Vedic Aryans and The Origins of*

Civilization (p.139), is near 2000 B.C. However, after including astronomical data from the *Ashvalayana Grihyasutra, Shatapantha Brahmana*, etc., the date can be brought farther back to near 3000 B.C., near the time of the *Mahabharata* War and the compilation of the other Vedic texts by Srila Vyasadeva.

With this view in mind, Vedic mathematics can no longer be considered as a derivative from ancient Babylon, which dates to 1700 B.C., but must be the source of it as well as the Greek or Pythagorean mathematics.

The Vedic form of mathematics is much more advanced than that found in early Greek, Babylonian, Egyptian, or Chinese civilizations. In fact, the geometrical formula known as the Pythagorean theorem can be traced to the *Baudhayana*, the earliest form of the *Shulbasutras* prior to the eighth century B.C. This confirms that the Greek philosopher owed much inspiration to India. In fact, Professor R. G. Rawlinson stated, "Almost al the theories, religious, philosophical, and mathematical, taught by the Pythagorians were known in India in the sixth century B.C."

Recognition of the superiority of the Vedic mathematics was also recorded as long ago as 662 A.D. by Sebokht, the Bishop of Qinnesrin in North Syria. As reported in *Indian Studies in Honor of Charles Rockwell* (Harvard University Press, Cambridge, MA. Edited by W. E. Clark, 1929), Sebokht wrote that the Indian discoveries in astronomy were more ingenious than those of the Greeks or Babylonians, and their numerical [decimal] system surpasses description. (N. S. Rajaram, p. 157, 1995)

It was this Indian system that originated the decimal system of tens, hundreds, thousands, etc., and the procedure of carrying the remainder of one column over to the next. It also provided a means of dividing fractions and the use of equations and letters to signify unknown factors. These Indian numbers were used in Arabia after 700 A.D. and then spread to Europe where they were mistakenly called Arabic numerals. It is only because Europe changed from Roman numerals to these Arabic numerals that originated in India that many of the developments in Europe in the fields of science and math were able to take place.

The first propounder of modern Calculus was the Indian Bhaskaracarya (1150 A.D.), which most people consider to be the contribution of Newton or Liebnitz. The practice of algebra, trigonometry, square and cube roots also first started in India. The simple formulation of "0" in particular, which is the product of extraordinary scientific thought from India, made possible many of the mathematical developments we have today. And it was Aryabhatta (497 A.D.) who calculated "pi" as 3.1416. Many of these mathematical methods are scattered throughout works such as the *Shatapatha Brahmana, Baudhayanasutra*, etc.

Looking at the *Puranas*, they contain a variety of information on the creation of the universe, its maintenance, and destruction. Other subjects include astrology, geography, use of military weapons, organization of society, duties of different classes of men, characteristics and behavior of social leaders, predictions of the future, analysis of the material elements, symptoms of consciousness, how the illusory energy works, the practice of yoga, meditation, spiritual experiences, realizations of the Absolute, and much more.

The *Vedas*, written thousands of years ago, also completely disprove the theory of modern scholars who think that all ancient civilizations thought the earth was the center of the universe and the stars and sun revolved around it. In the Vedic description of the cosmological arrangement, it is explained that all planets, as well as the sun, have their own particular orbits of travel through the universe. We can also find in the *Yajur-veda* a description of how the earth is kept in space because of the superior attraction to the sun. The theory of gravitation is also described in the *Siddhanta Shiromani* centuries before the birth of Newton, the western discoverer of the law of gravity.

Some experts have written that evidence of astronomical observations were noted in the *Rig-veda*, over 4,000 years ago. However, some assign these observations from between 12,500-1,500 B.C.

Within the *Surya-Siddhanta* are recordings of star coordinates that date back to a remote period. The knowledge of this classic astronomical treatise is said to have been originally known as long as 13,000 years ago. Ravindranath Ramchandra Karnik dates it back to 13,902 B.C. in his book, *Ancient Indian Technologies*. Others, using present day calculations based on the proper motions of these stars, suggest that some of the coordinates noted in it must have been recorded as far back as 50,000 B.C. Modern scholars date the book to around 490 A.D. In any case, it was quite advanced for its day. For example, it says (12.54) that though people may view the world as flat, the earth is actually a globe. The thirteenth chapter describes the process of map making, even to the level of creating an actual sphere with lines or wires depicting the latitudes and longitudes.

So what does this mean? According to anthropologists, the first positive evidence for the existence of modern man in Europe or the Middle East dates back to only 40,000 years ago, and the development of agriculture and village life did not take place until 10,000 to 7,000 years ago. So from this viewpoint, it seems that people would not have had the intellect or concern to have measured or recorded positions of the stars as far back as 50,000 years ago. Therefore, these descriptions in such books as the *Puranas* or the *Surya-Siddhanta* make it clear that the Vedic civilization was much more highly organized and advanced than many people think. The way the ancient Brahmins and *rishis* used astrological calculations was to determine the most auspicious dates for religious ceremonies, and when to expect changes in the earth and the consciousness of society.

In another point regarding the advanced nature of the Vedic system of astronomy, the *Srimad-Bhagavatam* (10.82.2) explains that Krishna and Balarama once went to Samanta-pancaka (Kuruksetra) in preparation for the approaching eclipse to earn pious credit. In fact, people from all over India went there to participate in bathing at the sacred lakes while the eclipse took place. This means, as the verse relates, that everyone knew of the eclipse in advance. Thus, the system of astronomy used by the Vedic astronomers 5,000 years ago enabled them to predict eclipses of the sun and moon in advance just as well as our modern astronomers today.

Furthermore, in the earliest of Vedic writings, such as the *Atharva-veda*, we find a number of verses that deal with the uses and benefits of electricity, such as this one: "That very electric power may be our peaceful friend, providing us with the horse-power to drive our machines, light to light our houses, and power to produce grains in the fields. Let it bring on prosperity and well-being for us by flowing into numerous currents." (*Atharva-veda*, Book 20, Hymn 7, verse 3)

Other sciences are mentioned in the *Yajur-veda*, such as the following verse:

"O disciple, a student in the science of government, sail in oceans in streamers, fly in the air in airplanes, know God the Creator through the *Vedas*, control thy breath through yoga, through astronomy know the functions of day and night, know all the *Vedas*, *Rig*, *Yajur*, *Sama*, and *Atharva*, by means of their constituent parts.

"Through astronomy, geography and geology, go thou to all the different countries of the world under the sun. Mayest thou attain through good preaching to statesmanship and artisanship, through medical science obtain knowledge of all medicinal plants, through hydrostatics learn the different uses of water, through electricity understand the working of ever-lustrous lightening. Carry out my instructions willingly. . ." (*Yajur-veda*, 6.21)

Among all the different sciences mentioned in the above verse, it may be surprising to find a reference to airplanes, or *vimanas*. But, actually, the mention of airplanes is found many times throughout Vedic literature, including the following verse from the *Yajur-veda* describing the movement of such machines:

"O royal skilled engineer, construct sea-boats, propelled on water by our experts, and airplanes, moving and flying upward, after the clouds that reside in the mid-region, that fly as the boats move on the sea, that fly high over and below the watery clouds. Be thou, thereby, prosperous in this world created by the Omnipresent God, and flier in both air and lightening." (*Yajur-veda*, 10.19)

In the *Brihad Vimana Sastram* with Sanskrit verses and English translations, edited by late G. R. Josyer of Mysore, we can find descriptions relating to 37 models of these *vimana* airships with equipment to collect information by wireless devices, and with the ability to make themselves invisible. It also describes the types of food to be used by the navigators and vessels for traveling from planet to planet. The *Rig-veda*, *Ramayana*, *Mahabharata* and many other Vedic texts also contain numerous references to a variety of *vimanas*, flying machines, and even flying cities. In the *Raghuvamsham*, Kalidasa provides a vivid and accurate description of Lord Rama's flight from Sri Lanka to Ayodhya on a flying vehicle. With the additional scientific knowledge provided in the Sanskrit texts, it becomes obvious that the art of flying on machines was known in ancient India. (More information about *vimanas* is supplied in the Appendix in back of the book.)

Other discoveries of modern technology is that of atomic energy and its by-products. Most people agree that no civilization before us had knowledge of such things. But time and again we find in the Vedic literature descriptions of weapons, such as the *brahmashtras*, that had a similar amount of energy as the atomic bombs of today. To what else would these next few verses from the *Atharva-veda* refer if not a description of the basic principles of atomic energy?

"The Atomic Energy fissions the ninety-nine elements, covering its path by the bombardments of neutrons without let or hindrance. Desirous of stalking the head, i.e., the chief part of the swift power, hidden in the mass of molecular adjustments of the elements, this atomic energy approaches it in the very act of fissioning it by the above-noted bombardments. Herein verily the scientist know the similar hidden striking force of the rays of the sun working in the orbit of the moon." (*Atharva-veda*, 20.41.1-3)

Another point illustrating the advanced nature of the Vedic Aryan civilization is their conception of the universal time scale. The time factor is calculated as affecting various levels of the universe differently. For example, it is said that a day for the demigods is equal to six months for humans on planet earth. And a year is calculated as 360 human years, while 12,000 years of the gods are said to be but one blink of the eye of Maha-Vishnu. For Lord Brahma, the highest of all the demigods, his day equals one thousand cycles of the combined four ages of Satya, Treta, Dvapara, and Kali-yugas. This amounts to 4.3 billion years, at the end of which is his night of equal duration when there is a partial annihilation of the universe, which includes the earth. After his night, Brahma's day begins again, and that which is destroyed is again created or revived. Interestingly, modern science has estimated that the age of the earth is about 4 billion years. Whether this fits into the Vedic scheme or not, scholars feel it is uncanny that the Vedic Aryans could have conceived of such a vast span of time over 3,500 years ago that would be similar to the same figure considered by science today.

Regarding time and long calculations, even Dr. Carl Sagan wrote in his book, *Cosmos* (Balentine Books, New York, 1980), "The Hindu religion is the only one of the world's great faiths dedicated to the idea that the cosmos itself undergoes an immense, indeed an infinite number of deaths and rebirths. It is the only religion in which the time scales corresponds, no doubt by accident, to those of modern scientific cosmology. Its cycles run from our ordinary day and night to a day and night of Brahma, 8.64×10^9 years long, longer than the age of the earth or the sun and about half the time since the Big Bang."

Of course, we do not accept that such calculations were found by accident. From what imagination could such a figure come when it agrees with modern science? Such figures have been mentioned by Lord Krishna in the *Bhagavad-gita* and other *Puranas*, so it could hardly be accepted as an accidental figure. So how could the ancient Vedic knowledge contain such calculations?

The reason why this is possible is not because of speculative thoughts about life by the sages thousands of years ago, but because the Vedic knowledge is, as we have previously explained, established by the Supreme so that the living entities can understand their position in this world. Thus, this knowledge has been descending down through time, ready to be utilized by anyone qualified to do so. Through the above examples, we can see that many of the sciences and inventions that we feel proud of today, thinking they are but recent achievements, were known many years ago. Therefore, we should be careful not to feel that no civilization before us has ever been so advanced. From the Vedic literature it is quite evident that we have failed to see that what has been known for many years we are now, at great expense and with much research, only rediscovering.

The Vedic Aryans were also quite advanced in sea travel. While the European sailors and traders were mostly unaware of the sea-routes from Europe to India up to the sixteenth century A.D., the Indian literature and epics describe the shape of the earth and the continents and oceans thousands of years before this. And ancient Indians knew how to reach the foreign shores by the sea-routes.

As pointed out in *World-Wide Hindu Culture* by Dr. S. Venu Gopalacharya (p. 102), it is well-known that large Indian ships used to carry sailors and merchandise from India to its colonies in Java, Sumatra, Borneo, the Philippines, etc., from times immemorial up to the naval supremacy of the Europeans in the Indian Ocean in the 18th century. India was more than proficient at sailing and traveling beyond its water borders on three sides. The quoting of the scriptural injunction that a holy man, and others, should not travel by sea to another country relates only from the 14th century A.D. onwards. This was because the people of Malaysia and Indonesia had been converted to Islam and sea-travel became difficult due to the fact that it might result in such travelers to other lands being forced to give up their faiths or even their lives.

The *Yuktikalapataru*, a Sanskrit work of the pre-Christian era, gives rules to construct different models of ocean-going ships. The *Jatakas* describe that the ruler Simhabala of Bengal went to Sri Lanka in the sixth century B.C. in a ship carrying his son, Vijaya, and seven hundred co-sailors. Simhabala had another ship following him which carried 1,000 carpenters. So this was no small ship. Their ships are said to have carried the Matsya Yantras, which were magnetic needles that floated in oil that showed the proper direction. This has been developed into the modern compass. However, the western sailors came to know of the mariner's compass only after the 16th century, probably after having contact with the sailors of India.

That the Indians excelled in shipbuilding was especially noted by the British, who were well attentive to everything related to naval architecture, and who noted any Indian ships worth copying. Sir John Malcolm had written that India vessels, "are so admirably adapted to the purpose for which they are required that, not withstanding their superior science, Europeans were unable, during an intercourse with India for two centuries, to suggest or at least to bring into successful practice one improvement."

In regard to military science, the *Ramayana* and the *Puranas* make frequent mention of *Shataghnis*, or canons, being placed on forts and used in times of emergency. A canon was called "Shataghni" because it meant the fire weapon that kills one hundred men at once. They ascribe these *agniyastras*, or weapons of fire, to Visvakarma, the architect of the Vedic epics. Rockets were also Indian inventions and were used in native armies when Europeans first came in contact with them. As per Dante's *Inferno*, Alexander mentioned in a letter to Aristotle that terrific flashes of flame showered on his army in India.

The *Shukra Neeti* is an ancient text that deals with the manufacture of arms such as rifles and guns. In *The Celtic Druids* (pp. 115-116), Godfrey Higgins provides evidence that Hindus knew of gun powder from the remotest antiquity.

The ancient Vedic culture also had an advanced system of medicine. Some of the earliest references to Indian and herbal medicine for curing diseases are found in the *Rig-veda* (Book Ten, Chapter 97, and 145). Fever is also mentioned in the *Atharva-veda* (5.22.12-14 & 7.116.1-2), and descriptions of various kinds of fever are listed in the *Vajasaneyi-Samhita* [*White Yajur-veda*](12.97). The *Taittiriya Samhita* (2.3,5) points out the importance of food and breath. Knowledge of veins and arteries is mentioned in the *Atharva-veda* (1.17.1-4), and surgery is discussed in the *Rig-veda* (1.116.15) in which the Asvins fitted an artificial iron leg to Vispala, an amputee who lost her foot in a war, and helped the lame to walk and the blind to see (1.112.8), and cured broken bones (10.39.2). The development of the *Ayurveda* took the first medical science to newer levels.

Within the science of medicine was the science of Embryology. The earliest writing regarding embryology is found in the *Rig-veda* and *Atharva-veda*. Although these are not developed discussions, we do find in Chapter 31 of the Third Canto of the *Bhagavata Purana* a very thorough description of how the living being enters the womb at the time of conception, and how the semen mixes with the ovum and the embryo is formed, and its growth in the womb up to its birth. It even discusses the child's thoughts and feelings while in the womb, and even how it is affected by the emotions of the mother and the types of foods the mother eats, and how it feels pain when the mother consumes spicy foods. Other texts, such as the *Garuda Purana* and the *Manu-Samhita*, discuss ways of ensuring whether a baby will be a boy or a girl. With the help of these books and additional information in other texts, such as the *Aitareya Aranyaka* and *Chandogya Upanishad*, we find a fairly complete system that explains how semen is formed all the way up to the birth of a child. This confirms that Vedic scientists in ancient times had a sound understanding of embryology even when people of most countries were in ignorance of it.

Dorothea Chaplin mentions in her book, *Matter, Myth and Spirit, or Keltic and Hindu Links*, (pp.168-9), "Long before the year 460 B.C., in which Hippocrates, the father of European medicine was born, the Hindus had built an extensive pharmacopoeia and had elaborate treatises on a variety of medical and surgical subjects. . . The Hindus' wonderful knowledge of medicine has for some considerable time led them away from surgical methods as working destruction on the nervous system, which their scientific medical system is able to obliviate, producing a cure even without a preliminary crisis."

The importance of this observation is that the Vedic system of *Ayurveda* medicine is a divine system whose treatment is based on laws of nature. It is also inexpensive, least ostentatious, very efficacious, and the least painful. It also aims at curing the disease instead of merely treating the symptoms or alleviating the pain. However, when in some cases surgery was necessary, the ancient Indian surgeons were very skillful. Even from the time of the *Rig-veda* (1.116.15) it appears that they knew the art of surgery to care for battle wounds and could even fit artificial metal limbs onto the bodies of amputees. As explained by A. L. Basham in his book, *The Wonder That Was India* (p. 502), "Indian surgery remained ahead of European until the 18th century, when the surgeons of the East India Company were not ashamed to learn the art of rhinoplasty from the Indians."

In pages 30-31 of *Bharat (India) As Seen and Known by Foreigners* by G. K. Deshpende (1950), Dr. Sir William Hunter observed, "The surgery of the ancient Indian physicians was bold and skillful. They conducted amputations, arresting the bleeding by pressure, a cup-shaped bandage and boiling oil; practiced lithotomy, performed operations in the abdomen and uterus; cured hernia, fistula piles; set broken bones and dislocations and were dexterous in the extraction of foreign substances from the body. A special branch of surgery was devoted to rhinoplasty, an operation for improving deformed ears and noses and forming new ones, a useful operation which Europeans have now borrowed. The ancient Indian surgeons also mention a cure for neuralgia, analogous to the modern cutting of the 5th nerve above the eyebrow. They were expert in midwifery, not shrinking from the most critical operations."

Mr. Oak goes on to explain in *World Vedic Heritage* (p. 360), "The prostrate gland operation performed by modern, Western surgeons follows step by step the exact procedure laid down by the Hindu surgeon, Sushrut, thousands of years ago. Even the term prostate gland is the Sanskrit term *Prasthita granthi*, signifying a gland located in front of the urinal bladder."

Plastic surgery was also practiced in India hundreds of years ago. This is explained in a letter to the editor of *Gentleman's Magazine* (available in the library of the "Wellcome Institute for History of Medicine," 183 Euston Road, London). It explains that there once was a Maratha bullock-cart driver, Cowasjee, who served with the British Army in India in 1792. Being taken prisoner by Tipu Sultan's army, they chopped off his nose as per the usual barbarous Muslim torturing and maiming tradition. After his return to his home in Pune a year later, a local Hindu Ayurvedic surgeon furnished him with a new nose. British doctors Thomas Cruso and James Trindlay were two fascinated witnesses. They testify to such miracle operations being very common in India even in their days.

On pages 369-70 of *World Vedic Heritage*, Mr. Oak provides a comparison between English and Sanskrit words. This shows how much western culture has inherited from Vedic/Sanskrit knowledge on medicine as well as how many Sanskrit words have been inherited into English.

English	Sanskrit
fever	jwar, which becomes jever, then English fever
entrails	antral
nasal or nose	naas
herpes	serpes
gland	granthi
drip, drop, drops	drups
hydrocephalus	ardra-kapaalas (damp brain)
hiccups	hicca
muscle	mausal (fleshy)
malign, malignant	mallen
osteomalacia	asthi-malashay (contamination of the bones)
dyspepsia	dush-pachanashay (bad digestion)
surgeon	salya-jan (one yielding a sharp instrument)
fertility	falati-lti (one which yields fruit)
anesthesia	anasthashayee (one lying in improper state)
homeopathy	Samaeo-pathy (treatment parallel to symptoms)
allopathy	alag-pathy (treatment different from symptoms)

In conclusion to this section, I include the quote from Mr. Oak from page 371 of his *World Vedic Heritage*, wherein he explains: "Thus a close study of allopathic terminology, whether of ailments, physical organs, symptoms, remedies, or instruments will be found to be based on *Ayurveda* because during the universal unitary Vedic administration it was only *Ayurveda* which was the sole Vedic medical system which was used throughout the world. With the shattering of the world medical system after the *Mahabharata* War, fragments of *Ayurveda* surviving in different parts of the world assumed the form of tribal remedies or as rival systems such as homeopathy and allopathy. This has a parallel in theology and religion too inasmuch as after the break-up of the world Vedic theology, cults of different gods and goddesses, such as Mithraism, Jainism, Judaism, Buddhism, and Shaivism, not hostile or dissimilar to Vedic culture, at first cropped up. However, later even hostile and militant faiths such as Christianity and Islam made their appearance."

MORE ANCIENT GLORIES OF VEDIC CULTURE

There are many other unique developments and inventions that few people realize came from Vedic society. P. N. Oak points out many of these items in his *World Vedic Heritage*. He observes, "The gossamer-thin muslin of Dhaka; the gold studded gorgeous, rich, colorful, royal saris of Varanasi; the thin needles manufactured in England by an Indian; the massive and towering buildings standing over the ancient world; the records of inter-stellar travels and inter-continental missiles; wonder vehicles hovering on air-cushions or zooming through the skies, the orbiting satellites such as Trishanku; the wonder medical science of *Ayurveda*; the mastery of the mysterious science of yoga; the administrative control of a united humanity throughout the world for millions of years; and the propagation of a single universal language, Sanskrit, are some of the unsurpassed glories of Vedic culture.

"Public memory being proverbially very short, all such stupendous evidence has been ignored and forgotten. Moreover, just as an ancient thing is assailed by different pests, Vedic culture is often misunderstood and misinterpreted by its detractors."

Many things that we enjoy everyday can be traced back to the Vedic culture. For example, music originated from the *Sama-veda*. The *Sama-veda* lays the ground rules for music since many of the verses of this *Veda* were used by the priests to sing at the Vedic fire rituals. Many of the Vedic divine personalities are also shown with instruments with them, such as Lord Krishna with His flute, Saraswati with her vina, as also the cosmic sage Narada Muni. And Shiva is often depicted dancing to the beat of the drum, or playing his drum.

German author Weber writes in his book, *Indian Literature* (p. 297), "The Hindu scale--Sa, Re, Ga, Ma, Pa, Dha, Nee has been borrowed also by the Persians, where we find it in the form of do, re, ma, fa, so, le, ci. It came to the West and was introduced by Guido d' Arezzo in Europe in the form of do, re, mi, fa, sol, la, ti. . . even the 'gamma' of Guido (French gramma, English gamut) goes back to the Sanskrit gramma and Prakrit gamma and is thus a direct testimony of the Indian origin of our European scale of seven notes."

More information on how the Indian system of music traveled to Europe is provided by Ethel Rosenthal's research in her book *The Story of Indian Music and its Instruments* in which she observes, "In *The Indian Empire*, Sir William Wilson Hunter remarked that a regular system of notation had been worked out before the age of Panini and the seven notes were designated by their initial letters. This notation passed from the Brahmins through the Persians to Arabia, and was then introduced into European music by Guido d' Arezzo at the beginning of the 11th century. . . Hindu music after a period of excessive elaboration, sank under the Muhammadans into a state of arrested development. . . "

This not only explains how the Indian system of music traversed to Europe, but it also counters the view that India was benefitted by Islamic art and music. As explained by P. N. Oak in *World Vedic Heritage* (p. 411), "Aurangzeb, the 17th century Moghul emperor of India, had forbidden his courtiers from attending any musical programmes. Consequently, the courtesans of Delhi lost their clientele. That put a number of musicians out of employment in Delhi. To bring their plight to the notice of the emperor, the music fraternity organized a funeral procession in which they carried on a bier an effigy representing the muse of music. As they proceeded along the thoroughfare they set up a loud wail as though grieving for a departed soul. When the emperor inquired about the cause for such loud public mourning, he was informed that the musicians put out of business were carrying the muse of music for burial. Aurangzeb was mighty pleased. Consequently his message conveyed to the mourners was that music should be buried so deep as never to be able to raise its head ever again any more. Aurangzeb regarded himself a deputy of Allah on earth, and in banning music he was only carrying out Allah's wish. Islam thus stands for a total negation of all art and finer sentiments of human nature. The only art it admits is calligraphy, and that too is confined to the Koran. The Muslim contribution to the development of music is thus. . . zero. . ."

There were also numerous forms of technological advancement in many branches of learning in the Vedic literature. The iron pillar at the Kutab Minar near New Delhi is a testimony to the scientific knowledge of ancient Vedic times. Evidence shows that the pillar was once a Garuda Stambha from a Vishnu temple. Some date it back to the fourth century A.D., while others date it to over 4000 years old. The pillar is 16 inches in diameter and 23 feet tall. In spite of it being outdoors for centuries, it has never rusted. It is made of pure iron, which even today can be produced only in small quantities by electrolysis. Such a pillar would be most difficult to make even today. Thus, the pillar defies explanation.

The Vedic Aryans also had attained mastery in the fields of astronomical mathematics, yoga and breath control, architecture and town planning. Texts such as the *Mayamata*, *Samarangana-sutradhara* (dating to the 11th century A.D.), and the *Vishnudharmottara* (450-650 A.D.) elaborately deals with the science of architecture. The *Munasara* (dating to the 11th to 15th century in its present form) also mentions a 12-storeyed palace for a monarch. So sky-scrapers were not unknown at the time. Furthermore, the *Arthashastra* (2.3,4) includes information on the building of ramparts, tower gates, *gopurams*, palaces, temples for Deities, and residential quarters for different kinds of people.

The *Shilpa Shastra* is also a Vedic classic on architecture, house construction, and town planning. More of the latter is found in the *Vastu Vidya*. Some of the information in the *Vastu Vidya* is in the *Jataka* stories and Buddhist Pali cannons. This similarity confirms that the *Vastu Vidya* existed during the time and after the death of Lord Buddha, from 500 B.C. to 100 A.D. Furthermore, when we consider the descriptions of the opulent buildings and the town planning of Dwaraka city in the Tenth Canto of the *Bhagavata Purana*, we can understand that such knowledge had already been established and utilized several thousand years ago.

The *Vastushastra*, along with references in the Vedic epics, the *Arthashastra*, and *Jatakas* also make mention of building materials and that different sizes of bricks and stones were used for the building of pillars, lintels, and the construction of dome roofs. The *Vrikshayarveda* portion of the *Agni Purana* discusses forms of irrigation by means of canals.

The science of agriculture was explained in a scattered form in the *Brihatsamhita*, *Arthashastra*, and more exclusively in the *Krishiparashara*. This work explained everything from sowing seeds to planting saplings to the harvest and storing of grains. The *Vrikshayarveda* of the *Agni Purana* also discusses forms of irrigation, the development of canals, watering of plants, and diseases of plants and their cures, etc.

The science of Botany was also well known in the ancient Vedic times long ago. Ancient Vedic books like the *Rig-veda* (10.97.21) and the *Mahabharata* explained that plants have life and can feel. It was Sir J. C. Bose who scientifically proved it in a laboratory. Other works, such as *Upavanavinoda* of the *Sharngadhara-paddhanti* of the 13th century, along with portions of many of the *Puranas*, such as the *Agni, Padma, Matsya, Bhagavata,* and *Arthashastra, Brihatsamhita,* etc., deals with the treatment of plants and their diseases. The information described included the use of fertilizers to nourish trees and plants, causes and cures of diseases, how to make barren trees fruitful, how to make fragrant flowers, plants' reactions to heat, cold, thunder, smell, and touch, and how to use water and wind and the art of grafting. Even the idea of the rotation of crops was discussed in the *Taittiriya-samhita* (5.1.7.37). Also, the use of herbal medicines such as opium for an anesthetic was first used in India.

The science of jewels and lapidary can be found in the *Garuda* and *Agni Puranas,* which had the first written descriptions of the quality and grading of jewels, how they are found and mined, and even how they can be used to counteract the astrological influence of planets.

There are also explanations of the divisions of time, molecules, atoms, and missiles, all of which are Sanskrit terms. The scripture known as the *Agastya Samhita* contains verses that explain how silk is a perfect material for balloons and parachutes because of its elasticity. Another verse explains that one can soar in the skies with an air-tight cloth filled with hydrogen. Other verses in the Vedic texts explain the process for making cords and cables, air-tight textiles, batteries, motors, and a process for electroplating. Furthermore, the *Silpa Samhita* describes the telescope in this way: "First manufacture glass through roasted earth. Fix those glasses at either end and in the middle of a hollow tube. This is as useful as the turi-yantra in observing distant celestial bodies."

Other Vedic texts also point out how to make things that we take for granted today, but have a difficult time imagining that they were available thousands of years ago. For example, a copy of the *Silpa Samhita* manuscript in the Jain library at Anhilpur, Gujarat, as reported by P. N. Oak in *World Vedic Heritage* (p. 152), describes how a thermometer may be made with the help of mercury, thread, oil, and water. The text known as *Bhoj-Prabandh* mentions a wooden horse owned by King Bhoj which could travel 22 miles in 24 minutes, and a fan which could rotate without manual help to give a sharp breeze. The *Gayachintemani* mentions an aircraft shaped like a peacock. Bharadwaja's ancient volume titled *Anshubodhini* has a special chapter on aircraft, *vimanas*. And his ancient *Vimaanika Shastra* gives detailed descriptions of how these various machines are put together. Some of them are described with several floors and are quite large.

There was also a description of eight kinds of machines that operated with the use of 1. Electricity, 2. Natural elements (air, water), 3. Steam, 4. Gems, 5. Air power, 6. Oil (petrol, diesel), 7. Solar energy, and 8. Magnetic power. So these kinds of machines were not unfamiliar to those knowledgeable in the Vedic literature. The point of all this is that if these various Vedic texts that are hundreds and thousands of years old cover these numerous topics, it would be extremely hard to say that this comes from anything but an advanced civilization. Therefore, we reach a point of having to acknowledge the supremacy of Vedic culture.

THE VEDIC ION MACHINE

One more very interesting account of the advanced nature of Vedic science in action was reported in *Ancient Skies*, a bi-monthly magazine published by the Ancient Astronaut Society in Highland Park, Illinois. An article by Bhalchandra Patwardhan, reproduced in the *Annual Research Journal--1997* of the Institute For Rewriting Indian (And World) History, describes the Vedic Ion Engine.

It turns out that there are verses in the tenth chapter of the *Rig-Veda* that refer to the Art of Flight, and the means by which it can be capable. The great Rishi Bharadwaja wrote a commentary, called *Yantra Vidya* (Science of Machines), in which he describes the mechanism which provides the impulse needed for propulsion, involving the combination of eight sub-assemblies and using the interaction principally of solar energy and Mercury. The ancient text known as the *Vymaanika-Shastra* contains detailed instructions on building a mercury vortex engine. It turned out that a Sanskrit scholar, Shivkar Bapuji Talpade, used his Sanskrit knowledge and creativity to construct such an aircraft according to the *Rig-veda* description. In fact, he demonstrated the capability of the aircraft on a beach in Bombay, India in 1895. The demonstration was attended by such people as Maharaja Sayajirao Gaekwad of Baroda, and was reported in a leading Marathi daily newspaper, called *The Kesari*. Let us remember that this was eight years before the Wright Brothers achieved their first flight at Kitty Hawk, North Carolina. Mr. Shivkar Bapuji Talpade used this flying machine, the Vedic Ion Engine, to reach an altitude of 1500 feet.

The basis of the Vedic Ion Engine is to use a stream of high-velocity electrified particles instead of hot gases to propel the aircraft. Interestingly, the National Aeronautics and Space Administration (NASA) was planning to send a space probe to meet with Halley's Comet in 1980 which was to be powered by such an Ion Engine. As Bhalchandra Patwardhan's article explains, "The theory of the Ion Engine has been credited to Robert Goddard, long recognized as the father of Liquid-fuel Rocketry. It is claimed that in 1906, long before Goddard launched his first modern rocket, his imagination had conceived the idea of an Ion rocket."

However, this is still after Talpade had already demonstrated what he could do by using the Vedic information to build a flying machine without additional research and development to perfect it. Nonetheless, as the article continues, "The engine now being developed for future use by NASA, by some strange coincidence, also uses Mercury bombardment units powered by solar cells [much like the Vedic description]. Interestingly, the impulse is generated in seven stages. The Mercury propellent is first vaporized, fed into the thruster discharge chamber, ionized, converted into a plasma by combination of electrons, broken down electrically, and then accelerated through small openings in a screen to pass out of the engine at velocities between 20,000 and 50,000 metres per second."

This description is much the same as that for Talpade's machine. The big difference is that NASA's machine was yet to produce more than one pound of thrust, while Talpade's machine lifted his aircraft 1500 feet into the air. It seems that NASA could have used some pointers directly from the ancient Vedic information to more quickly perfect their machine. The point is that regardless of how much progress any civilization has made in the area of flight, the reality is that such scientific thought originated in the Vedic civilization much earlier than in the West. Furthermore, Vedic society had already produced results using principles that we are now only rediscovering.

Although early India had many scientific advancements, there were several major reasons why they began to fade. One of course was the great *Mahabharata* war at Kuruksetra. This started the many factions and disruptions in the global Vedic empire that kept and funded many educational institutions from which they spread their knowledge and continued their developments. Later, the many foreign invasions also interrupted their progress. From this came the urge for secrecy that kept new advancements in knowledge from spreading. Furthermore, the invasions put so much pressure on the people in general, as well as the local rulers, that they had other things with which they were concerned, and, thus, many people became introverted toward their own concerns and apathetic to the scientific advancements that once made India so prominent in the world. Therefore, the scientific research that had been developed in ancient India was reduced in time to be considered as merely antiques. Nonetheless, it has proved to be a great contribution to the world and an essential part of the development we have continued to make in this day and age.

Even the spiritual sciences and technologies we are learning today were clearly understood in Vedic times. As we can recognize in what some people may call the "New Age" teachings, or new insights in life after death through the out-of-body and near-death experiences people are having, much of this describes information and experiences that were already known and explained thousands of years ago in the Vedic teachings. Even the techniques for relaxing, expanding our consciousness, visualization and meditation, tuning into higher energies and higher benevolent beings, the present fascination with angels, or preparing for death--the final transition, is all old science. It is nothing knew when you look back into the ancient teachings found in the Vedic literature. That is where the roots of all this can be found. We are only relearning what was previously known thousands of years ago.

CHAPTER FOUR

The Origins of Vedic Society: Source of the World's Spiritual Heritage

With only a small amount of research, a person can discover that each area of the world has its own ancient culture that includes its own gods and legends about the origins of various cosmological realities, and that many of these are very similar. But where did all these stories and gods come from? Did they all spread around the world from one particular source, only to change according to differences in language and customs? If not, then why are some of these gods and goddesses of various areas of the world so alike?

Unfortunately, information about prehistoric religion is usually gathered through whatever remnants of earlier cultures we can find, such as bones in tombs and caves, or ancient sculptures, writings, engravings, wall paintings, and other relics. From these we are left to speculate about the rituals, ceremonies, and beliefs of the people and the purposes of the items found. Often we can only paint a crude picture of how simple and backwards these ancient people were while not thinking that more advanced civilizations may have left us next to nothing in terms of physical remains. They may have built houses out of wood or materials other than stone that have since faded with the seasons, or were simply replaced with other buildings over the years, rather than buried by the sands of time for archeologists to unearth. They also may have cremated their dead, as some societies did, leaving no bones to discover. Thus, without ancient museums or historical records from the past, there would be no way of really knowing what the prehistoric cultures were like.

If a few thousand years in the future people could uncover our own houses after being buried for so long and find television antennas on top of each house wired to a television inside, who knows what they would think. Without a recorded history of our times they might speculate that the antennas, being pointed toward the heavens, were used for us to commune with our gods who would appear, by mystic power, on the screen of the television box inside our homes. They might also think that we were very much devoted to our gods since some houses might have two, three, or more televisions, making it possible for us to never be without contact with our gods through the day. And since the television was usually found in a prominent area, with special couches and reclining chairs, this must surely be the prayer room where we would get the proper inspiration for living life. Or they might even think that the television was itself the god, the idol of our times. This, of course, would not be a very accurate picture, but it reflects the difficulty we have in understanding ancient religion by means of analyzing the remnants we find. However, when we begin comparing all the religions of the world, we can see how they are all interrelated and have a source from which most of them seem to have originated. And most of them can be traced to the East.

Most scholars agree that the earliest of religions seems to have arisen from the most ancient of organized cultures, which are either the Sumerians along the Euphrates, or the Aryans located in the region of the Indus Valley. In fact, these two cultures were related. C. L. Woolley, one of the world's foremost archeologists, establishes in his book, *The Sumerians*, that the facial characteristics of the Sumerian people can be traced to Afghanistan, Baluchistan, and on to the Indus region. The early Indus civilization, which was remarkably developed, has many similarities with Sumer over 1500 miles away, especially in regard to the rectangular seals that have identical subjects on them, and are similar in the style of engraving and inscriptions. There are also similarities in the methods used in the ground plans and construction of buildings. Woolley suggests that, rather than concluding too quickly that the Sumerians and Indus civilization shared the same race or political culture, which may actually have been the case, or that such similarities were merely from trade connections, the evidence at least indicates that the two societies shared a common source.

The researcher and scholar L. A. Waddell offers more evidence to show the relation between the Aryans and the Sumerians. He states in his book, *The Indo Sumerian Seals Deciphered*, that the discovery and translation of the Sumerian seals along the Indus Valley give evidence that the Aryan society existed there from as long ago as 3100 B.C. Several Sumerian seals found along the Indus bore the names of famous Vedic Aryan seers and princes familiar in the Vedic hymns. Therefore, these Aryan personalities were not merely part of an elaborate myth, like some people seem to proclaim, but actually lived five thousand years ago as related in the Vedic epics and *Puranas*.

Waddell also says that the language and religion of the Indo-Aryans were radically similar to that of the Sumerians and Phoenicians, and that the early Aryan kings of the Indian *Vedas* are identical with well-known historical kings of the Sumerians. He believes that the decipherment of these seals from the Indus Valley confirms that the Sumerians were actually the early Aryans and authors of Indian civilization. He concludes that the Sumerians were Aryans in physique, culture, religion, language, and writing. He also feels that the early Sumerians on the Persian Gulf near 3100 B.C. were Phoenicians who were Aryans in race and speech, and were the introducers of Aryan civilization in ancient India. Thus, he concludes that it was the Aryans who were the bearers of high civilization and who spread throughout the Mediterranean, Northwest Europe, and Britain, as well as India. However, he states that the early Aryan Sumero-Phoenicians did not become a part of the Aryan Invasion of India until the seventh century B.C. after their defeat by the Assyrian Sargon II in 718 B.C. at Carchemish in Upper Mesopotamia. Though the Sumerians indeed may have been Aryan people, some researchers feel that rather than being the originators of Vedic Aryan culture, or part of an invasion into India, they were an extension of the Vedic culture that originated in India and spread through Persia and into Europe.

THEORIES ON THE ARYAN ORIGINS

This brings us to the different theories that scholars have about the origins of the Aryan society. Though it seems evident that an Aryan society was in existence in the Indus Valley by 3100 B.C., not everyone agrees with the dates that Waddell has presented for the Aryan Invasion into India, and whether the Aryans were actually invaders is doubtful. Obviously, different views on the Aryanization of India are held by different historians. Some scholars say that it was about 1000 B.C. when Aryans entered Iran from the north and then occupied the Indus region by 800 B.C. In this scenario, the Aryans had to have entered India sometime after this. But others say that it was between 1500 and 1200 B.C. that the Aryans entered India and composed hymns that make up the *Rig-veda*. So some people calculate that the *Rig-veda* must have been composed around 1400 B.C.

Mr. Pargiter, another noted scholar, contends that Aryan influence in India was felt long before the composition of the Vedic hymns. He states that the Aryans entered India near 2000 B.C. over the Central Himalayas and later spread into the Punjab. Brunnhofer and others argue that the composition of the *Rig-veda* took place not in the Punjab, but in Afghanistan or Iran. This theory assumes that Aryan entrance into India was much later.

Even Max Muller, the great orientalist and translator of Eastern texts, was also a great proponent of speculating on the dates of the compilations of the *Vedas*. He admitted that his ideas on the dates of the *Vedas* could not be dependable. He had originally estimated that the *Rig-veda* had been written around 1000 B.C. However, he was greatly criticized for that date, and he later wrote in his book, *Physical Religion* (p.91, 1891), "Whether the Vedic hymns were composed 1000, 1500 or 2000 BCE, no power on earth will ever determine."

So, as we can see from the above examples, which are just a few of the many ideas on the Aryan origins, analyzing these theories can get rather confusing. In fact, so many theories on the location of the original Aryans or Indo-Europeans have been presented by archeologists and researchers that for a time they felt the location could change from minute to minute, depending on the latest evidence that was presented. In many cases over the years, archeologists presumed they had located the home of the Sumerians or Aryans any time they found certain types of metal tools or painted pottery that resembled what had been found at the Sumerian or Indus Valley sites. Though such findings may have been of some significance, further study proved that they were of considerably less importance than had been originally thought, and, thus, the quest for locating the original Aryan home could not be concluded.

WAS THERE EVER AN ARYAN INVASION?

One of the major reasons why a consideration of the idea of an Aryan invasion into India is prevalent among some Western researchers is because of their misinterpretation of the *Vedas*, deliberate or otherwise, that suggests the Aryans were a nomadic people. One such misinterpretation is from the *Rig-veda*, which describes the battle between Sudas and the ten kings. The battle of the ten kings included the Pakthas, Bhalanas, Alinas, Shivas, Vishanins, Shimyus, Bhrigus, Druhyas, Prithus, and Parshus, who fought against the Tritsus. The Prithus or Parthavas became the Parthians of latter-day Iran (247 B.C.–224 A.D.). The Parshus or Pashavas became the latter-day Persians. These kings, though some are described as Aryans, were actually fallen Aryans, or rebellious and materialistic kings who had given up the spiritual path and were conquered by Sudas. Occasionally, there was a degeneration of the spiritual kingdom in areas of India, and wars had to be fought in order to reestablish the spiritual Aryan culture in these areas. Western scholars could and did easily misinterpret this to mean an invasion of nomadic people called Aryans rather than simply a war in which the superior Aryan kings reestablished the spiritual values and the Vedic Aryan way of life.

Let us also remember that the Aryan invasion theory was hypothesized in the nineteenth century to explain the similarities found in Sanskrit and the languages of Europe. One person who reported about this is Deen Chandora in his article, *Distorted Historical Events and Discredited Hindu Chronology,* as it appeared in *Revisiting Indus-Sarasvati Age and Ancient India* (p. 383). He explains that the idea of the Aryan invasion was certainly not a matter of misguided research, but was a conspiracy to distribute deliberate misinformation that was formulated on April 10, 1866 in London at a secret meeting held in the Royal Asiatic Society. This was "to induct the theory of the Aryan invasion of India, so that no Indian may say that English are foreigners. . . India was ruled all along by outsiders and so the country must remain a slave under the benign Christian rule." This was a political move and this theory was put to solid use in all schools and colleges.

So it was basically a linguistic theory adopted by the British colonial authorities to keep themselves in power. This theory suggested, more or less, that there was a race of superior, white Aryans who came in from the Caucasus Mountains and invaded the Indus region, and then established their culture, compiled their literature, and then proceeded to invade the rest of India.

As can be expected, most of those who were great proponents of the Aryan invasion theory were often ardent English and German nationalists, or Christians, ready and willing to bring about the desecration of anything that was non-Christian or non-European. Even Max Muller believed in the Christian chronology, that the world was created at 9:00 AM on October 23, 4004 B.C. and the great flood occurred in 2500 B.C. Thus, it was impossible to give a date for the Aryan invasion earlier than 1500 B.C. After all, accepting the Christian time frame would force them to eliminate all other evidence and possibilities, so what else could they do? So, even this date for the Aryan invasion was based on speculation.

In this way, the Aryan invasion theory was created to make it appear that Indian culture and philosophy was dependent on the previous developments in Europe, thereby justifying the need for colonial rule and Christian expansion in India. This was also the purpose of the study of Sanskrit, such as at Oxford University in England, as indicated by Colonel Boden who sponsored the program. He stated that they should "promote Sanskrit learning among the English, so as 'to enable his countrymen to proceed in the conversion of the natives of India to the Christian religion.'"

Unfortunately, this was also Max Muller's ultimate goal. In a letter to his wife in 1866, he wrote about his translation of the *Rig-veda*: "This edition of mine and the translation of the *Veda*, will hereafter tell to a great extent on the fate of India and on the growth of millions of souls in that country. It is the root of their religion and to show them what the root is, I feel sure, is the only way of uprooting all that has sprung from it during the last three thousand years." (*The Life and Letters of Right Honorable Friedrich Max Muller*, Vol. I. p.346)

So, in essence, the British used the theory of the Aryan invasion to further their "divide and conquer" policy. With civil unrest and regional cultural tensions created by the British through designations and divisions among the Indian society, it gave a reason and purpose for the British to continue and increase their control over India. This will be explained further elsewhere in the book.

However, under scrutiny, the Aryan invasion theory lacks justification. For example, Sir John Marshall, one of the chief excavators at Mohenjo-Daro, offers evidence that India may have been following the Vedic religion long before any so-called "invaders" ever arrived. He points out that it is known that India possessed a highly advanced and organized urban civilization dating back to at least 2300 B.C., if not much earlier. In fact, some researchers suggest that evidence makes it clear that the Indus Valley civilization was quite developed by at least 3100 B.C. The known cities of this civilization cover an area along the Indus river and extend from the coast to Rajasthan and the Punjab over to the

Yamuna and Upper Ganges. At its height, the Indus culture spread over 300,000 square miles, an area larger than Western Europe. Cities that were a part of the Indus culture include Mohenjo-Daro, Kot Diji east of Mohenjo-Daro, Amri on the lower Indus, Lothal south of Ahmedabad, Malwan farther south, Harappa 350 miles upstream from Mohenjo-Daro, Kalibangan and Alamgirpur farther east, Rupar near the Himalayas, Sutkagen Dor to the west along the coast, Mehrgarh 150 miles north of Mohenjo-Daro, and Mundigak much farther north. Evidence at Mehrgarh shows a civilization that dates back to 6500 B.C. It had been connected with the Indus culture but was deserted in the third millennium B.C. around the time the city of Mohenjo-Daro became prominent.

The arrangement of these cities and the knowledge of the residents was much superior to that of any immigrating nomads, except for military abilities at the time. A lack of weapons, except for thin spears, at these cities indicates they were not very well equipped militarily. Thus, one theory is that if there were invaders, whoever they may have been, rather than encouraging the advancement of Vedic society when they came into the Indus Valley region, they may have helped stifle it or even caused its demise in certain areas. The Indus Valley locations may have been one area where the Vedic society disappeared after the arrival of these invaders. Many of these cities seemed to have been abandoned quickly, while others were not. However, some geologists suggest that the cities were left because of environmental changes. Evidence of floods in the plains is seen in the thick layers of silt which are now thirty-nine feet above the river in the upper strata of Mohenjo-Daro. Others say that the ecological needs of the community forced the people to move on, since research shows there was a great reduction in rainfall from that period to the present.

We also have to remember that many of the Indus sites, like Kalibangan, were close to the region of the old Sarasvati River. Some Hindu scholars are actually preferring to rename the Indus Valley culture as the Indus-Sarasvati culture because the Sarasvati was a prominent river and very important at the time. For example, the Sarasvati River is glowingly praised in the *Rig-veda*. However, the Sarasvati River stopped flowing and later dried up. Recent scientific studies calculate that the river stopped flowing as early as around 8000 B.C. It dried up near the end of the Indus Valley civilization, at least by 1900 B.C. This was no doubt one reason why these cities were abandoned. This also means that if the Vedic people came after the Indus Valley culture, they could not have known of the Sarasvati River. This is further evidence that the *Vedas* were from many years before the time of the Indus Valley society and were not brought into the region by some invasion.

As a result of the latest studies, evidence points in the direction that the Indus sites were wiped out not by acts of war or an invasion, but by the drought that is known to have taken place and continued for 300 years. Whatever skeletons that have been found in the region may indicate deaths not by war but by starvation or lack of water. Deaths of the weak by starvation are normal before the whole society finally moves away for better lands and more abundant resources. This is the same drought that wiped out the Akkadians of Sumeria, and caused a sudden abandonment of cities in Mesopotamia, such as at Tell Leilan and Tell Brock. The beginning of the end of these civilizations had to have been near 2500 B.C. This drought no doubt contributed to the final drying up of the Sarasvati River.

Regarding Mohenjo-Daro, archeologists have discovered no sign of attack, such as extensive burning, or remains of armor-clad warriors, and no foreign weapons. This leaves us to believe that the enemy of the people in this region was nature, such as earthquakes, flooding, or the severe drought, or even a change in the course of rivers, and not warrior invaders. So again, the invasion theory does not stand up to scrutiny from the anthropological point of view.

The best known archeological sites of the Indus cities are Mohenjo-Daro and Harappa. Excavation work at Mohenjo-Daro was done from 1922 to 1931 and 1935 to 1936. Excavation at Harappa took place from 1920 to 1921 and 1933 to 1934. Evidence has shown that temples played an important part in the life of the residents of these cities. The citadel at Mohenjo-Daro contains a 39-by-23 foot bath. This seems to have been used for ceremonial purposes similar in the manner that many large temple complexes in India also have central pools for bathing and rituals. Though deities have not been found in the ruins, no doubt because they were too important to abandon, images of a Mother goddess and a Male god similar to Lord Shiva sitting in a yoga posture have been found. Some of the Shiva seals show a man with three heads and an erect phallus, sitting in meditation and surrounded by animals. This would be Shiva as Pashupati, lord or friend of the animals. Representations of the *lingam* of Shiva and *yoni* of his spouse have also been easily located, as well as non-phallic stones such as the *shalagram-shila* stone of Lord Vishnu. Thus, the religions of Shiva and Vishnu, which are directly Vedic, had been very much a part of this society long ago and were not brought to the area by any invaders who may have arrived later.

Another point that helps convince that the Vedic religion and culture had to have been there in India and pre-Harappan times is the sacrificial altars that have been discovered at the Harappan sites. These are all of similar design and found from Baluchistan to Uttar Pradesh, and down into Gujarat. This shows that the whole of this area must have been a part of one specific culture, the Vedic culture, which had to have been there before these sites were abandoned.

More information in this regard is found in an article by J. F. Jarrige and R. H. Meadow in the August, 1980 issue of *Scientific American* called "The Antecedents of Civilization in the Indus Valley." In the article they mention that recent excavations at Mehrgarh show that the antecedents of the Indus Valley culture go back earlier than 6000 B.C. in India. An outside influence did not affect its development. Astronomical references established in the *Vedas* do indeed concur with the date of Mehrgarh. Therefore, sites such as Mehrgarh reflect the earlier Vedic age of India. Thus, we have a theory of an Aryan invasion which is not remembered by the people of the area that were supposed to have been conquered by the Aryans.

Furthermore, Dr. S. R. Rao has deciphered the Harappan script to be of an Indo-Aryan base. In fact, he has shown how the South Arabic, Old Aramic, and the ancient Indian Brahmi scripts are all derivatives of the Indus Valley script. This new evidence confirms that the Harappan civilization could not have been Dravidians that were overwhelmed by an Aryan invasion, but they were followers of the Vedic religion. The irony is that the invasion theory suggests that the Vedic Aryans destroyed the Dravidian Indus townships which had to have been previously built according to the mathematical instructions that are found in the Vedic literature of the Aryans, such as the *Shulbasutras*. This point helps void the invasion theory. After all, if the people of these cities used the Vedic styles of religious altars and town planning, it would mean they were already Aryans.

In a similar line of thought in another recent book, *Vedic Glossary on Indus Seals*, Dr. Natwar Jha has provided an interpretation of the ancient script of the numerous recovered seals of the Indus Valley civilization. He has concluded that the Indus Valley seals, which are small soapstone, one-inch squares, exhibit a relation to the ancient form of Brahmi. He found words on the seals that come from the ancient *Nighantu* text, which is a glossary of Sanskrit compiled by the sage Yaksa that deals with words of subordinate Vedic texts. An account of Yaksa's search for older Sanskrit words is found in the *Shanti Parva* of the *Mahabharata*. This may have been in relation to the Indus Valley seals and certainly shows its ancient Vedic connection.

The point of all this is that the entire *Rig-veda* had to have been existing for thousands of years by the time the Indus Valley seals were produced. Therefore, the seals were of Vedic Sanskrit origin or a derivative of it, and the Indus Valley sites were part of the Vedic culture. This is further evidence that there was no Aryan invasion. No Aryan invasion means that the area and its residents were already a part of the Vedic empire. This also means that the so-called Indo-Aryan or Indo-European civilization was nothing but the worldwide Vedic culture. From this we can also conclude, therefore, that the so-called Indo-Aryan group of languages is nothing but the various local mispronunciations of Sanskrit which has pervaded the civilized world for thousands of years.

Another interesting point is that skeletal remains found in the Harappan sites that date back to 4000 years ago show the same basic racial types in the Punjab and Gujarat as found today. This verifies that no outside race invaded and took over the area. The only west to east movement that took place was after the Sarasvati went dry, and that was involving the people who were already there. In this regard, Sir John Marshall, in charge of the excavations at the Harappan sites, said that the Indus civilization was the oldest to be unearthed, even older than the Sumerian culture, which is believed to be but a branch of the former, and, thus, an outgrowth of the Vedic society.

One more point about skeletal remains at the Harappan sites is that bones of horses are found at all levels of these locations. Thus, the horse was well known to these people. The horse was mentioned in the *Rig-veda*, and was one of the main animals of Vedic culture in India. However, according to records in Mesopotamia, the horse was unknown to that region until only about 2100 B.C. So this provides further proof that the direction of movement by the people was from India to the west, not the other way around as the invasion theory suggests.

Professor Lal has written a book, *The Earliest Civilization of South Asia*, in which he also has concluded that the theory of an Aryan invasion has no basis. An invasion is not the reason for the destruction of the Harappan civilization. It was caused by climactic changes. He says the Harappan society was a melting pot made up of people from the Mediterranean, Armenia, the Alpine area, and even China. They engaged in typical Vedic fire worship, *ashwamedha* rituals. Such fire altars have been found in the Indus Valley cities of Banawali, Lothal, and Kalibangan.

He also explains that the city of Kalibangan came to ruin when the Saraswati River dried up, caused by severe climactic changes around 1900 B.C. Thus, the mention of the Sarasvati River also helps date the *Vedas*, which had to have existed before this. This would put the origin of Sanskrit writing and the earliest portions of Vedic literature at least sometime before 4000 B.C., 6000 years ago.

In conclusion, V. Gordon Childe states in his book, *The Aryans*, that though the idea of an Asiatic origin of the Aryans, who then migrated into India, is the most widely accepted idea, it is still the least well documented. And this idea is only one of the unfounded generalizations with which for over seventy years anthropology and archeology have been in conflict. In fact, today the northern Asiatic origin of the Aryans is a hypothesis which has been abandoned by most linguists and archeologists.

THE INDUS VALLEY CIVILIZATION
WAS A PART OF THE ADVANCED VEDIC CULTURE

Besides what we have already discussed, more light is shed on the advanced civilization of the Indus Valley and how it influenced areas beyond its region when we consider the subject of Vedic mathematics. E. J. H. Mackay explains in his book, *Further Excavations at Mohenjo-Daro*, that the whole basis of Vedic mathematics is geometry, and geometrical instruments have been found in the Indus Valley which date back to at least 2800 B.C. The Vedic form of mathematics was much more advanced than that found in early Greek and Egyptian societies. This can be seen in the *Shulbasutras*, supplements of the *Kalpasutras*, which also show the earliest forms of algebra which were used by the Vedic priests in their geometry for the construction of altars and arenas for religious purposes. In fact, the geometrical formula known as the Pythagorean theorem can be traced to the *Baudhayans*, the earliest forms of the *Shulbasutras* dated prior to the eighth century B.C.

The *Shulbasutras* are the earliest forms of mathematical knowledge, and certainly the earliest for any religious purpose. They basically appear as a supplement to the ritual (*Shrauta*) aspect of the *Kalpasutras*. They essentially contain the mathematical formulas for the design of various altars for the Vedic rituals of worship, which are evident in the Indus Valley sites.

The date of the *Shulbasutras*, after comparing the Baudhayana, Apastamba and Katyayana *Shulbas* with the early mathematics of ancient Egypt and Babylonia, as described by N. S. Rajaram in *Vedic Aryans and The Origins of Civilization* (p.139), is near 2000 B.C. However, after including astronomical data from the *Ashvalayana Grihyasutra*, *Shatapantha Brahmana*, etc., the date can be brought farther back to near 3000 B.C., near the time of the *Mahabharata* War and the compilation of the other Vedic texts by Srila Vyasadeva.

With this view in mind, Vedic mathematics can no longer be considered as a derivative from ancient Babylon, which dates to 1700 B.C., but must be the source of it as well as the Greek or Pythagorean mathematics. Therefore, the advanced nature of the geometry found in the *Shulbasutras* indicates that it provided the knowledge that had to have been known during the construction of the Indus sites, such as Harappa and Mohenjo-Daro, as well as that used in ancient Greece and Babylon.

It is Vedic mathematics that originated the decimal system of tens, hundreds, thousands, and so on, and in which the remainder of one column of numbers is carried over to the next column. The Indian number system was used in Arabia after 700 A.D. and was called Al-Arqan-Al-Hindu. This spread into Europe and became known as the Arabic numerals. This, of course, has developed into the number system we use today, which is significantly easier than the Egyptian, Roman, or Chinese symbols for numbers that made mathematics much more difficult. It was the Indians who devised the methods of dividing fractions and the use of equations and letters to signify unknown factors. They also made discoveries in calculus and other systems of math several hundred years before these same principles were understood in Europe. Thus, it becomes obvious that if the Europeans had not changed from the Roman numeral system to the form of mathematics that originated in India, many of the developments that took place in Europe would not have been possible. In this way, all evidence indicates that it was not any northern invaders into India who brought or originated this advanced form of mathematics, but it was from the Vedic Aryan civilization that had already been existing in India and the Indus Valley region. Thus, we can see that such intellectual influence did not descend from the north into India, but rather traveled from India up into Europe.

Additional evidence that it was not any invaders who originated the highly advanced Vedic culture in the Indus Valley is the fact that various seals that Waddell calls Sumerian and dates back to 2800 B.C. have been found bearing the image of the water buffalo or Brahma bull. Modern zoologists believe that the water buffalo was known only to the Ganges and Brahmaputra valleys and did not exist in Western India or the Indus Valley. This would suggest a few possibilities. One is that the Sumerians had traveled to Central and Eastern India for reasons of trade and for finding precious stones since Harappa was a trading center connected by way of the Indus river with the gold and turquoise industry of Tibet. Thus, they learned about the water buffalo and used images of them on their seals. The second and most likely possibility is that the Aryan civilization at the time extended from Eastern India to the Indus region and farther west to Mesopotamia and beyond, and included the Sumerians as a branch. So, trade and its Vedic connections with India naturally brought the image of the water buffalo to the Indus Valley region and beyond.

Further evidence showing the Vedic influence on the region of Mohenjo-Daro is a tablet dating back to 2600 B.C. It depicts an image of Lord Krishna as a child. This positively shows that the Indus Valley culture was connected with the ancient Vedic system, which was prevalent along the banks of the Rivers Sarasvati and Sindhu thousands of years ago.

THE VEDIC LITERATURE SUPPLIES NO EVIDENCE OF AN ARYAN INVASION

As we can see from the above information, the presence of the Vedic Aryans in the Indus region is undeniable, but the evidence indicates they had been there long before any invaders or immigrating nomads ever arrived, and, thus, the Vedic texts must have been in existence there for quite some time as well. In fact, the Vedic literature establishes that they were written many years before the above mentioned date of 1400 B.C. The age of Kali is said to have begun in 3102 B.C. with the disappearance of Lord Krishna, which is the time when Srila Vyasadeva is said to have begun composing the Vedic knowledge into written form. Thus, the Rig-veda could not have been written or brought into the area by the so-called "invaders" because they are not supposed to have come through the area until 1600 years later.

One of the problems with dating the Vedic literature has been the use of linguistic analysis, which has not been dependable. It can be safe to say, as pointed out by K. C. Verma in his Mahabharata: Myth and Reality–Differing Views (p.99), "All attempts to date the Vedic literature on linguistic grounds have failed miserably for the simple reason that (a) the conclusions of comparative philology are often speculative and (b) no one has yet succeeded in showing how much change should take place in a language in a given period. The only safe method is astronomical."

With this suggestion, instead of using the error prone method of linguistics, we can look at the conclusion a few others have drawn by using astronomical records for dating the *Vedas*. With the use of astronomical calculations, some scholars date the earliest hymns of the *Rig-veda* to before 4500 B.C. Others, such as Lokmanya Tilak and Hermann Jacobi, agree that the major portion of the hymns of the *Rig-veda* were composed from 4500 to 3500 B.C., when the vernal equinox was in the Orion constellation. These calculations had to have been actual sightings, according to K. C. Verma, who states, "it has been proved beyond doubt that before the discoveries of Newton, Liebnitz, La Place, La Grange, etc., back calculations could not have been made; they are based on observational astronomy." (*Mahabharata: Myth and Reality–Differing Views*, p.124)

In his book called *The Celestial Key to the Vedas: Discovering the Origins of the World's Oldest Civilization*, B. G. Sidharth provides astronomical evidence that the earliest portions of the *Rig-veda* can be dated to 10,000 B.C. He is the director of the B. M. Birla Science Center and has 30 years of experience in astronomy and science. He also confirms that India had a thriving civilization capable of sophisticated astronomy long before Greece, Egypt, or any other culture in the world.

In his commentary on *Srimad-Bhagavatam* (1.7.8), A. C. Bhaktivedanta Swami, one of the most distinguished Vedic scholars of modern times, also discusses the estimated date of when the Vedic literature was written based on astronomical evidence. He writes that there is some diversity amongst mundane scholars as to the date when *Srimad-Bhagavatam* was compiled, the latest of Vedic scriptures. But from the text it is certain that it was compiled after Lord Krishna disappeared from the planet and before the disappearance of King Pariksit. We are presently in the five thousandth year of the age of Kali according to astronomical calculation and evidence in the revealed scriptures. Therefore, he concludes, *Srimad-Bhagavatam* had to have been compiled at least five thousand years ago. The *Mahabharata* was compiled before *Srimad-Bhagavatam*, and the major *Puranas* were compiled before *Mahabharata*.

Furthermore, we know that the *Upanishads* and the four primary *Vedas*, including the *Rig-veda*, were compiled years before *Mahabharata*. This would indicate that the Vedic literature was already existing before any so-called invasion, which is said to have happened around 1400 B.C. In fact, this indicates that the real Aryans were the Vedic kings and sages who were already prevalent in this region, and not any uncertain tribe of nomadic people that some historians inappropriately call "invading Aryans" who came into India and then wrote their Vedic texts after their arrival. So this confirms the Vedic version.

Another point of consideration is the Sarasvati River. Some people feel that the Sarasvati is simply a mythical river, but through research and the use of aerial photography they have rediscovered parts of what once was its river bed. As the *Vedas* describe, and as research has shown, it had once been a very prominent river. Many hundreds of years ago it flowed from the Himalayan mountains southwest to the Arabian Sea at the Rann of Kutch, which is north of Mumbai (Bombay) in the area of Dwaraka. However, it is known to have changed course several times, flowing in a more westerly direction, and dried up near 1900 B.C.

Since the *Rig-veda* (7.95.1) describes the course of the river from the mountains to the sea, as well as (10.75.5) locates the river between the Yamuna and the Shutudri (Sutlej), it becomes obvious that the Vedic Aryans had to have been in India before this river dried up, or long before 2000 B.C. The *Atharva-veda* (6.30.1) also mentions growing barley along the Sarasvati. And the *Vajasaneya Samhita* of the *Yajur-veda* (*Shuklayajur-veda* 34.11) relates that five rivers flow into the Sarasvati, after which she becomes a vast river. This is confirmed by satellite photography, archeology, and hydrological surveys that the Sarasvati was a huge river, up to five miles wide. Not only does this verify the antiquity of the Aryan civilization in India, but also of the Vedic literature, which had to have been in existence many hundreds of years before 1900 B.C. So this helps confirm the above date of 3102 B.C. when the Vedic texts were compiled.

Furthermore, the ancient *Rig-veda* (10.75.5; 6.45.31; 3.59.6) mentions the Ganges, sometimes called the Jahnavi, along with the Yamuna, Sarasvati, and Sindhu (Indus) rivers (*Rig-veda*, 10.75.1-9). So the rivers and settlements in the Ganges region did have significance in the Vedic literature, which shows that the *Vedas* were written in India and not brought into the Ganges area after they had been written at some other location.

The *Manu-samhita* (2.21-22) also describes Madhyadesa, the central region of India, as being where the Aryans were located between the Himavat and Vindhya mountains, east of Prayaga and west of Vinasana where the Sarasvati River disappears. It also says the land that extends as far as the eastern and western oceans is called Aryavata (place of the Aryans) by the wise. This means that the center of Vedic civilization at the time was near the Sarasvati River.

The point of this is that here is more evidence that the Vedic Aryans could not have invaded India or written the *Rig-veda* after 1800 B.C. and known about the Sarasvati River. In fact, for the river to have been as great as it is described in the *Vedas* and *Puranas*, the Aryans had to have been existing in the area for several thousand years, at least before the river began to dry up. And if the Aryans were not the first people in this area, then why are there no pre-Aryan names for these rivers? Or why has no one discovered the pre-Indus Valley language if it had been inhabited by a different people before the Aryans arrived? And why is there no record of any Aryan invasion in any of the Vedic literature?

In this regard, Mr. K. D. Sethna points out on page 67 of his book, *The Problem of Aryan Origins From an Indian Point of View*, that even scholars who believe in an Aryan invasion of India around 1500 B.C. admit that the *Rig-veda* supplies no sign of an entry into the Indian subcontinent from anywhere. There is no mention of any such invasion. From our research and evidence, the *Rig-veda* can be dated to at least around 3000 B.C. or much earlier. Thus, for all practical purposes, there is little reason to discuss any other origination of the Vedic Aryans than the area of Northern India.

This is corroborated in *The Cultural Heritage of India* (pp. 182-3) wherein it explains that Indian tradition knows nothing of any Aryan invasion from the northwest or outside of India. In fact, the *Rig-veda* (Book Ten, Chapter 75) lists the rivers in the order from the east to the northwest, in accordance with the expansion of the Aryan outflow from India to the northwest. This would concur with the history in the *Puranas* that India was the home of the Aryans, from where they expanded to outside countries in various directions, spreading the Vedic culture. The *Manu-samhita* (2.17-18) specifically points out that the region of the Vedic Aryans is between the Sarasvati and the Drishadvati Rivers, as similarly found in the *Rig-veda* (3.24.4).

Any wars mentioned in the Vedic literature are those that have taken place between people of the same culture, or between the demigods and demons, or the forces of light and darkness. The idea that the term "Aryan" or "Arya" refers to those of a particular race is misleading. It is a term that means anyone of any race that is noble and of righteous and gentle conduct. To instill the idea of an Aryan invasion into the Vedic texts is merely an exercise of taking isolated verses out of context and changing the meaning of the terms. Even the oldest written Vedic book, the *Rig-veda*, contains no mention of a wandering tribe of people coming from some original holy land or any mountainous regions from outside India. In fact, it describes the Indian subcontinent in recognizable terms of rivers and climate. The Sarasvati River is often mentioned in the *Rig-veda*, which makes it clear that the region of the Sarasvati was a prime area of the Vedic people. Furthermore, it describes no wars with outsiders, no capturing of cities, and no incoming culture of any kind that would indicate an invasion from a foreign tribe. Only much later after the Vedic period do we have the invasion of India by the Muslims and the British, for which there is so much recorded evidence.

The Vedic literature is massive, and no other culture has produced anything like it in regard to ancient history. Not the Egyptians, Sumerians, Babylonians, or Chinese. So if it was produced outside of India, how could there not be some reference to its land of origination? For that matter, how could these so-called primitive nomads who came invading the Indus region invent such a sophisticated language and produce such a distinguished record of their customs in spite of their migrations and numerous battles? This is hardly likely. Only a people who are well established and advanced in their knowledge and culture can do such a thing. In this way, we can see that the Vedic texts give every indication that the Vedic Aryans originated in India.

Therefore, we are left with much evidence in literary records and archeological findings, as we shall see, that flies in the face of the Aryan invasion theory. It shows how the Vedic Aryans went from India to Iran, Mesopotamia, Anatolia, and on toward Europe in a westward direction rather than toward the east. The invasion theory is but a product of the imagination.

MORE EVIDENCE FOR THE ORIGINAL HOME
OF THE VEDIC ARYANS

The Brahmin priests and Indian scholars believe that the Sarasvati and Ganges valley region are the origin of Indian civilization and the Aryan society. This can be given some credence when we look at the cities in this region. For example, North of Delhi is the town of Kuruksetra where the great battle of the *Mahabharata* took place when Sri Krishna was still on the planet over 5,000 years ago. There is also the old city of Hastinapura that was once situated along the Ganges until the river changed its course and swept the city away in 800 B.C. This is the old capital of the Kuru dynasty in the *Mahabharata*. Pottery remains have been found near this location that are traced back to at least 1200 B.C. In New Delhi we find the Purana Qila site, which is known to have been part of the ancient city of Indraprastha. An interesting quote can be found in the ancient *Srimad-Bhagavatam* (10.72.13) which can give us some idea of how prominent Indraprastha had been. It states that during the time when Sri Krishna was on this planet 5,000 years ago, King Yudhisthira sent his brothers, the Pandavas, to conquer the world in all directions. This was for bringing all countries to participate in the great Rajasuya ceremony that was being held in ancient Indraprastha. All countries were to pay a tax to help the performance of the ceremony, and to send representatives to participate. If they did not wish to cooperate, then they would have to engage in battle with the Pandavas. Thus, the whole world came under the jurisdiction of the Vedic Aryan administration.

South of New Delhi are the holy towns of Vrindavan and Mathura along the Yamuna River. Both of these towns are known for being places of Krishna's pastimes and Vedic legends that go back thousands of years, which are also described in the Vedic literature. Farther south, located on the Yamuna, is the ancient city of Kaushambi. This city still has the remains of massive defense structures from the tenth century B.C. that are very similar to buildings in Harrappa and the Indus region that use baked brick for construction. The *Yajur-veda* (*Vajasaneyi Samhita* 23.18) also mentions the town of Kampila, which is located about halfway between Hastinapur and Kaushambi. The next city is Allahabad (Prayag) where we find the confluence of the Yamuna and Ganges. This location abounds with importance and Vedic legends that are so remote in antiquity that no one can say when they originated. Then there is Varanasi along the Ganges that is another city filled with ancient Vedic legends of importance. A short distance north of Varanasi is Sarnath, where Buddha gave his first sermon after being enlightened. A four-hour train ride north of Varanasi is the town of Ayodhya, where Lord Ramachandra had His capital, as fully described in the ancient *Ramayana*. And, of course, there are the Himalayan mountains that have many Vedic stories connected with them. Furthermore, there are numerous other places that could be mentioned that are connected with the Vedic legends throughout the area. (Most of these have already been described in the *Seeing Spiritual India* sections in my previous books.)

Though some archeologists claim they have discovered no evidence for the ancient existence of the Vedic Aryan culture in this Gangetic region, even a casual tour through this area, as mentioned above, makes it obvious that these towns and holy sites did not gain importance overnight, nor simply by an immigration of people who are said to have brought the *Vedas* with them. These places could not have become incorporated into the Vedic legends so quickly if the Vedic culture came from another location. Therefore, the argument that the early Vedic literature was brought from another region or describes a geographical location other than India cannot so easily be accepted. The fact is that the whole of India and up through the Indus region was the original home of the Vedic Aryan culture from which it spread its influence over much of the rest of the world.

THE VEDIC EXPLANATION OF THE ORIGINAL ARYANS
AND HOW THEIR INFLUENCE SPREAD
THROUGHOUT THE WORLD

How the Aryan name was given to those who are said to have invaded the Indus region is regarded as uncertain, and, as I have shown, whether there really was any invasion is no longer a legitimate consideration. Nonetheless, the term *aryan* has been applied to those people who occupied the plains between the Caspian and Black Seas. The hypothesis is that they began to migrate around the beginning of the second millennium B.C. Some went north and northwest, some went westward settling in parts of the Middle East, while others traveled to India through the Indus Valley. Those that are said to have come into India were the "invading Aryans."

The Vedic literature establishes a different scenario. They present evidence that ancient, pre-historical India covered a much broader area, and that the real Aryans were not invaders from the north into the Indus region, but were the original residents who were descendants of Vedic society that had spread over the world from the area of India. Let us remember that the term *aryan* has been confused with meaning light or light complexion. However, *Aryan* refers to *Arya*, or a clear consciousness toward God, not white or white people. In the Vedic *sutras*, the word *aryan* is used to refer to those who are spiritually oriented and of noble character. The Sanskrit word *aryan* is linguistically related to the word *harijana* (pronounced hariyana), meaning one related to God, Hari. Therefore, the real meaning of the name *aryan* refers to those people related to the spiritual Vedic culture. It has little to do with those immigrants that some researchers have speculated to be the so-called "invading Aryans." *Aryan* refers to those who practice the Vedic teachings and does not mean a particular race of people. Therefore, anyone can be an Aryan by following the clear, light, Vedic philosophy, while those who do not follow it are non-Aryan. Thus, the name Aryan, as is generally accepted today, has been misapplied to a group of people who are said to have migrated from the north into India.

Some call these people Sumerians, but L. A. Waddell, even though he uses the name, explains that the name *Sumerian* does not exist as an ethnic title and was fabricated by the modern Assyriologists and used to label the Aryan people. And Dr. Hall, in his book *Ancient History of the Near East*, says that there is an anthropological resemblance between the Dravidians of India and the Sumerians of Mesopotamia, which suggests that the group of people called the Sumerians actually were of Indian descendants. With this information in mind, it is clear that the real Aryans were the Vedic followers who were already existing throughout India and to the north beyond the Indus region.

To help understand how the Aryan influence spread through the world, L. A. Waddell explains that the Aryans established the pre-historic trade routes over land and sea from at least the beginning of the third millennium B.C., if not much earlier. Wherever the Aryans went, whether in Egypt, France, England, or elsewhere, they imposed their authority and culture, much to the betterment of the previous culture of the area. They brought together scattered tribes and clans into national unity that became increasingly bright in their systems of social organization, trade, and art. In seeking new sources of metal, such as tin, copper, gold, and lead, the Aryans established ports and colonies among the local tribes that later developed into separate nations which took many of their traditions and cultural traits from the ruling Aryans. Of course, as trade with the Aryans diminished, especially after the *Mahabharata* War in India, variations in the legends and cultures became prominent. This accounts for the many similarities between the different ancient civilizations of the world, as well as those resemblances that still exist today.

Another consideration is that since the Aryans were centralized in the Gangetic plains and the Himalayan mountains, from there they could have spread east along the Brahmaputra River and over the plain of Tibet. The Chinese, in the form of the Cina tribe, also are likely to have originated here since they have the legend of the sacred mountain in the west with four rivers. The ancient *Puranas* explain that Manu and his sons ruled over the area, over as many lands north of Mount Meru and Kailas as south. Other Aryans could have easily gone down the Sarasvati and Sarayu into north India. Others went from the Indus into Kashmir and Afghanistan, and into Central Asia. Others went into the areas of Gujarat and Sind, and over through Persia and the Gulf region. This is how the Sumerian civilization was founded, along with Babylonia. From there they went farther into Turkey and Europe.

After spreading throughout South India, they continued down the Ganges by sea east into Malaysia and Indonesia, founding the ancient Vedic cultures there. By sea they continued to China, meeting the Aryans that were probably already there. From China and the orient, they sailed over the Pacific Ocean and finally reached and colonized the Americas. Plenty of evidence of this is presented in the following chapters.

We can see some of the affect of this spread out of India in regard to the term *aryan*. The name *Harijana* or *Aryan* evolved into Syriana or Syrians in Syria, and Hurrians in Hurri, and Arianna or Iranians in Iran. This shows that they were once part of Vedic society. A similar case is the name Parthians in Partha, another old country in Persia. Partha was the name of Krishna's friend Arjuna, a Vedic Aryan, and means the son of King Prithu. So the name Parthian indicates those who are the descendants of King Prithu. Parthians also had a good relationship with the early Jews since the Jews used to buy grains from the Parthians. The Greeks referred to the Jews as Judeos, or Jah deos or Yadavas, meaning people of Ya or descendants of Yadu, one of the sons of Yayati. It is also regarded that the basis of the Kabbalah, the book of Jewish mystical concepts, as described in *The Holy Kabbalah* by Arthur Edward Waite, is linked with Kapila Muni, the Indian sage and incarnation of Krishna who established the analytical *sankhya-yoga* philosophy. Therefore, a connection between the early Jews and ancient Vedic culture is evident.

Another aspect of the connection between these various regions and the Vedic culture is explained in the Vedic literature. In the *Rig-veda* (10.63.1) Manu is the foremost of kings and seers. Manu and his family were survivors of the world flood, as mentioned in the *Shatapatha Brahmana* (1.8.1). Thus, a new beginning for the human race came from him, and all of humanity are descendants from Manu. The *Atharva-veda* (19.39.8) mentions where his ship descended in the Himalayas. One temple that signifies the location of where the ship of Manu first touched land after the flood is in Northern India in the hills of Manali. His important descendants are the Pauravas, Ayu, Nahusha, and Yayati. From Yayati came the five Vedic clans; the Purus, Anus, Druhyus, Turvashas, and Yadus. The Turvashas are related to India's southeast, Bengal, Bihar, and Orissa, and are the ancestors of the Dravidians and the Yavanas. Yadu is related to the south or southwest, Gujarat and Rajasthan, from Mathura to Dwaraka and Somnath. The Anus are related to the north, to Punjab, as well as Bengal and Bihar. The Druhyus are related to the west and northwest, such as Gandhara and Afghanistan. Puru is connected with the central Yamuna/Ganges region. All but Puru were known for having intermittently fallen from the Vedic *dharma*, and various wars in the *Puranas* were with these groups.

As explained by Shrikant Talageri in his book, *The Aryan Invasion Theory: A Reappraisal* (pp. 304-5, 315, 367-368), from these descendants, the Purus were the Rigvedic people and developed Vedic culture in north central India and the Punjab along the Sarasvati (*Rig-veda* 7.96.2). The Anus of southern Kashmir along the Parushni or modern Ravi River (*Rig-veda* 7.18.13) spread over western Asia and developed the various Iranian cultures. The Druhyus northwest of the area of the Punjab and Kashmir spread into Europe and became the western Indo-

Europeans, or the Druids and ancient Celts. A first group went northwest and developed the proto-Germanic dialect, and another group traveled farther south and developed the proto-Hellenic and Itallic-Celtic dialects. Other tribes included the Pramshus in western Bihar, and Ikshvakus of northern Uttar Pradesh.

Incidentally, according to legend, thousands of years ago Kashmir was a large lake surrounded by beautiful mountain peaks. It was here where the goddess Parvati stayed in her boat. One day she went to see Lord Shiva in the mountains. Then a great demon took possession of the lake. Kashyapa Muni, who was present at the time, called for the goddess to return. Together they chased the demon away and created an immense valley. It was called Kashyapa-Mira, and later shortened to Kashmir. This again shows the Vedic connection of this region.

Other tribes mentioned in the Vedic texts include the Kiratas, who are the mountain people of Tibet and Nepal, often considered impure for not practicing the Vedic *dharma*. The *Vishnu Purana* (4.3.18-21) also mentions the Shakas who are the Scythians of ancient Central Asia, the Pahlavas who are the Persians, and the Cinas who are the Chinese. They are all considered as fallen nobility or Kshatriyas who had been driven out of India during the reign of King Sagara.

To explain further, Yadu was the eldest of the five sons of Yayati. Yayati was a great emperor of the world and one of the original forefathers of those of Aryan and Indo-European heritage. Yayati divided his kingdom amongst his sons, who then started their own dynasties. Yayati had two wives, Devayani and Sharmistha. Yayati had two sons from Devayani: Yadu and Turvasu. Yadu was the originator of the Yadu dynasty called the Yadavas, later known as the Lunar Dynasty. From Turvasu came the Yavana or Turk dynasty. From Sharmistha, Yayati had three sons: Druhya, who started the Bhoja dynasty; Anu, who began the Mleccha or Greek dynasty; and Puru who started the Paurava dynasty, which is said to have settled along the Ravi River and later along the Sarasvati. Some say that this clan later went on to Egypt who became the Pharaohs and rulers of the area. These Aryan tribes, originating in India by King Yayati and mentioned in the *Rig-veda* and *Vishnu* and *Bhagavat Puranas*, spread all over the world.

The Yadava kingdom later became divided among the four sons of Bhima Satvata. From Vrishni, the youngest, descended Vasudeva, the father of Krishna and Balarama and their sister Pritha or Kunti. Kunti married the Yadava prince Pandu, whose descendants became the Pandavas. Kunti became the mother of Yudhisthira, Bhima, and Arjuna (Partha), the three elder Pandavas. The younger Pandavas were Nakula and Sahadeva, born from Pandu's second wife Madri. After moving to the west coast of India, they lived at Dwaraka under the protection of Lord Krishna. Near the time of Krishna's disappearance from earth, a fratricidal war broke out and most of the Pandavas were killed, who had grown to become a huge clan. Those that survived may have gone on to the Indus Valley where they joined or started another part of the advanced Vedic society. Others may have continued farther west into Egypt and some on to Europe, as previously explained.

This is further substantiated in the *Mahabharata* which mentions several provinces of southern Europe and Persia that were once connected with the Vedic culture. The *Adi-parva* (174.38) of the *Mahabharata* describes the province of Pulinda (Greece) as having been conquered by Bhimasena and Sahadeva, two of the Pandava brothers. Thus, the ancient Greeks were once a part of Bharata-varsa (India) and the Vedic civilization. But later the people gave up their affiliation with Vedic society and were, therefore, classified as Mlecchas. However, in the *Vana-parva* section of the *Mahabharata* it is predicted that this non-Vedic society would one day rule much of the world, including India. Alexander the Great conquered India for the Pulinda or Greek civilization in 326 B.C., fulfilling the prophecy.

The *Sabha-parva* and *Bhisma-parva* sections of the *Mahabharata* mention the province of Abhira, situated near what once was the Sarasvati River in ancient Sind. The Abhiras are said to have been warriors who had left India out of fear of Lord Parashurama and hid themselves in the Caucasion hills between the Black and Caspian Seas. Later, for a period of time, they were ruled by Maharaja Yudhisthira. However, the sage Markandaya predicted that these Abhiras, after they gave up their link with Vedic society, would one day rule India.

Another province mentioned in *Mahabharata* (*Adi-parva* 85.34) is that of the Yavanas (Turks) who were so named for being descendants of Maharaja Yavana (Turvasu), one of the sons of Maharaja Yayati, as previously explained. They also gave up Vedic culture and became Mlecchas. They fought in the battle of Kuruksetra against the Pandavas on behalf of Duryodhana and lost. However, it was predicted that they would one day return to conquer Bharata-varsa (India) and, indeed, this came to pass. Muhammad Ghori later attacked and conquered parts of India on behalf of Islam from the Abhira and Yavana or Turkish countries. Thus, we can see that these provinces in the area of Greece and Turkey (and the countries in between there and India) were once part of the Vedic civilization and had at one time not only political and cultural ties, but also ancestral connections. This is the Vedic version, of the origin of Aryan civilization and how its influence spread in various degrees throughout the world.

THE CHRONOLOGY OF EVENTS
IN THE SPREAD OF VEDIC CULTURE

Now I will piece together the basic chronological order of the spread of Vedic culture from India. According to the Vedic tradition, the original spiritual and Vedic knowledge was given to mankind by God at the beginning of creation. Thus, there would have been a highly advanced Vedic and spiritual civilization in the world. However, through various earth changes, such as ice ages, earthquakes, droughts, etc., the structure of the global cultures changed. Some of these events, such as the great flood, are recorded by most cultures throughout the world.

Many scholars feel that the global deluge happened around 13,000 years ago. Some think that it could have been a meteorite impact that triggered the end of the Ice Age and caused a giant meltdown that produced the water that flooded the planet. Much land disappeared, and the global flood swept away most of the world's population. Great lakes were formed, all lowlands disappeared, and lands like Egypt became moist with water. This means that the advanced civilization that had once populated the earth was now gone, and would be replaced by the survivors. It was the mariners, such as the Vedic Manu and his family, who survived the flood and colonized other parts of the world.

Further information of the last ice age and global deluge is briefly explained by Dr. Venu Gopalacharya. In a personal letter to me (July 22, 1998), he explained that, "There are eighteen *Puranas* and sub-*Puranas* in Sanskrit. According to them, only those who settled on the high mountains of Central Asia and around the Caspian Sea, after the end of the fourth ice age, survived from the glaciers and deluge. During the period from the end of the fourth ice age and the great deluge, there were 12 great wars for the mastery over the globe. They divided the global regions into two parts. The worshipers of the beneficial forces of nature, or Devas, settled from the Caspian Sea to the eastern ocean, and the worshipers of the evil forces of nature occupied the land to the west of the Caspian Sea. These became known as the Assyrians (Asuras), Daityas (Dutch), Daiteyas (Deutch or German), Danavas (Danes), and Danutusahs (Celts). Some of them migrated to the American continent. The Mayans, Toltecs, and the rulers of Palanque (Patalalanke), are considered to be the Asuras who migrated to the Patala (land below), or the land of immortals, *Amaraka*. [This is the original Sanskrit from which the name of America is derived. *Mara* in Sanskrit means death, *amara* means no death or beyond it.] In the deluge, most of these lands were submerged. Noah (Manu) and his subjects became known as Manavas, ruled by the monarchs of the globe. They were successors of his [Manu's] nine sons and one daughter."

Dr. Venu Gopalacharya continues this line of thought in his book, *World-Wide Hindu Culture and Vaishnava Bhakti* (pages 117-18). He explains further how this Vedic culture continued to spread after the great deluge. It was under the leadership of the Solar dynasty princes that a branch of Indians marched west of the Indus River and occupied the area of Abyssinia and its surrounding regions around the rivers Nile, Gambia, and Senagal. The names of Abyssinia and Ethiopia are derived from words that mean colonies of the people of the Sindhu and the Aditya or Solar dynasty. You can recognize many names of places in and around Ethiopia that are derived from the original Sanskrit. So after the great deluge, Vaivasvata Manu's nine sons [some references say ten sons] were ruling over the various parts of the globe. They and their successors were very concerned about establishing the Vedic principles of *Sanatana-dharma*, the uplifting way of life for regaining and maintaining one's spiritual identity and connection with the Supreme. This was the essence of Vaivasvata Manu's teachings. This was especially taught and strictly followed by the great rulers of the Solar dynasty who governed from Ayodhya. These principles included the practice of truth, nonviolence, celibacy, cleanliness, non-covetousness, firmness of mind, peace, righteousness, and self-control as exemplified by Lord Sri Rama and His ancestors like Sagara, Ambarisha, Dilipa, Raghu, and Dasaratha. This is explained in Kalidasa's *Raghuvamsha* as well as other *Puranas* and *Itihasas*. This standard became more popular with the ancient Indians than people in other parts of the world, and, thus, India became the center of this Vedic way of life since time immemorial.

The unfortunate thing is that many of the most ancient records, in which we may very well have been able to find more exact information about this sort of early history, were destroyed by the revolutionary fanatics at places like Alexandria, Pusa, Takshashila, and others in Central Asia, and Central and South America. They did so while declaring that such knowledge and records were unnecessary if they contained what was already in their own religious books, but should be destroyed if they contained anything different. This is why the mythologies of Egypt, Babylonia, the Jews, the Old Testament, and the holy Koran contain only brief accounts of the pre-historical facts beyond 2500 years ago, unlike those histories that hold much greater detail as found in the ancient Vedic and Puranic literature.

In any case, we can begin to see that the Vedic Aryans had been living in the region of India since the last deluge, from about 13,000 to 10,000 B.C. Thus, there could not have been any pre-Aryan civilization in this area that had been conquered by so-called "invading Aryans" in 1500 B.C.

Using the many types of evidence previously provided in this chapter, it is clear that the height of the Vedic Age was certainly long before 3100 B.C., even as early as 4000 to 5000 B.C. as some scholars feel. Bal Gangadhar Tilak estimates that the *Vedas* were in existence as early as 6000 B.C., based on historical data, while others say it was as far back as 7000-8000 B.C. Since the Vedic culture during this time was practicing an oral tradition, and the literature had still not been put into written form, the basic hymns of the *Rig-veda*, and even the *Atharva-veda* and others, could have been in existence for many thousands of years. These *Vedas* were used in everyday life for society's philosophy, worship, and rituals. Therefore, they were a highly sophisticated product of a greatly developed society, and must date back to the remotest antiquity. Or, as the tradition itself explains, the essence of Vedic knowledge had been given to humanity by God at the time of the universal creation and has always been in existence.

By 3700, all of the principal books of the *Rig-veda* were in place and known. Of course, this was still an oral tradition and additional books could still have been added. One point in this regard is that the father of the great Bishma was Shantanu whose brother, Devapi, is credited with several hymns of the *Rig-veda*. This could not have been much earlier than 3200 B.C. since Bishma played a

prominent role in the *Mahabharata* War at Kuruksetra, which is calculated to
have been around 3137 B.C. Further calculations can be accorded with the
dynastic list as found in the *Adi Parva* of the *Mahabharata*. With the help of the
list, from 3100 B.C. we get nearly an additional 630 years or longer going back
to Sudas and the Battle of the Ten Kings, as described in the *Rig-veda*. This takes
us back to about 3730 B.C. Therefore, the height of the Vedic Age can be dated
no later than 3700 B.C.

From the Vedic literature, we can also see that the Sarasvati River had to have
been at its prime around 4000 to 5000 B.C. or earlier. This is when it was
recorded in the *Rig* and *Atharva-vedas*. This was also when the Vedic culture was
spreading throughout the world, either because of reasons of trade, migration, or
because some of the degenerated tribes were driven out of the Indian region. Some
of the first tribes to have left India may include the Prithu-Parthavas (who later
became the Parthians), the Druhyus (who became the Druids), the Alinas
(Hellenes or ancient Greeks), the Simyus (Sirmios or ancient Albanians), the
Cinas (Chinese), and others. This could have been around 4500 B.C., as explained
by N. S. Rajaram in *The Vedic Aryans and the Origins of Civilization* (p. 210).
These were some of the earliest of Aryans who created the most ancient form of
Indo-European society. They took with them their Vedic customs, language,
rituals, etc., all of which gradually changed with time due to their lack of seriously
following the Vedic traditions, or because of their loss of close contact with the
orthodox homeland. This would certainly help explain the many similarities in
languages and culture that we find today between numerous regions of the world,
many of which we will explain later in this book.

During the fourth millennium, near 3800 B.C., North India had plenty of
water, with such great rivers as the Indus to the north, the Ganga to the east, and
the central Sarasvati-Drishadvati river system, which was fed by the Sutlej and the
Yamuna. The great Thar desert did not yet create a division between North India
and the western areas. So it was all one cultural entity. Thus, the central Vedic
society covered a much wider area and had greater influence than the mere
country of India today.

However, before the time of the *Mahabharata* War, the Yamuna had changed
its course and was no longer flowing into the Sarasvati, but emptied into the
Ganga. By the time of the *Mahabharata*, around 3100 B.C., the Sarasvati is
described in relation to Balarama's pilgrimage (*Shalya Parva*, 36-55) as still being
significant in its holiness, but from its origin it flowed only for a forty-day journey
by horse into the desert where it disappeared. All that was left were the holy places
that used to be on its banks (as also mentioned in 3.80.84; 3.88.2; & 9.34.15-8).
The *Mahabharata* also describes the geographical location of the river, saying that
it flows near Kurukshetra (3.81.125). Similar information along with the place
where the Sarasvati disappears, Vinasana, is found in the *Manu-samhita* (2.21).
Gradually, the desert expanded and the people of the western region continued to

migrate farther west, losing touch with their Vedic roots. This is what helped further the development of the Sumerian and Egyptian communities.

The next major time period of 3100 B.C. or earlier not only marks the era of the *Mahabharata* War, the disappearance of Lord Krishna, and the beginning of the Kali-yuga, but it also marks the beginning of the end of the Vedic Age. The war at Kurukshetra was the beginning of the breakdown of the Vedic culture and its global contacts. It is also the time when the remaining major portions of the Vedic literature were compiled, which was accomplished by Srila Vyasadeva, for which He had appeared in this world. And since there were no Aryan invasions coming into India or the Indus Sarasvati region, as we have already established, then this is also the time when the Harappan civilization began to form, or reach its prime if it was already in existence. Furthermore, this was also the time of the first and second dynasties of Egypt, which is corroborated by the fact that many scholars feel that the pyramids of Egypt were built at this time. Some scholars feel that the Step pyramid in Sakkara, 30 miles south of Giza, was built about 5,000 years ago (around 3000 B.C.), while others consider it dates back to 2650 B.C. This also suggests that the Sumerian civilization was entering its prime during this period as well. It was also when the Egyptians and Sumerians were depending on the mathematical systems and formulas of the *Shulbasutras* from India for their own architecture, altars, and town planning, as were the sites of the Harappan civilization.

From 3000 to 2000 B.C., as the people continued to spread out from India to the west, there was still much contact between India and such areas as Egypt, Sumeria, Mesopotamia, and others. However, the great 300 year drought in the area created intense difficulties for all of these civilizations. Many agree that the Harappan civilization ended around 2500-2200 B.C. This 300 year drought, not any invaders, caused the beginning of the end of the Harappan sites, as well as that of the Akkadian society. The ancient Egyptian civilization also could have met its end because of this drought, leaving us only with the remnants of its monuments and writings that we are still trying to fully understand today. Its people probably migrated in the search for better resources. Furthermore, 3000 to 2500 B.C. is also the period, according to British archeological estimates, that is believed to be when the Druids and their priests arrived in Britain. However, the English Druids claim their origin is from the east from as far back as 3900 B.C., which follows more closely to the Vedic version.

By 2000 B.C. the Sutlej had also changed its course and flowed into the Indus, while the desert relentlessly grew. This left the Sarasvati with few resources to continue being the great river it once was. Near 1900 B.C., the Sarasvati River finally ceased to flow altogether and completely dried up, contributing to the disbanding of the people of northwestern India to other places, and making the Gangetic region the most important for the remaining Vedic society. Once the Sarasvati disappeared, the Ganga replaced it as the holiest of rivers.

After 2000 B.C. was a time of much migration of the Indian Aryans into West

Asia, Mesopotamia, Iran, and further. There was the founding of the Kassites, Hittites, and Mittani, along with the Celts, Scythians, etc., who all participated in their own migrations.

The reason why the populace of Europe gradually forgot their connection with India was because contacts between India were reduced to the Greeks and Romans. Then when Alexander and the Greeks invaded India, contacts were reduced to almost nothing for centuries. Thereafter, the Romans became Christians, forcing the rest of Europe to follow. This left the Arabs as the primary traders between India and Europe, until the wars developed between the Christians and the growing Muslims. Once the Muslims captured Constantinople in Turkey, they controlled all trade routes between Europe and India, and forced Europeans to find a sea route to India. This lead to the "discovery" of America, Australia, and parts of Africa. Later, as the trade routes with India were opened, missionaries, new invaders, and so-called scholars became the new conquerors. With them also came the new versions of history brought about to diminish the real heritage and legacy of India.

CONCLUSION

This chapter provides evidence of the real origination of the Vedic Aryans. It also makes it clear that it is to the East, specifically the area of India, where the origins of advanced civilization and the essence of religion and spiritual philosophy can be traced. From there, the Aryan influence had spread to many other regions and can still be recognized in numerous cultures. Only a few open-minded people who look at the whole picture of this kind of religious development will understand the inherent unity the world and its history contains. Such unity is disturbed only by mankind's immature, dogmatic, and self-centered feelings for regional and cultural superiority. We have seen this in the propaganda that was effectively used by the Nazis and is presently used by neo-Nazis and white supremacist groups who now employ the modern myth that the original location of the Aryan race was in northern Europe. Thus, they imply that members of this race are superior over all other races in physique, language, mental capabilities, and culture. This myth must be seen for what it is because there is no doubt that the real Aryan people originated and spread from the region of India and the Indus Valley, not Europe.

As N. S. Rajaram so nicely explains in *Vedic Aryans and The Origins of Civilization* (pp. 247-8), "To conclude: on the basis of archeology, satellite photography, metallurgy and ancient mathematics, it is now clear that there existed a great civilization--a mainly spiritual civilization perhaps--before the rise of Egypt, Sumeria and the Indus Valley. The heartland of this ancient world was the region from the Indus to the Ganga--the land of the Vedic Aryans.

"This conclusion, stemming from scientific findings of the past three decades, demolishes the theory that nomadic Aryans from Central Asia swooped down on the plains of India in the second millennium BCE and established their civilization and composed the *Rig-veda*. The picture presented by science therefore is far removed from the one found in history books that place the 'Cradle of Civilization' in the river valleys of Mesopotamia. Modern science and ancient records provide us also a clue to a long standing historical puzzle: why since time immemorial, people from India and Sri Lanka, to England and Ireland have spoken languages clearly related to one another, and possess mythologies and beliefs that are so strikingly similar.

"The simple answer is: they were part of a great civilization that flourished before the rise of Egypt, Sumeria and the Indus Valley. This was a civilization before the dawn of civilizations."

May I also say that this corroborates the history as we find it in the Vedic literature, especially the *Rig-veda* and the *Puranas*. It therefore helps prove the authenticity of the Vedic culture and our premise that it was the original ancient civilization, a spiritual society, using the knowledge as had been given by God since the time of creation, and established further by the sages that followed. According to a recent racial study (*The History and Geography of Human Genes*), it has been confirmed that all people of Europe, the Middle East, and India belong to a single Caucasian type race. This means that they had to have come from the same source. Thus, we are all descendants of this great Vedic culture, the center of which is India. As more evidence comes forth, it will only prove how the testimony of the *Rig-veda* and the *Puranas* is confirmed, and will point to the area of northern India as the original homeland of the Vedic Aryans.

The point of all this is that even if Muslims, Christians, Jews, Buddhists, Hindus, etc., all keep their own ideology, legends, and traditions, we should realize that all of these legends and conceptions of God and forms of worship ultimately refer to the same Supreme God and lesser demigods, although they may be called by different names according to present day variations in region and culture. In other words, all these doctrines and faiths are simply outgrowths of the original religion and worship of the one Supreme Deity that spread throughout the world many thousands of years ago from the same basic source, and which is now expressed through the many various cultural differences in the world. Therefore, no matter what religion we may consider ourselves, we are all a part of the same family. We are merely another branch of the same tree which can be traced to the original pre-historic roots of spiritual thought that are found in the Vedic culture, the oldest and most developed philosophical and spiritual tradition in the world.

In the following chapters this will become more apparent as we begin to take a closer look at each individual culture and religion, and various locations throughout the world, and recognize the numerous connections and similarities they have with the Vedic traditions and knowledge.

CHAPTER FIVE

THE WHOLE WORLD WAS ONCE UNITED IN VEDIC CULTURE

As we established in the chapter on the creation of the material world, when the Supreme Being created the universe He also provided the Vedic knowledge and terminology by which humanity could live peacefully as well as advance spiritually. Even the Bible (*Genesis* 11:1) describes how originally during pre-Christian times, "the whole earth was of one language and one speech." And, as we can see from the evidence in the previous chapters, that language was Sanskrit.

Theologians in general agree that despite diverse scriptures and tales of various people experiencing or hearing the voice of God, the immanent Divinity is One. Even physicists agree that the ultimate source of all elements has to be one. History too began from a single point. This means that the origination of the universe as well as the beginning of mankind was a purposeful and arranged event. It was not a chance encounter, a random, freakish, or spontaneous beginning, but an expansion from the Absolute Truth.

THE VEDIC TRADITION IS THE PARENT OF ALL HUMANITY

Since there is but one ultimate source of everything, all human activity started from that divine beginning. And activity means thought and speech. As the Vedic texts explains, the original language was Sanskrit, as taught by the Supreme Himself. We find that even the 1951 edition of the Encyclopedia Britannica (P. 70, Vol 13) describes that some scholars gave up attempts to explain the origin of language and have fallen back to the religious explanation that the first language was given by God to man.

Some people, however, feel that ancient man was able to only slowly develop a language of his own. This is thought to have started from grunts and noises like animals until it somehow shaped into the different languages we find today. So does that mean that babies will also develop some kind of language of their own if they are given enough time and not taught one? As described in P. N. Oak's book, *World Vedic Heritage* (p. 130), the 16th century Moghul emperor, Akbar, had also questioned this. Being in such a position of authority, he was able to indulge in a heartless experiment. He ordered several infant children to be taken away from their mothers and be confined to a house. No one was permitted to speak anything to the children, even when clothed and fed. The result was that they all grew to be dumb adults. They could speak no language at all. Neither did they develop any form of communication between themselves. Therefore, the idea that man will eventually educate himself or even develop a language on his own is mistaken. All knowledge must be given by a superior, which is exactly what the Vedic literature says happened at the beginning of time. The Vedic references explain that human civilization began by the arrangement of the Supreme. Man was given an original consciousness by which he had knowledge of the Sanskrit language and was guided by Vedic information, as taught by Lord Brahma and the numerous sages that followed. Thus, the ancient Vedic culture is the primordial culture of the whole world and not exclusive to India, Arabia, or Sumeria. It is universal.

The philosopher and researcher Edward Pococke also wrote about this conclusion in his book *India in Greece* (page 251). He states: "Sir William Jones concluded that the Hindus had an immemorial antiquity with the old Persians, Ethiopians and Egyptians, the Phoenicians, Greeks and Tuscans, the Scythians or Goths, and the Celts, the Chinese, Japanese and Peruvians." The observance of this global connection between India and the rest of the world is actually an indication that the whole world was once under the influence of the Vedic culture. Thus, it was India who nurtured the rest of the world with her wisdom and Vedic knowledge.

Pococke continues in this vein in his observation: "Now the whole of the society of Greece, civil and military, must strike one as being eminently Asiatic, much of it specially Indian. . . I shall demonstrate that these evidences were but the attendant tokens of Indian colonization with its corresponding religion and language. I shall exhibit dynasties disappearing from India, western India, to appear again in Greece, clans who fought upon the plains of Troy." Therefore, since Greece is supposed to be the origins of European culture, and since Greece displays much of the same culture as India, we can say that the pre-Christian culture of Europe was Vedic.

In fact, it may be the case that without the connection with India, Greece may not have been a major contributor to the advancement of Europe. Godfrey Higgins writes in his book *The Celtic Druids* (p. 112), "In science the Greeks were pygmies. What would they have known of science if their Platos and Pythagorases had not traveled into the East! In science and real learning they were inferior to the Orientals [Indians], and were the greatest liars upon earth. They wilfully mis-stated everything or they foolishly confounded everything."

William Durant, author of the 10-volume *Story of Civilization*, wrote, "India was the motherland of our race, and Sanskrit the mother of European languages. She was the mother of our philosophy. . . of our mathematics. . . of the ideals embodied in Christianity. . . of self-government and democracy. . . Mother India is in many ways the mother of us all."

Interestingly, Sir Isaac Tailor, the author of *The Origins of the Aryans*, wrote in a similar way (page 1), "Adelung, the father of comparative philosophy. . . placed the cradle of mankind in the valley of Kashmir, which he identified with paradise. To Adelung we owe the opinion, which has prevailed so widely, that since the human race originated in the East, most westerly nations, the Iberians and Celts, must have been the first to leave the parent."

As explained in *World Vedic Heritage* (p. 115), this is also the conclusion of Mr. B. C. Chhabra, who is the ex-Assistant Director General of Archeology under the British administration in India. He writes, "I do not want to go deep into the larger question of the theory of evolution which is today at the base of archeological interpretations, but I must need say that the history of Indian civilization begins with knowledge and not barbarism. The kind of knowledge that has been preserved therein has stood the test of time and is still unsurpassed in certain respects. It believes in an evolution of limited extent only and that for a definite period of time in the history of man's life as also in that of a nation. To base the entire history of mankind, down to the present-day, on the ape-man and the archeological ages of Paleolithic, Neolithic, Bronze and Iron is a travesty of facts. Even in the present age of great scientific achievements the ape-man cannot produce the homosapiens, obviously because they are two different species. Recent archeologists have proved abundantly that these ages have no meaning because different cultural ages are found in different regions, and that sometimes they co-existed in the same region which cannot be explained on the basis of the theory of evolution." Thus, regardless of the classifications made by archeologists about the ancient history of mankind, as confirmed by the prehistoric records of the Vedic literature, India was the center from where spread the intellectually superior Vedic culture, and is, therefore, the source of humanity's spiritual heritage.

The Preface of Vol. VI of *Indian Antiquities* (pp 11-13) also points one in this same direction: "The Hindu religion probably spread over the whole earth; there are signs of it in every system of worship. . . the arithmetic, astronomy, astrology, the holidays, games, names of the stars, and figures of constellations, the language of the different nations bear the strongest marks of the same origin."

The discerning and honest Christian author Godfrey Higgins wrote in his book, *The Celtic Druids* (p. 61), about the basis of all human civilization originating from India and the Vedic culture. "The peninsula of India would be one of the first peopled countries, and its inhabitants would have all the habits of progenitors of man before the flood in as much perfection or more than any other nation. . . In short, whatever learning man possessed before his dispersion. . . may be expected to be found here; and of this Hindustan affords innumerable traces. . . notwithstanding all. . . the fruitless efforts of our priests to disguise it."

The above quotes would indicate that the Vedic culture was a global faith, a world influence. This may be given further credence in the remarks of Ctesias, the Greek writer (as found in *Historical Researches*, Vol. II, p.220), "The Hindus were as numerous as all the other nations put together."

This is further corroborated in P. N. Oak's *World Vedic Heritage* (p. 506) in which he presents evidence that, "In pre-Christian times the temples of Vedic Deities such as Vishnu, Shiva, the Mother goddess, Rama, Hanuman, and Krishna used to abound in all regions of the world. Evidence of this is found in the works of ancient authors such as Megasthenes, Strabo, and Herodotus. All those names are of Vedic origin, too. The term Megasthenes is Megh-Sthan-eesh, i.e. the Lord of the Region of the clouds. The name Herodotus is Hari-dootus, i.e. Messenger of [Hari] God."

In *Some Missing Chapters of World History* (p. 134), P. N. Oak also explains that Shiva was worshiped all over the world, even in the Vatican. The word *vatican* comes from the Sanskrit word *vatica*, which means a bower or sylvan hermitage. He explains that even the premises of the Vatican have many Shiva emblems buried in their walls and cellars. Many such emblems have been dug up in other parts of Italy as well. And some of those found in the Vatican are still preserved in the Vatican's Etruscan museum.

Another point is that the original worship of the Mother Goddess can be traced back to India. Whether this Goddess is called Ma, Uma, Mata, Amba, Shakti, Durga, Bhagavati, Parameshvari, Kali, Lakshmi, Saraswati, Astarte, Venus, Ceres, Mother Mary, Mariamma, Madonna, Notre Dame, etc., it can be traced to the Vedic culture where such worship originated.

Albert J. Edmonds, in his book *Buddhist and Christian Gospels*, also explains that, "Strabo considered all Asia as far as India to be consecrated to Bacchus where Hercules and Bacchus are called Kings of the East. The last religions of Babylon and Egypt were born there. Even the Greeks and the Romans were debtors thereto for the cult of Bacchus and Mithras."

Bacchus refers to Bakesh or Tryambakesh, Shiva. Hercules refers to Hari-culeesh, Lord Krishna. They were known as Kings or supreme deities of the East. Since the religions of Babylon and Egypt were born in Asia, and Greeks and Romans observed a similar version of the Bacchus cult and one of Mithras, the sun, it is obvious the whole world followed, or was influenced by, Vedic culture. The reason is that all of these deities can be traced back to India, or are directly Vedic deities. From this information we can begin to understand that Vedic culture was a cause of worldwide unity, or the parent culture of all humanity.

INDIA AND SANSKRIT: THE SOURCE OF WORLD LITERATURE

Sanskrit, being the original language since the creation, is the source of world literature. Laura Elizabeth Poor observes in her book, *Sanskrit and Its Kindred*

Literatures--Studies in Comparative Mythology, "I propose to write about the literature of different nations and different centuries. I wish to show that this literature is not many but one; that the same leading ideas have arisen at epochs apparently separated from each other; that each nation however isolated it may seem, is, in reality, a link in the great chain of development of the human mind; in other words to show the unity and continuity of literature. . . The histories of Phoenicians, Cartheginians, Romans or Greeks, were so many detached pieces of information. . . But the moment the mind realizes. . . that one nation is connected with all others, its history becomes delightful and inspiring. . . And it is to the Sanskrit language that we owe this entire change. . . Sanskrit was a spoken language at the time of Solomon, 1015 B.C., also of Alexander, 324 B.C."

In this same line of thought, it has been determined that the Sanskrit *Rig-veda* is the oldest piece of literature in the world. Reverend Morris Philip, in his book *The Teaching of the Vedas* (p. 213), concludes, "After the latest researches into the history and chronology of the book of Old Testament, we may safely now call the *Rigveda* as the oldest book not only of the Aryan community, but of the whole world."

A. A. Macdonell provides a few more details in his book, *India's Past*, about how various literature in the world are all connected. In fact, he explains that many of the world's fairy tales come from India. "The history of how India's fairy tales and fables migrated from one country to another to nearly all the people of Europe and Asia, and even to African tribes from their original home in India, borders on the marvelous. It is not a case of single stories finding their way by word of mouth. . . from India to other countries, but of whole Indian books becoming through the medium of translations the common property of the world. . . many fairy tales current among the various people can be traced to their original home in India."

When we begin to compare the ancient legends and stories of one country with another, and one time period with another, we can recognize how similar and yet different they are. The conclusion is that they had to have come from one basic source, one people that later became divided and spread out over a wide area. Each part of this society must have brought with them into the new lands their old legends that were once common to all. Many of these stories were later shaped and altered according to the place they lived, and the natural esthetic and artistic preferences they acquired, while the primary legends have been the most likely to maintain their storyline. Though various mythologies may have similarities, the most common traits can be seen between any of them and the Vedic traditions. These kinds of similarities between these myths and the Vedic legends makes it clear that the Vedic tradition is the original from which all others are derived.

An example of this is the Indian classic *Ramayana.* From India the *Ramayana* has traveled to many other countries who now claim their own versions of the epic. Indonesia, Malaysia, Thailand, even Jamaica and Africa have versions of the *Ramayana* that have slight differences from the Indian *Ramayana.* Thus, we can see how this early Sanskrit literature traveled throughout the world and became local versions of what originated in India. The next section further corroborates this point.

WORLDWIDE REMNANTS OF SANSKRIT

The basis of all accomplishments of the Vedic culture is its literature. Max Mueller, in his book *India--What Can It Teach Us* (p. 21), says that, "Historical records (of the Hindus) extend in some respects so far beyond all records and have been preserved to us in such perfect and such legible documents, that we can learn from them lessons which we can learn nowhere else and supply missing links."

In Volume I (p.163) of *Chips From A German Workshop*, Max Mueller continues his thoughts on the importance and primordiality of Vedic literature: "Sanskrit no doubt has an immense advantage over all other ancient languages of the East. It is so attractive and has been so widely admired, that it almost seems at times to excite a certain amount of feminine jealousy. We are ourselves Indo-Europeans. In a certain sense we are still speaking and thinking Sanskrit; or more correctly Sanskrit is like a dear aunt to us and she takes the place of a mother who is no more."

That the entire ancient literature of India is composed in Sanskrit provides compelling evidence that Sanskrit was the only language spoken and understood thousands of years ago. Not only that, but many other texts at the time, along with grants, orders, ordinances, religious prayers and sacraments, were also all in Sanskrit.

Scholar H. H. Wilson wrote in his Preface to his translation of the *Vishnu Purana*, "The affinities of the Sanskrit language prove a common origin of the now widely scattered nations amongst whose dialects they are traceable, and render it unquestionable that they must all have spread abroad from some central spot in that part of the globe first inhabited by mankind according to the inspired record."

Let us take a brief look at additional evidence to help verify the idea that Sanskrit was the original language of the world, and that it is connected with numerous countries and cultures.

The fact of the matter is that remnants of Sanskrit can be found worldwide in practically any language. Mr. P. N. Oak provides a great comparison of this in his book, *Some Blunders of Indian Historical Research* (p. 277). This is like a brief overview which we will elaborate further in another chapter. He explains that, "Latin and Persian are dialects of Sanskrit. Greek has borrowed a lot from Sanskrit. French and English are full of Sanskrit words, roots and speech forms. The use of a prefix 'a' for the negative as in 'amoral' is Sanskrit. The termination *stry* as in dentistry [and] chemistry, derives from the Sanskrit word *shastra* meaning science or branch of knowledge. Words fashioned from roots like *dant* (as in 'dental, dentistry'), *mrutyu* (as in mortal, mortuary, morgue, post mortem) are all Sanskrit. Vesture for apparel is the Sanskrit word *vastra*. Common words like 'door' (*dwar*), 'name' (*nama*) are all Sanskrit. Numerals like two (*dwi*), three (troika, tripartite, tripod) is based on the Sanskrit word *tri*. Four (*chatwar*), five (*panch* in Sanskrit), gives us such words as pentagon, pentecostal. 'Gon' is the Sanskrit *Kon* meaning angle. Six (*shat* in Sanskrit), seven (*sapta*), eight (*astha*), nine (*vava*), ten (*dasha*) gives words like decimal, decade. 'Christ-Mas' is really the month of Christ. In Sanskrit a month is called *mas*. The Sanskrit root *pada* meaning foot leads to words like biped, centipede, pediatrics, and tripod. 'Pedestrian' is almost a pure Sanskrit word which is explained in Sanskrit as *padais charati iti padacharaha*. The root *bhara* meaning weight gets formed in Latin into 'barus' and gives us words like barometer. The word *naktam*, meaning night in Sanskrit, has led to words like night, or 'naucht' in German and 'nocturnal.' The English word pedestal retains its almost original Sanskrit form *pada-sthala*. In French, the words 'roi, rene, deu, genou, naga' meaning king, queen, God, knees, and cobra respectively are all Sanskrit words. The river Nile is the corrupt form of the Sanskrit word *neel*, namely 'blue.' That is why it is called the Blue Nile. In Greenland the Sanskrit word *sambandhi* is used in its original Sanskrit sense meaning a relation. In Africa the word *simba* meaning a lion is the Sanskrit word *simha*. The Latvian language is based on Panini's Sanskrit grammar. Their capital *riga* is the very root we find in the word *Rigved*. Pushtu, the language of Afghanistan, is a dialect of Sanskrit as is Siamese, the language of Thailand. In German, the declension of nouns is based almost four-square on the Sanskrit pattern.

"The sequence of week days from Monday to Sunday is followed the world over as laid down by Sanskrit-speaking Indians. In the ancient world the new year began about March-April as in India and Persia even now. The names September, October, November, and December derive from the Sanskrit words *Saptama*, *Ashtama*, *Navama* and *Dashama*, i.e. the 7th, 8th, 9th and 10th (months). The deity 'Mitras' was worshiped in the ancient world is the 'Mitra' or the Sun God of the Hindus. Scandinavia is the abode of warriors (*Skand Nabhi* in Sanskrit) i.e. of the Vikings." I might also add that *Skand* comes from the name of the warrior son of the Vedic demigod Shiva, Skanda. And the Scandinavians were the mariner descendants of the Vedic Kshatriya warriors who worshiped Skanda.

In regard to Latin being a dialect of Sanskrit, Godfrey Higgins, in his book *The Celtic Druids* (p. 61), makes a similar conclusion that for some people would be quite controversial. He explains, "There are many objections to the derivation of the Latin from the Greek. Latin exhibits many terms in a more rude form than Greek . . . Latin was derived from Sanskrit."

In any case, not only are there many words connected with or derived from Sanskrit, there are many places around the world that also reflect their Vedic connection. For example, the places that end with the suffix *sthan*, which is the Sanskrit *stan*, reflect their Vedic connection as found in Baluchisthan,

Afghanisthan, Kurdisthan, Kafiristhan, Turkisthan, Ghabulisthan, Kazaksthan, and others, such as Arvasthan which was corrupted to Arabia. Countries like Syria and Assyria show their Sanskrit connection through the Sura and Asura communities mentioned in the Vedic epics. Those countries also spoke Sanskrit until they lost their connection with India or Vedic culture. Cities in England show their Sanskrit connection with their corrupted form of *puri* turned to 'bury' as in Shrewsbury, Ainsbury, and Waterbury.

Even the name "England" comes from the Sanskrit word *Angla-Sthan*. Herewith we can see that the suffix "land" also shows a corrupted form of Sanskrit and that places such as Deutschland, Greenland, or Iceland, show a Sanskrit connection. For example, the name Deutschland is derived from the Sanskrit *Daitya Sthan*. Daityas were an ancient, Sanskrit speaking people. They were known as Daityas for being descendants of the woman Diti, as explained in the Vedic texts.

The Caspian Sea and the region of Kashmir also derive their names from Sanskrit, being named after the great sage Cashyap, or Kashyapa Muni. Kashyapa was the ancestor of the Daityas who figures prominently in the Vedic epics. The Daityas were also referred to as the Danuv community. The Danube River, being a river that flowed through the land of the Daityas, or Danuvs, was later known as the Danube. Danu was one of the primary goddesses of the Celts, and was the wife of Kashyapa Muni.

Furthermore, the Red Sea is so named because that is merely the translation of the Sanskrit *Lohit Sagar* as was mentioned in the *Ramayana* when Rama's emissaries were searching for Sita. *Lohit* means red. This is similar to the name "White Sea," which is a mere translation of the Sanskrit *Ksheer Sagar*. We will see more of this kind of linguistic, geographical, and archeological evidence in the chapters that follow.

HOW SANSKRIT FADED FROM BEING A GLOBAL LANGUAGE AND WHAT SHATTERED THE GLOBAL VEDIC CULTURE

Sanskrit was an internationally known language even up to the time of the 15th century. This is corroborated by a footnote on page 28, Volume One, of *Marco Polo's Memoirs*. It explains that in the village of Kenyung Kwan, 40 miles north of Peking, beyond the pass of Nankau, under an archway, two large inscriptions were engraved in 1345 A.D. in six languages, including Tibetan, Mongol, Bashpath, Uighur, Chinese, one unknown language, and Sanskrit. Furthermore, another footnote on page 29 of the same volume explains that the annals of the Ming dynasty in 1407 A.D. mentions the establishment of a linguistic office for diplomatic purposes. This required the study of eight languages, including Sanskrit.

So Sanskrit was an important language. We can see that the farther we go back in time the wider and more frequent was its use. With so many languages displaying words that derive from Sanskrit, or are corrupted forms of it, we can understand that Sanskrit was the primary language from time immemorial up to the era of the *Mahabharata* War. So why did Sanskrit go from a global language to one that is presently sparsely used?

It would seem that the *Mahabharata* War at Kuruksetra (c. 3138 B.C.) caused the global, united Vedic administration to break up into factions and fragments. The war caused many once united portions of world society to take sides to either support the Pandavas or the Kurus. As explained in the *Mausal Parva* section of the *Mahabharata*, after the heavy carnage of the war, masses of people had to flee the area or take refuge in new and unfamiliar areas of the world. This caused the breakdown of the world-wide Vedic social, educational, and administrative system which helped usher in the chaos of the age of Kali-yuga.

As people fled to other areas of the world and splintered away from Vedic society, they, nonetheless, carried with them remnants and memories of the Vedic rituals and customs, as well as speech and language they once knew and practiced. However, bereft of the formal style of Vedic administration, and the educational system that accompanied it, after many generations of this, the forgetfulness of their ancient ways led them to speak in progressively more distorted forms of Sanskrit and develop their own peculiar regional forms of speech, customs, and mannerisms. Therefore, people in the British Isles, the Mediterranean, China, Japan, etc., all evolved their own style of vocabulary and remnants of Vedic customs. This is how various forms of language emerged out of Sanskrit, and why many languages and customs and religions have a thread of similarities running through them. The idea of some scholars that Sanskrit, Latin, and Greek are descendants of some previous language is unfounded and simply speculation.

With the dispersal of large masses of people there was the formation of regional states that became isolated and divided, which took the shape of Syria, Assyria, Babylonia, Mesopotamia, Egypt, China, etc. Mr. P. N. Oak provides an interesting explanation in this regard in his book, *Some Missing Chapters of World History* (p. 8): "Like the Vedic empire splitting into regional bits, Vedic society too broke into diverse cults and communities. Consequently their names are all Vedic Sanskrit. Thus, Syria is Sur, Assyria is Asur, Babylonia is Bahubalaniya, Mesopotamia is Mahishipattaniya, etc., while Stoics were Staviks (people given to meditation), Essenes were devotees of Essan (Lord Shiva), Samaritans were the Smartas (those whose lives were regulated by the *Smriti* Vedic texts), Sadduceans were the Sadhujans (monks), Malencians were Mlencchas, Philistines were followers of the Vedic sage Pulasti, Casseopeans were followers of sage Kashyap, etc."

This is why so many of the Vedic symbols, or distortions of such, are still important or highly recognized in various parts of the world. For example, the Aryan symbol of the Swastika is a famous sign for auspiciousness and good luck, which was later distorted into a symbol of a different meaning by Hitler and the

German army. The *Shakti-Chakra* or *Sri Yantra* was held sacred and turned into the six-pointed Star of Solomon by the Jewish people.

Furthermore, we can easily see the many similarities in ancient architecture all over the world. The Vedic culture was not interested in conquering foreign people into submission, but was interested in upgrading people everywhere. Thus, they also spread the ancient science of constructing buildings. Many of the ancient temples and stone mansions we find today are built to the specifications of the Vedic *Shilpa Shastras*. The reason for the similarity in buildings of the Indians, Iranians, Arabs, Mongols, and even in the Americas is explained in this way.

One western author who also reached this conclusion is E. B. Havell. In his book, *Indian Architecture--Its Psychology, Structure and History* (pp. 1 & 2), he writes that all historic architecture is absolutely Hindu (Vedic) in style, concept, and execution. Havell also wrote about the false idea that the beauty and precision of Indian building art must have come from outside India. "All these misconceptions have their root in one fixed idea. The belief that true aesthetic feeling has always been wanting in the Hindu mind and that everything really great in Indian art has been suggested or introduced by foreigners. . . This persistent habit of looking outside of India for the origins of Indian art must necessarily lead to false conclusions."

Interestingly, the principles of Vedic architecture can be found a lot closer to home than many people may think. P. N. Oak describes in *World Vedic Heritage* (p. 390) that the White House in Washington D. C. also follows the principles of Vedic architectural design. In the age old tradition, the king's palace was designated as the *Dhavala Gruha*, which literally translates into White House. The design for such a house is described in two famous Sanskrit classics, the *Harsha Charita* and *Kadambari*. Both texts were written by the Sanskrit pundit Banabhatta 1300 years ago during the reign of King Harshavardhan. "The traditional Vedic features enjoined for the Hindu Chief Executive's *Dhaval Gruha* have been reflected in every detail in the White House in Washington D.C. and the U.S. Embassy building in New Delhi."

So why can we not remember or find more sources of documented history of our connection with a global Vedic culture? Why do most histories of any country tend to fade out after 2500 years? There are several reasons, some of which we will mention later. But one reason is that before the process of fragmentation began after the *Mahabharata* War at Kuruksetra in 3138 B.C., all regions of the world had not developed a separate identity from the global Vedic Aryan culture. Thus, there was not a need to record a separate regional history other than what was already recorded as a global history, as we presently find in many of the ancient Vedic histories known as the *Itihasas*, or *Puranas*. This is one of the reasons why most regional histories tend not to go back farther in time then 2500 to 3000 years ago. Even the longest regional histories hardly go back farther than 3000 B.C., the time of the *Mahabharata* War.

VEDIC CULTURE IS THE ORIGINAL ANCESTOR
OF ALL RELIGIONS

Not only is the Vedic culture the source of architectural art, music, language, and most learning in the world, it is also the original or primary faith and basis of spiritual development of all humanity since the beginning of time. So no matter whether one claims to be Buddhist, Christian, Muslim, Jewish, Jain, Sikh, or whatever, he or she is still a descendant of Vedic culture. This is because all other genuine religions and spiritual paths have numerous traditions, legends, and names of God that have been carried over, or have been adopted, from the Vedic culture. However, we need to remember that they look different because as the once united Vedic world became fragmented, portions of the Vedic culture began to emerge in what became separate faiths and customs based on regional preferences. Thus, bits of the Sanskrit literature turned up in portions of other religious texts, as found in, for example, what became known as the *Talmud* of the Jews, the *Zend Avesta* of the Iranians, the *Eddas* of Scandinavia, and so on. So from the Vedic culture came many breakaway cults and creeds. Unfortunately, as previously discussed, many cultures have forgotten their histories and fail to understand their true origins and ancient connections with others. What is worse is that as this age of Kali-yuga unfolds, there will be an increase of societies splintering off from Vedic culture, or whatever is left of it. In fact, this is the prophecy as found in the Vedic literature, which I have especially elaborated in my book, *The Vedic Prophecies: A New Look into the future*. This means that there will be a continued decrease in moral standards, behavior, our spirituality, and less ability to see what we all have in common.

Another reason why many portions of history have been forgotten or buried is that it was typical of the conquering religions that make converts through military force for them to destroy any historical evidence of the previous culture. Especially when it displays loftier principles and more advanced levels of consciousness. So rampaging Roman Christian and Arab Muslim armies destroyed as much of any remaining Vedic culture they could. This, unfortunately, also helped plunge the world into what has been called the Dark Ages, which included terrible crusades, witch burnings of thousands of innocent women, and intense torture of any so-called infidels.

Consequently, the teaching of Vedic sciences suffered a severe setback. This meant that the further development of society also ceased to progress and was forced to discover things all over again that were previously known. This provided the basis of the glorification of the inventions and discoveries of such men as Galileo, Copernicus, and Newton, who really were discovering what the Vedic literature had described thousands of years before. Thus, there was a period of several hundred years, if not thousands, in which societies became more distanced from Vedic culture, and they also became more backward and underdeveloped. In fact, in some distant regions, humanity sank to a state of primitive living.

Theologically, however, the Vedic pantheon was shared by many breakaway religions and cults, each swearing allegiance to some particular form of Divinity. Many philosophies and religions that were started by societies that broke away from Vedic culture still kept many of their Vedic traditions. The difference is that the Vedic knowledge and traditions came at the time of creation, and can certainly be traced back many thousands of years, while the more modern scriptures, such as the Bible and Koran, were developed many years later, appearing comparatively recently within the last 2000 years. The *Vedas* were given to mankind by Lord Vishnu to Brahma, the demigod creator of the universe, and were later compiled by Srila Vyasadeva, an incarnation of the Supreme Being, for the benefit of humanity. The Bible was supposedly developed by men who were said to be inspired by God. However, the more scholars focus their research on historical evidence, the more they find that the formation of the Old and New Testaments is far different than what the Bible tradition claims. The Koran is said to have been given to Muhammad by the angel Gabriel. However, this is questionable because history records that Mohammad could not even read or write. So how could have the original writings of these revelations take place? Furthermore, the Koran was put into its official form years after the death of Mohammad.

In any case, the concepts and scope of the Vedic literature is much broader than that of the Bible, Koran, or other religions. The Vedic literature is a compendium of universal truths and knowledge. The Vedic texts contain a higher level of spiritual understanding and universal love between God and humanity compared with the Koran, which contains many threats and curses for those who do not follow it cent percent. The Bible and Koran are, therefore, local scriptures that pertain primarily to the people of its immediate region. Such scripture deals almost exclusively with the local prophets and customs of the people. This also causes a division between them and everyone else. In this way, we can understand that the Vedic texts are a universal scripture which are based on the principle of *sanatana-dharma*, the eternal nature of the soul regardless of where or what a person may be. It is this process which can provide the means for people to return to their natural, spiritual state of being, and find common ground with all people.

Nonetheless, Judaism, Christianity, and Islam incorporate many Vedic traditions, which we will discuss much further in the chapters that follow. Even much of Islamic religious terminology is rooted in Sanskrit. For example, the term "Allah" is a synonym for a goddess in Sanskrit, usually in reference to Durga or one of her forms. Also, one of the Indian *Upanishads* is the *Allopanishad.*

Another example is the origin of the word *Satan*, which both Muslims and Christians use in their scripture. The term "satan," or Shaitan as Muslims call him, comes from the Sanskrit word *Sat-na*, which means unreal or nontruth. *Sat* means the true and eternal, while *Sat-na* means the opposite. From that we get the word *Satan*, which takes on a personality in the Bible and Koran, indicating our attraction or temptation to that which is impermanent.

The word "prophet" is a synonym for the Sanskrit word *avatar*, or one who descends from heaven, from which comes the concept for prophet. The correct Sanskrit word is *pri-pata*, which is being pronounced as Prophet in English. *Pri-pata* is also similar to the Sanskrit word *pita*, which means father.

Another similarity deals with Abraham. In the Jewish tradition Abraham was one of the progenitors of the Jewish race. However, there are religious scholars who question historically if there ever was an Abraham. There are stories about him, but little historical evidence can be found. But this Abraham, who is accepted by the Jews, Christians, and Muslims, is a reference to none other than Brahma of the Vedic tradition. Brahma is explained in the Vedic texts to be the first progenitor of the human race. It is this Brahma who is referred to under the mispronounced name of Abraham, who then became one of the progenitors of the Jewish people, and associated with and the basis of many stories within the new cultures and their scriptures. Therefore, Abraham is another misunderstood carry-over from the Vedic tradition.

Even the story of the creation of the world, as explained in the Bible, has its roots in the Vedic tradition. In the first sentences of the Bible it states: "In the beginning God created the heaven and the earth. And the earth was without form and void; and darkness was upon the face of the deep. And the spirit of God moved upon the face of the waters." So herein we can see that the Bible begins with the same but summarized story as recorded in the Vedic texts, when Lord Vishnu was lying on the universal waters in a dark and empty universe and created all the universal elements to form heaven and earth.

This is continued in the New Testament, in the opening lines of the book of *John* which states, "In the beginning was the word, and the word was with God, and the word was God." That first word, as described in the Vedic texts and related earlier in this volume, was *OM*. That word was present at the time of creation and was with God, and is God.

Shortly after the creation, the Bible refers to the story of Adam and Eve, the first couple from whom the human race was born. However, this is similar to the previously recorded story in the Vedic texts of Svayambhuva Manu and his wife Satarupa who, after coming into being, were essentially advised by Brahma, the creator, to "Beget many children and rule over the earth, for you shall be the ruler of men." The Koran also follows the biblical tradition, accepting the lineage of the prophets.

The trinity of the Christians of Father, Son, and Holy Ghost has also been a derivative of the Vedic tradition of *Bhagavan* (the individual Supreme Being), *Paramatma* (the internal incarnation and expansion of God, the Son), and the great, all-pervasive *Brahman* (Holy Ghost). This trinity can also be compared to Vishnu, Brahma, and Mahesh (Shiva). Mother Mary of the Christian tradition also reflects the Vedic goddess Mari-amma, where *amma* designates mother. Even the Christian term Mater Dei is but a reflection of the Vedic term *Matri Devi*--Mother Goddess.

There are even similarities between Christian, Buddhist, and Vedic styles of meditation, such as with the use of prayer beads. The use of beads goes back to prehistoric times. The word *bead* comes from the word *bid*, to plead or petition, which is done to awaken the spirit of God, or to open the channel of communication between God and man. Thus, chanting the name of God is to invoke God Himself. The followers of the *Vedas*, the Vaishnavas, have 108 beads on their *japa mala* or rosary, while Buddhists also have 108, Catholics have 54, and Muslims have 99 plus one head bead. Vaishnavas, Buddhists, and Muslims use beads to chant the names of God. Catholics chant prayers to God, and sometimes they just chant the names, especially in the Eastern tradition. The names of Krishna, Rama, and Hare are the original names of the Supreme Deity before they were changed in their theosophical and linguistic forms through variations in location and cultural traits.

In other aspects of spiritual practices, many cultures provided a means of entering into the higher levels of knowledge, which was often kept secret from the uninitiated. The Persians, Egyptians, Syrians, Cretans, Greeks, Romans, Celts, Druids, as well as the Mayans and American Indians all had their rituals of initiation into the mysteries of the unknown after which, in many cultures, the initiates were called twice-born. This is identical to the earliest known practice of the Vedic *brahmanas* who are initiated into spiritual understanding and, thus, are called "twice-born" to signify their spiritual birth which is over and above the common animal birth that every ordinary creature undergoes when born from the womb.

* * *

Since there are so many similarities between the cultures of the world, the most ancient of which can be traced back to the primal Vedic traditions, a return to Vedic culture, or at least the realization that it is the original and primordial tradition of humanity as given by Divinity, should be helpful to establish peace and social unity. With the highest common factor and background among us all being the Vedic heritage, the recognition of this can surely help break down the regional barriers as well as the distinctions created by present-day organized religions. This should be done for ultimate peace, idealism, and happiness.

Many more of these similarities in words, traditions, rituals, stories, and architectural discoveries will be explained in the following chapters as we look deeper into each area of the planet. This will help prove the existence of a global Vedic Aryan culture that preceded all others.

CHAPTER SIX

More Sanskrit/Vedic Links With English Words and Western Culture

As we mentioned in the previous chapter, there are many examples that show how numerous western traditions have roots in the Vedic customs, and how many languages are derived from Sanskrit. So let's point out some of the more common and easily identifiable linguistic links.

In regard to personal names, we find many from Europe that are rooted in Sanskrit. For example, *Rita* means one who embodies truth. *Margarita* means one who follows or is devoted to the path of truth. Socrates is *Sucrutas*, meaning one remembered for meritorious deeds. Aristotle comes from *Aritataal*, the God who shields one from mishap and sorrow. George is rooted in *Garg* or Garga Rishi, the name of the Vedic sage. James refers to Yamas, the Vedic God of death. Names like the Roman Caesar, German Kaiser, and Russian Czar are all varieties of the Sanskrit term *Eswar*, meaning Great Lord.[1]

The English surname Roy is found both as Roy and Rai in India since it is a Sanskrit name signifying a king, lord, or master. Sheila is an English name of Sanskrit origin signifying a woman of character. The Name Sarah is a European abbreviation of the Sanskrit goddess Sarasvati. The term "Syr" in old Welsh and "Sir" in modern English are mispronunciations of the Sanskrit honorific *Sri*.[2] Since "Sir" comes from the Sanskrit *Sri*, an example of an English name like Sir Roy Henderson in Sanskrit would be Sri Rai Indrasen. The Vedic name of Hari, meaning Lord Krishna, is changed to the English Christian name of Harry. And by placing an "n" in the name, becomes Henry.[3]

The names of many countries still show their roots in the Vedic culture. Australia comes from the Vedic term *astralaya* (*laya*--land of *astra*--missiles). It may have gotten this name for being the practicing place for the *brahmastra* missiles that had been used in the *Ramayana* and *Mahabharata* wars. These missiles may have caused the destruction of the land and formed the deserts of Australia. The ancient name of Japan is Nippon, which refers to the Sanskrit *nipun*, which means dexterous, for which the Japanese people are noted. Siberia gets its name from the Sanskrit appellation of *Sibiria* or *Shibireeya*, which indicates a region of encampments. This refers to the inhospitable climate making it suitable for only temporary residences before people moved on to other places. The term Russia comes from the Sanskrit word *Rusheeya*, referring to a country of *Rushees* or *Rishis*, sages. And Soviet comes from the Sanskrit term *Svet*, interpreted as "white," like the land of snow. Romania is the Sanskrit word *Ramaniya*, meaning scenic or attractive. The Alps mountains get their name from the Sanskrit *Alpas*, meaning small as in the small brother (mountain range) to the Himalaya mountains. Palestine gets its name from Pulastin, a revered sage, some of whose progeny became cruel demons. The English word Philistine is in connection with this and signifies an uncultured, quarrelsome people. Guatamalaya means the abode of the sage *Gautam*, a sacred Sanskrit name.[4]

In the field of currency there are many Sanskrit terms still used today. This proves that Sanskrit was a world language for many thousands of years under the universal Vedic administration. For example, the Sanskrit term for coins is *panas*. This term took shape as *paisa*, another common word in India. It has two meanings, one of which is a basic copper coin, and another is all the wealth a person possesses. The French word *Piastra* is a corruption of the word *paisa*. In Spain and Spanish territories we see the same word pronounced as "peso." This term took shape as "pence" in British currency. The term "shilling" is in fact a corrupt form of the Sanskrit term *Shivling*, which indicates that pre-historic Britain had coins with the *Shivalingas* stamped on them. The "Pound Sterling" is a corrupt form of the Sanskrit term *Poundra Sterling*. In ancient Sanskrit tradition the term *Poundra* signified a high caliber or rating. The term "star" signifies the level, and "ling" implied the imprint of a *Shivling* or a sign. Therefore, the term "Pound Sterling" meant a high quality coin bearing the stamp of the *Shivaling* as a mark of its sanctity and purity.

The word "coin" itself took shape from the Sanskrit word *kanak*, which means gold. Gold was one of the important metals for coins. The English word "cash" originates in the Sanskrit word *kasa*. This refers to bronze, which was another metal used in the ancient system of coinage. The word "money" also comes from the Sanskrit term *mana*, which used to be an ancient gold coin. The Indian term "rupee" also comes from the Sanskrit word *raupyam* for "silver" in Sanskrit.

The Sanskrit term for ruler is known as *raya*. And the currency issued under his authority used to be termed *rayal*. The "Rial" is the Saudi Arabian legal tender, which is the Arabic pronunciation of the term "Rayal." This shows proof that in pre-Islamic times Arabia used to be administered by Sanskrit speaking Kshatriya *rayas*. Even the Russian "Rubble" gets its name from the Sanskrit compound *rajya-bal* or *raya-bal*, meaning "strength of the realm."[5]

In the system of time, the word "time" itself is a corruption of the Sanskrit *Samay* which was pronounced as "Tamay" and later became "Time." *Kala* is the Sanskrit word for time, and the word "calendar" comes from the Sanskrit term *kalantar*, which signifies a chart of the divisions of time. Likewise the word "clock" comes from the Sanskrit word *kala-ka*, meaning a recorder of time. The system of time itself is also from the Vedic culture. The 60-second, 60-minute calculation is also from Vedic mathematics. According to the Vedic computation, 60 *vipalas* make one *pala* and 60 *palas* make one *ghati* (24 minutes). The term "hour" is a mispronunciation of the Sanskrit word *hora*, which is two-and-a-half *ghatis*. Even the word "day" is the corrupt form of the Sanskrit word *din*. And the terms a.m. and p.m. have a Sanskrit root. In English they mean "ante-meridian" and "post-meridian." But ante or post-meridian to what? However, this is cleared up when we realize that the a.m. and p.m. terms are the initials of the Sanskrit expressions *Arohanam Martandasya* (the climbing of the sun) and *Patanam Martandasya* (the falling of the sun).

The days of the week also follow the order given by the Vedic tradition. For example, Sunday (named after the sun) follows Saturday (the day of Saturn). And Monday (named after the Moon) follows Sunday, etc.

The names of the months are also based on Sanskrit words. September is *Saptamber*, October is *Ashtamber*, November is *Navamber*, and December is *Dashamber*. *Ambar* is the name referring to the Zodiac, while *sapta*, *ashta*, *nava*, and *dasha* represents the 7th, 8th, 9th and 10th months respectively. Other months include January, named from Januarius, or the Latin Janus, which is the Sanskrit Ganesh. Januarius is linguistically connected to the Sanskrit *Gana-raya-eash*. Ganesh is worshiped at the start of any ritual or project, or in this case the beginning of every year. Thus, the first month of the year was named after Ganesh.

February was spelled by the Romans as Februarius, which is a mispronunciation of the Sanskrit *Pravaresh*. Consequently, Februarius was named after *Pravar*, which signifies a sage, or God as Lord of the sages. The term "March" comes for the Sanskrit *Marichi* which is one of the names of the sun. The term "August" and even the name "Augustus" are rooted in the name of the sage Agastya, who was a very sober person. Thus, the phrase "august personality" is derived from that.[6]

As previously pointed out, the system of mathematics primarily comes from India. In fact, the Arabic numerals came from India through Arabia. Even the word "arithmetic" comes from the Sanskrit *Artha-maatica*, meaning a computation of monetary transactions. The word "eometry" is Sanskrit *Jya-matra*, meaning a measurement of earth. The word "trigonometry" is from the Sanskrit *tri-gono-matra*, which means "three-dimensional measurement." It can also refer to *trikon-matra*, meaning a triangular measurement. The word "physics" is from the Sanskrit term *pashya*, which means seeing or perceiving with all senses. Other terms like "divide" come from the Sanskrit *dwivide*, and the term "add" comes from Sanskrit *adhik*.[7]

The science of botany has a name that comes from the Sanskrit term *buta*, which means a science concerning plants. This is especially found in the practice of *Ayurveda* in which the term *jadi-buti* means "roots and plants." The English terms "osteomalacia" and "osteoporosis" come from the Sanskrit *asthi-mala*, meaning bones that are diseased. The English termination "stry," as found in chemistry or dentistry, is a perverted form of the Sanskrit term of *shastra* or *shastri*, which means a science. The science of gerontology was previously studied in Vedic culture and comes from the Sanskrit terms of *gera* (old age) and *onto* (end of the living being). Even the English word "cough" can easily be traced back to the Sanskrit word *kaf* or *kapha*, which refers to phlegm or mucus.

The English word "disciple" comes from the Sanskrit *deekshapal*, meaning one who abides by the lessons taught. And "synonym" also comes from the Sanskrit *sama-nama*, meaning "similar name." "Moon" is linked to the Sanskrit term *mun*, which refers to the mind. Astrologically the moon represents the mind of a person. Also, the day named after the moon is Monday. The English word "ignition" comes from the Sanskrit *Agni*, referring to fire or god of fire. From the Sanskrit *Pitar*, the European pronunciation replaces the "p" with an "f" which makes it "fitar," which becomes "father."

Other English words that are connected with Sanskrit are as follows:

"Sport" is a corruption of the Sanskrit *spardh*, meaning competing. "Sing" and "song" come from the Sanskrit science of music known as *Sangeet*. "Regime" comes from the Sanskrit *rajyam*. "Royal" is from the Sanskrit *Raya* or *Raja*, meaning king. "Majesty" is from the Sanskrit *Maharaja-asti*, meaning High Sovereign. "Mister" comes from the Sanskrit *Maha-ster*, meaning a person of high order. "You" and "we" are forms of the Sanskrit terms *yuyam* and *weyam*. "Divinity" comes from the Sanskrit *deva-nity*, meaning way of life of the *devas*, or gods.

"Diction" comes from the Sanskrit *deekshan*, meaning guidance. Thus, the word "dictionary" comes from the Sanskrit *deekshantary*, meaning an aid to resolve difficult words. "Management" and "manager" come from the Sanskrit *manje-ment*, meaning one whose thinking is devoted to running a concern.

"Inspire" comes from the Sanskrit *intesphuran*, meaning idea coming from within. "Institution" comes from *intisdhyan*, denoting an organization toward which inspiration is imparted. "Enterprise" comes from the Sanskrit *enterpreraj*, defined as that which is begun by inspiration. Thus, "entrepreneur" is the perverted form of the Sanskrit *enterpreritnar*, which means a person who through inspiration began a commercial venture.

"Known" and "unknown" come from the Sanskrit *jnana* (pronounced gyan) and *ajnan*, which means the same as the English. "Sugar" comes from the Sanskrit *shakara*. "Hunt" and "hunters" come from Sanskrit *hanta*, referring to killer, and *hantarah*, several killers. "Sweat" comes from the Sanskrit *swed*.

"Pediatrics" comes from the Sanskrit term *pada*, denoting foot. And "pedestrian" comes from the Sanskrit *padachara*. "Dentist" and "dental" come from the Sanskrit *dant*, meaning tooth.

The prefix *para* as in parapsychology and paramilitary is Sanskrit. *Para* means "different kind of." *Rama* as in Panorama or cinerama is also Sanskrit. The prefix *mal* as in malevolent, malpractice, or malignant is Sanskrit which means bad, dirty, or contaminated. The word *debt* is Sanskrit indicating the amount given. Nouns like "dentistry" and "trigonometry" are from the Sanskrit *dant-shastra* and *tri-guna-matra*.[8]

Other interesting examples of English words that have links to Sanskrit include the following (as explained on pages 251-2 of Mr. Oak's book, *Some Blunders of Indian Historical Research*):

English	Sanskrit	English	Sanskrit
preach	prachar	adore	adar
path	path	Mater Dui	Matru Devi
he	sah	she	sa
go	gama	come	agama
untruth	unrita	cow	gau
two	dwi	three	tri
four	chatwar	five	panch
seven	sapta	six	shad
eight	ashta	nine	nava
decimal	dashmalava	decade	dashak
octago	nashtakon	pentagon	panchakon
vesture	vastra	hand	hasta
cent	shata	internal	antarik
terra	dhara	mind	mana
night	naktam		

There are many more examples of Sanskrit words in English, as well as in Latin, Persian, and Greek. Many other languages show the same influence, such as Lithuanian in which many words are the same as Sanskrit. The above examples, however, should be enough to show that the Vedic Aryan influence once held a powerful sway over many lands, and its influence can still be recognized today through this type of research.

NOTES
Several portions of the above information have been compiled by Mr. P. N. Oak and presented in his books, *World Vedic Heritage* and *Some Missing Chapters in World History*, as noted:
1. *Some Missing Chapters in World History* (p. 14-15)
2. *World Vedic Heritage* (p. 885)
3. *Ibid.* (p. 992)
4. *Ibid.* (p. 338-343)
5. *Ibid.* (pp. 422-424)
6. *Ibid.* (pp. 347-350)
7. *Ibid.* (pp. 430-31)
8. *Ibid.* (p. 911)

CHAPTER SEVEN

The Vedic Influence Found in the Middle East and Africa

As we investigate the region and countries of the Middle East, we find much evidence that shows the early influence of Vedic culture. Much of this influence still remains today. This justifies the fact that such influence would not be there if this region had not been at one time a part of the global Vedic Aryan culture and had been administered by Vedic rulers.

Numerous countries of the Middle East shared many of the same gods in various ways, although they called them by different names. They also had many similarities in the legends and stories which explained the creation of cosmological realities. Often these were variations or condensations of other neighboring traditions or previously established truths. By studying some of these connections and similarities we can see how many of these cultures are connected to each other and related to the earliest traditions that came out of the Vedic Aryan civilization. We can also recognize how the Vedic influence extended over a vast area and traveled west into Europe and other regions and affected these countries in greater or lesser degrees.

Ancient India no doubt covered a much larger area of land than it does today and spread much farther to the north and west. At least there are historical indications showing that the Aryan influence was felt over long distances. The Vedic gods, for example, were known over a wide area. V. Gordon Childe, in his book *The Aryans*, states that evidence makes it clear that the Aryans had been established in centers on the Upper Euphrates in 1400 B.C. These centers were similar to the cities of the Indus Valley and later in Media and Persia. In fact, Hugo Winckler, in 1907, identified the names of four Vedic gods (Indra, Varuna, Mitra, and the Nasatya twins) along with ten Babylonian and four Mitannian gods that were invoked as witnesses to a treaty signed in 1360 B.C. between the kings of Mitanni and the Hittites. There are also tablets at Tell-el-Amarna that mention Aryan princes in Syria and Palestine. But these Aryans were not necessarily permanent residents of the area but dynasts who ruled over the non-Aryan subjects of that region. This would explain why some scholars such as Jacobi, Pargiter, and Konow accept the deities of the Mitanni in the Upper Euphrates in Syria and

Palestine as being Indian, introduced to the area through a Sanskrit speaking people who came from the Punjab. Furthermore, L. A. Waddell claims that the first Aryan kings can be traced back to at least 3380 B.C. They had a capital north of the Euphrates near the Black Sea in Cappadocia in 3378 B.C., and these Hittite kings of Cappadocia bore Aryan names. This means that the Aryans had to have been very well settled in the area during this time.

THE HITTITES

In speaking of the Hittites, they are said to have invaded the area of Cappadocia near 1950 B.C. However, as the above evidence shows, they may have been there much earlier. The Hittites are mentioned in Egyptian and other records of the area, as well as in the Old Testament. Documents from Boghaz-Koi, Turkey, translated in 1917, showed they did speak an ancient, but unknown, Indo-European language. This no doubt had to have been related or derived from Sanskrit. The dialects they spoke include Luwian, Palaic, Lydian, Lycian, and others. The Hittite people were called the Khatti in the oldest documents. This could possibly be derived form the Sanskrit words Kshatriya or the Pali Khattiyo, as pointed out by D.D. Kosambi in *The Culture and Civilization of Ancient India*, (p. 77). The Hittites were known to have worshiped a god called Inar, most undoubtedly the Vedic Indra, which the *Larousse Encyclopedia of Mythology* (p. 85) mentions as a god who had come from India with the Indo-European Hittites. There is also a book that has been found in Anatolia on horse training that contains technical terms in perfect Sanskrit. Thus, the Hittites were certainly part of Vedic culture and a migratory wave out of the Indian region. This could have been due to lack of water in the area as the desert expanded.

THE MITANNI

The Mitanni were also eastern people forced to move farther west away from their Indian homeland. They appeared as ruling tribes of Mesopotamia, Syria and Palestine near 1400 B.C. This is another example of people in far North India who had to leave the region due to a lack of water and resources due to the growing desert. Though they took up the local language and culture of the region, they still left clay tablets at El Amarna in the 15th century B.C. that recorded the names of the Mitanni kings of Syria, namely Artatama, Artamanya, Saussatar, Sutarna, Subandu, Dusratta, Suwardata, and Yasdata. Later on, the treaties between the Hittite king Shubbiluliuma and the Mitanni king Mattiuza are shown to invoke the Mitanni gods Mitra (Vedic Mitra), Indaru (Indra), Uruwna (Varuna), and Nashattiya (the Nasatyas). Herein we can see that the Mitanni gods had names similar to the Vedic gods. The Mitanni people were also called the Maryanni.

Childe, in his book *The Aryans* (p.19), compares this name to the Sanskrit word *marya*, meaning young men or heroes. This word is used in the *Rig-veda* (3.54.13 & 5.59.6). Thus, it is likely that the Mitanni could hardly be anything but part of the Vedic culture and from India. However, as they moved from their native land, they shed their culture. The Mitanni people were a group from the Vedic Purus.

THE SUMERIANS

One widely held view about the Sumerians is that they arrived in Mesopotamia before 3000 B.C. when they acquired the prosperity of the inhabitants that were living there. However, another view is that the Sumerians were actually the earliest cultivators in Mesopotamia. They had a philosophy which was especially influential on the succeeding Babylonians and Assyrians who assimilated much of their beliefs. The Sumerians believed the universe and all within it reflected the supreme mind and supernatural activity. They believed that the universe was created from the primeval sea along with all the planets, stars, sun, and moon, each of which had its own orbit. After the creation of the planets came superhuman and invisible beings, who then made human, animal, and plant life. This Sumerian theology, which is very similar to the Vedic version, can still be found in the detailed texts dating back to 1900 B.C.

Though the Mesopotamian cities shared a common pantheon, not all of the gods were worshiped in all of the cities, neither were they known by the same names. And when the Semites invaded the area, they changed the gods' names, characteristics, and relations. So presently it is not clear which were the Sumerian gods or which were carry-overs from the Vedic Aryans, to whom the Sumerians at least were closely related if not a part of Vedic civilization.

The Sumerians had many temples, such as the temple of Enki at Eridu, and of Marduk at Babylon. The images of the gods were worshiped by being given offerings of food and drink, fruit, incense, and new garments on festival days. This is the same system used in worshiping the Vedic deities in India. Anu was the god of heaven and was at first the ruler of the other gods, such as Enlil (lord of the winds and creator of the sun, moon, and vegetation), Ninki (lady of the earth), and Enki (lord of the underworld). Anu was especially worshiped at Uruk, around 300 B.C., but was replaced by Enlil when the city of Nippur defeated Uruk, the biblical city of Erech and modern Warka. However, the god Marduk, son of Enki, replaced Enlil in Babylonia when his city of Babylon ruled Mesopotamia by the influence of a powerful dynasty, and was also replaced by Ashur in Assyria near the middle of the second millennium. The consort of Enlil, Ninlil, became the Babylonian Ishtar, who represented many earlier female deities and was also known to Syrians as Anat, and to Arabs as Atar, to Greeks as Astarte, and to Egyptians as Isis. In Assyria, Adad was the god who controlled the rain. In Syria he was called Ramman the thunderer, among the Hittites he was Teshub, and in the Vedic tradition he was called Indra. Thus, we can see the interconnectedness of the Sumerian culture with others of the region, most of which have roots that go back to India and the Vedic traditions. In fact, L. A. Waddell concluded that the Sumerians were Aryans in many ways. (More about the Sumerians and their Vedic connection is described in on page 37 in Chapter Four.)

PERSIA

The name Persia is actually a derivative of the Sanskrit name *Parasu*, which was the battle axe of Parashurama. Lord Parashurama had led 21 expeditions around the world to chastise the Kshatriya warriors who had swayed from the Vedic principles and became cruel and unruly. This was before the time of Lord Ramachandra. Persia was overrun by Lord Parashurama and his troops and succumbed to abide by his administration. According to E. Pococke on page 45 of his book, *India in Greece*, the land of Persia became known as Paarasika.

Pococke goes on the explain that the term "Chaldeans" comes from the Sanskrit term *Kul-deva* (often pronounced Kaldeo), which means "family gods" referring to a people who worshiped the gods of the Brahmanas. He also adds that the map of ancient Persia, Colchis, and Armenia provides distinct evidence that show a colonization of people from India of a massive scale. It also shows the truth of several main descriptions of the area as found in the *Ramayana* and the *Mahabharata*.

A British author, R. G. Wallace, mentions on page seven of his book, *Memoirs of India*, that Hindus are numerous throughout Afghanistan, as well as Arabia and Persia. These are not recent migrants but remnants from the local populations who were converted to Islam by force.

Lt. Gen. Charles Vallancy, on page 465 of his book *Collectania De Rebus Hibernicus*, quotes Sir William Jones as saying: "It has been proved by clear evidence and plain reasoning that a powerful monarchy was established in Iran, long before the Assyrian or Pishdadi government; that it was in truth a Hindu monarchy. . . that it subsisted many centuries and that its history has been ingrafted on that of the Hindus, who founded the monarchies of Ayodhya and Indraprastha. . ."

E. Pococke, on page 178 of his book *India in Greece*, explains that, "A system of Hinduism pervaded the whole Babylonian and Assyrian empires. Scripture furnishes abundant proofs, in the mention of the various types of the Sun-god, Bal-nath, whose pillar adorned every mound and every grove." Later, on page 182 of the same book, he explains that the term Syria is derived from the Indian tribes that under Sur or Surya, the sun, gave its name to the vast province of Surya, now Syria. This martial race is found in its greatest force in Palestine.

It is also explained that Babylonia is named after the Sanskrit Bahubalaneeya, meaning the realm of King Bahubali, a well-known king in the Vedic legends.

V. Gordon Childe points out more linguistic resemblances found in the Sanskrit of the *Rig-veda* and the Iranian of the *Gathas* of Zoroaster and Darius the Great. Both Indians and Iranians had called themselves Aryas and worshiped the same deities, such as Mitra, Aryaman, Indra, Varuna, Agni, and so on. They also once knew the same set of rivers, the Sarasvati and Hara 'uvatis, as well as shared the Soma ritual. Thus, one can conclude that they were once of the same background. Even the word *Iran* or *Ariana* means "Land of the Aryans" as pointed out by Hermann Kulke in his book, *A History of India*. All this signifies that the early Iranians were a part of or at least affiliated with the Vedic Aryan civilization.

Many of the Vedic Aryan concepts of God were adopted by Zoroastrianism. In fact, its basic doctrines and conception of its god, Ahura Mazda, can be traced back to the *Purusha-sukta*, which is in the *Rig-veda*. Furthermore, Zoroastrianism had a great influence on the Judeo-Christian religion. Waddell points out that the Adam of the Adam and Eve story of the Hebrew Genesis came about from the traditional history in late Babylonia that described the oldest kings known to the ancient world of the Aryan dynasties. The Hebrew rabbis who composed the book of Genesis (said to be a book of Moses) heard these histories of the great supermen Aryan kings. Not understanding them, they distorted the historical facts about the great king Adda (the Babylonian name of an early Aryan king who was also called Addamu) and simply changed the name Addamu into "Adam," the first created man said to have been formed by God in 3761 B.C. Thus, Waddell concludes that the story of the Hebrew genealogy of Adam, Cain, Enoch, Noah, and Japhet are variations of the names and distortions of the Babylonian history of the earliest recorded Aryan kings.

Waddell goes on to explain that the Hebrew Adam was the Sumerian Adar or Addamu and the Aryan Iksvaku. The name Cain is the English equivalent of the Hebrew Qain, who was called in Genesis by the title of Aysh, similar to Ayus of the Vedic epics. Cain is said to have built a city and named it after his son Enoch, which is the English version of the Hebrew name Hanuk. Biblical authorities say this city is identical to the old Sumerian seaport of Unuk in Lower Mesopotamia that Chaldeans later called Erek. And the name Enoch or Hanuck equates with Janak of the Vedic epics. Thus, the religion of the Jews and Christians is naturally similar in many respects to the Vedic tradition, though the Jewish people may have used distortions of neighboring histories to fabricate their own folklore. They also adopted various customs as well. For example, the baptism ritual that is practiced throughout Christianity originated in India in the form of immersion in the Ganges River for spiritual rebirth and purification.

AFGHANISTAN

The word "Sthan" is actually a Sanskrit derivative that means place or land. There are a string of countries to the west of India with the suffix of "sthan," including Baluchisthan, Kurdisthan, Siwisthan, Arvasthan, and Turgasthan

(Turkey). Until the 10th century A.D. Hindu kings ruled over Afghanistan, and thereafter still in parts of it. As mentioned in *Albiruni's India*, compiled and edited by Dr. Edward D. Sachau, although Kabul had passed out of Hindu hands, the Hindu kings were still allowed to have their coronation ceremony in Kabul.

Many of the names in Afghanistan are also of Sanskrit origin. Pushtu, the language of Afghanistan, is replete with Sanskrit words. Kabul is also derived from the Sanskrit root *Kubha*. Temples of Mahanubhavas and other Indian sects are found in Kabul to this day. The Bamiyan valley of Afghanistan has several colossal statues of the Buddha carved out of the mountainsides as well as numerous rock cut temples, similar to what we find in places of India such as Ellora and Ajanta. The name Jalalabad has been given to the town which earlier was known as Nagarhara; the town of Lord Shiva. This, along with the above information on Kabul, proves that all of the ancient palaces, forts, temples, mosques, and mansions which date back to the 9th century A.D. in Afghanistan were actually Vedic constructions, built by the Hindus, and the people were followers of the Vedic culture. The buildings that have since become mosques, or are now used for Islamic purposes, were captured during the invasions. Thus, it can be safe to say that it was not the Muslims who introduced the dome, lime, concrete, and the arch to India, but it was the Vedic Indians who introduced them to Persia. This is evidenced by the Muslim word "Gumbaj" for dome which comes from the Sanskrit word *Kumbhaj*, meaning the same thing.

In *Some Blunders of Indian Historical Research* (pages 244-6), Mr. Oak describes the early opulence of this area: "What is now Karachi was a famous Hindu city called Debal or Devalaya deriving its name from a lofty temple with a towering spire. Enclosed in rings of massive walls, this sacred site was repeatedly attacked during Mohammad Kasim's times. King Dahir--whose real name is not known--ruled over that region when Mohammad Kasim started his invasion of India.

"According to Arab chronicles of Mohammad Kasim's time, Sind, far from being a desert, teemed with lakes and forests and irrigated fields and gardens. It was only when the era of invasions started and these elaborate water works as well as verdant fields were repeatedly laid waste by marauding hordes that Sind and Baluchistan and Afghanistan became deserts. . . Until about the sixth century A.D., we find it mentioned in encyclopedias that Arabia too was a well watered and vegetated land. But about 1,300 years ago the people in Middle-Western countries were seized by a new philosophy, a new way of life by which they organized themselves into raiding bands and raided neighboring countries to live off the toil of other people.

"The place where Akbar was born is called Umarkot. It is situated in Sind. Akbar's father, Humayun, had sought the hospitality of a Hindu Rajput chief who ruled over Umarkot when Akbar was born. These instances should prove that Sind, Afghanistan and Baluchistan were regions where Indian Kshatriyas ruled until 1,000 to 1,200 years ago and the people used to be all Hindus."

IRAQ AND IRAN

The names Iraq and Iran are derived from Sanskrit. The common root is "Ir," such as found in the Irawati River in Myanmar (Burma). The name "Iranam" in Sanskrit, from which the name Iran is derived, applies to salty and barren lands. This was the name that was given to the region by the Sanskrit speaking Kshatriya rulers or administrators. The capital of Iraq, Baghdad, also has a name based on Sanskrit, *Bhagwad* or *Bhagwan Nagar*, which is referring to *Nagar* (a city) dedicated to *Bhagwan* (Lord Krishna). It was abbreviated to Baghdad, meaning simply the "City of God."

This also means that this was not the first of Muslim cities, said to have been built by Caliph Al-Mansur in one year, 762-63 A.D., but was one of the first *captured* Vedic centers. Otherwise, it would not have had a name derived from Sanskrit. Furthermore, it was a well planned city, which would have taken much longer than a year to build. This is also an indication of the typical falsification or suppression of real history that forceful religions use to hide whatever advancements existed in the previous culture.

Kurdisthan is a part of Iraq and is also a Sanskrit name. The Kurdi language and customs still bear unmistakable traces and the stamp of their Sanskrit and Indian origin.

An interesting thing is that the royal family of Iran, the Pehlavis, have their roots in the Vedic Kshatriya tradition. The name Pehlavi appears first in the *Ramayana* episode in which Vishvamitra attempts to drive away Vashista's sacred cow. The title "Shah" is also a Vedic name and is also a common Hindu surname. The Hindu king of Nepal also bears the title of "Shah." The Kshatriya king of Gwalior deposed by the Muslims was Ram Shah. The wealthy patriot who turned over his wealth to Rana Pratap to help defend India was Bhama Shah. Therefore, the title "Shah" in Iran is simply a reminder of the Indian Kshatriya tradition that once ruled the area of Iran. In fact, when Iran started to come under attack by the Islamic invasions, many of the common people ran away to India. Histories also record that the royal family at the time also considered leaving Iran to seek shelter in India. So the very fact that the people and the ruler of Iran thought of coming to India during the Islamic raids proves that they were Hindus, part of the Vedic culture.

The *Rig-veda*, being the most ancient scripture, and its language being Sanskrit, provides evidence that Sanskrit is the great ancestor of all known languages. Persian is also, therefore, a descendant dialect of Sanskrit. For example, many towns in Iran have Sanskrit names. The birth place of Omar Khayyam, a well-known Persian poet, is Nishapur, which is a pure Sanskrit name. Indian troops stationed in West Asia during World War I and II have reported seeing temples of Indian deities like Ganesh and Shankar (Shiva) in ruins in remote desolate areas of Iran, Afghanistan, and other countries. Iranian mythology also has links with ancient Vedic lore.

One of the more interesting pieces of evidence is that the Iranians also knew of Lord Rama, as noted by Koenraad Elst in his book, *Indigenous Indians: Agastya to Ambedkar* (Voice of India, New Delhi, 1993). He writes that according to Ghosh, the name of Rama appears in the earliest portion of the *Avesta* as god of peace, associated with Vayu, the wind god. This mention of Vayu is likely to mean Hanuman, Rama's close devotee and associate, the son of Vayu. Rama's guru, Vasistha is also mentioned as Vahista, who has his own *Gatha* dedicated to him, *Vahishte-Ishti-Gatha*. This was before the Zoroastrian revolution. Also, many of the Iranian rituals were similar to those of the Vedic customs, such as the wearing of the sacred thread. So this reflects a migration of the early Iranian people out of India from many years ago, no later than 1900 or 1800 B.C.

Further evidence is that the main demon in the Avesta is Angra Mainyu, the Rigvedic Angira and Manyu. The Angiras are seven prominent families of *rishis* in the *Rig-veda*, while Manyu is Indra in a destructive form in the *Rig-veda* (10.83 & 10.84). Names of Iranian gods were similar to the Vedic, such as these:

IRANIAN	VEDIC
Ahura	Asura
Mithra	Mitra
Naonhaithya (a demon)	Nasatya
Thrita & Athvya	Trita Aptya
Aspina	Ashvina
Yima	Yama
Vivanhant	Vivasvat
Indra (a demon)	Indra (the Vedic demigod)
Yashna	Yajna (pronounced Yagya, a ritual)
Athravan (a priest)	Atharvan
Haoma	Soma

THE KASSITES

Also in the region of Iran and West Asia we find the Kassites, just before 2000 B.C. These were an Indo-Aryan people in Iran. They invaded Babylon around 1760 B.C. They worshiped Vedic deities and ruled Babylon for over 500 years after they had removed the Hammurabi empire. Though they adopted the speech and traditions of Babylon, they still worshiped Surias (Vedic Surya), Maruttas (Vedic Marutas), and Indabugas (Vedic Indra and Bhaga, or Bhagavan). The Kassites were a group from the Vedic Purus. The Kassite gods were also named similar to the Vedic gods, as shown by these few examples:

KASSITE	VEDIC
Indash	Indra
Shuriash	Surya
Maruttash	Maruts
Bugash (word for God)	Bhaga, Bhagavan (name of God)

ISRAEL

The name "Israel" actually is derived from the Sanskrit word *Ishwaralaya*, which means the abode of "Isha," or Krishna, God. The name Jerusalem also is derived from Yerushaleim, or the Sanskrit *Yedu-Ishalayam*, which signifies a township of Lord Krishna. "Isha" means God, the Supreme Controller, and "Yedu" refers to Yadu and the Yadu dynasty, which is in relation to Krishna. Furthermore, "Yedu-ish" comes from a Sanskrit term signifying Lord Krishna as chief of the Yadu clan. Therefore, Judaism is nothing but a form or derivative of "Yeduism." Thus, there is the relation with this area to the followers of the Vedic tradition and the worship of Lord Krishna.

We also find on the west bank of the Jordan River in the Gaza strip in Palestine the city of Ramallah, meaning the city of Lord Rama. Jordan is also a distorted form of the Sanskrit name "Janardan," another name of Krishna meaning the controller of all living beings.

Nearby Palestine gets its name from the modern distortion of the name of the Vedic sage Pulestin who had his abode there. The hill on which he used to light his sacrificial fire dedicated to Lord Shiva still bears the name "Har Homa," referring to the Homa Vedic fire ritual. Many such Sanskrit names in the region show the Vedic connection this area once had.

ARABIA

Arabia was known as Arbasthan, which is a corruption of the Sanskrit word *Arvasthan*, which means "land of horses." The term *arva* is Sanskrit for horse. Members of Vedic society used to breed horses here.

Originally, Arabs are known as the Cushites and Semites. Sem is a perverted form of the Sanskrit name of "Shyam," which is another name of Krishna. Cusha or Kush was the son of Lord Rama. Africa and Arabia formed part of his empire. Thus, people of Arabia were the Vedic followers of Krishna and Rama.

To help illustrate the well established Vedic connection in Arabia there is an old poem to which we can refer. It is from page 257 of the *Sair-Ul-Okul*, the anthology of ancient Arabic poetry compiled in 1742 under the order of the Turkish Sultan Salim. It was written by Labi-bin-e Akhtab-bin-e Turfa who lived in Arabia around 1850 B.C., 2300 years before Mohammed, and pays devout poetic tribute to the *Vedas* and mentions each one by name. In English, the poem reads as follows: "Oh, the divine land of Hind (India), very blessed art thou! Because thou art the chosen of God blessed with knowledge. That celestial knowledge which like four lighthouses shone in such brilliance, through the (utterances of) Indian sages in fourfold abundance. God enjoins on all humans, follow with hands down the path the *Vedas* with His divine precept lay down. Bursting with divine knowledge are *Sama* and *Yajur* bestowed on creation, Hence brothers respect and follow the *Vedas*, guides to salvation. Two others, the *Rig* and *Athar* teach us fraternity, sheltering under their luster dispels darkness till eternity."

So even at that early stage, we can get an idea as to the respect that was given to the Vedic tradition in ancient Arabia. The *Vedas* were the only religious scriptures to which the Arabs owed allegiance. This shows the antiquity of the *Vedas* and the existence of Vedic Kshatriya rule over the entire region from the Indus to the Mediterranean. In fact, from Mohammed's time backwards through history to the remotest antiquity, Arabia shows the influence of Vedic rule and culture. So you could say that Arabs used to be Hindus.

Another poem that illustrates this point was written by Jirrham Bintoi, who lived 165 years before prophet Mohammed. In the poem he glorifies the character of King Vikramaditya who ruled 500 years before Mohammed. Vikramaditya's capital was Ujjayini (Ujjain), alias Avantika, in Central India. The poem appeared in a premier article in a magazine around 1945 on the occasion of the 2000th anniversary of the Vikram Era, greatly celebrated in Ujjain. This poem is also from the *Sair-Ul-Okul*, the anthology of ancient Arabic poetry. It is in Arabic, but when put in English, it reads as follows:

"Fortunate are those who were born (and lived) during King Vikram's reign. He was a noble, generous, dutiful ruler devoted to the welfare of his subjects. But at that time we Arabs, oblivious of divinity, were lost in sensual pleasures. Plotting and torture were rampant (amongst us). The darkness of ignorance had enveloped our country. Like the lamb struggling for its life in the cruel paws of a wolf, we Arabs were gripped by ignorance. The whole country was enveloped in a darkness as intense as on a New Moon night. But the present dawn and pleasant sunshine of education is the result of the favor of that noble king Vikram whose benevolence did not lose sight of us foreigners as we were. He spread his sacred culture amongst us and sent scholars from his own land whose brilliance shown like that of the sun in our country. These scholars and preceptors through whose benevolence we were once again made cognizant of the presence of God, introduced to His sacred knowledge, and put on the road to truth, had come to our country to initiate us in that culture and impart education."

The poet Jirrham Bintoi had received the topmost award for three consecutive years at the Meccan symposium. All three poems, including the one above, had been inscribed on gold plate and hung inside the Kaba shrine.

This poem shows the way that Arabia had been a part of the advanced Vedic culture, and how it had been appreciated by Arab people. From this we can understand that there were many of the Vedic sciences that had been incorporated into the Arab region for the advancement of the people. Such would include Ayurvedic health centers (as is apparent from the almost identical nature of the Arabic Yunani and *Ayurveda* systems), schools, Vedic forms of irrigation and agriculture, and an orderly and peaceful way of life. It is for this reason why we can also find today the Kurds and Iranians speaking Sanskritized dialects, fire temples existing in places like Baku and Baghdad thousands of miles away from India, scores of sites of ancient Vedic cultural centers like Navbahar in Iraq, and what was once numerous *viharas* (Vedic educational centers) in Soviet Russia and throughout the world. Ancient Vedic scriptures are also found from time to time in Central Asia.

This also explains why when starting from India and going towards the West we find so many names derived from Sanskrit in the region, such as Afghanistan, Baluchistan, Kurdistan, Iran, Iraq, and Arvastan. It has not been realized that it was the Indians who ruled this entire region in the ancient past who gave all these names to these countries. It is from ancient times that Indian Kshatriya royal families like the Pehlavis and Barmarks have held sway over Iran and Iraq.

Other names of places in Arabia that are derived from Sanskrit include the holy Islamic city of Mecca. The word *Mecca* is derived from the Sanskrit word *Makha*, which means place of fire-worship or the sacrificial fire, which the ancient Vedic followers and Brahmanas were known to do as a part of their rituals in worshiping the Supreme. This was widely prevalent as evidenced by the Parsis who also had fire temples. Ancient fire temples are known to exist in Baku, Baghdad, and other places. Mecca also refers to Makka, which is the shortened version of the name Makkheshvar, or Mahadeva, Shiva. This is in relation to the understanding that the Black Stone (Sangay Aswad) in the Kaba is originally a representation of Shiva in the form of a Shiva-*lingam*. This is further explained in the chapter on Islam.

On page 632 of *World Vedic Heritage*, Mr. Oak illustrates how some of the Arabs appreciated the Vedic culture. This is recorded by Abu Umar Jahiz of Basra (who died around 868 A.D.) in his chronicle *Risalt-i-Fakharussau-dan'al al-Baidan*: "I have found the Indian people extremely advanced in astrology and mathematics. . . they occupy a prominent position in the field of medical science and can cure serious ailments. They are experts at carving stone figures and make color decorations on building arches. They are inventors of chess which is one of the best intellectual sports. Their swords are very sharp and they are experts in swordsmanship. Their mantras can neutralize positions."

It has also been historically recorded that the Arabic numerals came from India. Arabs learnt the decimal system and every branch of mathematics such as algebra, geometry, and trigonometry from the Vedic Indians. From Arabia it was passed on to the western countries.

Another sign of Vedic influence in Arabia is the "Bakri Id" observance. "Bakra" in Arabic signifies a cow. Consequently, Bakri Id was a day set aside for revering the cows. In Vedic tradition supreme reverence is attached to the cow. She is regarded as the second mother for all humanity. Her milk is given for next to nothing, and it supplies the nutrients for making good brain cells by which we can understand spiritual knowledge. Cow's milk can be used throughout our lives. Even the cow's urine and stool have numerous curative and medicinal uses, and is an antiseptic, besides being used for fuel and manure. For years the bull has provided the strength for plowing the fields and agricultural development. So in Arabia the Bakri Id day was set aside to pay reverence to the cow. However, the Muslims, oblivious to the sacred tradition, have perverted the holiday and now slaughter and eat cows on Bakri Id.

Another example of the forgotten Vedic influence found in Arabia is the city of Petra. Lowell Thomas describes in detail about when he found such a city in his book, *With Lawrence of Arabia*. He relates about finding a rose-red city, the perfect ruins of a lost civilization that was carved out of the enchanted mountains of Edom, not far from Mount Hor. Mount Hor was named after Shiva, as closely related to his Sanskrit name of Har or Hara. It was reached by trekking nearly a hundred miles across a desert. The temple was carved out of the cliff almost 2000 years ago. The city was farther down and big enough in which several hundred thousand people must have lived. There are fortresses, palaces, tombs, and amusement resorts, all carved out of solid rock. Up one staircase to the El Dair Temple there is a gigantic urn decorated with the heads of Medusa. Up another staircase to the Mount of Sacrifice are two obelisks and two altars. Near the altars are two great monoliths each about 24 feet high, carved out of the rock.

The important points regarding this city is that the rose or saffron color of the city is typical of Vedic townships. The name *Petra* comes from the Sanskrit word *prastar*, which means stone. It was the "stone" city. Being carved out of the rock is also typical of many Vedic temples that are either carved out or made from carved rock as found all across India. The El Dair Temple is also named from the Arab mispronunciation of the Sanskrit word *Devalaya*, which means place or temple of the *Devas*, gods. The urn that was mentioned is an altar for the Vedic fire ceremony. Medusa is a reference to the Sanskrit name Mahadevas, or Shiva. The great monoliths are also Shiva emblems used in the worship of Shiva. Thus, this ancient city provides a strong reflection of the pre-Islamic, Vedic culture that pervaded the region at least 2000 years ago.

One of the points we can understand from the above information is that, just as the Kaba is a captured Vedic shrine turned into an Islamic center of worship (which we discuss in another chapter), many other buildings, palaces, fortresses, and ancient cities which have been given an Islamic identification are not really Islamic at all. Though such buildings may be presently used for Islamic purposes, they are remnants of the pre-Islamic, Vedic culture.

Why much of this information is not known is because, as related on page 228 of *Some Blunders of Indian Historical Research*: "As Encyclopaedias Islamia and Britannica tells us, Arabia obliterated all its past history by destroying images and records. We are now told that the 2,500-year history of Arabia before the founding of Islam has been ironically written off as an 'age of ignorance' though it was in fact the 'wise' successors to that age who chose to remain ignorant by a deliberate breakaway from the past."

In this way, Arab historians tended to wipe out all pre-Muslim history. This is the fact not only in Arabia, but also in Turkey, Iran, Afghanistan, Algeria, and

Morocco. Scholars who have tried to study the histories of these countries have invariably found that such histories merely gloss over all pre-Muslim details and go on to make false claims about the Islamic culture. This is the process they have used to discredit all other pre-Islamic cultures and mislead people about the so-called glories and advanced nature of their own culture. It is this process which attempts to erase all pre-Muslim history and create a hatred for all that is not Islamic. This became the standard in all countries that were forcibly made Muslim after the invasions. This is what has created a vast amount of Islamic writing of what is mostly historical fabrication and speculation about anything pre-Muslim.

The problem with this is that whatever advancement was made from previous cultures was forgotten. This leaves the new, dominating culture to rediscover what had been previously known but is now slighted or omitted. Therefore, much of the Muslim claims for contributing to world advancement is actually nothing more than grafting earlier forms of knowledge to the post-Muslim era. What actually happened, especially in regard to the Islamic motto that all that needs to be known is in the Koran, is that the rise of Islam deterred all Arab learning and development in the arts and sciences. This was also the case in the other countries that bowed to the Islamic force. Consequently, the incentive for strenuous learning was replaced by redirecting their energy toward raiding, looting, burning, and killing non-Muslims. This was the result of breaking off from the advanced nature of the Vedic culture.

One purpose of this was that as people were forced to convert to Islam, in a few generations there would be no more non-Muslims left to complain about the rape and murder of people and the land, and the horrid atrocities that were used to forcibly convert people. Then the population would be united in praising Islam.

THE PARSIS

One point is that the Parsis thought of coming back to India when threatened with conversion to Islam. This is because they were Vedic fire-worshipers. They also wear a sacred thread and have the thread ceremony for adolescents. They also draw patterns with stone powder in front of their houses as do the Hindus. And their names Ardeshir (one who holds his head high) and Nausherwan (Anushreewan) have Sanskrit origin. This shows that before Islam was forced on Iran and other countries of the Middle East, the inhabitants were followers of the Vedic way of life. The names of the Parsi deities, the months, and so on, are derived from Sanskrit and similar to those of the Vedic tradition. Parsis also have 33 main deities as do the Hindus.

THE DRUZE

The Druze is a sect usually considered to be affiliated with Islam, although they prefer to be distinct from Muslims. It is a Mid-east religion in Lebanon, Israel, and other countries, with roots in the Indian Vedic tradition. Their philosophy is very similar to the Vedic teachings.

The word "Druze" was formed by the Muslims, just as they coined the term "Hindu." It was formed as a derisive reference to the group by way of referring to their founder, El Drazi. He was a heretical Muslim almost 1,000 years ago, and from him came the foundation for what became known as the Druze.

Many Druze accept their roots as being from India. Their beliefs, unlike most Middle Eastern religions, are similar to the Vedic concepts, and they describe a history that dates back many millions of years. They also describe regular incarnations of God throughout history in accord with the Vedic descriptions of the *avataras*. They also accept transmigration of the soul and reincarnation as taught in *Bhagavad-gita*. It has also been reported that presently the Druze people read the Vedic texts to get a better understanding of their own traditions. It is also known that the original language of their early scriptures was Sanskrit. The late, renowned spiritualist of the Druze, Kamal Jumbalat, praised Krishna and spoke of the *Bhagavad-gita*, *Ramayana*, and other Vedic books and personalities in his writings. Unlike most Muslims, Jumbalat was a vegetarian, in accord with Vedic customs.

Today the Druze consider themselves as followers of the one true religion, known as Muwahidoon. This present Muwahidoon comes from al Hakim Bi-Amr Allah, the sixth Fatimid Caliph. He is said to have ruled Egypt in the late 10th and early 11th centuries. However, it is not sure how al Hakim died, and it is speculated that he may have left Egypt to go to India to engage in peaceful meditation in preparation for death. This is in accord with new evidence that strongly indicates how the Druze culture extended to India during this time.

EGYPT

The name Egypt comes from the shortened term of *Ajap*, which refers to the Sanskrit name *Ajapati*, signifying Lord Rama as the illustrious scion of the clan of Aja, since Aja was the grandfather of Lord Rama. Also, the Egyptian Pharaohs had such names as Ramses I, or Ramses II, because Rama was universally regarded as an ideal ruler. Ramses means Rama the God. And like the Vedic tradition, the Egyptians also considered their rulers as being representatives or even descendants of God.

In an article by Dr. S. K. Balasubramanian, *Hindu Mythology as Prehistory*, he relates that the history of Egypt goes thousands of years back to the time of Yayati. Yayati had married Devayani, the daughter of Shukracharya, the Vedic

Aryan preceptor of the Danava king Vrishaparva, whose daughter, Sharmistha, was Yayati's second wife. Yayati's story finds etymological support in the development of Judaism and its linkage with ancient Egypt. Yayati suffered loss of youth and became prematurely old as a result of a curse and begged his sons to relieve his old age by exchanging their youth with his old age. The eldest son of Devayani, Yadu, declined the request and was deprived of his birth rite to succeed his father. The other sons became similarly accursed. The last son, Puru (by Sharmistha), exchanged his youth for his father's old age and was later crowned the sovereign of the world superceding his elders.

Therefore, Puru's descendants, who were the Puravas, later became known as the Pharaohs of Egypt who ruled over his father's domain with his elder brothers subject to him. Yayati was deified as Yahweh by the descendants of Yadu who are identified with the Yadus, the Jews of the present day. Nonetheless, they bore bitter animosity to their ancestor Aryan Hindus because the Jews were subservient to the Pharaohs by the edict of Yayati. They resented their subordinate status and revolted against it, moving out of Egypt. Thus, they went on and created their own culture, legends, and histories.

The other sons of Yayati were also subject to the Pharaohnic suzerainty. Of these, Druhya was the leader of those who became the French Druids, the Druhyas. Anu went on to become the head of Anatolia, while Turvasu was the king of the Turanians in the area north of the Black Sea.

By the time ancient Egypt comes into our view in history, its extent had shrunk to the Nile valley. Others in that ancient Vedic culture had also asserted their independence. The Minoans, the Maltese, and the Greeks had developed along such independent lines. The Jews rose in revolt against the Pharaohs and moved into Palestine retaining a grudge against their forebears in Aryavarta and Egypt. They developed an iconoclast religion and were the first to attempt to "rewrite" history. They rejected the past to such an extent and with such bitterness that they even reversed the natural mode of writing from left to right. The Egyptians and the Greeks retained the pluralism of their ancestors and developed on more tolerant lines.

Historically, Egyptian religion is said to be traced back to 4000 B.C. to its basic forms of worship. However, the first established kingdom was under Menes around 3000 B.C. The Egyptian Old Kingdom is dated to around 2686-2181 B.C., centralized in Memphis. Then the Middle Kingdom was centered in Thebes, and dated near 2050-1786 B.C. Later, Egypt is said to have fallen to the Persians in 528 B.C. because of being less developed militarily. And then Egypt was conquered by Alexander the Great in 332 B.C. The rest is history.

Count Biornsttierna, from pages 43-46 of his book *The Theogony of the Hindus*, has a lot of information to give us on the Vedic culture in ancient Egypt. "It is testified to by Herodotus, Plato, Salon, Pythagorus, and Philostratus that the religion of Egypt proceeded from India. . . It is testified by Neibuhr, Valentia, Champollian and Weddington that the temples of upper Egypt are of greater antiquity than those of lower Egypt. . . that consequently the religion of Egypt, according to the testimony of those monuments. . . came from India. . . The chronicles found in the temples of Abydos and Sais and which have been transmitted by Josephus, Julius Africanus, and Eusebius, all testify that the religious system of the Egyptians proceeded from India.

"We have Hindu chronologies (besides those of the *Puranas* concerning the Yuga) which go still further back in time than the Tables of the Egyptian kings according to Manetho."

Professor Brugsch agrees with this view and writes in his *History of Egypt* that, "We have a right to more than suspect that India, eight thousand years ago, sent a colony of emigrants who carried their arts and high civilization into what is now known to us as Egypt." The Egyptians came, according to their records, from a mysterious land (now known to lie on the shores of the Indian Ocean)."

As reported in the *Nava Bharat Times* (April 18, 1967), on one of the excavations obtained from the Egyptian Pyramid, dated to 3000 B.C., an engraved verse from the *Bhagavad-gita* was found. The verse was *vasamsi jirnani yatha vhiaya*: "As a person puts on new garments, giving up the old ones, the soul similarly accepts new material bodies, giving up the old and useless ones." (*Bhagavad-gita*, 2.22) This find certainly boosts the idea that Egypt was either a part of the Vedic culture, or was formed by emigrants from India.

Furthermore, Aap (or Abu) signifies water in Sanskrit, and Sind refers to the Sindhu River. Therefore, Abusind, which becomes the name Abyssinia, signifies a colony of people who had come from the banks of the Indus. It is from this information that Count Biornstierna concludes that it was the early followers of Vedic culture that have a greater claim to the primary generation of religion as well as civilization than the people of ancient Egypt.

Max Mueller had also observed that the mythology of Egyptians (and also that of the Greeks and Assyrians) is wholly founded on Vedic traditions.

Eusebius, a Greek writer, as explained on page 20 of *Bharat (India) as Seen and Known by Foreigners*, has also recorded that the early Ethiopians emigrated from the river Indus and first settled in the vicinity of Egypt.

Further information is provided by Col. Olcott, a former president of the Theosophical Society, who explains in a March, 1881 edition of *The Theosophist* (page 123) that: "India sent a colony of emigrants who carried their arts and high civilization into what is now known to us as Egypt. . . Bengsch Bey, Egyptologer and antiquarian says. . . That they migrated from India long before historic memory. . . to find a fatherland on the banks of the Nile. The Egyptians came, according to their own records, from a mysterious land. . . on the shore of the Indian Ocean, the sacred Punt; the original home of their gods. . . that Punt can be no other than India."

More evidence and explanations are supplied by P. N. Oak in his *World Vedic Heritage* (pages 610-11). Egyptians called India the land of Punt, or rather Pankth, and regarded it as their divine land peopled by Punts, meaning Pundits, sages, seers, and gods. Further evidence on the Vedic roots of the area of Egypt is noticed when we understand that Rama was spelled as Rham in the West. Later the "R" was dropped and consequently African school text books asserting that Africans are Cushites (subjects of Cusha, the son of Lord Rama) mention Ham (instead of Rham) as the father of Cusha. The name Rama is pronounced in South India as Raman. Europeans spell it as Ramon, and Muslims as Rehman. The twin brother of Cusha was Lava. Thus, the region named after him was known in Sanskrit as Laviya. Currently it is being pronounced as Libya.

Count Biornsttierna, from pages 40-41 of his book *The Theogony of the Hindus*, explains further that, "On comparing the religious systems of the Egyptians and the Hindus we are struck by their resemblance to each other . . . The principle of trinity with that of the unity, the pre-existence of the soul, its transmigration, the division of castes into priests, warriors, traders and agriculturalists are the cardinal points of both systems. Even the symbols are the same on the shores of the Ganges and the Nile. Thus we find the Lingam of the Shiva temples of India in the Phallus of Ammon temple of Egypt--a symbol also met with on the head-dress of Egyptian gods. We find the lotus flower as the symbol of the sun both in India and Egypt, and we find symbols of the immortality of the soul in both countries. The power of rendering barren women fruitful ascribed to the temple of Shiva in India was also ascribed to the temple of Ammon in Egypt. . . Bedouin women may still be seen wandering around the temple of Ammon for the purpose of obtaining the blessing."

The word *Phal* in Sanskrit signifies fruit. *Phalish* refers to "Ish" or "Isha," meaning the Lord as giver of fruit. Lord Shiva is credited with giving every person what is his due. Thus, the term *Phalish* simply means the Father God, generally Lord Shiva, and not the male genital organ. It was the result of Greek ignorance that created the misrepresentation of this as an obscene symbol, which seems to continue with many westerners to the present day.

The Egyptians also conceived of the earth planet represented as a cow (as the Vedic tradition does) and a sphere balanced on the hoods of a huge cobra known as Shesh. This is also another Vedic concept that all of the planets maintain their orbits by being held in balance through the power of Lord Sheshanaga, the huge serpent upon whom Lord Vishnu reclines. The Pharaoh's crown was decorated with the symbol of the cobra, a Vedic sign for respect, and the power of the Kundalini within. The Egyptians also paid respect to their elders by bowing and touching the elder's feet, as is done in India. The Egyptians also studied astrology.

The Nile River bears a Sanskrit name, for Nile comes from the Sanskrit *Neel*, which means blue, which is always associated with divinity, such as the color of Krishna's complexion. In modern times, people call it the "Blue Nile" forgetting that this is simply a duplication of the same meaning. This is only because their connections with Sanskrit have been forgotten.

The discovery of the source of the Nile is also credited to the early Vedic explorers. Colonel John Speke explains in his *Journal of the Discovery of the*

Source of the Nile (page 13) that, "Colonel Rigby gave me a most interesting paper with a map attached to it about the Nile and Mountain of the Moon. It was written by Lt. Wilford from the *Puranas* of the ancient Hindus. It is remarkable that the Hindus had christened the source of the river Nile. This, I think, shows clearly that the ancient Hindus must have had some kind of connection with different parts of Africa. . . All previous information concerning the hydro-graphy of these regions originated with the ancient Hindus. . . *and all those busy Egyptian geographers who disseminated the knowledge with a view to be famous for their long-sightedness in solving the mysteries which shrouded the source of the Nile (the holy river) were so many hypothetical humbugs.*"

This fact that the discovery of the Nile's source happened only with the assistance of Vedic information should help awaken the world to the realization that the ancient Vedic scriptures are treasures of comprehensive knowledge meant for all human beings.

A close look at the Egyptian theology may also shed light on the ancient existence of Vedic civilization and its influence in the area of Egypt. In some ways it is confusing to get a grasp of exactly what their theology was because it changed according to locality. Egyptian theology was also forced through a number of changes because of the demands of different pharaohs who preferred the worship of one god over all others and ordered the people to follow accordingly. In various cities, different gods were held to be supreme and the theory of creation was presented differently according to which Egyptian text was consulted.

The premise of Heliopolis, the Lebanese city of Baalbek, presented Atum as the first self-manifested creator who is characterized as the sun-god Ra. Atum emerged from the primeval waters and by masturbation created Tefenet (moisture) and Shu (air) who manifested Geb (earth) and Nut (sky), and through the procreation of Geb and Nut came Osiris, Isis, Seth, and Nephthys.

In Memphis, the creator-god was Ptah, who created by means of his intelligence and spoken word. In the temple of Edfu the texts explain how the earth emerges from a lotus flower which rises from the primeval waters, a story with similarities to the Vedic version of creation. Furthermore, the animal of Ptah is Apis the bull, similar to Lord Shiva whose carrier is Nandi the bull.

At Thebes, in southern Egypt, the chief god was Amun, god of life. Later the chief god was Amun-Ra, uniting Amun and Ra. Nearly everyone also worshiped Osiris, god of fertility, and his wife Isis, the great mother goddess of the moon and agriculture, and their son Horus, god of the day.

In the 14th century B.C. the ruler Amenhotep IV banished all other gods but Aton and claimed that he was the one god. Aton was the god of love, peace, and beauty. Amenhotep, who changed his name to Akhnaton (spirit of Aton), wanted to spread peace and beauty throughout the world. But Akhnaton reigned for only 15 years, after which the worship of other gods resumed.

To explain briefly about the Vedic connection of the great Egyptian leader

Amenhotep the Third, he had a Mitanni mother. She was the daughter of the Mitanni king, Artatama. Amenhotep also married Tiy, daughter of Yuaa, who was a priest of the Egyptian fertility-god, Min, although himself a foreigner from Mitanni. Tiy gave birth to Akhnaton (or Ikhnaton, Amenhotep IV), the pharaoh who had given Egypt its one-God religion. So not only was Akhnaton's mother Mitanni, either part or full-blooded, his grandfather was Mitanni, and his grandmother was at least partly Mitanni. He was also known to have had a Mitanni grandmother. The Mitanni people are a Vedic Aryan society, so it can be presumed that Akhnaton was strongly influenced by the Vedic culture, which can be seen in his single devotion to the sun god, Aton, or the Vedic Surya.

Later, Akhnaton married the famous Nefertiti, a Mitanni princess, daughter of King Dashratta. Together they became the high Priest and Priestess of the worship of Aton. Akhnaton praised the sun as the eye of God, Aton. This is also in accord with the Vedic texts, such as the *Bhagavad-gita* and *Brahma-samhita*, both of which declare the sun as one of the eyes of God. The symbol for the sun was a disk with many rays proceeding from it. This is the same as the symbol still used in India, which can be seen in various temples today.

Now to continue with the theology of the Egyptians, they worshiped their temple deities in a similar fashion as that found in India. The priests practiced cleanliness, shaved their heads, and wore white cloth. They would take a bath early in the morning to purify themselves and at dawn they would enter the temple. Opening the sanctuary where the deity was, the priest would prostrate before the image and then sit and chant prayers and burn incense. Then he would bathe the deity and dress it in fresh clothes and offer it food and drink, and then clean the altar and temple. The temple priests also bathed and dressed the temple deities in opulent clothes and ornamented with jewels and gems, much the same as in India. The deities were also given rest in the afternoon, as is still done in India. They would sometimes take the deity of the Lord on a boat on the Nile and give it rides, something which is still practiced in India. In worship, the Egyptians used the Chattra, which is the Chamara fan in Sanskrit. This is a long handle in which a Yak tail or something similar is inserted to be used as a fan to honor the deity or royalty. In Egyptian paintings, Osiris is often depicted as black, similar to the dark color of Krishna. In some paintings, there are little snakes or *nagas* holding round disks or planets on their heads, similar to Lord Seshanaga supporting the planets as described in the Vedic literature.

The Egyptian philosophical teachings and rites for the initiates took place either in the secret parts of the temples or in the pyramids. It is now generally understood that the pyramids were not necessarily tombs but places where the secret and intense initiation rituals into the mysteries of Egyptian philosophy were performed. In the lower phases of initiation the candidates were taught the knowledge of the soul. They accepted the soul as eternal and that it would leave the body at death and reappear in another state of being, usually in higher realms. In the higher phases of initiation, direct realization of the soul and communion with the Divine was to be attained. This is practically identical with the knowledge provided in the Vedic literature and shows there must have been a strong connection between India and Egypt in the early part of Egyptian civilization.

Other similarities are in the names. The name of the Egyptian sun-god Ra is derived from Ravi, the Sanskrit name for the sun. The name Heru (Horus is the Greek pronunciation) or Nar Heru is derived from Hari, which is the Sanskrit name for the Supreme or Vishnu. Nar Heru is called Naar Ari in Hebrew, which is the Nara Hari in Sanskrit, another form of the name of Vishnu or Krishna.

The Egyptian God Ptah is named from the Sanskrit word *Pita*, which means father. So Ptah comes from the impression as God the father of the universe. The name of the Egyptian god Seb comes from a mispronunciation of Shib, or Shiva. The same with *Har*, which comes from the Sanskrit name *Hara*, another name of Shiva. His consort Hathor, also known as Seket, comes from the Vedic name of *Shakti*, Shiva's consort. The Egyptian god Aton gets its name from the Sanskrit word *Atman*. Osiris has a number of connections, but can also be linked with the name Eswaras, which means Lord Shiva.

One of the main Egyptian hieroglyphs representing Hari is the round disk, appearing either singularly or with other symbols such as the hawk. A disk with wings was often the representation of Hari. The hawk is the Egyptian hieroglyph for Hari and is also symbolized by a number of other birds like the peacock, swan, or parrot, which all play a prominent role in Egyptian hieroglyphics. The peacock was the symbol of Heliopolis, which was the capital for the worship of Ra or Re, or Hari, until 2100 B.C. when Thebes became the state capital. The peacock had been imported by Solomon and was the symbol for the house of David and sacred to Eli, the god of the Jews and Hebrews.

Egyptian civilization is said to have made rapid development, from primitive to advanced, around 3000 B.C. How old the Egyptian civilization may be is hard to say. Some scholars feel that the first pyramid built, the Step pyramid at Sakkara, 30 miles south of Giza, was constructed during this time 5000 years ago, while others consider that it dates back to 2650 B.C. However, the Great Pyramid of Cheops at Giza is said to have been built around 2900 or 2800 B.C.

One point that helps confirm the time when the Great Pyramid at Giza was built is the southern shaft in the King's Chamber. It points directly up at the stars of Orion's belt where they would have been in 2500 B.C. The arrangement and positioning of these pyramids on the ground directly reflect the formations of the stars in Orion's belt. The purpose was that if a pharaoh was to die in this chamber, the shaft would help point the way to the stars of Orion, which is the journey that would allow them to reach Osiris in the sky, where they would then become immortal. And what pharaoh would not want that? Anyway, this helps show that the Great Pyramid was built at least by 2500 B.C.

In regard to the Sphinx, many scholars feel that the Sphinx was built in 2500 B.C. during the fourth dynasty, about 4500 years old. However, the grooves that are cut in the sides of the Sphinx reflect damage that would have been caused by heavy rainfall when Egypt was much more wet, which would have been around 3000 BC. Still, others say the Sphinx was built five to seven thousand years ago.

However, in 1993 John Anthony West, an independent Egyptologist, made the claim that geological evidence indicates that the Sphinx is 12,000 years old. Furthermore, Robert Bauval, author of *The Orion Mystery*, uses astronomical evidence to conclude that the Sphinx was built in 10,500 B.C. He claims that some of the astronomical principles by which the pyramids were built include that the Sphinx looks directly east toward where the vernal equinox would have been in 10,500 B.C. That was the beginning of the age of Leo, which would have meaning if the Sphinx represents Leo the Lion.

In any case, the way the Great Pyramid is made shows the characteristics of an advanced society and that it contains many mathematical formulas in its construction. The only other civilization that had knowledge of such advanced mathematics during this time was India. There is evidence that shows that not only did elements of ancient geometry in Babylonia stem from a religious purpose similar to that of the *Shulbasutras* from the Vedic culture, but also that of Egypt. The *Shulbas*, being meant for designing distinct altars for Vedic purposes of ritual, supplied many mathematical formulas and techniques to build altars for securing appropriate results through their use. Research has shown that in all time ranges of the Egyptian monuments, common trapezoidal Vedic altars can be found. The reason is that the Egyptians, during the Middle Kingdom (2050-1800 B.C.), were using the *Shulba* systems for mathematics, which described the necessary calculations for building various altars. And this could have certainly been applied to the construction of the pyramids. When we consider that the descendants of Puru, one of the great Vedic leaders of India, were the Puravas, who later became known as the Pharaohs of Egypt, we can certainly understand why they would have known about and had been using the advanced mathematics found in the *Shulbasutras*, no doubt from the time of Egypt's beginning.

As N. S. Rajaram explains in *Vedic Aryans and The Origins of Civilization* (p. 145 & 163-4), "... We have found connections between the so-called Step Pyramid or the *mastaba* built c. 2650 BCE by Djoser [of the Third Dynasty] (c. 2686 to c. 2613 BCE) and the *smashana-cit* altar (i.e., cemetery shaped altar), as its name itself clearly indicates was connected with Vedic funerary rituals. Since all Egyptian pyramids were erected to serve as mausoleums, the connection is not only mathematical but also of religion and ritual."

The Step Pyramid at Sakkara was designed by the architect Imhotep for King Djoser in the Third Dynasty. It is a terraced structure rising up to 60 meters, the idea of which may have come from the *shmashana-cit*, or cemetery shaped, altar as described in the *Baudhayana Shulba*. The true pyramids, such as those in Giza, were designed in the Fourth Dynasty. The reason for the pyramid was for those who wished to gain prosperity in the Pitriloka planets (worlds of the forefathers), as described in the *Taittiriya Samhita*. Thus, the pyramid shaped Vedic shrine, the *shmashana-cit* altar, was to ensure the well-being of the person after death. When this is compared with the *Pyramid Texts*, as explained in *The Orion Mystery: Unlocking the Secrets of the Pyramids* by Robert Bauval and Adrian Gilbert (p. 87), the pyramids were for guaranteeing a rebirth for the dead king to rejoin the original Osiris and become a star god in the constellation of Orion, the realm of the dead inhabited by star beings. The influence of the *Taittiriya Samhita* can be seen in this Egyptian custom when we realize that the star beings in the realm of the dead are what the *Samhita* calls the forefathers, or the world of Pitriloka, which the Egyptian kings wanted to secure for themselves. Therefore, this is but one indication that ancient Egypt, from the Third Dynasty and earlier, had been influenced by and were in contact in numerous ways with the Vedic culture.

Some people question that if the Egyptians changed from primitive to advanced in only a century or two, then how did they become so developed in such a short time? This could have been during the time when the people from western India or the area of the Indus Valley sites, such as Harappa and Mohenjo-daro, were moving to better climates to find better resources. Leaving the Indus region and using the trade routes to travel to Egypt and taking their Vedic culture with them would not have been too difficult. And this certainly could have been the case, until the spreading drought effected Egypt as well. However, others say that people from Atlantis arrived and settled in the land of Egypt, and began teaching their knowledge to the Egyptians. Nonetheless, we know that the idea of the lost continent of Atlantis primarily came from Plato who wrote about it in his *Dialogues* called "Critias" and "Tamaceus." Plato heard about a sunken land from a man named Critias, who heard about it from Critias the elder, who heard about it from Solon, an Athenian statesman, who is said to have heard a description of it from an Egyptian priest named Neith Sais.

Atlantis may have actually existed, as some people think, but no archeological evidence has been found, not at least in the Atlantic Ocean. And since we are primarily focusing on historical, linguistic, or archeological evidence in this chapter, a review of any similarities between Atlantis and other cultures will have to wait.

Another explanation for the sudden rise in Egyptian civilization is found on a script of simple hieroglyphics located in a tomb, which was written during the time of the building of the first pyramids. The script tells of a sailor who survived a shipwreck and reached a land of abundant fruit trees and gardens of vegetables, and where many advanced and wise men resided. The land sank beneath the sea and the survivors fled in all directions. Some are said to have found a home in Egypt. The story writer suggests the land was near the coast of Africa. Where exactly, no one knows.

Whether this describes Atlantis or not, no one can be sure. However, it would correspond to the coastal city of Dwaraka located on the west coast of India across the Arabian Sea from Africa. Present day Dwaraka is situated on the mainland north of Mumbai (Bombay) and some distance south of the Indus river. Ancient

Dwaraka is described in the Vedic texts as an island city off the coast of India that was very advanced and organized for its time. The *Bhagavat Purana* relates that the outer wall of the huge fortress covered as much as 96 square miles. Within the city were paved roads, gardens, and palatial buildings made of gold with rooms decorated with the finest of gems on the walls and floors. It was the heavenly city where Lord Krishna lived part of the time while on earth. It was also the capital of the Yadu dynasty, said to have had a population of one billion people. It is also recorded that it did sink into the ocean after Krishna departed from the planet about the time of 3100 B.C. This is near the era when the pyramids were supposed to have been built and when Egyptian culture made great progress.

A 3500 year old wall has been discovered not far off the island of Bet Dwaraka in the Gulf of Kutch. It was discovered on December 11, 1987, and belongs to the now sunken city of ancient Dwaraka. This 250 meter long wall runs along the coast and then circles around for another 50 meters. The length of the wall gives an idea of the large dimensions the city must have had. The wall can be seen above the water's surface during low tide, and gets submerged by as much as four meters of water during high tide. Also, artifacts such as seals with post-Harappan inscriptions, pottery, and stone anchors have been discovered in the area.

Other remains of buildings and huge fort walls of the sunken city have been found off the coast of present day Dwaraka. Professor S. R. Rao of the National Institute of Oceanography has found under the sea such items as pottery, seals, inscribed jars, a coppersmith's mold, as well as copper and bronze articles, etc., proving that a sophisticated city did exist there. Other structures and walls have been found further beneath the sea, buried under sediment. On the island off the coast the remains of a massive wall some 550 meters in length, usually submerged, proves that it was a fortified structure. Excavations near the sea by the present city have revealed that a settlement had been established there from at least the 15th century B.C. where the people built great temples and buildings. And on the beaches at low tide, people can be seen panning for gold, and, indeed, finding it. People say it washes onto the beach from the ancient city.

It would be feasible then that survivors from the sunken city of Dwaraka could have sailed across the sea to northern Africa. Or they may have traveled north toward the Indus Valley where another advanced society was begun or already in progress. From there some could have crossed Mesopotamia over trade routes and gone on to Egypt to the Nile where they shared their knowledge with the local inhabitants and started the Egyptian culture with variations in the Vedic traditions, legends, and local names for the demigods. However, Waddell, in *The Makers of Civilization*, claims that it was indeed the early Aryan kings who became the pre-dynastic Pharaohs of Egypt. This is also corroborated in the Vedic version which describes that the family of Puru became the Pharaohs of Egypt. This would explain why there are hardly any Egyptian records of how the culture began or who the earliest rulers were, since accurate Egyptian records were not kept until after the dynastic Pharaohs had been established. It would also explain why much of the spiritual aspect of Egyptian philosophy is so similar to that of the Vedic teachings.

L. A. Waddell establishes in his book, *Egyptian Civilization*, that Menes, the original founder of Egypt's first dynasty, was the pre-dynastic Aryan Pharaoh that united Egypt. Menes is the Manasyu mentioned in the *Mahabharata* (specifically the Calcutta edition published in 1834, Volume One, Section 94, verses 3695-3697) to which Waddell refers. Manasyu is described as the son of Pravira or Pravireshvara, the son of Puru, and is in the line of the Prabhu of Gopta, or Pharaoh of Egypt.

Manasyu was known as Manis or Manas in Mesopotamia (the affix *yu* means the *Uniter* in Sanskrit), and some of the seals found in the Indus Valley region refer to Kings Puru and Manis as rulers of the area, including Egypt. Waddell and other Egyptologists contend that Manasyu or Menes took his military and naval forces and sailed from the Indus region across the Arabian and Red Seas and entered Egypt east of Koptos or Abydos. Koptos was a town known as an ancient center for trade and still has some of the oldest statues of Egyptian gods. There are also illustrations of ships on the ebony labels at Menes' tomb at Abydos which signifies the importance of his sea travel. The inscriptions about Menes at his tomb, found by Sir F. Petri, are the earliest of hieroglyphs which are in Sumerian script and language.

After Menes' arrival, he began organizing Egypt and establishing the Aryan culture, especially in regard to its metal industry, irrigation systems, its form of tombs, and system of writing. The Egyptian hieroglyphs are a modified form of the Sumerian-Aryan picture-writing which was used during the rule of Menes. Many of the important Egyptian words are of Sumerian-Aryan origin, though many were changed years later because of the influence of the Semitic speech. Menes also adopted the sun-hawk as his royal emblem in Egypt because he engaged in sun-worship as was common amongst Aryans at the time. All this indicates that the first rulers of Egypt were indeed the Aryan monarchs. Even the Egyptians accepted the idea that their culture originated from across the sea to the East. Where else would this be but India?

It is also suggested that Menes is the same King Minos of Crete of the Greek fables. The reasoning for this is that Sir A. Evans, the great explorer of ancient Cretan culture, places the beginning of Cretan civilization at the same time as the First Dynasty Period of Egypt. He further believes that Cretan civilization was of an independent origin appearing within Crete that brought the sudden rise of the Copper or Bronze Age to the area. Like Menes, Minos was a sea-emperor of the Mediterranean who established laws over the land. Menes and Minos both used writing on clay tablets, had ceramic ware and painted pottery of similar design. The drain-pipes in ancient Crete are also similar to those found in Sumerian Ur and the cities of the Indus Valley. This could not be possible without some connection between Crete and the Aryan culture.

Waddell, however, stands alone in respect to the dates he sets for Manasyu's or Menes' invasion into Egypt. He suggests that Menes traveled to Egypt around 2704 B.C. But other Egyptologists suggest dates ranging from 5869 B.C. to 4400 B.C., which seem to corroborate more closely to the descriptions in the Vedic literature. Furthermore, some researchers say Minos arrived in Crete near 4000 B.C. Besides, bronze and copper casting was well established in the Middle East by 3500 B.C., so if Minos was Menes who brought the Bronze Age to Crete, it must have been before 2700 B.C. So Waddell's dates for Menes' invasion may have to be placed much earlier than 2704 B.C. The next few paragraphs may shed more light on this.

Another interesting point is that the great early Vedic Aryan King Ikshvaku may have become known as the god Osiris in Egypt. Ikshvaku was referred to as Asaru in Sumerian, which is changed to Asar or Asir in Egyptian, and then to Osiris. Ikshvaku originally may have been simply honored as a great ancestor and king by the early Aryan rulers, which is very likely in the Aryan tradition, only to later become the deified Father-god whom became the basis of many stories and legends embellished from whatever was heard of him at the time. Osiris is also known for being a legendary ruler of pre-dynastic Egypt and is said to have provided the people with knowledge of agriculture and civilization, things that were very important to the Aryans.

Ikshvaku's position is described in *Bhagavad-gita* (4.1). It is explained that the Supreme Being originally instructed the spiritual science of yoga to Vivasvan, the sun-god, who then instructed it in Treta-yuga to Manu, who is considered the father of mankind. Manu instructed this knowledge to Maharaja Ikshvaku who was the king of the earth planet many hundreds of years ago, and the forefather of the Raghu or solar dynasty, which he started in Ayodhya. Many years later Lord Ramachandra appeared in this dynasty. This is further explained in the *Mahabharata* (*Shanti-parva*, 348.51-52). Thus, the spiritual knowledge of the Vedic literature, whether in written form or not, has existed in human society from the time of the great Aryan King Ikshvaku.

This information also indicates that Vedic culture has been in existence many more years than most scholars think. According to the Vedic tradition, Treta-yuga lasts 1,200,000 years. After this is Dvapara-yuga which lasts 800,000 years. And we have now gone through 5,000 years of Kali-yuga. So if this spiritual knowledge was taught by Manu sometime in Treta-yuga, we can get some idea of how long it has been in existence on this earth. So this discourages us from accepting the time frame Waddell presents for the first time Egypt was ruled by the Vedic Aryans. In fact, there could have been many times when the area of Egypt and the Mediterranean had been influenced or colonized by Aryan emperors over many hundreds or thousands of years.

One other account of how the Egyptian culture began goes back to the prehistoric times of Lord Parashurama in India. It is recorded in the Vedic literature that Parashurama killed all the ruling kings in India who were cruel, sinful, and against the Vedic brahminical culture. It is explained in the *Mahabharata* that the earliest kings of Egypt were originally the miscreant kings and warriors who had fled India due to their fear of Lord Parashurama. Once they settled in Egypt, they started their own distorted version of the Vedic culture.

It is also interesting that some people believe that the Egyptian pyramids were built to help guide planes or spaceships to the area. The Vedic literature has many references to flying vehicles. No Hindu today is unfamiliar with the idea that flying planes, called *vimanas*, existed 5000 years ago, although they were powered much differently than the planes of today. Did the early Vedic rulers use spaceships or planes to reach and colonize different areas of the planet? Were they possibly the same men and flying machines described in other tribal legends of men coming from the sky and helping the local inhabitants? No one can say for sure, but planes played a big part in the Vedic legends and many of the ancient battles that are described. So this would indicate that it is a possibility. After all, the ancient *Bruhad Vimana Shastra* by the Vedic sage Bharadvaj describes the construction of these *vimanas*.

AFRICA

In ancient Vedic lore, Africa was known as KushaDeep, or Kushadvipa. Two reasons for this is because large stretches of land were covered by the tall grass known as *kusha* grass in Sanskrit, and after the war between Rama and Ravana, the continent was under the administration of Rama's son Kush, or Cusha. African school text books also describe Africans as Cushites, testifying to the above information.

Swami Krishnanand once visited the Abyssinian monarch Haile Selassie and presented a copy of the *Ramayana*. He thought the Christian rulers were not likely to have heard of the book, but was pleasantly surprised to hear the monarch's remark, "This is nothing new to us. We Africans are Cushites." This is what motivated Krishnanand to search the African school text books and find references of Africans designated as Cushites. The text books provided more evidence of Africa's ancient administration of Cusha. However, the text books wrongly mention Cusha's father as Ham instead of Rama. As previously explained, that is because Rama was spelled in western regions as Rham. In course of time the "R" was dropped and what was left was "Ham."

Other strong Ramayanic links with Africa can be recognized in the island of Mauritius off the eastern coast of southern Africa. The island gets its name from "Marichas," meaning the island of Marichi, who was one of the generals in the army of the demon Ravana, and also a name for the sun. Rama, however, routed all the demons out of the area during the war with Ravana, and made Marichi flee to the stronghold of the demons.

In a book by Drusilla Dunjee Houston, titled *The Wonderful Ethiopians of the*

Ancient Kushite Empire (in three volumes), she indicates that the ancient name for the landmass of Africa was Kushadvipa. This is also a name mentioned in the *Bhagavat Purana*. Furthermore, in the *Ramayana*, which records the activities and pastimes of Lord Ramachandra. Some people feel He appeared at least one million to two-and-a-half million years ago. Lord Rama had two sons, Lava and Kush (or Cush). Each son was given half of the earth planet to rule after the great war between Rama and the demon Ravana. Africa was an area that was under the rule of Lord Rama's son, Kush, for which it became known as Kushadvipa. For this reason the African people were also known as Kushites, also spelled as Cushites. Thus, Kush is the ancient Vedic name known for Africa. So the Vedic connection with Africa goes back no less than to the Ramayanic times.

Another reference in this regard is found in the Bible in the book of *Numbers*, Chapter 12, verse one, in which it is said, "And Miriam and Aaron spoke against Moses on account of the Cushite wife he had taken, for he had taken a Cushite wife." This means that Cush and Cushites were a distinct and recognized culture and people that existed from before the time of Moses. It also shows that Moses had taken a woman from this country as a wife. Most biblical scholars associate Cush with the area of Ethiopia. In the above verse, Miriam and Aaron spoke against Moses for having taken the woman as a wife because she was ethnically different from them.

Africa in ancient times was also known as Shankadvipa. The word *dvipa* is Sanskrit for island, and *Shanka* is Sanskrit for conch. This was because Africa was like a large island in the shape similar to a conch shell. The English word conch is a derivative of the Sanskrit *shank*. This also shows how the Vedic rulers were so familiar with Africa that they knew its shape as seen from miles above it.

The African Swahili language and other local dialects bare the remnants of its original Sanskrit. For instance, the Swahili word "simba" for lion is the Sanskrit word *simha*.

The name of the country Abyssinia gets its name from the corruption of two Sanskrit words; *App-Sindhu*, meaning the waters of the Sindhu River, the modern Indus. This signifies that this area was once a settlement of people who had come from the Indus region.

Elsewhere in Africa we find that Somalia is named after Soma, and whose people worshiped the moon. Tanganyka (from the Sanskrit term *Tung Nayak*, meaning "the great leader") and Zanzibar (a corruption of the Sanskrit name *Kanchipur*) have merged to become Tanzania. The port city Dar-es-Salaam is the Sanskrit term *Dwar-eeshalayam*, which means the "Gateway to the Temple of God." This also shows how the Vedic culture was in Africa.

E. Pococke, in his book *India in Greece* (page 205), mentions that Philostratus concluded that the Ethiopians were originally an Indian race. They were compelled to leave India for the sin of killing a certain monarch to whom they owed allegiance. Pococke goes on to say that another Egyptian remarked that he had heard from his father that Indians were the wisest of men and that the

Ethiopians, a colony of the Indians, preserved the wisdom and usages of their fathers, and acknowledged that this was their origin. He also found the same conclusion had been made at a later period by Julius Africanus, from whom it had been preserved by Eusebius and Syncallus. Thus, Eusebius had also stated that the Ethiopians migrated from the Indus region and settled in the vicinity of Egypt.

When we analyze the religions of Africa today, we can still recognize that the basic concepts regarding God and life on earth in the traditional African religions are in line with the essential principles of Vedic culture. Such things as the methods of divination and the rites of passage are similar to that found in Vedic traditions. Also, contact with the Divinity was a major factor in life in the Kushite culture. Most all traditional African religions accept a Supreme Being, but His function differs according to region. They also accept lesser gods, respect the ancestors, and practice magical rituals.

The Mbuti Pygmies believe in a supreme Creator in the form of an old man as lord of the sky. They also have reverence for the moon. There is also a benevolent god of the forest to whom many pray and who exists in the trees. They also have ritual dancing and feasting at festivals for religious purposes, and at the puberty rites for the boys and girls. The Bushmen in Southern Africa believe in celestial spirits and have legends that explain their characteristics. The personifications of natural forces are also accepted, and these forces are invoked when the need arises, as in the case of rain.

From Kalahari and the Congo to Tanzania there is the belief in an omni-present supreme Creator who punishes and rewards people according to their works. But there are few organized religious societies and no big temples to regularly offer formal worship to the Supreme. However, the general belief is that anyone can pray to God in time of need, and He oversees all the functions of nature and the earth. Belief in life after death is found everywhere. Part of the funeral ceremony often contains rites to make sure the dead will remain at peace and not become a restless ghost, all of which is common Vedic knowledge.

The ancient African religions have faded as Islam (130 million followers) and Christianity (160 million followers and six thousand sects) continue to spread, but many of the old rituals and beliefs have simply merged with these new religions.

* * *

This concludes our presentation of much, but not all, testimony on the Vedic influence in the Middle East and further into Africa. No matter whether every scholar agrees completely with all of this information, it nonetheless provides much evidence for considering the numerous links of the religion and civilization in the Middle Eastern regions to that of the ancient Vedic and Indian society. The Middle East was a part of the original Vedic empire that pervaded the area, and still remains greatly influenced by that Vedic tradition today.

CHAPTER EIGHT

Islam and Its Links with Vedic Culture

When studying the Middle East, we should also include a separate study of Islam itself. Such a study will provide additional evidence of the Vedic influence found within the area of the Middle East, and in Islam.

THE BASICS OF ISLAM

The word *Islam* is generally accepted to mean surrender or commitment, signifying one's proper relation to God. Islam demands total surrender to the one God, which they accept as Allah. The path of Islam is straight and narrow, contrasting sharply with the Vedic way, which is broad and allows one to progress from whatever station of life one finds him or herself. Islam demands its followers to have complete faith in the Koran and the prophets. There are 28 prophets in Islam, 18 of whom are of the Old Testament. The prophets include Abraham, Moses, Jesus, John the Baptist, and Mohammed, the founder of Islam. Mohammed said that all the prophets teach the same essential truths. However, Mohammed established himself as the last and most important of the prophets, and that belief in and obedience to him were necessary for salvation.

Muslims are prohibited from gambling, stealing, killing, committing adultery, eating pork, and drinking alcoholic beverages. Islam forbids the worship of images or idols; yet, some exceptions to this can be found in India where some Muslims still take care of deities. Islam expects its followers to also honor their parents, give help to those who are helpless, protect widows, be honest, look on all men as brothers, especially other Muslims, and treat servants and animals kindly.

One of the reasons for treating animals nicely is that Mohammed had a love for them and did not approve of anyone ill-treating camels or other kinds of animals. As noted by his biographers, Mohammed preferred to eat vegetarian foods, living mostly on a diet of barley, bread, dates, water, and sometimes milk and honey. He instructed those who ate meat to wash out their mouths before praying. He also encouraged his followers to be vegetarian, but did not force the issue. So, presently, most Muslims have forgotten about this concern and eat the flesh of many kinds of animals, except when they are on pilgrimage when, according to the Koran (9.1), all Muslims are forbidden to eat meat.

The Five Pillars of Islamic faith are the basic elements that make up Muslim worship. The first is *shahadah*, confession of one's faith by which the Muslims declare, "There is no God but the one God, and Mohammed is His prophet." This is repeated several times a day. The second pillar is *salat*, the prayer said while bowing towards Mecca five times a day: at dawn, noon, late afternoon, sunset, and after dark. The third pillar is *zakat*, alms given to the needy based on a percentage of the kinds of property a Muslim owns. The fourth is *sawn*, the fast during the month of Ramadan in which no food is taken between dawn and sunset. The fifth pillar is *haji*, the pilgrimage to the Kaba in Mecca which every good Muslim is expected to do at least once in a lifetime.

Mohammed was born between 570 and 580 A.D. in the Bani Hashim, a poor but noble clan of the Quraysh tribe of Arabia. His father had died before his birth and his mother died shortly thereafter. Mohammed was raised an orphan by his uncle Abu Talib. Mohammed's education was very basic, and what he learned mostly came from his uncle. While he and his uncle were on a journey to Syria when he was 12 years old, he came in contact with Christianity for the first time, which left a philosophical impression on him. Yet his direction in life was not clear. He was a shepherd and a camel driver for a time, and learned business and trade from his uncle. When he was 25 years old he led a caravan to Syria for the wealthy widow Khadijah who soon offered to marry him, which he did. She was 15 years older than he, but it was a good marriage and they had two sons and four daughters. However, the boys died at a young age. He continued to work until he was 40 when his interest in religion and meditation became quite strong. He often retired alone to Mount Hira near Mecca for meditation. During this time he had also been influenced by Jewish and Christian teachings.

It was after Mohammed's fortieth birthday, said to be in 610, while in meditation, when an angel appeared and commanded him to recite in the name of God. According to tradition, Mohammed did not respond, so the angel grabbed him by the throat and shook him, repeating the command. When Mohammed still did not respond, the angel choked him until Mohammed did as he was told. Thus began Mohammed's prophethood and the writing of Muslim scripture, the Koran. For a long time Mohammed felt unsure about the vision or from where the channeled revelations of the Koran were really coming. Finally, however, Mohammed gained a clear understanding of what his mission was and then determinedly began preaching the divine message.

For over ten years Mohammed preached in Mecca but was mostly ignored. His earliest followers were his family, Khadijah, and others from the lower classes who formed a small sect. During this time Mohammed once entered the Kaba and announced, "There is but one God," which immediately angered the Meccans who were used to worshiping a number of gods and goddesses. Mohammed could have been killed, but his uncle protected him. His followers fled the place and sought refuge in Abyssinia. After the incident, his uncle tried to make him give up his preaching, but he continued anyway. Hostility and opposition to Mohammed increased until Mohammed entered Yathrib where he, in 621, was able to find a place for himself and his followers. Later, Yathrib became known as Medina, the city of the prophet. This emigration became the starting point of the Islamic calender. By this time his faithful wife, Khadijah, had died.

At Medina, Mohammed occupied himself with strengthening his position. The continuing revelations that were being compiled in the Koran began to provide answers to criticism of Mohammed, and it also condemned as hypocrites those people of Medina who remained non-Muslim. Mohammed became especially angry with the Jews of the area for refusing to accept him as a prophet and for criticizing him, claiming that he distorted the stories in the Bible of former prophets. Eventually, most of the Jews were either banished or massacred by him and his followers. Mohammed also condemned the theory of the Christian Trinity on the grounds that it made God appear like He had partners in His Divinity. He also proclaimed that Jesus was not the Savior nor a part of the Divine Nature. For this reason Christians sometimes consider Islam a heresy.

As his position became stronger, he displayed his military force to bring alliances with the Bedouins and other tribal groups. He also took as many as 15 wives, though he had preached that a Muslim should take no more than four. Several of these marriages served to strengthen his relations with various tribes. He also began attacking the Meccan caravans that were a source of wealth and strength to Mecca. Mohammed soon engaged in armed conflict with the Meccans in 624, who saw him as a threat to their city. But they were not good fighters, and Mohammed was victorious.

Mohammed gained possession of Mecca without a fight due to his military strength and diplomatic abilities in 630. He then destroyed the deities of the Kaba and forced the people to stop worshiping the other gods and goddesses and worship only Allah, and accept him as Allah's prophet. Actually, the deity of Allah was known to the Bedouin Arabs long before the appearance of Mohammed, but Allah's function at the time was not clear; so, he did not play a prominent role in their religious practice. Even then, the Kaba in Mecca was an important place of pilgrimage, and Hubal was the principal god. Other deities were also established there since each clan would place their own deity in a sacred area of the shrine. Although Mohammed destroyed these "idols" later on, still many of the religious functions at the time were incorporated into modern Islamic practice.

Mohammed also declared that the Black Stone in the sacred shrine had been given by God to Abraham, and it has been worshiped to this day, though the real origin of this stone is not clearly known. The Islamic tradition says that the Hajar Al-Asvad, the holy Black Stone, is supposed to have fallen from paradise when the original couple fell into sin. The stone had once been white but turned black due to the sins of the pilgrims who touched it. The Black Stone is in the south-east corner, 1.5 meters from the ground. It is black with reddish tones and yellow particles. It is an ovoid shape, about 11 inches wide and 15 inches high.

Prior to Mohammed's take over of the Kaba, numerous tribes had brought many deities into the Kaba over the years, to the point where there was some 360 images. (Some of these will be explained in the next section of this chapter.) Muslim tradition says that people at the time worshiped anything and had lost the true concept of religion. When Mohammed conquered Mecca, he ordered the removal of all images except a few. Thus, Mohammed is given credit for stopping the practice of all false worship of fabricated idols. However, gradually it became accepted that it was forbidden to worship any deities, regardless of whether they were genuine or not. Thus, the worship of deities was completely discarded and rejected, which had formerly been a common Vedic practice throughout the region. Nonetheless, all images, even paintings and art, were given up.

Mohammed also forbade the use of music or musical instruments, which had been another integral part of the Vedic tradition in devotional expression there at the time. It was considered a sensual art. Thus, was lost the many artists, musicians, writers, libraries, and scholars, that are valued under a Vedic administration, under the pretext that all that was needed to be known was the Koran.

Tradition has it that Mohammed also ordered the removal of all paintings from the interior of the Kaba as well, except for those of the Virgin Mary and Jesus. However, it must be asked why the Kaba had paintings of Mary and Jesus since it is understood that the Kaba, during pre-Islamic times, was not a Christian temple. It housed 360 non-Christian images. So from what bias does such an assumption come that this painting was of Jesus and Mary? Having been a Vedic shrine, it is very likely that these paintings were actually of baby Krishna and His mother Yashoda. Such paintings of Krishna and Mother Yashoda were quite popular throughout the Vedic empire, and are still well-liked today and can be seen anywhere in India. It is this painting from which the Christian images of baby Jesus and Mother Mary was fashioned so many years ago.

In any case, this victory in Mecca gave Mohammed enormous gain in prestige, and Bedouins and Arabs from all over came to pledge their allegiance to him. After Mohammed took over the Kaba and seized the riches within, he started the spread of his religion with the use of his modus operandi: conquering by force and destruction. First, he had to begin abolishing all remnants of the previous Vedic religion that had been there, and begin changing the rituals into something that was meant to be exclusively Muslim. So, he destroyed all 360 images in the Kaba and kept only Allah, along with the Shiva-*linga*, which has become known as the Ashwet, or black stone. However, some of his followers broke the stone into seven pieces, showing their fanatical dedication to their new religion, and later patched it together with a silver band and nails. Mohammed also kept the Vedic practice of circumambulating the Kaba seven times, but changed the rotation from clockwise to counterclockwise. In this way, his campaign began.

Just before Mohammed's unexpected death in 632, he was easily the most powerful man in Arabia and he demanded that everyone bow to the Islamic ideals. After Mohammed died, Abu Bakr, the first caliph or successor of Mohammed, continued to use military force in attempts to hold together the tribes who had entered into Islam. For the next ten years, the Muslims attacked Syria, Palestine, Damascus, Jerusalem, Iraq, and Egypt. Through the years they continued their attacks into other areas such as across North Africa and Spain in 711, which was later lost in the 15th century. They were stopped in France in 732. In the 11th century Sultan Mahmud of Ghazni started attacking into the mountainous regions of Afghanistan and continued into India. Mohammed Ghori, 150 years later, kept up the conquest of North India to bring that area under Islam rule, an area where political and religious unrest has continued ever since. When the Muslims entered India, they slaughtered thousands and thousands of Hindus and Buddhists alike, and took pride in destroying many hundreds of temples.

As the Muslims expanded, they faced new problems with new and often much more sophisticated people who had religious systems that were far more developed than their own. They found that the conquered people did not quickly agree that the Muslims were bearing a new and superior religion. Thus, to solve these additional problems, the Muslims began to resort to the old traditions as the best examples to follow. However, as old customs could not always be cited to solve various issues, they often concocted new traditions in order to justify their needs or actions.

It became obvious that the Koran needed to be further expanded with additional authority to handle the new problems with which Muslims had to deal. Thus, new books were compiled from the traditional practices of the prophet that were called *Sunnah*. The *Sunnah* were known according to oral descriptions of the prophet's activities and sayings. This oral tradition was known as *Hadith*. Several collections of *Hadiths* were made during the first few centuries of Islamic history. The *Hadiths* are accepted as an accurate authority by the more conservative and fundamental Muslims; yet, modern scholars point out contradictions in the *Hadiths* and say that they are not a reliable source of information about Mohammed and merely reflect the general attitude of Muslims during the third Islamic century. Some modern Muslims have now rejected the *Hadiths* and their usage in Islamic tradition and rely only on the Koran as their authority.

For Muslims in general, the Koran is the infallible word of God and is said to be a transcript of a tablet found in heaven. The Koran is traditionally considered to have been given to Mohammed by the angel Gabriel and was gradually revealed over a period of twenty years. It was thought that earlier prophets had been given portions of this heavenly tablet who had then written it for mankind's guidance in the form of scripture, such as the Injil or Gospel of Jesus, Psalms of David, Torah of Moses, and so on. The reason for Mohammed to reveal another book was that the Arabs needed a prophet of their own and a scripture in their own language dealing with their own spiritual needs rather than through the Christian and

Jewish books. It was also considered that Mohammed was the last of all prophets. Even though Mohammed had been influenced by Jewish and Christian teachings, the Koran accuses the Jews of distorting the scripture and the Christians of worshiping Jesus as the son of God rather than directly worshiping God as God had commanded. And all such people, as is so often the message in the Koran, go to hell.

The name *Koran* means that it must be recited. Every Muslim is expected to read the entire Koran. It is divided into 114 chapters, which all begin with the phrase, "In the name of Allah, the Compassionate, the Merciful." It is understood that Mohammed could not read or write. And the Koran as we find it today was put together only after Mohammed's death. It was Zayd ibn Thabit who gathered all the various writings from the many people in the community who had copied or collected them. An official version of the text was then produced under the order of Uthman, the third caliph or head of Islam. Because of this, some scholars have questioned the validity and authority of the Koran, and how much of it really was received from the angel Gabriel.

Ultimately, the Koran demands surrender to the one supreme God. This is actually the basis and conclusion of any bona fide religion, as especially enunciated in the Vedic literature. Although the Koran primarily considers the impersonalist conception of God, in the end it refutes impersonalism and establishes the personal form of the Lord. According to the Koran, the Lord has a spiritual, blissful body and is the all-pervading, eternal being from which everything originates. The Koran, although seeming to prescribe various methods, briefly describes what are aspects of *karma-yoga* and *jnana-yoga* and acknowledges that the ultimate position of everyone is to worship and offer prayers (or *bhakti*) to the spiritual form of the Lord, the Supreme Person. Thus, though not always recognized, devotional service to the supreme spiritual form of the Lord is actually the perfection of correctly following the Koran. Though the methods may vary, this is exactly in line with the Vedic principles.

As anyone who reads the Koran will see, in comparison with other scripture, it is not a book which focuses much on theology or spiritual doctrine. It does not dwell on describing our eternal spiritual identity, the characteristics of the soul, or the spiritual nature of God. In fact, it provides a harsh view of God, when compared to other religious texts like the Vedic literature. It presents God, Allah, as a God who gives out much punishment with no mercy for those fallen ones who do not follow the Islamic path.

The fact of the matter is that Islam and the Koran, as presented by Mohammed, provides guidance for daily practice, but no practical spiritual philosophy. The Koran is mostly a book that instructs what is expected of a Muslim and warns of what can happen to those who do not follow it. It is a book which leaves many matters unclear and incomplete. Whatever Islamic theology we find today was developed after Mohammed's death and has, more or less, been added to it. Even as theological premises were developed, many thousands of

Islamic sects appeared, and many disappeared, which accepted or rejected various portions of this theology and thus modified their lifestyles, worship, meditation, and zealous attitudes accordingly. Sometimes these sects became locked in dispute with other sects for many years. Some that appeared were the Sunni, Wahhabi, Sufi, and Shiah, while the no-longer existing Assassin sect and the present Druze sect are Ismailis, which are subsects of the Shiah.

The real development of theology in Islam did not start until the third Islamic century with the appearance of a small group of Muslim philosophers called the Mu'tazilah. They tried to convey a rational understanding of Islam. They taught that there was only one God and no evil force or Satan, although there are verses in the Koran that refer to Satan. They also said that the Koran was created and was not a transcript of an eternal tablet in heaven. They also denied that God could be perceived by man or that God had human attributes, as referred to in the Koran. The Mu'tazilah school eventually passed out of existence sometime after it lost the favor of the Abbasid rulers. But from that time, Islamic theology has continued to transform and evolve as different people tried to present a variety of views to solve the various philosophical problems with which Islam had to deal. In this way, we can see how Islam has continually changed in its attempt to justify itself through tradition and philosophy, and develop a theology which can show its superiority to other societies.

Islam does, however, have a developed mystical tradition, beginning with Mohammed's experiences that are now incorporated into the Sufi sect. Up to the present, Sufism is considered the real meaning of Islam for most Muslims. According to tradition, Sufism was developed by Mohammed through Ali Ibn Abi Taleb, the fourth caliph. Some say the word *sufi* means one whose heart is pure. Others say sufi comes from *saff*, meaning one who is close to God through spiritual development. Others say it comes from the word *suf* (wool), meaning to wear simple woolen garments, which was begun as a protest against the theological forms and worldliness of the Muslims at the time.

It was Hasan al-Basri of Iraq who first engaged in the asceticism that was taken up by others, later known as Sufis, who wanted to experience the presence of God as Mohammed did by performing mystical practices. They believed that all being is one, all entities emanate from the divine, and before being created they exist in Allah's mind as ideas and are, therefore, eternal with God. They also accept, like the Islam faith in general, that there is one God, there are angels, there are prophets, there is a day of resurrection when one is judged by God, and there is fate. They also accept that the universe is primarily good, but evil comes from selfishness or desires which separate oneself from God. All of this is very correlative with the Vedic point of view.

The Sufi process of development is broken down into stages, of which the first is practice of asceticism and detachment to worldly affairs and the body and bodily possessions. Silent meditation is an important practice. The second stage consists of studying with a teacher to acquire the esoteric knowledge that accompanies mystical experience. The worship usually consists of chanting the 99 names of Allah on the 99 beads of their rosary. The third stage consists of attaining enlightenment of the experience of love between God and man, which leads to ecstasy. This is very similar to the element of *bhakti* found in Vaishnavism, the Vedic worship of Vishnu, Krishna. This is why many Sufis who had been persecuted as heretics in Arabia moved east into India where their lifestyle was quite similar and better received.

Presently, there are over 700 million Muslims in the world, and the expansion of Islam is making gains by peaceful means, especially into sub-Saharan Africa and other areas of the world. But for many years, as we can see historically, the expansion was based on zealous military strength rather than spiritual purity and goodness. Except for some of the sects like the Sufis, much of Islam has been a fighting religion and continues to be so to this day. This certainly seems to go against some of the basic tenets of Islam, such as treating others with kindness, helping those who need it, etc. Yet, such recent leaders as Ayatollah Khomeini announced that Islam was a religion of fighters for freedom who must comply or be obliterated. This outlook does not seem to leave the followers of Islam much choice in how to conduct their lives. And pity the person who does not comply, as was seen by all the executions and torture of those who opposed Khomeini, such as the Bahai sect which has a much more humanitarian philosophy. Many had to flee the country to avoid the repressive Islamic government. Thus, not all Muslims are so extreme in their attitude. In fact, most of them are content with simply trying to live in harmony with God and their fellow man as best they can in following the Muslim path.

Since the death of Khomeini in June of 1989, countries like Iran are becoming more liberal with new reforms under way. This provides the means for increased individual and social freedoms, but there is still a very long way to go. Artists, writers, and musicians still fear censorship and imprisonment if they should incur the wrath of any Muslim cleric or government official. Obviously, this is still a religion that is evolving and going through dramatic changes, depending on who its leaders are and how mature is their spiritual understanding, and in which countries the followers are located. And, as previously stated, as long as the foundation of a religion is not based on real spiritual knowledge that can be realized by its followers on a practical level, such a religion is bound to remain in flux, ever-changing along with everything else that cannot rise above the influence of temporary material nature.

THE VEDIC CONNECTIONS IN ISLAM

As we have seen in the previous section to some degree, much of the religion of Islam still contains the influence of the pre-Muslim Vedic culture. It also adopted many of the Biblical principles. However, many of those also can be traced back to the Vedic traditions. For starters, the name of God in the Muslim religion is Allah. Although Allah is a masculine God in Islam, the name Allah is a Sanskrit name and a reference to the Mother Goddess as found in the names Amba, Amma, Akka, and others. It appears in Sanskrit chants in praise of Goddess Durga, who is also called Chandi, Bhavani, etc. The Vedic names such as Alagiri Swamy and Alladi Krishnaswamy incorporate the name of Allah. This is a clear pointer to the Islamic adoption of the name or prior worship of this Vedic form of Divinity. There is even a Minor *Upanishad* called the *Allopanishad*, proving the Vedic link with the name Allah.

Other Vedic texts that relate to Islam can be found in the *Bhavishya Purana* (Parva 3, Khand 3, Adya 3, texts 5-6) which actually predict the appearance of Mohammed. Therein it states: "An illiterate teacher will appear, Mohammed is his name, and he will give religion to his fifth-class companions." Mohammed was indeed illiterate and gave religious principles to those around him of the lower classes. This also shows the universal nature of the Vedic texts, as opposed to those scriptures that focused on specific regions. Another Vedic reference that some feel is a prediction of Mohammed is found in the *Atharva-veda* (Kanda 20, Shukta 127, Mantra 1-3). However, I have found this not to be so clear.

Even the name "Islam" is derived from the Sanskrit word *Is-alayam*, which means the abode or temple of God. *Isha* is one of the Sanskrit references for God, and *alayam* refers to the place of God. Often the name Islam is interpreted as "surrender," or "peace," but this is in reference to its Arabic interpretation when the word is compared to the twin Hebrew word "Shalome." However, Shalome also shows its linguistic connections to the Vedic word *Isha-alayam* when we simply remove the "I" and it becomes "Shalayam," and then "Shalome." Even the name *Koran* is a corrupted form of the Sanskrit word *Karana*, referring to the *Vedas*. Muslim mythology also mentions that there were four boxes of knowledge, similar to the four *Vedas*, and Allah took some sentences out of them and put them into the prophet's mouth.

In *World Vedic Heritage* (pp. 682-3), Mr. Oak gives some other examples of Muslim names that derive from Sanskrit. In reference to a list of kings written and preserved on a silk cloth in a fortress at Nagarkot, he says that, "Names like Subuktagin and Alaptagin are Sanskrit *Su-bhakta-gun* (one possessing the qualities of a good devotee), and *Alipta-gun* (a person who has cultivated mundane detachment). Consequently fancied Muslim names ending in 'gin' must be recognized to have a pre-Islamic Vedic connotation. They must not be mistaken to be Muslim names only because the latter-day successors of that dynasty had been forced to accept Islam. The ferocity and barbarity of Turkish conduct ever since Turks became Muslims should serve to highlight the immense importance of Vedic culture, alias Hinduism, to humanity.

"Similarly, the title 'Shah,' alias 'Shahi' as in Badshah or Shershah is not Muslim. In Sanskrit the term 'Shah' connotes 'shining.' A person of royal descent 'shines' because of his wealth, status, power and personality. Even the English words 'shone' and 'shine' are variations of the same Sanskrit term. The Hindu ruler of Nepal is called 'Shah.' Similarly, 'Shah' is also a common Hindu surname. Therefore historians must realize the Hindu origin of dynasties styling themselves as Shahs."

Islam began only 1400 years ago. And, as we have already established, the Vedic culture was global and had great influence in the Middle East. So Islam's ancestors were once Hindu, or people who were associated with the Vedic Aryan culture. Even Mohammed's relatives were connected with the Vedic culture. Have doubts about this? Then let us review some evidence.

Mohammed's family name was Kureshi, which is Sanskrit signifying they were from a branch of the Indian Kuru dynasty that once ruled India. The city of Cairo commemorates that name, being a distortion of the name Kuru. This alone provides evidence that the Kurus ruled and administrated the Middle East regions of the world 5000 years ago before the *Mahabharata* war, as the Vedic histories explain.

It is also known that Mohammed's uncle and family were engaged in making temple deities. The *Encyclopaedia Islamia* explains that Mohammed's grandfather and uncles were hereditary priests of the Kaba temple which housed 360 deities. Mohammed destroyed most of the deities in the Kaba. However, the central object of worship in the Kaba remains the sacred black stone. Shiva worship was once prevalent amongst the Arabs, and Shiva-*lingas* are made of black stone. Even the title Mehdi of a Muslim chief is a mispronunciation of the name Mahadeva, which is another name of Shiva. Thus, the black stone Shiva-*linga* was allowed to remain in the Kaba because that was the faceless deity of Mohammed's family.

The *Encyclopaedia Islamia* goes on to relate that among the 300 Hindu deities that were housed at the Kaba were images of Lat, Manat, Uzza, Saturn, and the moon. Lat is a sacred Hindu name which can be recognized by the fact that the author of an ancient Vedic astronomical text is Lat-Dev. Furthermore, worship of the nine planets, still in vogue in India, includes Saturn and the moon. This shows that the worship of the planets was also practiced in the Kaba, signifying its Vedic influence.

From additional research found in *Bhakti-yoga and Islam*, by Airavata dasa, we find that the early pre-Muslim people believed God gave various functions of the universe to different gods and goddesses, very much like the original Vedic tradition. People would pray to these demigods to invoke their blessings for all kinds of undertakings. The "Goddess of Fortune" and consort of Allah was Al-Manat, similar to Lakshmi, the Vedic Goddess of Fortune and wife of Lord Vishnu. Al-Lat was the "Goddess of Sky," and Al-Uzza was the "Goddess of Venus." The sun was also worshiped by the people of Yemen, and the moon was worshiped by others. There were also additional deities worshiped by various tribes. For example, at the temple of Wad, north of Hijaz, there was a deity that closely resembled, if not in fact was, Lord Ramachandra. The deity was made of stone in the shape of a man covered with two mantles, carrying a sword, a bow on his shoulders, a quiver of arrows on his back, and a spear in his hand with a small flag near the top. This is typical of the way Lord Ramachandra appears in Deity form or paintings even today. As in the Vedic tradition, the early Arabs also sculpted the deities and then performed special rituals and worship to call in and install the personality of the god or goddess into the deity.

More information about the deities in the Kaba is provided by Sir W. Drummond from page 439 onward of Volumes III & IV of his book *Origines*. It is related that one image in the Kaba was a bird. Most likely this was Garuda, Lord Vishnu's eagle carrier, which is found in most Vishnu temples in India today. Allat was a deity mentioned in the Koran as a female deity. Allah could be that same deity. The Deity named Bag was obviously the shortened form of saying Bhagwan--Lord Vishnu. Kabar was the deity Kubera. Dsu al Chalasat was Devi Cali, Goddess Kali. Madan was Madan-Mohana, Krishna. Sair was Shree, or Sri Lakshmi, the Goddess of Fortune. Saad was the deity of good fortune, which comes from *sadhaka*, spiritual practice. And Sawara was Eswara, Shiva. This illustrates the familiarity of the Arab people with the entire Hindu pantheon before the spread of Islam.

Umar bin-e Hassham, Mohammed's uncle, is the family member most known for being devoted to the Vedic custom of deity-making, and was a staunch devotee of Lord Shiva. Much of this sort of history about Mohammed and Arabia has been hidden or destroyed. However, page 235 of the famous anthology of ancient Arabic poetry titled *Sayr-ul-Okul* provides the poem that relates this history. In fact, an extract of the page has been reproduced in black ink on a red stone column of the fire-worship pavilion in the backyard of the Birla Lakshmi-Narayan Temple on Reading Road in New Delhi. The poem describes the devotion that Mohammed's uncle felt for Lord Shiva and India. The English translation is as follows:

> The man who may spend his life in sin
> And irreligion or waste it in lechery and wrath
> If at least he relent and return to
> Righteousness can he be saved?
> If but once he worship Mahadeva with a pure
> Heart, he will attain the ultimate in spirituality.
> Oh Lord Shiva exchange my entire life for but
> A day's sojourn in India where one attains salvation.
> But one pilgrimage there secures for one and all
> Merit and company of the truly great.

Umar bin-e Hassham's poetry shows the Arabic people's appreciation for Vedic culture and India. It also shows that the Arab people were familiar with the worship of Lord Shiva. Therefore, it is logical to recognize that the first battles between Hinduism and Islam were fought in the very land which has been flaunted as the exclusive and original cradle of Islam.

Evidence in the form of al-Biruni's (973-1048 A.D.) compilation   of
Patanjali's *Yoga Sutras,* called *Kitab Patanjali,* and his *Kitab al-Hind,* a treatise
on Indian culture, shows that Muslims studied and were fascinated by the
philosophy of Vedic India. Even the name *Namaz,* referring to the practice of
bowing toward Mecca five times a day, is derived from the joining of two Sanskrit
words, *Nama* and *Yaja,* which means to bow and worship. In the Foreword of
Ashraf F. Nizami's book, *Namaz: The Yoga of Islam,* he points out that when
impartially analyzed, the practice of Namaz is the daily practice of yoga. He
concludes that those who do the Namaz everyday are unconsciously doing yoga.
According to Nizami, since the Namaz is presumed to have been started by
Mohammed and entails specific yoga postures, it is obvious that Mohammed must
have practiced yoga, or been aware of it, and taught it to his followers in the Kaba.

Additional insights into the Vedic connection with Islam is that the name of
the Islamic month of "Rabi" is derived from the Vedic word "Ravi" because the
Sanskrit letter "V" changes into the Prakrit "B." One festival that occurs in this
month is the Gyarahavi Shareef, which is the eleventh day of the month when a
special Manavrat initiation ceremony used to be held. In the Vedic tradition, the
11th day after the new or full moon is the sacred *Ekadashi* day. This is the custom
that is still commemorated in the Muslim Gyarahavi Shareef. The Muslim
observance of Miladul Nabi is also the same as the Vedic celebration of the vernal
equinox, which signifies a reunion with God. Other Muslim festivals are also
dependent on the citing of the moon, which is derived from the Vedic tradition.

Another festival was the Islamic Shabibarat, the name of which is the corrupt
form of the Vedic festival known as Shiva Vrata or Shivaratri. Since the Kaba had
been an important Shiva temple, the Shivaratri was an important time of
celebration.

The custom of the Islamic month of Ramadan comes from the Sanskrit
Rama-dhyan. Dhyan means to meditate, and Rama, or Ramachandra, is an
incarnation of God who was known to the Arab people. Thus, Ramadan refers to
a time to meditate on God, especially in the incarnation of Lord Rama, although
most Muslims have forgotten this aspect of it. In the Vedic tradition, the 9th day
of the bright half of the month of Chaitra is Rama's birthday. The pre-Islamic
Arab tradition has retained the 9th month of the year for meditating on Lord
Rama. Also, fasts are always associated with Vedic worship, and Islam has
retained that fasting tradition for Ramadan.

Another obvious connection between India and Arabic Muslims can be
recognized when we consider that much of the Islamic knowledge of astronomy
came from India, as did their system of mathematics, the Arabic numerals, and the
decimal system. Furthermore, Islam has continued to be guided by the lunar
calendar, the same as the Vedic tradition. The Muslim month of "Safar" signifies
an extra month, identical with "Adhik" or the extra month of the Vedic calendar.

As pointed out in *World Vedic Heritage* (p. 690) by Mr. Oak, we can find an
exact translation of a verse from the *Yajur-veda* in the Koran along with other

Vedic references to astronomy, as explained by research scholar Pandit S. D. Satawalekar of Pardi in one of his articles: "The Vedic description about the moon, the different stellar constellations and the creation of the universe have been incorporated from the *Vedas* in the Koran, Part 1, Chapter 2, stanzas 113 to 115 and 158, 159: Chapter 9, stanza 37, and Chapter 10, stanzas 4 to 7. That indicates that the *Vedas* used to be recited in Mecca and in the Kaba itself even during Mohammed's boyhood days." This helps show how the Vedic tradition was quite popular and dominant in the area before the changes made by Islam. And even after Islam was established, more philosophical changes and developments took place in its philosophy to help smooth out whatever controversies emerged.

Historically we have to remember that the Koran was not officially compiled until after Mohammed's death. This is also pointed out by Colin Maine in an article from the Rationalist Association (of N.S.W. 58 Regent Street, Chippendale, N.S.W. 2008, Australia). He states: "The Koran was written down 20 years after Mohammed's death, and the first *Hadith* (Saying of Mohammed) 220 years after his death. Many *Hadiths* were invented in the intervening years to support a particular course of action."

This is historically the way the Koran itself unfolded: Illuminations came from Mohammed as there arose particular controversies in his clan. These illuminations were recorded by others and only after his death were they collected to form the Koran. The point is that hardly anyone really could remember well enough exactly what Mohammed said to compose the *Hadiths* 220 years after his death. Therefore, it is hard to say how many *Hadiths* were composed by people who wanted to incorporate their own philosophical purposes and then stamp them with the name of Mohammed.

Incidentally, we can still see the Vedic influence in the word *Hadith*. It comes from the Sanskrit word *Satya*, which means truth. However, the Arabic pronunciation changes the "S" to "H," turning *Satya* to Hatya, and then to *Hadith*.

THE KABA WAS A VEDIC SHRINE

Now let us focus our attention on the Kaba, the holiest shrine of Islam. It was entirely rebuilt as it now stands in 1627 A.D. The name *Kaba* comes from the mispronunciation of the Sanskrit word *Garbha Graha*, which was shortened to Gabha. This refers to the sanctum, which the Kaba is in Islam. Just as the Sanskrit word *Gow* or *Gau* becomes "cow" in the West, with the "G" becoming "C," the word Gabha became Kaba in Arabic. Thus, we can begin to understand that before Mohammed invaded the Kaba and destroyed most of the deities there, the Kaba was known as the *Garbha Graha*, and was an international Vedic shrine. To help confirm this, let us remember that the Kaba is also known as Haram, which comes from the Sanskrit word *Hariyam*, which means "The Shrine of Hari, Lord Vishnu."

In *World Vedic Heritage* (p.123) Mr. Oak describes the floor plan of the Kaba as that of a square box-like building within the courtyard of a octagonal structure. Octagon was a typical Vedic pattern in architecture. Each corner of the building was meant for enshrining one of the major Vedic deities, eight altogether. The central sanctum in the Kaba housed the reclining form of Lord Vishnu.

Even now the Vedic custom of circumambulating the Deity is practiced at the Kaba. All pilgrims circumambulate the entire building at least eight times. This is strange in that there is no modern mosque where circumambulation of the shrine is practiced. So walking around shrines is generally not an Islamic custom, although it is quite common in Vedic society. Therefore, this is another carry-over from the original Vedic culture that once pervaded the Middle East and Arabia, and proof that the Kaba was once a Vedic temple.

Another Vedic tradition at the Kaba is this one: Just as every Shiva temple has a sacred water spring that represents the holy Ganga (Ganges) River, there is the Zam Zam spring near the Kaba. The two "Gs" in the word Ganga are replaced with "Z" which makes the name Zamza or Zamzam. Furthermore, Shiva is often shown with a crescent moon on his head, and Shiva temples have a crescent on top of the temple. The crescent moon on the pinnacle on the Kaba is but a remnant of its Vedic origin.

The Black Stone is the main point of worship in the Kaba. What remains of it is a cylindrical shape. It had been cut into seven pieces but is now rejoined. It is half buried in the outer surface of a corner wall of the Kaba. So half of it is covered in the wall. Even a good portion of the curved outer half is covered with silver foil. Thus, the pilgrim gets to view only a small portion of the original stone that is left uncovered by the silver sheet.

It is also said that the Black Stone (Sangay Aswad) is originally a representation of Shiva, Mahadeva, in the form of a Shiva-*lingam*. Shiva is also known as Makkheshvar, to which the name Makka or Mecca refers. This *linga* stone was retained by Mohammed as a formless symbol of the Divinity, although its pedestal has been lost. However, it is known that Mohammed smashed the other deities, except for that of Allah, and buried them in the cellars of the temple. The Black Stone is black with reddish tones and yellow particles. It is an ovoid shape, about 11 inches wide and 15 inches high. This is the typical shape and color similar to the black Shiva-*lingas* that are popular in India today. There is a story from India that relates that if anyone should enter the Kaba and pore Ganges water over it, which is the traditional Vedic way of worshiping a Shiva-*linga*, the incident would somehow cause the decline and mark the beginning of the end of Islam. If that is true, then this would be another reason why there is so much secrecy and protection regarding who is allowed to enter the area of the Kaba.

This is further corroborated in *The Wanderings of a Pilgrim in Search of the Picturesque* (p. 403, Vol. 1), by Fanny Parks, in which she relates, "The Hindus insist that the Black Stone in the wall of the Kaba, or sacred Temple of Mecca, is no other than a form of Mahadeo [Mahadeva, Shiva]; and that it was placed there by Mohammed out of contempt; but the newly converted pilgrims would not give up the worship of the Black Stone, and sinistrous portents forced the ministers of the new religion to connive it."

Furthermore, as described in *World Vedic Heritage* (page 677), "The general belief that the Kaba is only a Shiva temple is not true. It originated as a Vedic shrine depicting the Vedic version of the creation with a reclining Vishnu's navel forming the centre of the cosmic theme. Vishnu was surrounded by a whole pantheon of Vedic gods. Mohammed destroyed them all. The Shiva-linga stone wrenched away from its base was retained as a sacred symbol because it was the special patron and a faceless deity of Mohammed's Kuru-ishi household. He was a Shaivite. That was why those insisting that the caliphate remain in his family are known as Shaivas, now called Shias [Shiites]."

In conclusion, Mr. Oak, in *World Vedic Heritage* (pp. 121-2), relates: "An ancient Sanskrit scripture known as *Harihareshwar Mahatmya* has [a couplet] which mentions Lord Vishnu's holy footprint to be at three main centres in the world, namely one in Gaya (India), the other in Mecca, and the third near Shukla Teertha.

"This information when coupled with the information from Muslim sources that there were 360 idols in the temple, indicates that Lord Vishnu was surrounded by an entourage of other deities of which Lord Shiva was one. But the Muslims, being iconoclasts, destroyed the idols of other deities while Shiva's emblem, a round cylindrical dark, black-red stone, they retained as a central featureless object of reverence."

The verse from the *Harihareshwar Mahatmya* reads:
> *ekam padam gayayantu*
> *makkayaantu dwitiyakam*
> *tritiyam sthapitam*
> *divyam muktyai shuklasya sannidhau*

This relates to Lord Vishnu whose lotus feet were consecrated at the three holy places of Gaya, Mecca, and Shukla Tirtha. Worshiping the impressions of the Lord's feet is an old Vedic tradition. However, it is not a Muslim custom. Those that do so, thinking that it is Mohammed's footprint, are only carrying on with something that is foreign to their religion and is but a carry-over from the Vedic standard that used to be at Mecca.

Also, in reference to the Kaba we find the Haj, which is a continuation of the ancient festival that used to be held at Mecca during pre-Islamic times. Mr. Oak points out in *Some Blunders of Indian Historical Research* (pages 232-3) that there is a famous library called Makhtab-c-Sultana in Istanbul, Turkey. It has the largest collection of ancient West Asian literature. In the Arabic section there is an anthology of ancient Arabic poetry that was compiled from an earlier work in 1742 A.D. under the order of the Turkish ruler Sultan Salim. This is the anthology known as *Sayar-ul-Okul* which was compiled and edited by Abu Amir Abdul Asamai who was the Poet Laureate of Harun-al-Rashid's court. The first modern edition of the anthology was printed and published in Berlin in 1864 A.D. Another was published in Beirut in 1932. This work is regarded as the most important anthology of ancient Arabic poetry. The point of it is that it throws considerable light on the social life, customs, manners, and forms of entertainment in ancient Arabia. The book also contains an elaborate description of the ancient Mecca shrine and the annual fair which used to be held every year, known as Okaj. This fair later became known as the annual Haj of the Muslims and the pilgrimage to the Kaba. Thus, the Haj is merely a continuation of the old pre-Islamic fair and not a new practice.

However, the ancient Okaj was far from a carnival. It provided a means by which people and the learned could discuss the social, religious, and other aspects of Vedic culture which pervaded Arabia. Arabia was known then by its Sanskrit name, Arvasthan--Land of Horses. The *Sayar-ul-Okul* asserts that the conclusions of such discussions were highly regarded throughout Arabia in the same way that such discussions were regarded in Varanasi. This was another place in India where the learned would gather for discussing the means to attain spiritual bliss. The principal shrines in both places in ancient times were Shiva temples.

Today, one of the traditions for entering the Kaba is that Muslim pilgrims have to shave themselves, have a bath, remove their clothes and wear two white sheets, all of which are Vedic customs that are still often followed by pilgrims in India before entering a temple. No animal is allowed to be slaughtered, and no meat allowed in the Kaba during pilgrimage. Also, pilgrims are expected not to eat any meat during the pilgrimage. The pilgrims circumambulate the temple, but no one is allowed to enter the interior of the Kaba, which is kept heavily shrouded. The secrecy is being maintained, it is believed, because the interior walls have Sanskrit inscriptions etched on them, and possibly some traces of the earlier deities and paintings which have remained unexplored. This could give a clue to the pre-Islamic origin of the Kaba. Also, non-Muslims coming by land are stopped outside a 35-mile radius from the Kaba, another way of guarding the true nature of the building.

Other Encyclopedias also tell us that there are inscriptions on the inside of the Kaba walls. What they are nobody has been allowed to study. But according to hearsay, at least some of them are verses from the *Bhagavad-gita*. This would indicate a definite connection with its Vedic past, and another reason for the secrecy that shrouds the Kaba.

Further testimony that there were paintings inside the Kaba is found in the book *Islam* (page 13), wherein Alfred Guillaume records, "It is credibly reported that when Mohammed entered Mecca in triumph in the year 630, paintings of Jesus and the Virgin Mary among others were still visible on the inner walls of the Kaba. He ordered all paintings except that of the Virgin and the Child to be expunged; this painting was seen by an eye-witness as late as 683 when so much of the Kaba had been destroyed by fire that it had to be rebuilt."

This becomes even more interesting when we consider, as previously explained, that what Christian writers mistook to be paintings of Jesus and Mary were actually paintings of Krishna being held in the arms of His foster mother Yashoda. The style of painting with Jesus being held by Mother Mary is practically the same as those of Krishna being held by Mother Yashoda. The difference is that history of Krishna goes back 3,000 years before the time of Jesus. The Kaba was, basically, a Vedic temple. Even the Arabic greeting "Salam walekum" is also the garbled Sanskrit expression *Ishalayam Balakam*, which means obeisance or holy remembrance of the "Child-God (Krishna) consecrated in the temple." *Isha* means God, *Alayam* means the place or temple of, and *Bala* means child. Krishna was the only ancient, non-Christian form of the Divine that was worshiped in His form as a child.

Furthermore, let us remember that the Kaba was not a Christian shrine before Mohammed captured it. Therefore, the paintings in the temple could not have been of Jesus and Mary because the Kaba temple had been in possession of Mohammed's family. They were not Christians. That family was a branch of the Vedic Kuru dynasty and were hereditary priests of the temple. Mohammed's uncle is known for being a maker of deities. The temple had 360 of such images, and Christianity has no where near 360 images to worship. Therefore, as is the usual Vedic custom, the temple had many images of demigods and sages surrounding the central Deity of Vishnu, along with many paintings on the walls and ceiling of Vedic personalities and episodes from the Vedic epics and *Puranas*. These included depictions of the life and pastimes of Lord Krishna. That is why the Kaba is also known as Haram, or Hariyam, the abode of Hari, the Lord. Thus, it was no doubt paintings of Krishna and Yashoda that had also made their way to Mecca and into the Kaba, with which the people of Arabia were familiar. In course of time, and with numerous attacks by vandals, all of these images and paintings were destroyed. What paintings and inscriptions exist today in the Kaba nobody knows because the temple is never opened to outsiders.

There have, however, been several Europeans that have visited the Kaba and lived to tell about it. One such visitor was John Lewis Burckhardt who provides insights to visiting the Kaba in his book, *Travels in Arabia*. On page 172 he describes, "In passing under the insulator arch in front of the Kaba, called Bab-as-Salam, certain prayers are said. Other prayers are recited in a low voice, and the visitor then places himself opposite the black stone and prays two Riktas [Rikta is obviously Richa, a Vedic stanza] at the conclusion of which the stone is touched with the right hand or kissed. The devotee then begins the Towaf, [the] walk around the Kaba (anti-clockwise). This ceremony is to be repeated seven times. . . Every circuit must be accompanied with prescribed prayers, which are recited in low voice and appropriated to the different parts of the building that are passed: the Black Stone is kissed or touched at the conclusion of each circuit."

As related in *World Vedic Heritage* (page 703), another visitor was a Spaniard, Juan Badia Seblis, who temporarily converted to Islam and visited the Kaba in 1807. His two-volume travel account, *Travels of Ali Bey*, was published in 1816. On page 86 he records: "The basement (of the Kaba) which surrounds the building is of marble." He goes on to describe that the interior of the Kaba is a big hall with two central pillars, each about two feet in diameter. The ceiling is shrouded by a sheet of costly cloth, so are the walls up to about a height of five feet from the floor. The cloth is rose-colored, lined with white silk, with silver embroidered flowers. There is a permanently barred staircase in the northern corner leading to the terrace. It is near that corner where the sacred Black Stone is fixed. Opposite that is a marble-paved basement. Praying in it is considered very holy because Mohammed is supposed to have prayed there. He goes on to explain that houses in old Mecca are constructed in the ancient Indian-cum-Persian ornamental style. Mecca has no flowers, no artists, no sculptors, and not even cobblers. Footwear is imported from Turkey and Egypt. No music is ever heard in Mecca. That is how Ali Bey described it at the time.

Even now in Islam, especially in the Middle Eastern and Arabic countries, many avenues of expression of thought are forbidden. This makes research and development into new areas of benefit for human existence extremely stifled. Thus, Muslim contributions to the sciences, art, music, dance, engineering, medicine, and the general welfare of the world are negligible, especially when compared to contributions of the Vedic culture. The Islamic rhetoric is that it is the fastest growing religion in the world. But most Islamic countries allow no other religion, worship, temples, or schools for any but Muslims. All others are excluded. These are not democratic countries. And even Muslim student organizations in such countries as England and the United States are becoming more militant against non-Muslims. This naturally creates an increasingly divisive and disruptive situation. Even the different sects within Islam engage in murderous fights among themselves. If this is a sign of the future, then until Islam can recognize its common Vedic roots or its similarities with other cultures and give up this divisive and separatist mentality, it may very well be a inconsequential contribution to civilized life.

* * *

All of the above evidence surely shows the Vedic traditions and influence in Islam. We have to realize that the ancestors of the Muslims were Hindus, followers of the Vedic culture. This is not only the case in Arabia but also in India. Therefore, each Muslim should research back through the generations of his family to find out which of his ancestors were converted to Islam, and under what circumstances. It is also known that many converts to Islam were not made due to the purity of the religion, but due to the violence that Islam forced on people.

Nonetheless, history also records that besides the ancient Vedic culture in Arabia, many years ago there were numerous godless tribes and practices as well. Only a person like Mohammed could have purged the area of such people and customs. However, for those who were sincere practitioners of the Vedic culture and real religion, violence was an unnecessary force that drove the high and lofty spiritual ideals and knowledge of the Vedic system out of the land.

The motivation of those who used violent attacks and killings to convert all others to their religion and wipe out whatever original culture had been there was simply for political dominance and military suppression of all opposition. Consequently, Islam was spread primarily through the means of violence by the Arab, Iranian, and Turkish hordes. No matter how such a religion is spread, without genuine spiritual purity, no such culture can be expected to produce truly peaceful or spiritual results. They can only be but passing religions subject to whatever set-back and decay that will force it to change and fade. Thus, we should not take it for granted that the Islamic tradition itself has predicted such an eventuality and foretold its own demise after a span of 1400 years from the time of Mohammed, which it has just completed. How this may happen, only the future will tell.

CHAPTER NINE

The Philosophical Origins and Vedic Links in Judaism

While investigating the area of the Middle East, we should also take a closer look at the prominent culture of Judaism, and the Vedic influence and links that are found within it. There is evidence that Judaism contains much influence from the Vedic culture. Some people even consider it as an ancient off-shoot from the Vedic system. There is enough evidence to make this worth considering, and it is rather convincing.

THE HISTORY OF JUDAISM

As mentioned in a previous chapter, the Jews were some of the first to use the technique of rewriting history to help establish the uniqueness of their culture. They often had to use the legends of neighboring countries and cultures and then embellish them to ascertain the special traits of Judaism. However, as we can see from the evidence within this chapter, there are different versions of their history even within their own writings. This can cause confusion as to which version to believe, and at the very least shows that they were not as unique as their tradition may seem to convey.

Judaism is said to have originated with a compact between God and Abraham. Legend has it that this began in the city of Ur, where the nomadic tribes that had captured the town from the Sumerians worshiped nature spirits and made many deities of them in their temples. These were likely some of the demigods from the Vedic pantheon. According to tradition, Terah, a man who made such deities, had a son, Abraham, who had many dreams and visions that made him feel that deity worship was wrong. So he would smash the deities his father made. He also had a dream in which God instructed him to take his people west to Canaan, which he did around 2100 B.C. when they began many years of wandering. This is

128

described in *Genesis*, Chapter 12, in which God instructs Abraham to leave his father's house and go to the land God would show him. There He would make him a great nation and bless him. However, there have been some doubts amongst scholars as to whether Abraham was actually a historical figure or simply a character in the Jewish myths. The original pact between Abraham and God is probably in reference to the pact between God and Brahma as related in the Vedic texts, when God agreed to give Brahma the power to create after Brahma did penance.

According to tradition, the beginning of the Jewish nation started with Abraham who had a son, Isaac, who also had a son, Jacob. It is said that God appeared to Isaac as well as Jacob and gave Jacob the name Israel and told him to give up all strange gods. Jacob, or Israel, had twelve sons whose names were the names of the twelve tribes of Israel. The word *Judah*, from which it is said came the name *Judaism*, is supposed to come from the name of Jacob's fourth son. Judaism later meant those people who lived in the southern half of Palestine when it was divided into the two kingdoms of Judah and Israel. After some time, Judaism was known as the faith of all who worshiped Yahweh or Jehovah.

It is said that when the first Jewish people went south to Egypt to live in Goshen for 400 years, they greatly multiplied. They kept to themselves, but the Egyptians became fearful of their growing population and enslaved them. However, some researches of the early history of Israel have concluded that only a small portion of the ancient Israelites were actually slaves in Egypt. These could have been the Levites because it is among them in which we find people with Egyptian names. Names such as Moses, Hophni, and Pinehas are Egyptian, not Hebrew. They worshiped God as Yahweh while in Egypt and Sinai and only later, after arriving in Israel and meeting the Israelite tribes, did they worship God as El and become the priests of the religion. Nonetheless, tradition goes on to explain that the Jewish people multiplied in Egypt until one Pharaoh, trying to curb this growth, ordered that the oldest male child of each family should be cast into the Nile. It was during this time that one Hebrew woman placed her son in a small reed basket and let it float down the river. The daughter of the Pharaoh found and adopted the baby, naming him Moses.

Moses lived in the palace for 40 years, learning the highly regarded wisdom of Egypt. But after killing an Egyptian in a fit of rage, he fled to the desert. After 40 years of living as a shepherd, it is said that he saw God as a burning bush who instructed him to deliver his people from Egyptian slavery and take them to the promised land of Canaan after leaving Egypt. It took another 40 years of wandering before they returned to Canaan to capture the land from the Semite people who were living there.

Let us remember, from the Vedic histories it is related that it was the Vedic king Puru whose descendants were the Puravas, later to be known as the Pharaohs of Egypt. Puru ruled over the domain of his father, Yayati, with his elder brothers subject to him. Yayati was deified as Yahweh by the children of Yadu who are identified with the Yadus, or Yadavas, some of whom became the Jews of the present day. These Jews bore bitter animosity toward their ancestor Aryans, the Pharaohs of Egypt. The Jews were subservient to the Pharaohs by the old edict of Yayati, who had declared that the Yadus would not have a kingdom, and that Puru would rule over the other sons of Yayati and their descendants. They resented their subordinate status and revolted against it, moving out of Egypt, wanting to be totally separate. Thus, they went on and created their own culture, legends, and histories.

As the Jewish people traveled to Canaan, they conquered and killed many people in the cities they encountered. The reason is that they felt they had a God-given right to do so, as explained in *Deuteronomy* (20.10-18) where the Jewish God instructed that when they came near a city they should offer terms of peace, and if the people accept, then the Jews could put the people to forced labor. And if the people make war, then everyone should be killed except for the women and children, which could be enjoyed as the spoils of the enemy. Thus, they should utterly destroy the Hittites, Amorites, Perizzites, Hivites, Jebusites, and Canaanites. Even after the Jewish people kicked out or killed the original residents of their new land where they had settled, they still waged war and killed many others amongst the neighboring cultures while their nation expanded.

Moses also gave the quarreling Jewish people the God-given law that he received on Mount Sinai. This is one of the most significant incidents in Jewish history. The Jews feel that since God revealed His law to them through Moses, they must be the chosen ones to play an important part in the coming of God's kingdom, which would be preceded by the arrival of a personal Messiah.

This written law forms the essence of the Hebrew Bible, which is a collection of books written over a period of 1,000 years in which Judaism has its roots. The commandments are a part of the written law. We know the biblical story of how Moses went up to Mount Sinai and communed with God who appeared to him in the form of a great dark cloud that covered the Mount. It was there that God gave Moses the stone tablets that contained the commandments. However, the ten commandments that were traditionally given by God to Moses were in fact not given by God, but were simply a summary of laws that had been known in the area for years long before Moses' time. Although Hebrew tradition relates how Moses received the law from God on top of a mountain, this is said to have also happened to Zoroaster many years previous. Zoroaster had earnestly prayed on the mountain, was given enlightenment by God, and then descended with the book of law, which developed into the *Zend Avesta*. It is said that even Minos, the law-giver of the Cretans, climbed a mountain and received the law from Zeus. In fact, the proposal that the laws for mankind were given by God has been propagated in a variety of cultures in order to give them more authority. This is also seen with Mohammed, who said he was called by God to be the prophet for the Arabs and was given the *Koran* by mental telepathy, or by channeling the angel Gabriel. This is an example of the Jewish writers adopting the legends of other cultures as their own.

A vastly different description of how the Jewish law was originally developed is given in the *Book of Jasher*, a lost book of the Bible. Jasher was the son of Caleb, one of the close associates of Moses, who is said to have written a simple book that records many of the incidents that took place during the wanderings of the early Jewish people. The *Book of Jasher* is also mentioned in *Joshua* and *The Second Book of Samuel* in the Bible. Therefore, even though the *Book of Jasher* is not well-known, it has authority.

In the *Book of Jasher*, it is related that long before Moses went onto Mount Sinai he had a meeting with Jethro, his Midianite father-in-law, in which Jethro described the commandments for the people of Israel to follow and how they should be judged accordingly. Moses wrote down all these rules. When Moses wanted to establish these customs, he was met with resistance by Miriam, his sister, and the people who felt they did not need the customs of the Midianites. Moses became very angry with Miriam and had her arrested. But the people demanded that she be released.

Miriam had become highly respected by the people because it was she who found water for the tribes of Israel when they were dying of thirst during their sojourn from Egypt. The Bible describes how Moses struck a rock with his staff and the people drank the water that flowed from it, but in the *Book of Jasher* this does not occur. Instead, what is described is that Miriam discovered a spring under the shade of a tree. When Moses and a few others dug out the spring, it turned into a small rivulet leading them to a place where there were 12 wells. The people all went there and drank and praised Miriam for having found the water needed to refresh them.

So upon the demand of the people, Moses released Miriam after arresting her, but after some time she died and the people greatly mourned over her death. Then Jethro, seeing the opportunity, visited with Moses again because Moses could now carry out the instructions of Jethro without anyone's intervention. First, as Jethro had instructed him, Moses made the people of Israel choose 70 elders. Then he placed Aaron and Hur in charge of the people while he took Joshua, Nadab, Abihu, and the 70 elders up on Mount Sinai to stay for 40 days and nights. There he met Jethro who instructed Moses and the others how to build a tabernacle to their God and establish priests. Moses then decided to let Aaron and his sons, the Levites, be set aside as the priests of the tribes of Israel. During the remaining 40 days, Jethro, Moses, and the elders decided on all the statutes and ordinances that were to be observed. Then they wrote them all down in a book for remembrance.

During this time the people of Israel at the foot of the mount murmured against Moses, rightly speculating that he was cunningly trying to set himself up as a king of all the people. Aaron sent messengers to Moses and the elders to tell them of this disturbance among the people. After hearing the news, Moses became very angry, sent the messengers away, and suggested to the elders that they tell the people that they had seen and communed with God on the mount and that the commandments are actually from God as He had spoken them. All the elders agreed to accept this plan except for Nadab and Abihu who were then cut off from the assembly and returned to the people below.

When Moses and the elders came down from the mount, they were greeted with rebellion. Then Moses met with Aaron to tell him that God had chosen Aaron and his sons to minister before the Lord in the tabernacle and that they should separate themselves from the rest of the people. The next day, Moses told the sons of Levi to take up swords and kill all those who were rebellious to Moses' plans. So they went through the camp and killed Nadab, Abihu, and another 3000 people. After the slaughter, the rest of the people became humble with fear and promised to follow Moses.

Under Moses' instructions, a tabernacle was built and Aaron and his tribe were established as the priests. From the tabernacle Moses read the book of commandments before the congregation, saying that these were the laws given by God. In this way, many rules were given, prefixed with the words, "Thus saith the Lord." This was completely misleading and deceitful on the part of Moses since most of the rules had originally been set forth by Jethro and then agreed upon by the council of elders while on the mountain. The group had not actually seen God on the mount, nor had there been a dark cloud that covered the mount, nor had God ever given Moses the commandments on a stone tablet as the Bible describes. These commandments were simply old rules of the Midianites.

After Moses had established the priesthood in Aaron's house, Korah, Dathan, Abiram, On, and 250 other renowned and respected men of the congregation objected to this. They asked why only the tribe of Levi should be favored with doing little work, being clothed in soft raiment, and eating sumptuously everyday from the remnants of the sacrifices. After all, were not all people holy? And should not all people help till the ground? So, the next day Moses ordered these men to appear before the tabernacle and then commanded the Levites to slay them with fire. Thus, all 250 respected men were burned to death in front of the tabernacle by the Levites, and because of this slaughter great fear fell on all of the people. This is the way Moses used force and fear to stabilize his rule. However, in the book of *Numbers* this incident has been written to describe that Korah, Dathan, Abiram, and their families were swallowed up by a pit that opened in the earth. After that it is explained that a fire came from the Lord that burned up the other 250 men. In this way, the Hebrew writers described the event to appear like a supernatural occurrence.

Thereafter, according to Jasher, Moses established many types of animal sacrifices, saying that they were ordained by the authority of the Lord. Moses made it so that the sacrifices had to be performed by the people in order for them to become cleansed of various sins. Oxen, bulls, rams, and even doves would often be sacrificed to God in the tabernacle as a means of atonement. Even a woman who gave birth to a child was expected to offer a lamb for sacrifice in order to become cleansed. Of course, this is totally illogical when viewed with real knowledge of *karma* and the soul. The killing of animals does not cleanse the soul, but only implicates one more deeply in sinful reactions. This only displays the ignorance of the customs and the mentality of the people, and how little they understood of anything really spiritual. Later, the Bible indicates that God condemned such sacrifices:

> To what purpose is the multitude of your sacrifices unto me? Saith the Lord: I am full of the burnt offerings of rams, and the fat of fed beasts; and I delight not in the blood of bullocks, or of lambs, or of goats. . . When ye spread forth your hands, I will hide Mine eyes from you: yea, when ye make many prayers, I will not hear, for your hands are full of blood. . . If ye be willing and obedient, ye shall eat the good of the land. But if ye refuse and rebel, ye shall be devoured with the sword: for the mouth of the Lord hath spoken it. (*Isaiah* 1.11,15,19-20)

The son of Shelomith, showing a little genuine spiritual understanding, accused Moses in front of the congregation of misleading the people. He said all these sacrifices and things that Moses had established were not actually said by God, but were imaginations of evil. Moses obviously knew the man was correct, but, again calling on the Levites, Moses commanded that the son of Shelomith be taken from the camp and stoned to death, "for the Lord hath spoken." And so they did. Obviously, Moses was not a man with much tolerance, nor did he exhibit much spiritual purity or any inclination for philosophical debate. Force was the medium by which Moses established himself as the voice of the Lord.

In any case, these are the stories that are provided about the characteristics and qualities of the original patriarchs of Jewish culture. And we can see that the *Book of Jasher* gives a very different perspective of how the sacrifices and commandments were established when compared with the descriptions found in *Exodus* and *Leviticus*. Through the *Book of Jasher* we can see how the rabbis who originally compiled the books that are attributed to Moses included many embellishments to make the Bible stories more extraordinary. And we can only guess how many other stories were also given special treatment to make it appear as if God had directly conferred with Moses or shown special favor when actually such incidents may never have taken place at all.

Another example of this is in the story of the exodus. In *Prickard's Historical Records*, it is explained how Choeremon the historian recorded that while the Jews were living in Goshen, Egypt was infested with a disease. In order for Egypt to be rid of this disease, using the advice of Phritiphantes the scribe, the Pharaoh had the Jews driven out of the country.

Further elaboration is given in S. F. Dunlap's *Vestiges of the Spirit History of Man.* It is said that the Jews hated and did not worship the Egyptian gods, and the Egyptian people considered the Jews to be dirty and unclean foreigners, which, for all practical purposes, is confirmed when one regards the laws given in *Leviticus.* On the other hand, it is known that the Egyptians practiced a high level of cleanliness. The priests bathed every day, shaved their bodies, practiced circumcision, and wore clean white linen. They looked on the Jews as being worth only the most menial of tasks. Leprosy was rampant among the Jewish people, and the disease was considered to be displeasing to the Egyptian gods. So, the Oracle of Ammon ordered the Pharaoh to purify the land by driving the Jews out into the wilderness. The more noble of Jews are said to have followed Cadmus and Danaus to Greece, while the rest of them followed Moses to Palestine. So here is another reason why the Jews carried a great deal of animosity toward their ancestor Hindus, the Pharaohs of Egypt. They were rebellious of the Egyptians, but they had also been driven out of the land. Here again we can see a vast difference between the legends that come from the Jewish tradition and the history of it from alternative sources.

In *Exodus* we read how the Egyptian Pharaoh pursued Moses and his people out of Egypt to the sea where the water magically divided to let the Jews pass through. Then while the Egyptians were in the midst of the sea, the water came together to drown all the Egyptians. But, historically, there is no Egyptian record of any Pharaoh taking his army to chase after the Jews, nor of any Pharaoh drowning in the Red Sea. Neither is there any record of any Pharaoh killing all the eldest sons of the Jews while they were in Goshen. Such events surely would have been recorded somewhere if they had actually happened. But why would an army chase after a group of people who had been ordered to leave the country because they were considered dirty and diseased? Thus, it is quite unlikely that this episode happened the way the Hebrew writers depicted. Furthermore, the mummy of the Pharaoh who reigned during the Jewish captivity in Egypt, King Ramses II, the third king of the 19th dynasty, was found in a cave near Thebes in August of 1881 in a state of near perfect preservation. So, obviously, he did not drown in the Red Sea. Therefore, the stories in *Exodus* must have been written and embellished in a way that would fit more closely with other extraordinary legends that the Jewish writers wanted to include in their scripture to establish the superior significance of their culture. After all, it is known amongst those who have studied the history of Jewish religion that the Hebrew writers had little history to use as their own and, thus, borrowed from many traditions and legends of neighboring cultures.

For example, in *Exodus* it is described how Moses performed many miracles. However, many of these are the same as those of Bacchus, one of the early Greek gods who is described in the hymns of Orpheus, the earliest of Greek poets. Bacchus also had a staff which could change into a serpent. He also passed through the Red Sea without getting wet. He also drew water by hitting a rock with his staff, and he was led by a light during the night, similar to the pillar of fire that is said to have led Moses and his people. Bacchus was also the law-giver of his people and the laws were written on two tables of stone, just as it is said to have happened later with Moses. And as a baby, Bacchus was also put into a boat on a river and was discovered by a woman who adopted him. Thus, there are significant parallels between the early legends of Bacchus and Moses which could not be merely coincidental.

Another legend was that of the great flood with Noah and his ark, which was supposed to have taken place near 2348 B.C., although histories of that period in Egypt and elsewhere make no mention of any great flood. The biblical flood was copied by the Hebrews from the Chaldean version, as was written by Berosus, the Chaldean historian, with the later biblical version having only a few differences. The Hebrews did the same with the story of the creation. The account of the creation found in *Genesis* is very similar to not only that described in the *Zend Avesta* of Zoroastrianism, but also to the Etruscan and Persian legends, as well as the Babylonian legend of creation which existed 1,500 years before the Hebrew version. Many aspects of these legends were carry-overs from the Vedic descriptions. Without such duplicating, the Jews were bereft of these histories in their own tradition.

Although the Pentateuch (from Greek, meaning "five scrolls") or the Torah (from Hebrew, meaning "instruction") is often referred to as being written by Moses (consisting of *Genesis, Exodus, Leviticus, Numbers,* and *Deuteronomy*), Moses actually had little to do with its writing, especially its present form. Though Moses was Hebrew, he had been raised as an Egyptian in his youth and was known to have been an adept in the ancient Egyptian mysteries. It is said that he used Egyptian hieroglyphics when he wrote the original portions of the Pentateuch, but the meaning of the hieroglyphs was soon lost. So when the Jews first compiled the Pentateuch and needed to translate it into Hebrew, it was an almost impossible task. Many errors were made, not only in the translation but also in the attempt to understand the highly esoteric meaning of the message itself. Thus, many things that were expressed in the language of the adepts, which the Jews were not, were misunderstood. So how were these books written and from where did the writers get their ideas and adaptations of legends to include in the Pentateuch?

Modern research has discovered that the first four books of the Bible were originally written by four authors. By noticing differences in style, language, phrases, interests, along with various contradictions within these four books, it becomes obvious that these books are not the writings of Moses, or even a single author. They were the works of several authors, with additional embellishments made to them later. The original works must have been written before the Assyrians destroyed and exiled Israel in 722 B.C. From the content of the books, some of them could have been written between 848 and 722, or even from 922.

Dr. Knappert, in his book *The Religion of Israel,* gives some additional indication of how this developed. First of all, there were three different periods in which the books of the Pentateuch were written and modified. The first period of writing was around 722 B.C. It was during this time that many of the Jews had been captives of Salmanassar, King of Assyria, when they learned the legends of the Babylonians, Persians, and others, and adopted many of these accounts into their own recorded history. Before this time the Jews had no divine or sacred scripture since the early tribes of Israel did little writing.

Nothing changed until 620 B.C. when a priest wrote another book of law that was included in *Deuteronomy* and labeled authoritative by King Josiah. It was Hilkiah who was probably the writer of the book he claimed to have found in the temple. To add authority to it, he said it was somehow written by Moses 800 years earlier. However, the phraseology was that of a recently written book, not of one 800 years old. Nonetheless, objections to this were ignored since Josiah had been won over by the Jews of the period. Thus, the book became part of the Pentateuch.

The third period of biblical writing was done by Ezra around 444 B.C. when he made additions to the Pentateuch in the form of various stories and laws that he had learned from the priests of Babylon. When he finished adjusting the Pentateuch, it stayed in that form and is what we find today. It is Ezra who is said to have rewritten the books of the Old Testament and claimed them to be Holy Scriptures, books given by the inspiration of the Spirit of God. Only from that time on were they considered divine. The Apocryphal book of *Esdras* has an account of this. Nonetheless, the Pentateuch underwent a few more changes when the King of Egypt, Ptolemy Philadelphus, ordered that it be translated into Greek in 287 B.C. In any case, the Pentateuch as we find it today was not written by any one writer, nor is it as old as many people like to believe, nor was it given by the inspiration of God. It is the result of slow and purposeful development.

Most scholars agree that the Old Testament was written by a wide variety of people, and sometimes describes contradictory accounts of the same events. Thus, it becomes very difficult to separate factual history from embellished legends.

The books of the Old Testament are divided into three sections. The section called the Earlier Prophets consists of *Joshua, Judges, Samuel,* and *Kings.* The Later Prophets include *Isaiah, Jeremiah, Ezekiel,* and twelve minor books. The Writings consist of *Psalms, Proverbs, Job, Song of Songs, Ruth, Lamentations, Ecclesiastes, Esther, Daniel, Ezra, Nehemiah,* and *Chronicles.* These books are said to have already been in existence before the time of around 287 B.C. in the forms of songs, letters, and prophetic books of the Persian kings that had been collected by Nehemiah. And according to Professor Breasted, a number of *Psalms* and the *Book of Proverbs* are based on the older Egyptian texts. Anyway, the followers of Ezra, the scribes in Jerusalem, collected and edited these texts and then added them to the other sacred books. Thus, by understanding how these books were put together, we can see that the Old Testament, rather than being the embodiment of Jewish history and law, is actually the retainer of much of the ancient Chaldean theology and many Babylonian legends, although it was embellished and molded in a Jewish fashion.

Looking at the history of Jewish society, we need to first see the conditions prior to the rise of the Jewish culture, between 1200 and 722 B.C. The area at this time had what people now would call the pagan religions. This was simply the carry-overs from the once ruling Vedic culture many years previous. Fifty thousand tablets were found at Ninevah alone, and another three thousand tablets were found at the Canaanite city of Ugarit. Through these, scholars can read the hymns, prayers, legends, places where they worshiped, and see how the gods were depicted in their art. The religion at the time was close to nature. Gods and objects of worship included the sky and wind, the sun, the sea, fertility, and death. In the Vedic culture these demigods would be Indra, Surya, Varuna, Durga, and Yamaraja. The deities that the people erected were like the icons you would find in a church or temple. The chief god at the time was El, a male and a ruler. He was the head of the other gods that were associated with nature. Later, the God of Israel was Yahweh, also a male and a ruler, which they accepted only after they had been in Egypt. The people of Israel spoke of him in terms of his acts in history, as if he had actually appeared on earth and influenced the people with his deeds. This would corroborate the historical perspective that it had been the ancient Vedic King Yayati who had become deified as Yahweh.

During the 11th through the 8th centuries B.C., it was under kings Saul, David, and Solomon, that the kingdom of Israel reached its zenith. David came from the tribe of Judah, the largest of the tribes. It was under David's rule in which Jerusalem became his capital. Before David captured the city, it had belonged to the Jebusites. Thus, the town had been a major city belonging to other cultures before David took it.

After Solomon's death in 977 B.C., the society broke in two. Ten tribes calling themselves Israel went to the north and made Samaria their capital. They gave up the law that was supposed to have been given by Moses and again worshiped the Canaanite gods. This kingdom lasted until 722 B.C. when the people were conquered by Assyrians and were taken away.

The tribes of Judah and Benjamin stayed in Palestine with Jerusalem as their capital. This kingdom lasted until 586 B.C. when Nebuchadnezzar came, destroyed Solomon's temple in Jerusalem, and took the people as captives to Babylon. It was during this time of their captivity and the destruction of the First Temple when they began to anticipate the coming of a Messiah descending from the house of David, who would reorganize their nation and bring the kingdom of God to earth. Some of them returned to Jerusalem after Cyrus freed them when he conquered Babylon in 538 B.C. Those who returned rebuilt the temple, but Greek thought with its more abstract concepts of God was already present then and political and religious factions developed. It was while the Jews were in Babylonia that they incorporated such ideas as the resurrection of the body and belief in

Satan, and it was only after the conquests of Alexander the Great (323 B.C.) did they begin to accept the precept of the eternality of the soul.

Thus, as we can see from the above information, the Jewish theology was slow to develop, and it was only due to their exposure to other cultures that helped them form it into a more comprehensive philosophy, and to develop their own embellished history. Judaism had long ago given up its connection with the Vedic knowledge and legends in its earliest stages, and especially during its travels through Egypt and the Middle East. Nonetheless, it still had to again, unknowingly, accept portions of it in order to have a more thorough and comprehensive philosophy, though it was adopted indirectly through its contact with Chaldean, Babylonian, Zoroastrian, and other neighboring cultures. It was these other cultures that held legends and knowledge that were more directly connected with the remnants of Vedic civilization.

MORE VEDIC LINKS IN JUDAISM

One of the primary connections between Vedic culture and Judaism is that the name Judaism is linguistically related to Yeduism, or Yaduism, which points to the Yadus, also known as the Yadavas, who were a clan that belonged to Krishna's tribe. The letter "Y" changes to "J" in popular pronunciation. Through the years the term Yadavas changed to Jadavas and then to Judaists and shortened to Jews. Even today in India we find variations of that name among its people in the form of surnames such as Yadav, Jadhav, and Jadeja.

One very interesting reference supplies evidence that the Jewish people originated in India. It is from a footnote from Volume I (p. 346) of *Marco Polo's Travels*, translated by Sir Henry Yule. It states: "Much has been written about the ancient settlement of Jews at Kaifungfu (in China). One of the most interesting papers on the subject is in Chinese Repository, Vol. XX. It gives the translation of a Chinese Jewish inscription. . . Here is a passage: 'With respect to the Israelitish religion we find an inquiry that its first ancestor, Adam, came originally from India and that during the (period of the) Chau state, the Sacred Writings were already in existence. The sacred writings embodying eternal reason consist of 53 sections. The principles therein contained are very abstruse and the Eternal Reason therein revealed is very mysterious, being treated with the same veneration as Heaven. The founder of the religion is Abraham, who is considered the first teacher of it. Then came Moses, who established the law and handed down the Sacred Writings. After his time this religion entered China."

Therefore, the Jewish writings, being held with the same veneration as heaven and handed down by Abraham, implies that these were originally the *Vedas* that had been handed down by the Vedic demigod Brahma. Brahma is spelled as

Abraham in the Jewish tradition. Thus, the essential Vedic laws and legends, or whatever the Jewish people kept of the Vedic tradition, reappears in the form of the Talmud. The Talmud was a study of the Mishna, which is said to encapsulate the oral tradition of Moses. The oral law had been handed down by Moses' successors. The Talmud includes Jewish law, but also topics of life after death, immortality, the will of God, etc, most of which can be traced back to the Vedic philosophy. Even the name *Talmud* is derived from the Sanskrit language. *Tal* signifies the palm, and *Mud*, from the Sanskrit *Mudra*, signifies the imprint or script. Therefore, Talmud refers to a palm-leaf manuscript. Tradition holds that the ancient Vedic scriptures were written on palm leaves, which, it is figured, the original Jewish people continued to do after they left India.

Further evidence of the outside influence on the Jewish people is presented by John M. Allegro in his book *The Chosen People* (p. 20). "The names of the patriarchal heroes, as that of God Himself, are non-Semetic. . . and go back to the earliest known civilization in the near East, indeed of the world." This is an important observation which points out that the names of the Jewish Deity came from other than the Jewish tradition and emanated from the oldest civilization, namely the Vedic culture.

Another example of outside influence is the Jewish emblem known as the Star of David. This consists of two interlocking triangles, one pointing up, the other down, which is a Tantric Vedic symbol. It is called Rangawali, or Rangoli. It is also a simplified form of the Sri Yantra, which is connected with the Goddess Sri, or Sri Lakshmi Devi, the goddess of fortune and wife of Lord Vishnu. Even its name *David* is the Sanskrit word Devi-d, meaning "bestowed by the Mother Goddess." This emblem is also drawn in front of many orthodox Hindu homes in rice powder or chalk every morning after the house is washed, and especially on holidays.

Even the name "Adam," the first created man according to the Talmud, is a name derived from the Sanskrit *aadim*, which means the first or most ancient man. The Islamic word "aadmi" is also derived in the same way, signifying a descendent of Aadim, or Brahma.

The name "Israel" is connected with the Sanskrit *Iswar-alaya*, meaning the "abode (*alaya*) of God (*Iswar*)." Similarly, even the holiest city of the Jewish community, Jerusalem, derives its name from Yerusaleim, which comes from the Sanskrit words *Yedu-Ishalayam*. *Yedu* refers to "Yadu," or Krishna who appeared in the dynasty of Yadu, *Isha* means God directly, and *Alayam* means "place of." Thus, the name simply means "the place of God, Krishna." In popular parlance in the West, "J" often replaces the "Y", and when "D" is replaced by the "R", the name *Yedu-Ishalayam* becomes Jerusalem. Jerusalem got its name as *Yedu-Ishalayam* because the town sprung up around the Dome of the Rock, the octogonal temple that was once a place for the worship of Lord Krishna.

Another theory that some people have considered about the Indian origin of the Jews, or Yadavas, is that they headed toward the region of Suria, now called

Syria, when they left the kingdom of Dwaraka in Gujarat after the *Mahabharata* war. Dwaraka submerged into the sea just after everyone left the island when Krishna left this world. All the tribes of people scattered from Dwaraka in various directions. The Yadavas moved toward what became known as Suria, which reflects that their chief Deity was "Sur," which means Divinity, God, or Krishna. The name Suria, or Syria, is also connected to the Vedic Surya, the sun-god, who is also accepted as a representative of the Supreme Deity.

Even the *Encyclopaedia Judaica* (p. 108, Vol. 9) mentions that the area of, "Erez Israel and (central-southern) Syria were referred to as Horru chiefly as an ethnic term after the Horites who inhabited the country." Horites is the mispronunciation of Harites, or those who worship Hari, Krishna. Thus, Krishna has been a universal Deity, which also proves the universality of Vedic culture. This realization should induce archeologists to review their finds to redraw the contours of world Vedic culture.

Though the Jews have long lost contact with their guardian Deity, Lord Krishna, and their Vedic spiritual heritage due to 5000 years of wandering and war, from the above evidence we can begin to understand the influence the Vedic culture initially had on them. We can see that originally they must have been descendants and a part of the Vedic culture and followers of its principles from many hundreds of years ago.

CHAPTER TEN

The Vedic Influence in Europe and Russia

In this chapter we will present information that will make it clear that Vedic civilization existed in pre-Christian times in England, France, Scandinavia, Russia, and all over Europe. The tendency of European scholars to bundle all prior civilization with the contemptuous labels of "heathen" or "pagan," and consequently nullify the legitimacy of all systematic study of it, is one of the most sinister characteristics of current Western scholarship. However, even the names "heathen" and "pagan" show a tendency toward Vedic culture. The word "heathen" is referred to those who live close to nature, plants and herbs. The name "pagan," which meant a country person, is linguistically connected to "bhagan" which becomes *Bhagwan*, the Vedic name for the Supreme Deity. So pagans were those connected with worshipers of *Bhagwan*, meaning Vishnu or Krishna, and the associated demigods. This is further verified in the fact that there is evidence that the Italians, Greeks, Iranians, and even the Slavonic people offered sacrifices to their gods through the fire as found in the Indian Vedic tradition. The Slavs also called the fire Ogon, similar to the name of the Vedic demigod of fire, Agni.

Before Christianity, Vedic culture had access to all lands around the globe. This is proved by several finds, such as the naval bell with a Tamil inscription found on the sea-bed off Australia. There was also a ship of the B.C. era with the image of Buddha on it found under the ice-bound sea near Denmark. Ancient statues and temples and cities bearing an identification with India and Vedic culture have been located in almost all continents and even in remote islands. References are available about Hindu naval experts assisting people in Africa and other continents to safely navigate the high seas. The chronicles of the Greek Periplus indicate that India shipped a variety of products to Greece. These included spices, high quality textiles, ivory, gems, and iron. Rome also supplied many products to India in these trades. While trading in the Mediterranean area, India did much trade with Egypt, as evidenced from the great stock of 14th century Egyptian and Syrian gold and silver coins found in Broach, Gujarat.

Images and paintings of Krishna in His mother's arms were worldwide. Only later was it adopted by early Christians to depict Mother Mary holding baby Jesus. Such images and the Vedic books and remnants of Vedic civilization throughout

Europe were destroyed by Christian invaders. Thus, in some ways you could say we have forgotten this knowledge of our ancient roots because we have been forced to forget it.

How this destruction took place is explained by Godfrey Higgins in his book, *The Celtic Druids* (p.164). He says that Christians did not always burn and plunder, but subtlety took in whole communities along with their customs and stamped them as Christian. "The monks of Roman and Greek churches were remnants of the sect of the Essenes converted to Christianity, and much degraded and corrupted from their excellent predecessors. . . When they became converts they formed an odd mixture of the two religions. In what they called monasteries, many of them built before the Christian era, a day had from time immemorial been dedicated to the god Sol (the Sun-god) as his birthday, and that he bore the epithet Lord. . . Thus came the 25th December, the heathen festival of the God Sol to be selected as the birthday of Christ, and the Druidic festival of the winter Solstice to become a Christian rite. . . the 'birth' of the Sun on 25th December was kept from India to the Ultima Thule. . . these ceremonies partook of the same character."

So from this it is apparent that many of the Christian festivals were carry-overs from the Vedic culture from India, which also recognized the importance of the sun, the solstices, and so on. Therefore, as the Vedic culture had reached all lands, all ancient people throughout the world, whatever may have been the name of their community or region, were united in a common culture and observed familiar festivals. It could be that the same festivals had different emphasis in different regions, but the main culture was the Vedic culture or a close derivative of it.

Other Vedic customs also were known in Europe, such as removing shoes when entering homes or temples. Removing the shoes before entering a temple or one's home is still the standard Vedic practice in India. In Chapter Three of the book of *Exodus* we read, "The angel of the Lord appeared unto him in a flame of fire out of the midst of a bush. He said, 'Moses, Moses put off thy shoes from off thy feet for the place whereon thou standeth is holy ground.'" The evidence about this in the Bible is a clear indication of the prevalence of Vedic customs in pre-Christian Europe.

Furthermore, old pictures of pre-Christian life in Europe reveal that people used to wear robes, such as the traditional *dhoti* and shoulder cloth commonly seen amongst holy men and temple priests of India. Such pictures also show a holy thread slung across the left shoulder and display marks of ash or sandal-paste on the foreheads and torsos. These are all unmistakable signs of the earlier Vedic influence.

Other traces of the ancient Vedic impact can be recognized throughout Europe. For example, in language, the word navy comes from the Sanskrit *naa-vi*, which means "a collection of boats," and navigability is a Sanskrit compound meaning "that which has the capacity to allow ships maneuverability." Places like

Solonica, Veronica, and Thessalonica refer to the presence of armies since the Sanskrit term *fonica* means an army. The same goes for Dorchester and Lancaster because the suffix *ster* is a Sanskrit term meaning "a place of arms." Places like Kilkenny and Kilpatric mean the place of forts because the Sanskrit prefix *kila* or *qila* means a fort. The name Atlantic is derived from the Sanskrit word *a-tal-lantic*, meaning "a sea of great depth." And Mediterranean in Sanskrit refers to a body of water in the middle of land since it divides Europe from Asia or Africa. Ramsgate in England is the same as the word *Ramsdvar*, meaning "door to the township of Rama," one of the incarnations of Lord Krishna. And Rome, which is spelled Roma in Italy, refers to Lord Rama. Paintings from episodes of the *Ramayana* found in early Italian homes support this conclusion. The city of Ravenna in Italy, said to be founded after Ravana, Rama's adversary in the *Ramayana*, also corroborates this. Germany calls itself Deutschland and in Holland the people are called the Dutch because of their ancestral link with the Daityas, the descendants of Diti who were generally opposed to the Vedic demigods. Budapest is the ancient Buddhaprastha, the Hungarian city dedicated to Buddha. And the name Hungary has a linguistic connection with the Sanskrit term *shringary*, meaning "a beautiful hilly country." The term *arya* is also connected to the word *eire* as found in the name Ireland, which is the land furthest west that is known to have been reached by the Aryans in ancient times. Many similarities exist in the Lithuanian language, which very closely resembles Sanskrit, as does Slavic. Thus, we can see how many references to Vedic influence throughout Europe remain to this day.

Many similarities in European religion and philosophy can be found in the Vedic teachings, one of which is the respect for the sun as a representative of the Supreme. Sun worship was central to many European cultures from ancient to Roman times. Considering the many resemblances between the old pre-Christian and Vedic cultures in language, religions, gods, goddesses, rituals, and legends, as well as the many similarities in modern Christianity, which I explain in the following sections and chapters, we can rightly conclude that the Vedic culture is the real spiritual heritage of the European people.

From the above evidence, which is only the beginning, we can surmise that the Vedic people from India either migrated into Europe, or conquered it after the great flood and ruled it for many years. Manu was the Vedic progenitor of the post-flood world. The word "man" is a reference to being descendants of Manu. Even the term "humanity" is derived from the Sanskrit term *su-man-iti*, which means being endowed with a good and balanced mind.

The reason why Europe became so disconnected from the Vedic culture is that the *Mahabharata* war of Kuruksetra, in which tribes from all over the world participated, caused a complete breakdown of the worldwide Vedic social, educational, and administrative system. The farther away an area was, the more cut off it became. So until around 3800 B.C., Europe, Russia, and other regions had an identical civilization. Thereafter, Europe, West Asia, Africa, and other regions and islands exhibited only broken bits of what once was a universal Vedic culture. After a few thousand years, along with numerous wars, came Christianity and Islam. Through terror and torture they converted large masses of people from whatever was left of the ancient Vedic system and traditions. Then Europe and Russia put whatever they remembered of their ancient Vedic culture farther behind them until they completely forgot what their connection once was.

As the influence of these new cultures and religions grew, the knowledge that had been provided by the previous Vedic culture was forgotten. On page 315 of *Collectania De Rebus Hibernicus* by Lt. Gen. Charles Vallancey, we find it mentioned that, "It is a remarkable circumstance on record that when the rest of Europe through ignorance or forgetfulness, had no knowledge of the true figure of the earth, in the 8th century the rotundity and true formation of it should have been taught in the Irish schools."

In view of this, the general notion that 400 years ago Galileo first discovered that the earth was round and moving turns out to be unworthy of credence. The Irish schools had already been teaching this. The rest of Europe had forgotten such ancient knowledge which had been known and taught in Vedic culture for thousands of years prior to Galileo's discovery. Furthermore, we can understand from this that it was Christianity that assisted in dismantling the ancient scientific, Vedic educational system throughout the world, especially in Europe, and ushered in an era of uninformed dogmas. For example, Christianity decided for itself that the world was created in 4004 B.C. (and whatever other dates that have been adopted and changed from time to time) and on that basis mounted its make-believe axioms with which to tutor the public. This is what helped bring in the "dark ages" that followed.

Another problem, as pointed out by Godfrey Higgins on page 14 of his book, *The Celtic Druids*, is that histories of early Europe that now exist, such as the Memoirs of Caesar's, have probably been copied by Christian priests. This would allow them to forge history in the most favorable way for them, as well as add various superstitious rituals to the earlier customs of the time that would seem most barbaric and inhumane. This would assist them in glorifying Christianity while condemning any previous culture as being pagan, heathen, or demoniac. Unfortunately, this aspect of European history seems to be inadequately known.

Nonetheless, the whole of Europe, including Russia, still bear indelible traces of its ancient Vedic culture. However, society seems to remain steeped in ignorance about its primordial Vedic past. Therefore, people need to be told about the pre-Christian Vedic knowledge and traditions that once pervaded the region. So, in this chapter we will begin to uncover the information that reveals how much the European region is still influenced by Vedic culture.

THE VEDIC INFLUENCE IN BRITAIN

How the Vedic influence was felt in such far away places as England and Scandinavia is explained in *The Aryans* by V. Gordon Childe. He relates that in Britain, shortly after 2000 B.C., a people conquered the territory who were noted for their use of battle-axes. It was during this time that a period of rapid development began. It is now understood that these people were mixed with Aryans who promoted what is now called the Western type of civilization that continued to develop.

L. A. Waddell also writes that the Trojans and their civilization were of Sumerian-Aryan origin. When the Trojan amulets were deciphered they were disclosed to be of the same religion with the same invocations and deity symbols as on the amulets of the seals of the Indus Valley. These symbols were also the same as those on the ancient monuments in Britain. And recorded history states that Britain was first colonized by King Brutus the Trojan in about 1103 B.C.

Further Vedic influence in Britain was also brought by the Celts. Celts were Indo-Europeans who first emerged as a separate people near the source of the Danube about 1000 B.C. They swept over central Europe and arrived in Britain about 800 B.C. Ward Rutherford, in his book *Celtic Mythology*, points out many similarities between the Celtic and the early Hindu or Vedic traditions. He suggests that though the Celts and Vedic followers were separated by a large mass of land, they nonetheless must have originally come from the same source. Furthermore, Waddell, in *The Makers of Civilization*, provides some evidence that Saint George, Saint Andrew, Saint Michael, and the legend of King Arthur and the Holy Grail, as well as the Thor-Odin legend of the Britains and Scandinavians, were of Sumerian-Aryan origin.

A point that further corroborates this is that according to Celtic mythology, the Celts worshiped two main gods, Dagda, or Eochaid Ollathair, as "Father of All," and Lug. The two primary goddesses were Danu, or Anu or Brigit, and Macha. Danu was known as the wife of the Vedic sage Kashyapa Muni, one of the early progenitors described in the Vedic texts.

As we look at one place to another, we often find that the present name of a country is related or a derivative of its original Vedic name. Such is the case with England. For example, the name Isle of Angelsey in Britain derives from the Sanskrit name of Lord Vishnu as *Angulesh*, meaning the Lord of the Anguli country. The British Isles were designated as *Angulisthan*, referring to a place (*sthan*) that is a finger-size country when compared to Europe, which is likened to a palm of a hand. It is this term, *Angulisthan*, that later came to be pronounced as Anguliand, and then England. The name Britain also comes from the Sanskrit *Brihat-sthan*, meaning a great place or great islands. Therefore, England was once under the Sanskrit speaking Vedic administration that gave it its original name.

Many names of England's cities also have Sanskrit affiliations. For example, London was a very ancient Vedic capital. Its ancient Sanskrit name was

Nandanium, which is Sanskrit for a pleasing habitation. In Roman times it was misspelled as Londonium. This was later abbreviated to London. In European language the letter "L" often replaces the Sanskrit "N." That is why the Sanskrit name *Svetanana* (the fair-faced) is pronounced in Russia as Svetlana.

Other names are in affiliation with Lord Rama, an incarnation of Krishna. Towns such as Ramston and Ramsgate are directly connected with Lord Rama, at least in name. Personal names such as Ramsey McDonald and Sir Winston Ramsay are akin to the Indian name Ramsahay. The word *ramrod* is derived from the stumps of huge trees that were used as rods by Rama's troops to break open the gates of Lanka.

The Sanskrit suffix of *puri*, as found in such Indian cities as Sudamapuri or Jagannatha Puri, is changed to "bury" in England, which means a township. We find this in the English cities of Shrewsbury, Ainsbury, and Waterbury. Salisbury's hilly topography is also proof that it is a corrupt form of the Sanskrit term *Shail-eesh-pury*, which means a hilly area with a Vedic temple. Canterbury is also linguistically connected to what would be the Sanskrit word *Sankarpury*, meaning a township of Lord Sankar, Shiva. This is when you pronounce the "C" as an "S" and replace the "T" with a "K" in the name Canter, which is not uncommon in changes between Sanskrit and English. This would also indicate that prior to the British Isles turning Christian in the sixth century A.D., Canterbury used to be the seat of a Vedic spiritual leader. Thus, the Archbishop of Canterbury used to be a Vedic priest and teacher, or a Sankaracharya, from which comes the name Sankarpury.

Another connection is the English termination of "shire," which is a corrupt form of the Sanskrit word *shwar*. This is in reference to Indian towns known for being ancient Shiva centers, such as Tryambakeshwar, Lankeshwar, Ghrishneshwar, and many others. In England we find towns such as Lancashire, Pembrokeshire, Hampshire, and Wiltshire. Devonshire comes from the Sanskrit *Devaneswar*, meaning Lord of the gods. Such towns very well may have had large Shiva temples, which is why they are still named the way they are.

In Scotland we find the town of Marayshire, the name of which is a corruption of the Sanskrit deity Moreshwar. The place is an ancient Vedic site as can be determined from the figures of bulls still seen carved in the rocks. The bull Nandi is the carrier of Lord Shiva. The place must have had many Shiva temples that have since been destroyed by Christian zealots.

We can also compare the name of Edinburgh to Sanskrit. The *Veda* had come to be pronounced as Eda after the advent of Christianity in Europe. The *Eddas*, Scandinavia's ancient-most scripture, is an echo of the Sanskrit *Vedas*. Edinburgh in Scotland is a corruption of the Sanskrit term *Vedinpur*, meaning City of the *Vedas*.

In India, walled townships and forts are known and pronounced as "Cote," which is the same as *Kot* as in Siddhakot, Agrakot, Lohakot, Bagalkot, and Amarkot. In England, too, walled townships and castles still bear the Sanskrit names "Cote" as may be seen in names like Charlcote, Northcote, Heathcote, and Kingscote.

The famous horse races at Ascot are not a chance sport of that place. The name Ascot comes from the Sanskrit name *Aswacot*, meaning city of horses, which is a legacy of the ancient Vedic Kshatriya administration.

This shows these names were given by ancient Sanskrit-speaking people when they ruled over this region. So it is not surprising that parts of England should still bear the Sanskrit terminations even after all historical traces of India's sway over England have been seemingly wiped out.

There are many more English words with their roots in ancient Sanskrit, as explained in *Some Blunders of Indian Historical Research*, page 251. *Pada* is Sanskrit for "foot," which is connected with a range of English words, such as Pedeatrics, pedestal, pedestrian, and biped. Another Sanskrit root is *dant*, which means tooth, from which we get dentist, dentistry, and dental. Another Sanskrit term is *mrityu*, which means death, from which we get mortuary, morgue, mortal, and immortal. The word "man" derives from the Sanskrit word *manas*, meaning the mind, or a thinking and rational being. The English "door" is Sanskrit *dwar*. The English term "Monarch" comes from the Sanskrit term *Manawarka*, which means the sun among humans. In Vedic tradition the monarch was regarded as the sun of glory, power, and sustainer of the realm. A list of some more comparable words include the following:

ENGLISH	SANSKRIT
Ca-tholic	Sa-Devalik (he or she being a temple devotee)
Friar	Pravar (sage)
Convent	Sonvent (holy establishment)
David	Devi-da (bestowed by the goddess)
Church	Churcha (place of religious discourse)
Churchill	Churcha-cholak (one who conducts sermons)
Papa or Pope	Papa-ha (absolver of sin)
Constantine	Kaunsa-Daityan (Kaunsa of the Daitya clan, adversary of Krishna)

A whole unsuspected host of Sanskrit words continuing to exist in English is very strong evidence of the Vedic Indians having once held sway in Europe. More of such examples can be found in Chapter Six of this volume.

More evidence of England's Vedic heritage can be recognized by the fact that while rebuilding the war-ravaged areas of London after World War II an image of the Indian demigod Mitras, the sun, was found buried under the foundation of an old building. It has been said that Romans had introduced sun worship in Britain during their rule there. All this means that either Vedic Indians themselves had traveled to England, or the Vedic culture traveled to England via Greece and Rome.

In a similar vein, the British Museum of London has an exhibit of a peacock mosaic that had been dug up in the British Isles. Though the peacock belongs to tropical regions and is considered sacred, and is also the mount of goddess Sarasvati and Lord Murugan in the Vedic tradition, it was a popular motif in ancient, Vedic Europe. This is one of the visual proofs of the Vedic past of Great Britain.

Furthermore, evidence of the Vedic practice of cremation being prevalent in ancient Britain is found in the form of urns containing sacred ashes preserved under elaborate stone shrines.

Such religious carry-overs can be seen in other ways too, as explained on page 12 of *Some Missing Chapters of World History* by P. N. Oak. "St. Paul's cathedral in London, rebuilt by Christopher Wren after the great fire of London over 300 years ago, still retains several pre-Christian traditions. St. Paul's used to be a Gopal or Chrisn [Krishna] temple. Here are some of the proofs: Its central altar is separated from the backside wall by a narrow perambulatory passage. [This was for allowing the people to circumambulate around the altar, a typical custom in Vedic temples.] The main altar enshrines not Jesus but the eight directional Vedic cross. In front of the altar, some distance away, is a golden eagle on a stand. The eagle is the [Garuda] mount of Lord Chrisn. Overhead on the curved rafter ledge supporting the ceiling are Latin prayers beginning with the Vedic incantation OM painted in bold block capitals. Along the walls inside are sketched in bold relief sages and others taking a holy dip in the river Ganges." Therefore, this would seem to indicate that many of the most important of present-day Christian holy places or churches were once Vedic holy shrines and temples.

The practice of tucking a feather in the European hat, and the feather seen even in Muslim crowns originates in the imitation of Lord Krishna who is the ancient-most person known to wear a (peacock) feather in his cap or crown. That shows how the ancient world revered Lord Krishna.

It is also understood that the ancient Vedic Kshatriya administrators had in their employ traditional singers and poets who were known as *Bhaats* or Bards. It is those same words which continue to be used in English as Poet (a mispronunciation of the Sanskrit word *Bhaat*) and Bard. The tradition originated in the East and then traversed to the Greeks and then Latins. The Vedic King Prithviraj's court poet, Chand, was known as "Bardai," which is spelled as "Bard" in English. The continuance of this poet or bard tradition in Britain is one very significant proof of the Sanskrit-speaking Vedic rulers having administered the British Isles in ancient times.

STONEHENGE AND THE DRUIDS

Another place to consider in regard to its Vedic influence is Stonehenge, a mysterious place standing on the Salisbury plain in Wiltshire. The name of

Stonehenge comes from the Sanskrit *Stavankunj*, which means meditational bower. The original name actually has nothing to do with the huge boulders standing there. A few miles away is the place known as Woodhenge. The Sanskrit equivalent of "wood" is *vana*, pronounced as "bon." Thus, the Sanskrit name for the place would be *Vanakunj*, meaning a "forest bower." This provides some insight into the Sanskrit origin of the names ending with "henge."

The Druids, who are connected with Stonehenge, were the priests who played a great part in social life in ancient Europe. The term *Druid* is a European variation of the Sanskrit term *Dravid*. One of the connections the Druids had to the Vedic culture is explained by P. N. Oak on page 221 of *Some Missing Chapters in World History* in which he relates: "The European community called Druids are the ancient Hindu Dravids. The dictionary describes them as an ancient religious order in ancient Gaul, Britain, and Ireland. In the Irish and Welsh sagas, and later Christian legends, the Druids appear as conjurers and not as priests and philosophers. This is a clear indication that the Druids of Europe are the same as Dravids of India. They are not racial groups. They are a religious group of priests and philosophers who were deemed to perform miracles through their chants and worship. Incidentally, it should be noted here that it is wrong to characterize the Aryans and Dravids as rival racial groups. They are not. They are [different] ancient Hindu communities both well-versed in Hindu religious worship, lore and Vedic practice. They spread to Europe when Indian Kshatriyas ruled the world. As in India so in European communities we come across the terms Aryans and Druids. They are not exclusive to each other. Druids are a group professing the Arya Dharma that is the Arya way of life. Hence when the world says that the Europeans are Aryans what it should realize is that the Europeans have been Hindus. The Druids, alias Dravids, formed a religious group in that Arya community believing in and practicing the same Arya Dharma."

The term *Dravid* relates to the earliest of sages at the start of the Krita-yuga. The root *Dra* signifies Drashta, one of the original seers, while the latter syllable *vid* relates directly to the knower, or the sage himself. Thus, they are from India, as also related on page 483, Volume II of *Asiatic Researches* by Reverend Thomas Maurice: "The Asiatic origin of the Druids has long been an acknowledged point in the world of antiquities. Mr Reuben Burrow, the great practical astronomer of India, was the first person who, after a strict examination and comparison of their mythological superstitions and their periods, directly affirmed them to be a race of emigrated Indian philosophers."

Reverend Maurice continues this line of thought on page 246, Part 1, Volume I of his *Antiquities of India*: "These priests (the Druids), Brahmins of India, spread themselves widely through the northern regions of Asia, even to Siberia itself, and gradually mingling with the great body of Celtic tribes (Kalatoya people to the South of Kashmir) pursued their journey to the extremity of Europe and finally established the Druid that is the Brahmin system of superstition in ancient Britain. This I contend was the first Oriental colony settled in these (British) islands."

This is very similar to what Navaratna S. Rajaram explains in his book, *Vedic Aryans and the Origins of Civilization*. He says that the Druids are recorded in the Vedic literature as the Druhyus. They were driven out of India in a number of campaigns by rulers of the fourth millennium B.C., even by Mandhatr as early as 4500 B.C. This is in agreement with the Druid tradition which traces their origins from Asia to as early as 3900 B.C. The Druhyus, who were from India's northwestern regions were led back into the heartland by their king, Angara. Mandhatr drove them back out of the Punjab and into Afghanistan. Thereafter, Puranic records indicate that they went farther north and then west into Europe, where they eventually became the Druids.

On page 11 of *The Celtic Druids*, Godfrey Higgins relates that, "Caesar. . . says, speaking of the Druids, that they did not think it lawful to commit the secret of their religion to writing." This means that in the way they passed down their knowledge to others they kept the Vedic oral tradition. Sanskrit learning was always committed to memory prior to it being written. And to keep it in memory, the Druids used to regularly chant the *Vedas* and other Sanskrit scriptures.

From page 154 of *Matter, Myth and Spirit or Keltic Hindu Links*, Dorothea Chaplin explains, "The Dravidas were Kshatriyas and all Kshatriyas were Aryas. . . Manu in verse 43-44 of the tenth chapter of the Samhita designates ten Kshatriya tribes as Vrishalas, among whom are the Dravidas."

On pages 179 to 183 she continues to explain that the Druids took no part in war, nor did they pay ordinary taxes for that purpose. They were exempt from such taxes. Large numbers joined the priesthood for which they were sent by their parents to undergo the necessary training. At the age of five the student was sent to the hermitage of the guru for 12 to 20 years of education and learning the sacred Vedic hymns. They would memorize large numbers of lines. The heart of their study was to understand the eternality of the soul and the process of reincarnation. Other study was astronomy, geography, different branches of philosophy, and problems of religion. Thus, the Druid system of education was also Vedic.

These similarities to the Vedic system makes it obvious that the Druids were in fact the Druhyu clan from India, part of the Vedic culture who guided and exercised supervisory control over contemporary European society. In the same book, Chaplin explains that the Druids colonized the British Islands and established centers in many places in the British Isles, the most important of which were Avebury, Stonehenge, Woodhenge, Malvern, Mona, Tara, and Iona. Even the Celtic people were subject to the authority of the Druids. However, not only did the Druids prosper in Britain, but in *The Complete History of the Druids* (page 27), it explains that, "The religion of the Druids flourished a long time, both in Britain and Gaul (France). It spread as far as Italy, as appears by Augustus's injunction to the Romans, not to celebrate its mysteries."

As recorded on pages 182-183 of *Caesar's Commentaries on the Gallic War*, translated by T. Rice Holmes, Julius Caesar explains that the god for whom the Druids had most reverence was Mercury. He was regarded as the inventor of all arts and pioneer and guide of travelers, and promoter of commerce and acquisition of wealth. They also had reverence for Apollo (dispeller of disease), Mars (the Lord of war), Jupiter (topmost of the celestials) and Minerva (originator of industries and handicrafts). In the Sanskrit tradition these same deities are known as Surya, Mangal, Budha, Indra, and Lakshmi.

On page 161 of *The Celtic Druids*, by Godfrey Higgins, it is also explained that the festival of December 25th was celebrated with great fires on the hilltops. The evergreens and particularly the mistletoe betray the Druidical origin of the custom.

The Druids were not the only people from India, or of Vedic orientation, who were in Britain. From page 113 of *Matter, Myth and Spirit or Keltic Hindu Links*, Dorothea Chaplin explains, "The kingdom of Kent was founded by the Jat brothers. Both the people of Kent and of the Isle of Wight are the offspring of the Jats." The Jats are another Kshatriya clan from India and helped administer Vedic culture in other parts of the world.

IRELAND

Other parts of the British Isles also display much evidence of their being influenced by Vedic culture. The name "Ireland" is a mispronunciation of the Sanskrit term *Aryasthan*, meaning a land of Aryan (Vedic) culture.

On page twenty of the Preface of *Collectania De Rebus Hibernicus*, by Lt. Gen. Charles Vallancey, he explains that the Druid religion of the Britons was founded on that of the ancient Irish, which was in great part that of the Brahmins. . . by no other means could the deities of the Brahmins have been recorded in the Irish manuscripts." If this is the case, this would mean that *the pre-Christian manuscripts in England, Wales, Scotland, and Ireland were all of Hindu, Vedic, Sanskrit scriptures*. Vallancey further notes on page 22 of his book that, "Sir William Jones allows the Irish language great affinity with the Sanskrit." This means that much of Irish tradition is merely remnants of Vedic culture.

So whatever happened to these great Irish manuscripts? Vallancey notes on page eight of the Preface of his book, "The Irish and Welsh complain of the devastation of their manuscripts by the first Christian missionaries, by the Danes, Norwegions and others. . ." This explains how the evidence of Vedic culture was systematically wiped out by Christianity in Ireland as well as the whole of Europe. Later when scholars tried to collect such manuscripts and other evidence of the ancient European Vedic culture, these attempts were also stifled by hostile Christian elements.

The deities of the Irish were also the same as those of the Vedic Aryans, as Vallancey explains on page 32-34 of his book: "The Pagan Irish had most of the deities of the Hindus. . . Their altars still exist in Ireland under their names. By the mode of argument used by Dupuis, the Irish may be said to be Hindus. In the preface to my *Prospectus of an Irish Dictionary*, page XXIII, is a list of 18 deities, in common with the Pagan, Irish and the Brahmins. . . It is worthy of remark that the two greatest rivers in Ireland, the Seanon (Shannon) and the Suir, are the names of the two greatest rivers in India, viz. the Ganges and the Indus or Sindh. . . The Euphrates in Babylon was named Sur."

Speaking of the ancient Vedic temples in Ireland, Mr. Oak explains on page 906 of *World Vedic Heritage* that: "Near Killarney in the county of Kerry is an Aghadoe Church. It has an imperfect Ogham inscription obviously disfigured by Christian invaders. The deity's name inscribed is Som. As in India, that was a Somnath temple of Ireland. It is currently looked upon as a church. *Agha* in Sanskrit means Sin, and 'Doe' alias *Dev* means God. Therefore that edifice is obviously an ancient Vedic temple of Lord Shiva who is an absolver or a refuge from sin. The name Killarney too is Sanskrit. The term *Killaarnav* in Sanskrit connotes a fort commanding the sea or close to the sea."

One more point, the name Scotland itself is an English corruption of the Sanskrit term *Kshatra-Sthan*. This means a land of Kshatriyas, the administrators of Vedic culture. Therefore, from all this evidence we can understand that much influence on the British Isles, which can still be seen today, came from India and the Vedic empire, of which it was a part.

FRANCE

The Vedic influence in France can be recognized in *Caesar's Commentaries on the Gallic War* on pages 180-1, in which he explains that everywhere in Gaul (France) two classes of men existed; the Druids and the knights. The Druids officiated in the worship of the gods, regulated rituals, and expounded questions of religion. Large numbers of men resorted to them for study and many people held them in high respect. They also acted as judges in disputes and made decisions of award or punishment. In this way, we can see that the Druids were very much the Brahmins of the area, and that the early culture of France was very similar to that of Britain.

Mr. Oak relates on page 831 of *World Vedic Heritage*, "Prior to English developing as a separate language it is well known that the British spoke the same language as the French. That was because the language or languages spoken all over Europe were variations of Sanskrit.

"In this context Godfrey Higgins observes [in *The Celtic Druids*], 'Speaking of the Gauls, Caesar says, that they had all the same language, with some little variation in their dialects. But he says it was usual with them to pass over to Britain to improve themselves in the discipline of the Druids, which almost proves that the two countries had the same language. And Tacitus says expressly, that the language of Gaul and Britain was not very different. . . ' That is why French continued to be the language of the British Isles for a long time.

"This indicates that not only France and England but the whole of Europe and the entire world once spoke the common language Sanskrit. With the eclipse of the world Vedic empire, continents, regions, and later still individual countries drifted apart mistaking their mannerisms and corruptions of Sanskrit as their own separate languages."

In regard to the name "France," it is from the Sanskrit root *pra*, pronounced as "fra" in modern pronunciation. The Sanskrit root *pra* retains its connotation in modern European parlance as "pro," meaning "tending towards." A Vedic monk is known in Sanskrit as *pravarh*, which means tending toward *var*, the superior caliber of spirituality. The *pravar* of Vedic terminology is still in use in Europe as "Friar." The addition of the "nce" in the name "France" signifies the plural of "Fra," which consequently means a group of people (Vedic Friars or Druids) in the region who are tending toward spiritual freedom. This is the Vedic aim of life. Consequently, the use of the name Friar by Christians also proves its Vedic connection.

The name of Paris also has a Vedic derivative, and is the shortened version of the name of the Vedic goddess Parameshwari. During Roman times Paris was spelled as Parisorium, which is a corruption of the Sanskrit name *Parameswarium*, meaning the abode of goddess Parameshwari. This means that there must have been a temple to the Vedic goddess Parameshwari on the banks of the Seine River. The town that grew around it became known as Parameswarium. After the *Mahabharata* War at Kuruksetra and the international disruption of Vedic administration, the Sanskrit name came to be called Parisorium. Then after Roman rule ended, the name was abbreviated to Paris. Frenchmen have further shortened it to "Pari." This is but an indication of how names of localities have changed and how the French have forgotten their Vedic roots.

Out of respect for their homeland, the Seine River was originally called the Sindhu by the people who came from India and colonized France. The French later dropped the last syllable and what remained was Sind or Seine, which is what it is called today.

There are many other similarities between French and Sanskrit. For example, Frenchmen usually pronounce "S" as "Z." Thus, you find the Sanskrit word *Ishwar*, meaning "Great Lord" used to signify temporal rulers in various parts of the world, pronounced as Caesar, Kaiser, Czar, and Azar in Egypt. The French surname Aron is the Sanskrit term *Arun*, signifying a red, rising sun. The Sanskrit word *tu* has assumed the softer pronunciations as "the" in English and "des" in French.

Another example that gives an insight into early Vedic culture in France is the name of the town Cannes. The "C" is pronounced as "K" but can also be used for "S." So the name Cannes could be spelled as Sannes, which immediately is connected with the Sanskrit term *Sanis* for Saturn. Thus, this could have been the center for the worship of Saturn, and the large cathedral there would have been the site for an ancient Vedic Saturn temple.

The term "Notre Dame" is usually translated to mean "Our Lady," but actually it should mean "Our Mother." Some feel that Notre Dame was once the site of a temple to the Vedic Mother Goddess, Bhagavati or Parameshwari. It is still a temple to the Mother Goddess but in the twelfth century it was converted to a Christian church. The evidence is that it still has various geometrical patterns on it, such as squares, hexagons, octagons, and circles with 12 or 24 spokes. Such esoteric designs are known as *Yantras* in the worship of the Vedic Goddess. These patterns represent many of the creative forces used during the process of creating the universe, in which the Vedic Mother Goddess participates. You can also find the 12 zodiacal signs of Vedic astrology on its edifice. Vedic astrology deals with the past and future births of the human soul and its *karma*. If the cathedral was originally a Christian building, astrological signs would not have been there because astrology has no place in Christianity. Christianity claims no knowledge of past and future births, nor does it know anything about the law of *karma*. The Zodiacal signs also indicate that, according to tradition, there had no doubt been images of the nine planets installed within the temple in pre-Christian times.

You can also see the temple spire covered with figures of saints, nuns, birds, beasts, and demons. Decorating temple towers in this way is also a Vedic tradition. You find this especially in the area of South India.

On page 25 of *Matter, Myth and Spirit or Keltic Hindu Links* by Dorothea Chaplin, she explains that, "At Atun in France, a deity thought to be a Keltic fertility God is overcoming a serpent." This is obviously Krishna subduing the Kaliya serpent. The label of Him being a fertility god is another presumption on the part of Christian scholars to conveniently create a subtle prejudice in the minds of the people. The fact is that the Puranic episode of Lord Krishna overcoming the multi-hooded serpent Kaliya was extremely popular among all people from India. They naturally would have brought these stories and Vedic texts with them, as well as establish temples to their Vedic Deities, such as Lord Krishna. Therefore, Atun obviously had an ancient Krishna temple at the spot occupied by its main cathedral.

On pages 822-3 of *World Vedic Heritage*, Mr. Oak explains that Strabo, the ancient geographer, records in his Geography of Marseilles that it had a protective wall around it. There had also been a temple to the Delphian Apollo, a sun temple. A Vedic sun temple is also called *Marichalayas*. Thus, the name Marseilles is a derivative of that word.

Verseilles gets its name from the Sanskrit *Vareshalayas*, which means shrine of the Great Lord. This would indicate either Vishnu or Shiva. The ancient central cathedral was the place of that original Vedic temple.

The name of the town Sable is also a short form of Shibalaya, which is a distortion of the Sanskrit name *Shivalaya*. The chief cathedral in that town must have been the place of the original Vedic Shiva temple. In light of this, the late Dr. V. V. Pendse, head of the Dyanaprabodhini Institution in Pune, India, peeped through a window of one of the corner sanctums at the cathedral, which is kept permanently locked as very sacred and secret. Within he saw that the interior bore all signs of an uprooted Shiva-*linga*. This is further proof that pre-Christian France once practiced and was a part of ancient Vedic culture.

SCANDINAVIA

The name Scandinavia itself is an indication of the Vedic, Sanskrit roots of the region. Scanda (or Skanda) is the warrior son of Lord Shiva and the Commander-in-Chief of the divine army. The Sanskrit word *naviya* signifies a naval expedition and settlement. This region is thus a Vedic settlement initiated by a naval expedition in the name of Scanda. Such an expedition was undertaken by the Vedic Kshatriya warriors who obviously populated the region. On page 53 of his book *India in Greece*, Edward Pococke observes that the European, Scandinavian, and Indian Kshatriya warrior castes are identical. This shows that the same warriors from India who immigrated through Europe also went to Scandinavia. The Vikings of the region who later appeared inherited this tradition. In fact, the last syllable of Viking (King) comes from the Sanskrit word *simha* which means lion. *Simha* is pronounced as "singa," then changing the "S" to a "K" it becomes king. Thus, the Vikings were considered lion-like warriors.

The whole of Europe was administered in ancient times by a Sanskrit-speaking Vedic clan known as the Daityas. Danu and Merk were two leaders of that ancient clan of Daityas. It is those two names which are combined into the term Denmark. Count Biornstierna, himself a Scandinavian, is no doubt right in determining in his book *The Theogony of the Hindus*, "It appears that the Hindu settlers migrated to Scandinavia before the *Mahabharata* War."

The ancient names Sveringe for Sweden and Norge for Norway come from the Sanskrit terms *Swarga* and *Narka*. The term Sweden in Sanskrit means a place of no perspiration, and *narka* means hell. A town in Norway is actually named Hell.

Scandinavian names such as Amundsen and Sorensen also exhibit characteristics of Vedic tradition. The term *sen* in India is generally used as a surname, but also as a personal name, such as Ugrasen and Bhadrasen.

The ancient *Vedas* that the Kshatriyas followed were also transported to Scandinavia. Later they became the *Eddas*, which still remains the ancient-most scripture of the region. However, due to the discontinuation of the Vedic form of education, the content of the *Eddas* has all been changed from the ancient Sanskrit texts to the fairy tales of the local modern language. Nonetheless, close study reveals many similarities in the tales of the *Eddas* and Vedic and Puranic legends.

The Norse ballad about Sigfried, a hero who was born with a coat of horn, is the European relic of the story of Karna. He was born with an armor-plated body as described in the *Mahabharata*. Also, the story called "Hildebrand Lied," the oldest in Norse mythology, is an episode from the ancient *Ramayana*.

Similar to the Vedic time line, in the Norse region it is said that ancient peoples lived for hundreds of years. There was also a set of ages, or time periods, during which conditions would continue to deteriorate with increasing violence into a time called the knife and axe age. After this final age would be what is called Ragnarok, the period of annihilation. However, after this would be a time of restoration in which the world would return to a time of goodness. During the Ragnarok, the world would be destroyed by flames that come from a being named Surt. It is he who lives in an underworld, Hel. This is quite similar to the Vedic version (*Bhagavatam* 3.11.30) in which the world is destroyed by the flames that come from the mouth of Lord Sankarshana, who is an expansion of Lord Krishna who is seated in the lower regions of the universe.

The Vedic gods and heroes are also the same as those found in Scandinavia, although different names may have been given to them in the *Eddas*. We find on page 27 of the footnote of Volume I of the text *Aryatarangini*: "Even today, the study of Sanskrit is a treasured objective among the Finns and the Lithuanians and the legendary gods of these people can be mostly identified with Vedic deities."

For example, Scandinavian Woden and the Germanic Odin are similar to the Vedic Varuna. Woden was the god that ruled by magic and took an interest in the universal purpose, and not merely in the world of men. Odin provided the laws for society. Varuna was also concerned with universal order and gave moral codes for the world. Woden's and Odin's form of royal dress and residence is similar to that of Varuna's golden mantle and flowing robe and residential mansion of gold (*Rig-veda* 5.67.2).

Donar/Thor was also the thunder-god of the Scandinavians, armed with a thunderbolt. This is quite similar to Indra, the god of rain and thunder who is also armed with a thunderbolt, and, thus, an early god of battle. Donar/Thor also had the ability to drink more than anyone else. Similarly, Indra was known for drinking huge quantities of Soma (*Rig-veda* 5.29.7 & 3.48.2).

Even symbolism was derived from the Vedic culture. The existence of the elephant in Scandinavian symbolism is a sure indication of the prevalence of Vedic culture in pre-Christian Scandinavia. There were no real elephants in Scandinavia, but the elephant was considered a symbol of wisdom and sacred strength in the Vedic tradition. Its image is found adorning many Vedic temples and palaces.

Another piece of evidence is the Gundestrup Cauldron. This is a huge silver cup that dates back to 150 B.C. that has been found in Denmark. It displays an image of Pushupati, Lord Shiva as the friend of animals. This indicates that he must have been a common deity of pre-Christian Europe. The cup provides further evidence for the migration of Vedic Aryans out of India and through Iran and on into Europe.

There have also been accounts which have appeared in newspapers of ships salvaged from the depths of the Arctic ocean containing Vedic images. So the Vedic Kshatriyas and sages must have gone farther north of Scandinavia in their explorations of the world.

More information is supplied in this regard on pages 267-9 in *Sanskrit and Its Kindred Literatures: Studies in Comparative Mythology* by Laura Elizabeth Poor: "The Norsemen were converted to Christianity so much later than any other European nation that their cosmogony and mythology have been preserved to us in a perfectly unaltered condition. . . Their literature is both grand and poetic. Their sacred books are the two *Eddas*, one poetic, the other prose, written in that old Norse tongue which was once spoken by the four families throughout the Scandinavian Peninsula. The word *Edda* means great grandmothers by repetition. The poetic *Edda*, which is the older of the two, is a collection of 37 sagas. Some of them are religious, and give an account of the creation of the world, of the gods and men, some of them historical telling of the heroes of the nation; one of them gives a series of moral maxims.

"The ballads were written before the 6th century but they were collected together in 1086 A.D. by a Christian priest named Soemund. Scholars think Soemund was a name given to him in reference to this, for it means the mouth which scatters seeds. . . "

With the Christian invasion of Europe, Olaf was the first Scandinavian king to be turned into a Christian. As soon as he was baptized, he let loose his army in 1030 A.D. to forcibly convert all other Scandinavians to Christianity. Thereafter, the Vedic gods of old were stigmatized and misrepresented as demons and devils.

LITHUANIA

Lithuania was one of the last Vedic countries to be converted to Catholicism. The kingdom of Lithuania (or Lietiva) at the time extended from the Baltic to the Black Sea and to the Urals in the East. The last of the pre-Christian rulers before Lithuania was forcibly taken over by Christianity was Grand Duke Gediminas of the 14th century. Although he defended his country against the force of the Christians, he had the wisdom to announce that the Pagans of Lithuania, Catholics, and Orthodox Christians all worshiped the same Supreme Being, although in different forms. Even though he had guaranteed religious freedom in Lithuania, his liberal attitude did little to help his country from being conquered by the Christians who then suppressed the native pagan religion. Of course, pagan in this instance refers to the ancient Vedic culture, or the remnants of it. In any case, it was only 50 years after Gediminas' rule that Lithuania was taken by the Christian crusaders. The Lithuanian king at the time, Jogolia, married the Polish princess Jadvyaga and converted her to Catholicism. Then pagan temples were destroyed and Christian churches built in their place. The last pagan temple was closed in 1790.

That, however, did not bring a swift change in the people of Lithuania. Many of them held on to their pagan beliefs and rituals, much to the dismay of the church missionaries. After all, to the native people, the Christians were but foreign invaders. Even the Soviet occupation after World War II did not overpower the national pagan church--Romuva. The church was kept alive through the 1980s, during the nation's independence. Even today you can find the pagan rituals still being held with participants circling the fires singing *Dainas*, the Lithuanian Vedic chants. The name *Dainas* is linguistically connected to the Sanskrit word *dhyanam*, which means meditation. So these chants were and still are considered a way of meditation in the same way the Vedic chants have always been used. The fire goddess is still held in reverence, and her name is Gabija or Ugnis, related to the Sanskrit fire god *Agni*. Another similarity between the modern pagan rituals and Vedic culture is that the priest uses some of the ashes from the fire to smudge the third eye area on the forehead of the participants, as often done during the Vedic fire rituals.

The Lithuanian language was not Slavik but was based on Sanskrit. This is why there are so many Sanskritic words in the Lithuanian language. A short example can be seen in the words for God, day, and son, which are *devas, dina*, and *sunu* in Sanskrit, and *dievas, diena*, and *sunus* in Lithuanian. The numerals are also very similar. There is a large Sanskrit Department in the University of Vilnius. Since the language has changed less than others over the centuries, it clearly shows its linguistic link to the past.

In Kaunas, the second largest city of the country, there is a museum called the Museum of Devils. Featured in it are images of Mahakali and Hanuman, and other Vedic deities. The name of the museum is no doubt an aspect of the Christian attempt to discredit and forget the Vedic past of Lithuania.

GERMANY

The area of Germany has many points that relate to its connection with its primordial Vedic culture. In regard to names, the name "Prussia" is from "Pra-Russia." Russia simply refers to the Sanskrit *Rishiya*, or a land of Rishis, and Prussia is an extension of the *Rishi* Country. Its other name, Deutschland, is a corruption of the Sanskrit term *DaityaSthan*, which refers to the land of the Daitya clan, or those born of Mother Diti and Kashyapa Muni. This is why Germany is called Deutschland. The term "Titan" is the European pronunciation of the Sanskrit word *Daityan*. The Dutch people of Holland also share in the same name of *Daitya*.

The name German is a corruption of the Sanskrit term *Sharman*, which is applicable to the Sanskrit scholars in Vedic terminology. You can find many Indian people with the surname of Sharma, which is in reference to this.

Other examples of Sanskrit words in German are easily found. In the German names like Heidelburg, "burg" signifies a fort. Heidelburg is the Sanskrit compound *Haya-dal-durg* meaning a fort garrisoned by a contingent of horses. Hindenburg is another such example, which simply means the fort of the Hindus.

The German word of thanks is *Danke*, a mispronunciation of the Sanskrit *Dhanya*, which is commonly used in India. The German suffix "maan" in names like Hermann and Hahnemann comes from the Sanskrit word *Manav,* meaning man. Hahnemann is also a derivative of the name Hanuman from the *Ramayana.*

We also find personal and place names that derive from the Vedic incarnation of Lord Rama, such as Ramstein, the site where the first American Pershing missile was located in November, 1983. "Stein" is similar to *sthan*, which means a spot or place.

Tacitus, an ancient Greek writer, has also testified to the ancient Hindu, Vedic culture in old Germany. Furthermore, Col. James Tod records on page 63 in Volume I of *Annals and Antiquities of Rajasthan*: "The first habit of the Germans upon rising was ablution, which must have been of Eastern origin and not of the cold climate of Germany, as also the loose flowing robes, the long and braided hair tied in a knot at the top of the head, so emblematic of the Brahmins."

One of the more obvious signs of Vedic culture was the Swastika. The Swastika was found widely all over Europe as an important Vedic symbol in the pre-Christian era. The very term *Swastika* is Sanskrit meaning an emblem of well-being. It is a symbol of the sun and earth and cosmos in a dynamic whirl. It represents *karma* and action in consonance with the whirling cosmos. It also represents the divine energy which pervades the universe in the eight directions which are important in Vedic tradition.

As explained further by Mr. Oak on page 745 of *World Vedic Heritage*: "The notion that the Nazi Swastika being forked to the left was different from the real, Vedic, Indian variety is not true. India too has left-forking Swastikas inlaid in stone, displayed high on the entrance of the majestic, seven-storied ancient Hindu palace in Sikandra (six miles north of Agra) where Akbar is said to have been buried later. Vedic Tantric designs include Swastikas of either variety. . . In the ancient rift between Devas and Daityas (alias Danavs) the Swastika forking to the right was chosen by the gods as their symbol while the one forking to the left was preferred by the Daityas, as is apparent from the left-forked Swastika rooted in German (Deutschland) tradition since hoary antiquity."

Another interesting point Mr. Oak goes on to explain is in reference to the wording of property deeds. "The land-grant deeds of ancient Germany are identical with those of India. Both contain an invocation addressed to divinity, the names of witnesses, a description of the gifted land, names of the donor and donee, reason for the grant and a direction that the grant will be enjoyed by the donee in perpetuity and that the donee's right to unhindered enjoyment of the property will be guarded and guaranteed. Such identity of wording, sequence and form of the contents is emphatic proof that both Germany and India were part of a universal Vedic administration in the ancient past."

Germany also observed the same worship of Lord Shiva as in India. West Germany issued a 30-Pfennig postal stamp depicting a Shiva-*linga* covered in gold sheet. This had actually been found during an excavation in the city of

Schifferstadt. Further evidence is in a town known as Czestochowa in Poland where exists an ancient temple of the Vedic Mother Goddess known as the Black Virgin, meaning Goddess Kali. The Asna Gora monastery in which that holy icon is consecrated is actually in reference to the Sanskrit term *Isan-Gouri*, which means Lord Shiva and his consort Gouri. Sanskrit is the mother of the Polish language. The Poles once regarded India as their cultural mother. One can recognize this in their saying, "Kto poznal India, poznal coly swiat," which means "He who sees India has seen the whole world."

Another indication of Vedic culture in the region is that in Amsterdam the biggest hotel is named after Lord Krishna as Krisnapolsky. Even the name "Amsterdam" is from the Sanskrit word *Antardham*, which means a region below sea-level. The term Netherlands, although English, has the same meaning.

CENTRAL EUROPE

The area of Czechoslovakia, Yugoslavia, and Hungary all have signs of ancient Vedic or Sanskrit influence. As Mr. Oak explains on page 756 of *World Vedic Heritage*, "The terms Czechs, Czechoslovakia and Czestochowa originate in the term 'shak,' an ancient clan of Vedic Kshatriyas who as a branch of the Daitya clan administered parts of Europe. The Saxenas of India, Saxons of Europe, and the Anglo-Saxons of Britain are part of the same stock. Consequently the term Czechoslovakia is the Sanskrit term *Shakaslavakiya*. Slavak is another ancient sub-clan."

The Slav language is a dialect of Sanskrit, too. Similar words are *agni*, meaning fire; *malka* (Sanskrit *mallika*) meaning mother; *sestra* is sister; *brat* is brother; *syn* is son; *nos* is nose; *dom* (*dham*) is house; and *dvar* is door. Many of their personal names are also Sanskrit, such as Sudhakant, Asha, Meenakshi, and Ramkali. In Scopte, a city in Yugoslavia, there live over 50,000 Ramas, or families with names referring to Vedic connections.

The Slavik people also worshiped the same Vedic deities. Their chief deity was Bog, which is a relic of the Sanskrit name *Bhag* or *Bhagavan*. "Swarog" is another name for that deity, which is for Sanskrit *Swarga*, meaning heaven. "Ogon" is their pronunciation of the Vedic demigod Agni, the god of fire, and "Parun" is their pronunciation of the Vedic demigod Varuna.

Slavik festivals also have Vedic origins, such as the one falling on January 13/14, known in the Punjab of North India as Lodi and also Sakranti. This is almost the same as the "Lada" of the Slavs. The Slavs celebrate the end of winter in the spring by building a bonfire. Peasants dance and sing songs to Loda, the goddess of spring and festivity. The Christians have since renamed this festival as Butter Week. This is another indication of how the Christians have tried to place their identity on age old Vedic festivals to make them look deceptively Christian.

As Mr. Oak further explains (page 768, *World Vedic Heritage*), the Slavs were forced into Christianity and to abandon Vedic culture in the 9th century. "For a long time Christianity suffered to exist. However, Vladimir, the Charemagne of Russia (who ascended the throne in 980 A.D.) proclaimed Christianity as the state religion by himself toppling a statue of the Vedic deity Varun, alias Parun. Thereafter, all Vedic temples and schools in the region were turned into Christian churches and monasteries. At his baptism the name Vladimir was changed to Wassily. The Russo-Greek church has since hailed him as St. Basil. This is yet another instance of the Christian and Muslim practice of raising to sainthood persons who wielded the sword and resorted to terror and torture to eradicate worldwide Vedic culture and force people to become Christians and Muslims."

As we go on to Hungary, the name "Hungary" is a corruption of the Sanskrit term *Shringeri*, implying a scenic, hilly region. The "S" and "H" have been interchangeable, as seen in the names Sindhu and Hindu. The name of Hungary's capital, Budapest, comes from the Sanskrit term *Buddhaprastha*, meaning the city of Buddha.

In Bulgaria we find the dictionary replete with Sanskrit words. When the Bulgarian Government was informed of this by the Indian Embassy, Bulgaria promptly set up courses in Sanskrit in numerous schools. Sofia University has a special department for Sanskrit studies. At an Indian film festival held there some years ago, it was discovered that Bulgarian audiences could easily understand Sanskrit words in the dialogue.

SPAIN

The name Spain originates from the Sanskrit word *spand*, meaning throbbing or pulsating. Words like spin, spun, and spindle come from the same Sanskrit root. Spain gets its name from being an ancient pulsating or thriving Vedic center that linked Europe with Africa.

Although the Vedic history of Spain seems to be completely wiped out and forgotten, it should be apparent that when the rest of Europe followed and was a part of Vedic culture, Spain could be no different. First the Christians came in and overran the country, and then later the Muslims invaded and did the same thing. About 600 years later, the Spanish people drove away the Muslims and retrieved their Christian heritage. However, farther back in time is their own Vedic heritage, which they seem to have forgotten. Nonetheless, some still feel that there are remnants of the Vedic history in Spain.

For example, Mr. Marvin H. Mills is the adjunct professor in the School of architecture in the City College of The City University of New York. He made a preliminary study of the buildings of Spain for a doctoral thesis under Columbia University. He has written to Mr. Oak (in a letter dated November 15, 1983): "My belief, though it remains to be confirmed, is that the most important alleged Moslem buildings in Spain are not Moslem at all. They probably precede the

Moslem era dating from 711 A.D. Much like in India the Moslems came as looters and conquerors, preying on a superior culture where they found generous amounts of buildings to choose from without the need of the ability to construct new ones. Thus I would guess that the (so-called) Mosque of Cordoba, the Alhambra, and the palace city of Azhara outside of Cordoba as well as buildings in Seville and elsewhere will turn out to be non-Moslem. In short, there is need to rewrite Spanish history as well as Indian history."

More evidence of the Vedic culture in Spain is that the promontory near Cadiz was known as holy because it abounded in temples of Lord Krishna and other Vedic deities. This has been recorded by Herodotus as well as Strabo (p. 253, Vol. I, *Strabo's Geography*) in which he says that it had many temples of Rhadamanthus. That term is from the Sanskrit name of Krishna as Radharamana, the Lord of Radha's heart. So Spain engaged in and had knowledge of the worship of Lord Krishna.

ITALY

The name Italy (from Etaly) in Sanskrit signifies a country situated at the bottom of the continent now called Europe. As the Vedic culture had crossed through the mid-eastern countries and into Greece and Italy, the Vedic gods were still a primary factor in the worship and legends of the land. However, the names had changed in the local jargon to emphasize various characteristics that had more emphasis with the people of the region. We can recognize this in regard to how the popular Roman god Mithra can be traced to Mitra of the *Vedas*, who came to the Mediterranean through Asia Minor by the military forces who had been impressed with the Vedic philosophy.

Furthermore, many other Roman gods originated from the east, especially from the Greek tradition who were further traced and characterized after the Vedic deities. For example, Zeus is Dyaus, Jupiter is Diupeter (or Dyaus Pitar, the Vedic Indra), Minerva is Pallas Athen, Diana is Artemia, Venus (the Vedic Lakshmi) became Aphrodite, Neptune is Poseidon, Vulcan is Hephaestus, Ceres is Demetri, Liber is Dionysus, Mercury became Hermes, and Hermes was formerly the Egyptian god Thoth. An interesting point concerning Hermes is described by Dr. Ginsburg in *Life of Levita*. It is mentioned that the way the god Hermes was worshiped was as a phallus, standing on a flat stone, which was anointed with oil, similar to the worship of the Shiva *linga*. But the Shiva *linga* is anointed with Ganges water, representing the way Shiva accepted the pounding force of the Ganges river on his head as it descended from the heavenly region to earth.

One of the reasons why so many Vedic deities can be found here is that Rome had been engaged in trade with India for many years. An example of how extensive trade was between Rome and India can be seen at Sisupalgarh. This was a fort located on the far eastern side of India, three miles south of Bhubaneshwar.

It was built around the third century B.C. and abandoned in the fourth century A.D. Excavations revealed Roman and Indian coins that date back to the first and second centuries.

Another example of this is given by Franz Cumont on page 110 of his book, *Oriental Religions in Roman Paganism*. Therein he explains, "It was easy for the divinities of the Phoenician Coast to cross the seas (into Rome). Among them were Adonis whom the women of Byblos mourned; Balmarcodes 'The Lord of the Dances,' who came from Beruit; Marna, the master of rain, worshiped at Gaza; and Maiuma whose nautical holiday was celebrated every spring on the coast near Ostia as well as in the Orient."

The Lord of the Dances is generally known as Shiva, or Nataraja. However, Shiva, like Krishna, has hundreds of other names, too. Balmarcodes refers to *Balmukundas*, a Sanskrit name of Lord Krishna as the child who gives liberation. Maiuam is the Mother Goddess Uma, consort of Lord Shiva. The nautical holiday was because mariners participated in her worship. Marna is a corruption of Maruna, referring to the name of Varuna.

Even today we can see the image of Lord Shiva standing over a public fountain in the square at Bologna, Italy. Although he may be portrayed with more Roman physical characteristics, you can still see him holding his trident, and the hoods of two snakes on his shoulders that are coiling around his neck. Throughout Italy can be found images of Ganesh, Shiva, and other Vedic deities in archeological digs. These give away the ancient Vedic past of Italy, although such findings are never publicized by the Christian regime.

Not only did the early Italians worship Lord Krishna and Shiva, they also knew the *Ramayana* and painted episodes of the *Ramayana* on plaques and vases. Hundreds of such paintings of Ramayanic episodes inside ancient homes have been discovered all over Italy in archeological excavations and displayed in books and reports. However, the Christian scholars are blissfully unaware of what the paintings depict. Mr. Oak has in his personal collection reproductions of those ancient Etruscan paintings. Some of the scenes include Rama, Sita and Lakshmana walking through the forest, one behind the other, as described in the *Ramayana*. Another shows Rama's brother Bharat proceeding to meet Rama. Another shows Vibhishan entreating Ravana to release the sorrowing Sita. There is one of Kausalya sharing the holy fertility potion with her two co-wives, Kaikeyi and Sumitra. Another painting depicts the sons of Rama, Lava and Kusha driving away with the sacrificial horse released by Rama. One more shows the monkey chiefs Vali and Sugriva coming to blows over the possession of Ruma, the wife of Sugriva.

On page 812 and 813 of *World Vedic Heritage* we can see pictures of what the early Italians and Etruscans looked like. These pictures both appear in *History of Rome* by Mr. Smith, and *Long Missing Links* by Iyengar. One shows Pompey, the Consul of Rome, wearing the distinct mark of the Vedic "V" *tilok* on his forehead. The other painting shows an early Etruscan emperor (2nd century B.C.) wearing the same Vedic *tilok* insignia on his forehead and neck as well as a *dhoti*, the traditional Indian robe.

The city of Rome (pronounced as "Roma" in Italy) is also named after Lord Rama. The Sanskrit letter "A" is replaced with "O" for the European pronunciation, just as *Nasa* in Sanskrit is spelled as "nose" in English. This indicates that the entire Roman empire was originally part of the empire of Lord Rama.

As further related on page 255 of *Some Missing Chapters of World History*: "An additional proof is that the date of the founding of Rome remains firmly rooted in the memory of Italians as 21st of April, 753 B.C., which is very unique since perhaps no other city of the ancient world is so very exact about its founding date. Why and how then Rome alone remembers the exact date of its founding? That is because the date of Ramanavami (Rama's birthday celebration) in 753 B.C. was April 21.

"Yet another proof is that another Italian city, Ravenna, is named after Ravana, the great adversary of Rama. Since Rama and Ravana were enemies of each other, Rome and Ravenna are situated diametrically opposite each other, one on the western coast and the other on the eastern coast of Italy."

As Roman culture spread westward, it incorporated more gods and goddesses, such as those of the Celtics, like Sulis, the goddess at Bath, who was identified with Minerva. Maponus was identified with Apollo, and Mars (the Vedic Skanda) had many similarities with other gods. The name of the Roman god Janus was the Latin word for the Vedic demigod Ganesh. A description of the worship of Janus is practically a duplicate of how Ganesh is worshiped.

All this indicates that the ancient Italians were part of the Vedic culture, or were Hindus, worshipers of Lord Rama and Krishna. Their legends were Vedic, they worshiped the Vedic pantheon, and their head priest, the Pope, administered Vedic rites because he had originally been a Vedic priest.

THE POPE AND THE VATICAN

In Sanskrit *Paap* means sins. Adding the syllable "ha" to it, as in *Papa-ha*, signifies one who removes sin. Consequently, *Papa-ha* was the title and the function of the supreme pontiff attached to the Vedic administration in Europe. From this came the shortened European pronunciation of Pope. Other words connected with this Sanskrit origin are papacy and papal, which refers to dealing with sin, or the guidance from acquiring it. *Pa* is the Sanskrit root meaning to protect, from which the term Pope means father, like the father protecting his children. The term Pontiff is a corruption of the Sanskrit term *pundit* or *puntah*.

As the royal Vedic priest, the Pope used to live in his bower or hermitage, which in Sanskrit is *Vatica*. Even now it is still called Vatican, which reveals the Sanskrit and Vedic source of the position. Unfortunately, under the orders of

Constantine, who had just converted to being a Christian, the Roman troops crushed all vestiges of Vedic culture and forced everyone to accept Christianity and renounce everything else. It was also during that stage that the chief Vedic priest of the region, the *Papa-ha* or Pope, the deliverer from sin, was forced to succumb to these same threats. It is likely that he was killed by Constantine around 312 A.D. who then installed the Bishop of Rome, a priest of the tiny, newly-formed group of Christians. The Vedic records and histories of the time obviously were quickly carried away, hidden, or destroyed. From that point, the Vedic Vatica became the Christian Vatican.

Further evidence that the Vatican was once a Vedic post is found in the Vatican's Etruscan Museum. Therein is preserved and on display five Hindu Shiva-*lingas*, some of which the Hindu Pope used to worship, as well as images of Shiva with a cobra raising its hood over Shiva's head. Many others are said to be hidden in the Museum and in the cellars of the Vatican. If such is the case, then it is also likely that there were many other images and deities of Lord Krishna, Rama, Ganesh (known as Janus), Lakshmi (known as Shree and then Ceres), Brahma (known as Abraham), Vishnu (known as Vista), etc. There must have been many Vedic temples throughout the area before they were destroyed.

Much of the present-day Pope's rituals are rooted in Vedic customs. The chanting of hymns, the purification with incense, the offering and distributing of food, and even the washing of feet are remnants of the full Vedic rituals that used to be practiced by the Pope. Ceremonial washing of the feet at important religious ceremonies of a person held in high reverence is a pre-Christian practice. Washing of the feet was never a Christian custom when Christian congregations are bedecked with socks and shoes. However, it has been practiced from time immemorial to this day within the Vedic tradition when religious leaders and spiritual masters allow their feet to be washed or worshiped in a display of respect and reverence. Therefore, such rituals as washing the feet in Christianity is a carry-over from the pre-Christian Vedic ceremonies. However, even the present-day Pope does not seem to understand the Vedic source of such practices.

GREECE

In looking at the Greek culture, we find many connections between it and the Vedic civilization. Many people and scholars tend to view Greece as a source of western civilization. However, it is seldom realized that the original Greek culture was itself Vedic. This is not to say that no one has recognized the similarities. Even as far back as 1830 we can find on pages 61-2 from Volume II of *Narrative of a Journey Overland From England to India*, by Mrs. Colonel Elwood, where she sees the Vedic influence in Greece. "The striking analogy between some of the Hindoo fables with those of the Greeks, would induce us to believe that the Greeks and Hindoos must, at an early age, have had much intercourse, and possibly

Pythagorus, with the doctrine of the Metempsychosis, may have imported some of the adventures of the Indian Gods and ascribed them to the Greek deities.

"Indra whirling his thunderbolt appears to be the same with Jupiter. Chrisn [Krishna] and his nine Gopis are evidently Apollo and the Muses. The beautiful Camadeva is a more interesting being even than the Greecian Cupid, while the lovely Maya, the Goddess of beauty, the Venus, sprang from the bosom of the ocean, Surya and Arjuna resemble Phoebus and Aurora, and the twin sons Aswinau, Aswini-cum-arau, or the Daul, Castor and Pollux; Lachshemi crowned with ears of corn appears to be Ceres; Kali, Hecate or Proserpine; and Narad, the eloquent messenger of the Gods, is Mercury. Sir William Jones identifies Ganesh with Janus, whilst Hanuman and his monkey attendants, resemble Pan and his Sylvan deities."

The fact that Krishna was the God of Greece is proved by the silver coins made by Agathaclose, a Greek ruler of the 2nd century B.C. These coins bear the imprint of Lord Krishna and His brother Balarama and are on display in several museums. Furthermore, a large mosaic of a young Krishna playing the flute, standing cross-legged under a tree while grazing cows, hangs in the museum in Corinth. This was obviously salvaged from a local Krishna temple which proves this city was once a center of Vedic culture with temples to Krishna.

We can recognize that as the Vedic culture moved from India to Egypt to Greece, etc., much of the philosophy stayed the same, although the names and artistic characteristics of the gods changed with time. The features of the deities would change because as they moved west the esthetic standards would be adjusted since the priests would emphasize certain aspects of the images according to regional and cultural preference. The early Greek sculptures seem to have been carved by the priests for the temples. In other words, they were the temple deities and were probably dressed rather than left naked, and then worshiped in the temples. Many of the early forms were almost always carved as a boy of 15 to 17 years of age with long hair like Krishna. Furthermore, Zeus, Jupiter, and Amon were all blue bodied, not because they were sky-gods like some say, but because they are related to the image of Krishna who is blue, which signifies His spiritual nature.

More examples of Vedic deities in Greece include Helios who was the sun-god or Greek form of Ravi or Hari, and Helios contains the name of Eli, which is the name of the Jewish form of God the Father. The Sanskrit name Hari is linguistically related to the name Eli, and Elohim is the plural form of Eli which refers to the demigods or lesser representatives of the Supreme Deity.

One of the most important of the Greek gods is Zeus, the god of the heavens and earth (the Vedic Indra). Hades is god of the underworld (similar to Lord Shiva). Poseidon, the Greek god of the sea, refers to *Pati dhana* in Sanskrit, which is a by-name of Seshanaga. *Dhana* means the support or the one who holds up the universe. The Greek Prometheus comes from the word *Pramathes*, which is a name for Lord Shiva. The Greek name of Patar Ouranos, that is translated into

"Heavenly Father" in the New Testament, refers to Pitar Varuna, the Vedic demigod Varuna.

Greek writers like Pliny referred to Hari Krishna as Heracles. This is traced back to the way the early Greek writers who visited India said that the city they called Klessleboro (Mathura) was the capital of Krishna worship. The Greeks pronounced the name Krishna as *klessle*, and Hare or Hari as *hera*. Thus came the name of Heraklessle, or Heracles and Hercules, who is the muscular man who played prominent roles in the Greek myths. Interestingly, Krishna is also known for His mighty deeds, such as lifting Govardhana Hill with the little finger of His left hand while still a young boy.

The Greeks recorded that Heracles, Krishna, had lived 138 generations before Alexander, whose time was around 325 B.C. Therefore, if you calculate 20 years or more for each generation back from the time of 325 B.C., it would take us to somewhere around 3085 B.C. Let us remember that the Age of Kali started when Lord Krishna left this planet, which is accepted to be in the year 3102 B.C. So this is quite close to that time. This means that the Greek records are in accord with the Vedic standard and shows their connection with the Vedic culture.

Further information about the Greek deities and linguistic similarities is related on page 776 of *World Vedic Heritage*. Mr. Oak explains, "The Greek name Bacchus is the truncated Sanskrit name Tryambachesh (the three-eyed Lord) of Lord Shiva. In European usage the first syllable 'Tryam' got dropped off while the remainder continued to be spelled as Bacchus. And curiously enough, just as some wayward persons in India smoke and consume intoxicants (such as Bhaang) in the name of Lord Shiva, the Greeks too regarded Shiva as the deity presiding over drinking parties. This again shows how the Greeks were wayward Hindus.

"Mount Olympus of the Greeks is supposed to be the heavenly abode of their Gods. Eliminating the last syllable 'pus' one may notice that the first syllable 'olym' is the Sanskrit word *Alayam*, meaning 'abode' as in *Granthalayam* (abode of books, i.e. library) and *Devalayam* (abode of Gods). The Greek Mount Olympus is a regional substitute for the Vedic tradition which considers the Himalayan peaks such as Mount Kailas as the abode of its deities."

Other linguistic similarities can be found. For example, the word paradise in English is related to *paradisio* in Greek, which is related to *pardes* in Hebrew (meaning the garden beyond), which is related to *paradesha* in Sanskrit, meaning the far away place of Para or Vishnu. The Greek word *propheto* referred to the Egyptian high priest at the sacrifice. This was derived from the Sanskrit word *purohito*, which is the name of the high priest officiating at the fire sacrifice or Deity worship in the Vaishnava tradition. This is the origin of the English word prophet. There is also a linguistic similarity between the Christian word *Amen* and the Sanskrit *Om*, and *Abraham* and the Sanskrit words *brahmana* and Brahma.

You could say that practically the language of ancient Greece was Sanskrit, or a derivative of it. Later, after the disruption of the *Mahabharata* War, the universal Vedic educational system broke down and local mannerisms led to changes in pronunciation to form what we now call the Greek language. However, we can still see many of the similarities between Greek and Sanskrit in the following examples:

GREEK	SANSKRIT
Demetrius	Deva-Mitras (a friend of the gods)
Alexander	Alaksyendra (the invisible God)
Menander	Meenendra (Lord of the fishes)
Aristotle	Arishta-taal (God as the warder of calamities)
Parthia	Parthia (the land of Partha--Arjuna)
Theodorus	Devadwaras (doorway to Divinity)
Macedonia	Maha-Sadaneeya (a region of great mansions)
Socrates	Sukrutas (one whose conduct is helpful and meritorious)

The Greek greeting "Hari Tutay," also means "May Hari bless you" and refers to Lord Krishna as Hari. It is equivalent to the Hindu greeting of "Rama Rama" or "Hare Krishna." The name Hercules also means *Hari-cul-eesh* in Sanskrit and refers to the Lord in the lineage of Hari, Lord Krishna. The legendary feats of Hercules is patterned after the activities of Lord Krishna, such as slaying the demon King Kamsa and lifting Govardhan mountain when Krishna was a child. Thus, the Greeks simply plagiarized the story. This means that the Greek civilization, along with its traditions and culture, are of Vedic origin.

Lord Shiva was also given high regard in Greece. The name of the city Cyprus is an Arabic mispronunciation and shortened version of the Sanskrit name *Shivaprastha*, signifying a center of Shiva worship. Sun-worship was also prominent in Greece, in regard to which the name Heliopolis is derived from the Sanskrit *Suryapuras*, meaning the city of the sun. Changing the "S" to "H", and the "R" to "L," which is often the case when changing from Eastern to Western pronunciations, Suryapura becomes Huryapulus, and then Heliopolis.

Even in nearby Turkey there was the lake known as Ramsar. The name is from the Sanskrit *Ramasagar*, which signifies Rama Lake or Lake of Lord Rama.

Additional evidence of the Vedic influence in Greece can be recognized in the ancient Vedic records, which relate that Greece was the area of the Yavanas. This word can be broken into the Sanskrit meaning in this way: *Vana* means forest, and *Ya* means departed. So thousands of years ago, this region was for those who had departed from following the Vedic principles. However, it had been administered by Vedic rulers, and much of Vedic culture still remained in ancient Greece.

This is described by E. Pococke on pages 9 to 12 in his book *India in Greece*. He relates that there was perfection in the arts and the abundance of gold with elegant workmanship. There was beauty in textiles and ornaments. There was social refinement and comforts, and magnificent palaces of Alcinous and Menlaus. There also was constant use of the war chariot. He concludes that, "The whole of this state of society, civil and military, must strike anyone as eminently Asiatic; much of it specifically Indian. Such it undoubtedly is. . . these evidences were but the attendant tokens of an Indian colonization with its corresponding religion and language. . . the whole of Greece, from the era of the supposed godships of Poseidon and Zeus, down to the close of the Trojan war (was) Indian in language, sentiment and religion, and in the arts of peace and war."

Even though Mr. Pococke feels Greece was Indian in so many ways, there are others who feel that India was far superior to Greece. In *Bharat (India) As Seen and Known by Foreigners* by Babasaheb Deshandey, he explains that, "In respect of philosophy, the Hindus were far in advance of the philosophy of Greece and Rome, who considered the immortality of the soul as problematical. . . the Egyptians derived their religion, mythology and philosophy from the Hindus and the Greek philosophy too was indebted almost wholly to the Hindu philosophy. . . the resemblance between (them) is too close to be accidental. The Hindus being far more advanced must have been the teachers, and the Greeks the disciples. . ."

Another point about Greek philosophy is that many people think Pythagorus was one of the most noteworthy philosophers that came from that country. However, evidence shows that Pythagorus himself was a product of the worldwide Vedic culture. For example, his name comes from the Sanskrit *Peeth Guru*, which signifies a *guru* working at a *peeth*, or an educational establishment. And his system of mathematics that he is most noted for had already been in existence in India. His system of teaching and his standard for living were the same as found in the Vedic culture.

In light of this, considering the strong influence of Greek philosophy on western culture, we should also look briefly at the philosophers of Greek civilization. Many of them had ideas on life that were very similar to the Vedic view. Pythagoras (582-507 B.C.), one of the earliest Greek philosophers, taught that the soul wandered through many lives in this material creation, living even within the bodies of plants and animals. Thus, the goal of the soul, according to Pythagoras, was to attain freedom from the cycles of reincarnation through the performance of virtuous acts. These would attune the soul to God and bring deliverance. This philosophy is parallel to the Vedic knowledge of the soul and law of *karma*. Even the many mathematical theories that Pythagoras taught had already been known in the older Vedic times of India.

To help people purify themselves spiritually, Pythagoras set up communities that had laws similar to those of India and stressed vegetarianism and the wearing of simple clothes. He also taught that a person's life should be divided into four divisions, which were the same as the four *ashramas* in the Vedic plan of life. India no doubt had a great influence on Pythagoras. In fact, it has been said that in the travels of Pythagoras, India was one of the places he visited. And it was noted by his followers that he had been initiated into Vedic philosophy while studying in Ellora, India. It was no doubt while he was in India that he got many of his ideas on mathematics.

Socrates (469-400 B.C.) was the next great philosopher of Greece. From the *Memorabilia* written by Xenophon we get a picture of Socrates as a man wandering the streets of Athens talking to anyone about various aspects of life. There is every possibility that men from India had reached Athens by this time for purposes of trading spices and metals. Trade between India and the Tigris-Euphrates region goes back to ancient times. This was done by using land routes or by crossing the Indian Ocean and sailing up the Red Sea. Babylon was a center where those of the West and East would meet to trade their goods. It is here that Greeks and Indians may have discussed not only prices of goods, but also philosophies of life. And if there were any intellectual Indians in Athens, surely Socrates would have met them and engaged in lengthy discussions. In fact, Eusebius writes in his *Praeparatio Evangelica* (XI.3), written in 315 A.D., about an account told by Aristoxenus, one of Aristotle's pupils, of a meeting between Socrates and a group of Indian Brahmins. Such a meeting surely would have influenced Socrates' philosophical views.

Socrates' pupil, Plato (428-347 B.C.), had a philosophy of the soul that was also very similar to the Vedic conception. Plato believed in an immortal soul and a universal or Supersoul as well as a God or Supreme Creator of the physical world. He believed that God was the perfect being and, therefore, changeless. The unfortunate thing is that the philosophers of this era had a habit of not acknowledging their sources of information, which may give a reason as to why Plato never mentions India in his writings. However, Plato must have been aware of India because Plato's pupil Aristotle did mention India in his writings, signifying he knew where it was.

Aristotle (384-322 B.C.) also had strong spiritual beliefs which were very similar to the teachings of the *Vedas*. Aristotle believed that God was the being who directed the world and that God's existence could be proven. His analysis was that every moment or "now" implied that there had to be a "before." In other words, everything that makes up the present was caused by what happened previous to that moment. Thus, time and motion, in respect to past, present, and future, must be eternal. Therefore, absolute reality is eternal without a creation. So if change is a constant factor, there must be an eternal cause of change which implies, according to Aristotle, that there is a prime mover who would be the cause (cause of all causes as the Vedic literature describes) that imparts motion or the affects of time without himself being moved or affected. This would be the absolutely perfect Supreme Being who moves the world through love.

Aristotle's conception of the soul was that the soul is divided into two parts. One part was the rational aspect or the intellect, while the other part is the irrational aspect where are the desires. This would correspond to the Vedic analysis of the difference between the rational intelligence and the irrational mind, which is the center of the senses and sensual desires. Aristotle concluded that the intellect could control the desires through developing reasoning and moral discipline. Such development leads a person to wisdom and understanding.

Aristotle, by stressing this kind of progress, viewed self-realization as the purpose of life. This, of course, was also the ultimate goal of Vedic philosophy by which the Greek philosophers seemed to be strongly influenced.

Another point that shows Greek civilization was influenced by India is the use of animals in the Greek fables by Aesop. Such fables with animal characters are easily found in India in books like the *Panchatantra*, *Hitopadesa*, and *Jatakas*. The *Panchatantra* was written in the second century B.C., but the stories are much older, having appeared in earlier Sanskrit texts written many years before Aesop's time. Thus, some scholars, such as Max Muller, believed that renditions of these fables came to Greece from India. The reason for this opinion is that many of the characters in these fables are animals like the lion, jackal, elephant, peacock, tiger, monkey, and crocodile, which are found in India but not in Greece.

Furthermore, many of the fairy tales that are told in different countries and in different periods are so similar that they show they must have, at some distant time, originated with a common source, in one culture. But, as with spiritual knowledge, these stories must have undergone change as the people divided and moved and carried these tales to new localities. However, these legends of ancient heroes and stories that preserved and elaborated on spiritual truths that were clearly understood in the Aryan culture of India gradually became transformed into supernatural and unintelligible myths as they traveled through Persia, Greece, Italy, and then up through Germany and into Scandinavia. In other words, by comparison we can see how the original Aryan culture and its legends became more and more distorted as each region changed the stories as well as the names and activities of the characters within them and the traditions that were described.

There is also undeniable archeological evidence that signifies that the Greeks were impressed with the Vedic culture as far back as 200 B.C. We can see this evidence in what is called the Heliodorus column which was erected by the Greek ambassador to India in 113 B.C. at Besnagar in central India. The inscription on the column, as published in the Journal of the Royal Asiatic Society, says:

> This Garuda column of Vasudeva (Vishnu), the god of gods, was erected here by Heliodorus, a worshiper of Vishnu, the son of Dion, and an inhabitant of Taxila, who came as Greek ambassador from the Great King Antialkidas to King Kasiputra Bhagabhadra, the Savior, then reigning prosperously in the fourteenth year of his kingship. Three important precepts when practiced lead to heaven: self-restraint, charity, conscientiousness.

This shows that Heliodorus had become a worshiper of Vishnu and was well versed in the texts and ways pertaining to this religion. It can only be guessed how many other Greeks became converted to Vaishnava Hinduism if such a notable ambassador did. This conclusively shows the Greek appreciation for India and its philosophy.

The column also establishes archeological proof that knowledge of Krishna and the Vaishnava tradition antedated Christianity by at least 200 years. This disproved claims of the Christians and British that the stories of Krishna in the *Puranas* were modern and merely taken as adaptations from the stories of Jesus.

All of the above evidence bears witness to the fact that Greece was but a part of Vedic culture and repeated what it and its philosophers had learned from the Vedic sages rather than being a source of the higher levels of philosophy as some people think. In other words, without its connection with the Vedic knowledge, it would not have been considered as important to Western thought as it is for which it is presently given credit.

RUSSIA

There is much evidence that connects the area of Russia with Vedic culture. Take the name of Russia itself. *Russi* (also spelled as *Rishi*) is the Sanskrit word for a sage. Thus, the term Russia (or Russiya) signifies the land of the Rushis, or *rishis* and sages.

Russian phraseology and language also bears close resemblance to Sanskrit. Take, for example, the Sanskrit word for a daughter-in-law is *Snusha*. The Russian term is *Snokha*. The word for fire is *agni* in Sanskrit and *agone* in Russian. Many Russian names are also Sanskrit. The Russian name Andropov signifies one belonging to the family of Indra, the Vedic demigod of heaven (pronounced as Andro in Russian). The name Lebedev is the Sanskrit name Lava-dev, meaning Lava, the son of Lord Rama.

The name Moscow also has a Sanskrit origin. When we change the places of the "C" and the "S" the name is spelled as Mocsow, pronounced as Moksow. This is in fact the Sanskrit word *Moksha*, which means salvation. This is the chief goal of life of all Rushis, sages. This should give further evidence that the area once known as Russia used to be the chosen haunt of sages because its atmospheric severity ensured undisturbed seclusion.

While we are dealing with names, the term Soviet is from the Sanskrit *Svet*, which means the white (snow-covered) region. Similarly, Stalin's daughter's name, Svetlana, is a local corruption of the Sanskrit name *Svetanana*, meaning fair-faced. The term Bolshevik is the Sanskrit term *Bal-Sevik*, signifying Rushis (sages) who sought the attainment of (spiritual or temporal) power.

Names of townships ending with the suffix "grad" are also of Sanskrit origin. "Grad" comes from the Sanskrit *graam*, which means township. Stalingrad and Leningrad signify towns of Vedic origin, although called after recent leaders. However, they should more appropriately be spelled as Stalingraam or Leningraam. In a more Vedic tradition, there is a town in Siberia, about 2000 miles east of Moscow, named Krasnoyarak. Since the "i" is pronounced as an "a," "Krasno" signifies that it is named after Krishna.

There were also Vedic temples in Russia as well. On the Caspian Sea is the busy port of Baku, you can find the ancient temple of the Goddess of Effulgence (Jwalamai). Buried under the heaps of ashes are inscriptions left there by the Vedic fire-worshipers. On the walls of the temple the sacred *Gayatri mantra* is written in Devanagari script. Even up to the time of World War II a lone Vedic monk would station himself there in the austere surroundings to maintain the place. Local Indian Hindu merchants would bring donations for the upkeep of the temple and monk. How many more Vedic temples may be scattered throughout the area of Russia that are now camouflaged as Christian churches?

Even the *Evening News* in Mumbai, a "Times of India" publication, on August 30, 1982 reported the discovery of stone carvings depicting a Vedic chariot in the region of Tajikistan. Ancient Vedic sages were known to live in mountain caves with their disciples. Many of these caves were not natural but carved out by hand. Thousands of such caves can be seen in India. A similar complex of rock-cut caves has been discovered recently in the Armenian Republic.

S. K. Malhan writes in the *Indian Express* of Sunday, November 27, 1983 about the Vedic remains found in Russia. "When Soviet archeologists stumbled on the remains of a giant Buddhist cave-monastery inside the Kara-Tepe hill during excavation-work in Termez in Southern Uzbekistan, fresh light was once again thrown on the possibility of a cultural relationship between Soviet Central Asia and India."

More descriptions by Malhan certainly connect India with Russia. "Although excavations have been carried out only on the southern tip of the three-summit hill. . . it is already clear now that the Buddhist center situated there included dozens of separate complexes. Each of these consisted of a number of cave constructions and other buildings, i.e. temples, shrines, cells, yards, etc., sometimes arranged in two rows. In some yards there were *stupas* while in others there were columned porticos called *aiwan*. The cave-temple and the *aiwans* were often embellished with ornamental and genre paintings of various deities and donors. . . and also with scenes from legends.

"Of particular interest among the Kara-Tepe finds are the inscriptions in different languages--in the so-called Kushan script (based on the Greek alphabet), the Brahmi, the Kharoshtri, the Middle Persian, as well as the yet unidentified writing of Aramaic origin.

"Researchers found ancient frescoes--many of which were done by Indian masters--and statues of the Buddha which looked very much like those in India. The expedition also found and bought from the local population several Sanskrit manuscripts, silk and paper pieces. . . and other ancient items."

This description provides some very positive evidence of the Vedic culture and the offshoot of it--Buddhism--being a very influential part of society in these regions of Russia. Mr. Oak continues to explain this aspect of research on page 732 of *World Vedic Heritage:* "To continue with Malhan's observations, he informs us that yet another gigantic statue of Buddha was discovered in a temple in Kuva in Farghana (Uzbekistan). It had on it a third eye. Malhan has missed its implication, namely that the Buddha there had obviously displaced an earlier gigantic Shiva statue because it is Shiva who has the legendary third eye."

Then on page 738 of *World Vedic Heritage*, Mr. Oak relates the significance of other discovered artefacts. "A Russian Orientalist, Asimov, points out that some artefacts of the Adighai, a Vedic community surviving in Russia from ancient times, such as bronze axes and images of Lord Vishnu, are on display in Russian museums. The decorative patterns and pictures carved on those axes have their counterparts in India. Among those decorative figures are elephants, though elephants were never native to the cold Russian region. The elephant design is a sure sign of the Indian, Vedic connection. . . Russian archives have preserved over 600 manuscripts of those ancient times which are in Sanskrit as well as its later variations and corruptions."

The Russians also knew of the *Ayurveda*, the ancient Vedic medical science. A Sanskrit text of *Ashtang Ayurveda* that was discovered in Russia, along with a bronze image of the Vedic deity of longevity, is on display at the International Academy of Indian Culture, 22-Hauz Khas, New Delhi. Representatives of the academy who toured Siberia around 1968 reported that people of the Siberian region are also familiar with common Ayurvedic household preparations such as Triphala and Hingashtak powders. The people also hold a strong respect for Ganges water. The reason this area holds a stronger tie to Vedic culture than other parts of Russia is because, as the International Academy of Indian Culture points out, Christianity was not able to easily penetrate the inhospitable Siberian region. This is strong evidence of ancient Indian educators, administrators, and medicine men having worked and taught the people of the region since time immemorial.

The very word *Siberia* is also of Sanskrit origin. Though spelled as Siberia, the local people still call their land *Shibir*, which is the exact Sanskrit word meaning encampment or temporary habitation. Since Siberia is so inhospitable, people usually live there only temporarily. The name was given to the area by Indian explorers who first charted the land.

In the town of Samarkand is a palatial building said to house the grave of the conqueror Tamerlain. There is some confusion about whether the building was a captured Hindu palace or whether the Muslims built it as the grave for Tamerlain. On the arch over the doorway you can see two drawings of a rising sun shining on a tiger and a deer. Muslims never included pictures or images of living animals on their buildings. The Russian women guides describe the pictures as "Soor-Sadul." This is actually the Sanskrit term of *Surya-Shardul*, meaning the sun and tiger. This was obviously the emblem of the Vedic rulers who administered in that region. Therefore, this building is actually an ancient Hindu palace in Vedic architecture that had been captured by Muslims and then used to house the grave of Tamerlain.

Another strong point about the Vedic connection with Russia is the mention of the *Russian Veda*. In a book called *Diary of a Traveling Preacher* by

Indradyumna Swami, a member of Iskcon (International Society for Krishna Consciousness), the author describes how he met a professor while visiting Ekaterinburg. Professor Alexander Vasilyevich Medvedev is from the State University of the Urals and the Chairman of the Religious Affairs Committee of the Ural Region, which investigates new religious movements. While meeting the professor at his office, Indradyumna Swami describes on page 57 of his book the conversation between him and the professor:

"The problem among our leaders may not so much be in having to accept your movement, but to accept the fact that the Vedic culture could have very well been the original culture here in Russia. You know, in Russia practically all scientists accept that the Vedic culture once flourished here, the center being in the Volga River region. The debate among our scientists is only if the Aryans came from India, or they originated here. There is much evidence to the fact that the Vedic culture existed here, most notably the *Russian Veda*."

"The *Russian Veda*," I [Indradyumna Swami] interjected.

"Yes. It is famous among our people. It is as old as Russia, and the stories are exactly like those found in the Vedic scriptures. The central figure of the *Russian Veda* is a personality called Krishen. He is the upholder of spiritual truth and the killer of many demons. His killing of a witch and a snake are exactly like the history of child Krishna killing the Putana and Agasura demons in the *Bhagavat Purana*. But the *Russian Veda* is not intended for children. It is full of spiritual truths.

"The Vedic culture was once all over the world. Did you know that in the former Yugoslavia there is a very ancient cave drawing with Lord Jesus Christ in the robes of a *brahmacari* [Vedic monk]? My theory is that He went to India, and among other things learned mystic powers from the yogis there. This would explain why He didn't die on the cross and was able to leave His tomb. India has always been the motherland of religions."

With the above words coming from a Russian professor, I could not have said it better myself. Herein we can understand that the area of Russia most certainly had been a part of the Vedic, Sanskrit culture. This shows the essential premise of this book: That the Vedic culture was once a worldwide culture, and the whole world still shows the influence that this lofty culture had on it. The Vedic culture is the spiritual heritage of the world, the source from which came all original spiritual knowledge, and the culture from which we are all descendants. That is our common heritage.

One last note on this common, global, Vedic heritage that is found in Russia is the name of Professor Medvedev. The name Medvedev is obviously a Russian corruption of the name Madhava or Madhavadev, which is another name of Lord Krishna. It seems that the influence of Vedic culture has touched closer to the Professor than he realizes.

CHAPTER ELEVEN

Christianity and the Vedic Teachings Within It

After investigating the Vedic influence found throughout Europe, which is presently so effected by Christianity, we need to take a closer look at how Christianity itself has been effected and continues to hold many of the teachings, legends, and customs found in the Vedic philosophy, which had already been in existence for many thousands of years.

A BRIEF LOOK AT CHRISTIANITY'S BEGINNINGS

At the time of Jesus' appearance there were many cults in Judaism. There were the Pharisees, the Sadducees, and another was the Essenes who were very pure in their habits. They were frugal and were strict vegetarians, eating no meat of any kind and drinking fresh fruit juices or water. They believed in working in harmony with nature and the forces that surround the world and all within it.

The name Essene is supposed to derive from a Syrian word meaning physician, and they would practice the healing of the sick in mind, body, and soul. They had two main communities, one in Egypt, the other in Palestine near the Dead Sea. Another was in Syria. Their origins can be traced to the Far East, and their methods of prayer, meditation, and fasting were quite similar to Eastern or Vedic practices.

Their membership was open to all and they were a well respected order with many hundreds waiting to join. But their teachings were given only to members. To be a member of the Essene order, one had to pass a probationary period of one year and be able to fast for 40 days. Their school had three degrees, and few passed successfully through all. They divided themselves into two levels, consisting of those who were celibate and those who were married. The Essenes were a peaceful order of pious men and women who lived in asceticism, spending their days in simple labor and their evenings in prayer. They never became involved with political or military affairs. They never became merchants or entered into commercial life in the cities, but maintained themselves by agriculture and raising sheep for wool, as well as by crafts like pottery and carpentry. (And tradition holds that Jesus was a carpenter.) Any profits or harvests were not kept individually, but were given to the community and then divided.

More information is provided by H. Spencer Lewis who writes on page 28 of his book, *The Mystical Life of Jesus*: "Every member of the Essenes in Egypt or Palestine had to be a pure-blooded descendant of the Aryan race." This would indicate that the Essenes were a clan of Aryans and, as we know, the Aryans were followers of the Vedic principles. On page 29, Lewis explains further: "Immediately upon initiation, each member adopted a robe of white composed of one piece of material, and he wore sandals." This one-piece robe sounds very much like the Vedic practice of wearing a *dhoti*.

In a footnote (p. 31) of another book, *The Secret Doctrine of Jesus*, H. Spencer Lewis describes that, "Findings of such archeologists as G. Lankester Harding, Director of the Jordanian Department of Antiquities (viz. The) most startling disclosure of the Essene documents so far published is that the sect possessed, years before Christ, a terminology and practice that has always been considered uniquely Christian. The Essenes practiced baptism and shared a liturgical repast of bread and wine, presided over by a priest. They believed in redemption and immortality of the soul. Their most important teacher was a mysterious figure called the Teacher of Righteousness."

This makes it quite obvious that many of the so-called Christian practices and terminology, aside from those that Paul established, are a mere continuation of the pre-Christian Essene tradition. The Essenes were also followers or worshipers of Essan (Issan), which comes from the Sanskrit term *Isha*, which means God.

Jesus was a member of the Essenes and was apparently the head of one of the Essene temples. In all the Essene temples there was one leader and twelve assistants. When they had their ritual, which they had been doing many years before Jesus appeared, they would break bread and take wine. The leader would stand over the wine and bread and say, "This is my body, this is my blood," acting as a representative of God. Then he would distribute it. This is information from the Dead Sea Scrolls which were written long before Christ appeared. So we can see that this is a tradition previous to Christ that is still being carried on in the Christian churches today.

The philosophy of the Essenes was very exalted for that period of time. Traditionally, the Jewish doctrine for justice was an eye for an eye. But the Essenes, even before Christ, taught that one should simply turn the other cheek. So in many cases when Jesus taught, he was simply repeating the doctrine of the Essenes. It was not original. But considering the advanced level of the Essene philosophy in general, it would not be surprising if they had been influenced by the Vedic writings in some way. In fact, evidence of this can be seen when we consider that the school of the Essenes was originally conducted chiefly for the purpose of interpreting the Pythagorean symbols and teachings.

According to legend, Pythagoras was one of the many sages of antiquity for whom an immaculate conception is asserted. He was born between 600 and 590 B.C. and the birth was predicted by the oracle of Delphi. Pythagoras had traveled and learned the mysteries of the Greeks, Egyptians, Babylonians, Chaldeans, and even went through Media and Persia to Hindustan to study for several years under the learned Brahmin priests. This is accepted by some to be the same areas where Jesus later traveled and learned the Eastern spiritual philosophy.

One of the things Pythagoras had declared was that meat-eating clouded the reasoning faculties, and that judges should refrain from eating meat before a trial to assure that the most honest decisions would be made for those who went before them. He also taught that mortals who, during their earthly existence, had become like animals in their activities would return to earth again in the form of the beasts they had grown to resemble or act like. Pythagoras also taught the medicinal properties of plants and how to heal by the use of color, vibrations, music, herbs, etc. He also taught how there was a Supreme World, spiritual in nature, which pervaded all things. The material worlds existed within the nature of this supreme sphere, and people should try to recognize the spiritual nature in their surroundings. The Essenes taught many of these same points. They also believed in the eternality of the soul and the philosophy of reincarnation, as did the Pythagoreans and other groups of that time, and taught that rewards of righteousness must be earnestly striven for.

Jesus' brother James was one of the leaders of the Essenes in Jerusalem and was a strict vegetarian. It is said that never in his life did he eat meat, nor did he drink liquor. He was an ascetic. So if these two brothers were stalwart preachers of the Essenes and one was a staunch vegetarian, it is hard to imagine that the other one would not also be. Of course, if a person wants to establish Jesus as a meat-eater, they can repeat the biblical story in which he distributed many fish. But that was an emergency situation, and whether Jesus actually ate any fish is still in question. But, from an objective point of view, there is evidence that Jesus did not eat meat. In Isaiah (7.14-15) it is stated: "Therefore the Lord Himself shall give you a sign; Behold, a young woman shall conceive and bear a son, and shall call his name Immanuel. Butter and honey shall he eat, that he may know to refuse the evil, and choose the good." This shows that Christ was a vegetarian.

The founding fathers of the early Christian church, such as Tertullian, Pliny, Origen, St. John Chrysostom, etc., were also strict vegetarians. In fact, St. John Chrysostom advised that saints are loving not only toward people, but also to the beasts because they come from the same God who created mankind. Other saints who were either vegetarian or who at least made friends with animals or protected them from hunters include St. Francis, and Georgian saints like St. David of Garesja, St. John Zedazneli, and early Celtic saints like St. Wales, St. Cornwall, and St. Brittany. Therefore, a real "Christian" who follows Christ's doctrines should also extend their love to all of God's creatures as Christ had done. Otherwise, how can they be considered real followers of Christ?

The fact of the matter is that the Bible, in Genesis (1.26), states: "And God said, Let us make man in our image, after our likeness: and let them have dominion over the fish of the sea, and over the fowl of the air, and over the cattle, and over all the earth, and over every creeping thing that creepeth upon the earth." Herein, dominion does not mean to do whatever one wants to with other creatures, but to have dominion as a ruler of a country has leadership over the people he rules. It is not expected that a leader will torture and eat the people who inhabit his country. That is no leader at all, but is merely one who exploits others for his own interests. Furthermore, only a few verses after the one above we find that God expects us to be vegetarian: "And God said, Behold, I have given you every herb bearing seed, which is upon the face of all the earth, and every tree, in the which is the fruit of a tree yielding seed, to you it shall be for meat." (Genesis 1.29) Therefore, meat-eating should be avoided in Christianity.

Only after the Ecumenical councils at the time of Emperor Constantine, who was a meat-eater, did vegetarian Christians have to practice underground. It was either this or live in fear of having molten lead poured down their throat, which Constantine would do if he caught any vegetarian Christians. Of course, now this is no longer an issue in Christianity. Almost everyone considers that meat-eating is normal and that animals have no soul or feelings.

The idea that animals have no soul was started by Aristotle (384-322 B.C.). St. Augustine (354-430 A.D.) also supported this view because he favored meat-eating. Aristotle based his opinions on his speculations, but later Thomas Aquinas (1225-1274) unfortunately adopted Aristotle's philosophy, and the Church took Aquinas' teachings as dogma. And now most everyone in Christianity has followed suit. In fact, due to the expansion of Christianity in Ceylon and other parts of the East, meat-eating has spread, although the slaying of animals is forbidden in Buddhism and amongst those *lamas, yogis,* and Brahmins who are working to attain the highest spiritual development. Therefore, we can see how this destructive opinion that animals have no soul, which is based on a gross ignorance of spiritual knowledge, has spread.

The understanding that meat-eating is incompatible with spiritual progress can be seen more clearly in early Christianity and Eastern religious systems. In fact, such similarities between the Eastern and Western philosophies were more evident before the Ecumenical councils, which did away with many of the early Christian teachings that dealt with such things as reincarnation, *karma,* rebirth, and so on. Such Eastern influence was no doubt partly due to Jesus' travels through the Eastern countries, such as India, Ceylon, and a few of the Himalayan countries. But the modern Church often declines to discuss the fact that early Christianity shows every evidence of being influenced by the East. And the East, specifically India, has always been viewed as the land of spiritual knowledge since time immemorial. So it should not be considered too unusual that many philosophical ideas of Christianity are rooted in the Vedic literature. However, if it is ever established beyond a doubt that Jesus was an initiate of the so-called "pagan" Asiatic teachings, it could certainly have a considerable effect on the members of the Christian faith. However, more and more people are gradually becoming aware of this Eastern influence.

PAGANISM IN CHRISTIANITY

The name *pagan* means a country man. The name *heathen* comes from the word *heath*, which is a common name for a variety of evergreen shrubs that live in swamps or along mountain slopes. Thus, the name heathen simply referred to those who lived in the country near such plants. Therefore, the use of the name heathen or pagan originally was not meant in a condescending way. To be a heathen or pagan simply meant that one followed those religions that existed prior to Christianity, or that he or she participated in the nature religions, which primarily meant demigod worship. So paganism is simply a reference to following the old remnants of the Vedic Aryan culture. And people throughout pre-Christian Europe worshiped a variety of spirits and demigods, known by different names according to culture and region. The Romans and Greeks of that time also worshiped demigods. The sun-god, Mithra, was apparently considered the most exalted of the demigods. Even King Constantine (280-337 A.D.) was originally a devotee of the sun-god. His famous vision of the cross that he had while marching on Rome came to him from the sun. In fact, even after he was converted to Christianity, he remained a devotee of the sun-god, and because of that he continued to hold the Sabbath on Sunday, which traditionally was on Saturday.

According to Jewish tradition, the Sabbath was Saturday when God finished the creation and rested. So Saturday is the seventh day and Sunday is the first. Therefore, the Seventh Day Adventists, in a kind of protest, changed the Sabbath back to the original day. So even today the Sabbath is celebrated as a kind of pagan carry-over on the sun's day. In this way, each day was set aside for different demigods, who are the presiding deities of different planets. Thus, Sunday is for the sun, Monday is for the moon, Tues is the Greek name for Mars, Wednesday is for Mercury, Thursday for Jupiter, Friday for Venus, and Saturday for Saturn.

We can trace many more similarities between Christianity, Judaism, and other cultures. The origin of one of the first stories in the Bible can be traced to Zoroastrianism. In Zoroastrianism we find where the Lord, Ahura Mazda, creates the world in six stages, and then creates the first man and woman and brings them to consciousness with the breath of life. Shortly afterward, Ahriman, the devil, convinces the man and woman to eat of the forbidden fruit, thus bringing sin and death into the world.

In other cases, the Jews, having such little information about their founders, borrowed ideas from the legends of neighboring cultures to make their own heroes look special. For example, the stories of Moses' activities are borrowed from the god Bacchus, who as a baby was found floating in a small boat in the water the way Moses was. Bacchus also emitted rays of light from his forehead, wrote laws on stone, crossed the Red Sea without getting his feet wet, and had armies that were led by pillars of fire. Other similarities can be found in the story of Lord Rama and in the activities of Zoroaster who is said to have lived many years before Moses.

Other customs, such as circumcision, that now most Christians practice, is not exclusively Jewish, but actually came from Egypt. It had been practiced by the Egyptian priests as far back as 4,000 BC, long before there ever was a Jewish tribe.

Baptism is another ceremony that is often considered exclusively Christian. However, this is far from true, as some authorities admit. Reverend J. P. Lundy, who made ancient religions a special study, relates on page 385 of his book, *Monumental Christianity*, that, "John the Baptist simply adopted and practiced the universal custom of sacred bathing for the remission of sins. Christ sanctioned it; the church inherited it from his example."

So from where did Baptism come? The fact is that it has been practiced in the form of immersion or by sprinkling for the purification of sins as a common rite in various countries far and wide, for many centuries, in religions that are the least connected. One of the oldest forms of baptism comes from and is found in India. It is here where people, for aeons, have bathed with the intent of spiritual purification in rivers that are considered sacred. Rivers like the Ganges and Yamuna, or sacred lakes and ponds, have long been accepted as sources of spiritual cleansing if one bathes in them with reverence, especially at important times or events. Even today you can visit holy towns along the Ganges where people, young and old, make special endeavors to take a holy bath in the river, in which they plunge three times into the water, or at least sprinkle drops on their heads. This ancient practice spread all over the world in various forms.

Ancient Persians also practiced baptizing their infants soon after birth, dipping the baby in a vase of water. The old Mithraic initiation ceremonies also included baptism. The Egyptians used baptism as a symbol and rite of spiritual regeneration. Baptism by immersion was also performed by the pagan Greeks, Romans, Mayans, Incas, and, of course, the Essenes and Jews, long before it became a Christian custom.

There are also events and miracles in the life of Jesus that were known to have happened to other special beings, such as Buddha several hundred years earlier. For example, Jesus was supposed to have radiated light after his birth. However, other personalities who also had light shining from them when they were born include Bacchus, Apollo, the first Zoroaster, Moses, and the oldest of which is Krishna. Furthermore, just as Jesus fasted for 40 days and was tempted by the devil, Buddha also fasted and was tempted by the demon Mara in a more severe manner than Jesus. And just as Jesus told the devil, "Get thee behind me, Satan," the Buddha also told Mara, "Get thou away from me." However, other personalities from various cultures were also tempted in a similar way, such as Zoroaster of the Persians, and Quetzalcoatl of ancient Mexico.

Actually, Paul was the fanatic who took whatever was known of Jesus and, while misinterpreting Jesus' teachings, made Jesus out to be the incarnation of God, the Messiah, that Jesus never wanted to be. As described in *Mark* (8.29-30), when Jesus asked his disciples who they thought he was, Peter said that he was the Christ. And Jesus charged them that they should tell no man of him. In fact, the term *Christ* was first used in relation to Jesus by Paul when Paul first started preaching in the city of Antioch. The name Christ was simply the Greek word for Messiah. It was not a person's name.

Paul was the person who developed Christian theology and ritual and simply wrote in the Epistles his own ideas of Jesus while never referring to what Jesus actually said. Paul also put many threats into the philosophy of Christianity and created an image of a fearsome and jealous God rather than one that was merciful and loving. But, according to Paul's version of Christianity, salvation was granted by God alone who would save you if you simply became a Christian because Christ had already died on the cross as a sacrifice for your sins. In this way, faith was all that was needed, and faith outweighed the need for good works. This may be a simple and comfortable concept for Christians but is not a true one and was never presented in the real teachings of Jesus. Jesus actually did emphasize the need for good works. So what we really find in Christianity are the teachings of Paul, which in some areas have little to do with what Jesus actually taught.

Paul also accepted Sunday as the day of rest from Mithraism rather than Saturday, the seventh day as found in the Hebraic tradition. Paul also took Easter from Mithraism as the day Jesus rose from the grave. Mithra is said to have died in battle on a Friday and was buried in a rock tomb from which, after three days, he rose on the festive occasion of the spring equinox, called Eastra, the Latin word for Astarte, the earth mother goddess. Interestingly, the 40 days before the spring equinox corresponding to Lent was the period for searching for the renewal of life in that tradition. Furthermore, the celebration for the resurrection of the Greek god Adonis is said to have taken place as late as 386 A.D. in Judea at the same time as the Easter observance of Jesus' resurrection. And the use of dyed Easter eggs was widely known by such people as the Egyptians and Persians who made presents of them, and by the Jews who used them in the Passover feast. These are some of the non-Christian traditions that became incorporated into the Christian Easter holiday and are still practiced today.

In regard to Jesus' crucifixion, he is supposed to have died and descended into hell, and on the third day rose again. However, if we look at other cultures, many of which are far older than Christianity, this is hardly an isolated event. The Persian Zoroaster, the Egyptian Osiris, Horus, Adonis, Bacchus, Hercules, and the Scandinavian Baldur, and the Mexican Quetzalcoatl all are supposed to have spent three days in hell after their death and then rose again. All these persons also performed many miracles that can be compared to the ones Jesus performed.

The Eucharist of Christianity was also a practice of the ancient Egyptians in commemoration of the death of Osiris. They would eat the sacred cake or wafer after it had been consecrated by a priest, after which it became the veritable flesh of his flesh. The Persian Magi also administered bread and wine in their worship of Mithra. The ancient Pagan Greeks celebrated the sacrament of the Lord's supper in honor of Bacchus, the god of wine.

A more ancient form of this practice is found in the Vedic culture in which the people and priests would offer opulent foodstuffs to the Deities, and then partake of the remnants as *prasadam*, which means the Lord's mercy. The food would be accepted as practically equal to God and extremely purifying and sacred. This custom is still widespread around the world among Vedic followers. From these ceremonies and observances came the practices now seen in the Christian sacrament.

We can easily recognize many more outside influences in Christianity if we take a closer look. For example, one of the basic doctrines of Christianity is the Trinity of the Father, Son, and Holy Ghost. But the holy trinity existed many years prior to Christianity as an Eastern tradition. The Trinity, as in God the Father, Son and Holy Ghost, is another concept which is far from being of Christian origin. It comes from outside Christianity and from a much earlier source. We find the trinity in many cultures, including the Chinese and Japanese Buddhists (in the form of Fo), the Egyptians (in God's form represented as the wing, globe and serpent, and in which the second aspect is called the Logos or Word of God), the Greeks (Pythagorus, Heraclitus, and Plato all taught the Trinity in their theological philosophy), Assyrians, Phoenicians, the ancient inhabitants of Siberia, as well as the Maya (Tezcatlipoca, Huitzlipochtli, and Tlaloc) and Incas. The Scandinavians worshiped Odin, Thor, and Frey. The Druids worshiped Taulac, Fan, and Mollac. The Romans' trinity was God, the Word, and the Spirit. The Persians had a trinity consisting of Ahura Mazda as the creator, Mithras as the son or savior, and Ahriman as the evil one, or destroyer.

The oldest and one of the most prominent forms of the Trinity is the *tri-murti* (meaning three forms in Sanskrit), which is the Vedic triad consisting of Brahma (the secondary creator), Vishnu (the preserver), and Shiva (the destroyer), often worshiped in a three-in-one Deity form or separated on individual altars in many temples of India. Even the Vedic form of the one Supreme Being has three forms or expansions as Bhagavan (the Lord's Supreme Personality, Krishna), Paramatma (the Supersoul that accompanies each individual soul), and Brahman (the spiritual energy or force that emanates from the body of God and pervades everywhere). A variation of that is Lord Vishnu as the universal father, His incarnations as the sons, and His form of the omnipresent Supersoul as the Holy Ghost.

Therefore, long before Christianity, God was worshiped in a Trinity form around the world. The idea of a Trinity is not Christian at all, but a "pagan" concept. So Christians, namely Paul, may have adopted the Trinity not out of a philosophical choice, but out of necessity to accommodate the majority view. Thus, the trinity was nothing new in the world when Christianity adopted it.

After the Trinity was accepted by the Christians, it was still not until the 2nd century when the Christians claimed Jesus to be the son in their Trinity. This idea is traced back to Justin Martyr who simply stated that he realized this understanding by God's special favor rather than by using biblical references to verify it. In fact, though it had been proclaimed by Paul, the very idea that Jesus was God in human form, and, therefore, a part of the Trinity, was not settled until 325 A.D. during the Councils of Nicaea and Constantinople. Controversy had developed in regard to whether there was a time when the Trinity did not exist and whether the Trinity was formed only after the birth of the son, Jesus. Emperor Constantine was forced to summon the Council of Nicaea in hopes of solving this problem. During the council it was resolved that never was there a time when the Son of God did not exist, and those who thought there may have been were anathematized by the Church. They denounced the teachings of Arius, who had taught that the Son of God was a created human being who appeared once only and was secondary to the Father. Thus, by a majority vote, the Church pushed the resolution through and those who did not agree or believe it were expected not to oppose it and to keep their thoughts to themselves.

In fact, it was at this Nicaean Council that all the bishops gathered to discuss what interpretations of Christian theology the Church would teach. This was an attempt to calm the many disputes that had been going on within the Church about its varied teachings. Once this was settled, all other teachings were thrown out and considered heretical, and to teach or follow them was punishable by excommunication or death. To solidify these essential teachings, the Church compiled and edited the New Testament, omitting what was not acceptable and adding new material to justify its viewpoints and fill in what it did not know. Thus, the Church presented itself as the only source of truth and salvation.

Another interesting point regarding pagan influence is that the crucifix or cross and its many variations was not exclusively a Christian symbol. Bishop Colenso explains in his book, *The Pentateuch and Book of Joshua Critically Examined* (Vol. 6, p. 113), "Of the several varieties of the cross still in vogue, as national and ecclesiastical emblems, and distinguished by the familiar appellations of St. George, St. Andrew, the Maltese, the Greek, the Latin, etc., etc., there is not amongst them the existence of which may not be traced to the remotest antiquity. They were the common property of the Eastern nations."

Prior to Christianity, history shows that the cross was an auspicious and mystical symbol amongst ancient Babylonians, Indians, Egyptians, Greeks, Romans, Druids, and even Laplanders and Scandinavians. For centuries, Indians used the cross in a variety of shapes, most notably as the swastika. For many years the Romans carried a cross with a dark skinned man on it as a standard. The crucifix was also known in ancient Mexico, as discovered by the Spanish monks who first went there. They were told that the Son of God, Quetzalcoatl, died on the cross for the sins of mankind. Even Tertullian, as late as 211 A.D., wrote that the Christians neither adored nor desired crosses, and criticized pagans for doing so and for putting a man on the cross, too. For pagans, a cross was a sign of eternity.

In the first several centuries of Christianity, Jesus was represented as a lamb, or as a shepherd with a lamb over his shoulders. It was not until the 6th synod of Constantinople that it was decided that the symbol of Christianity, which was confirmed by Pope Adrian I, would be represented from that time on as a man crucified on the cross. In fact, the earliest instances of any artwork that illustrates Jesus on the cross can be traced back only to the eighth or ninth century. Thus, the Christians adopted the crucifixion as a symbol from the pagans.

Another interesting point regarding pagan influence is within one of the first principles of Christianity: the virgin birth of Jesus from Mary. Chapter 19 of the Koran explains Mary's pregnancy, which some interpret to mean she was impregnated by an angel of the Lord, said to be Gabriel. But the idea of a virgin birth for a highly revered personality is not exclusive to Christianity. Those who are said to have had a miraculous birth, or were born from a virgin, include Buddha, the Siamese Codom, the Chinese Fo-hi (said to be born 3468 B.C.), Lao-tzu (604 B.C.), the Chinese sages Yu and Hau-ki, as well as Confucius. In India everyone knows of Krishna who was born of a virgin without the need of any sexual exchange. In Egypt, there is the god Ra, and Horus born of the virgin Isis. Also Zoroaster of Persia. The Greek Hercules, Bacchus, Amphion, Prometheus, and Perseus are all said to have been fathered by the gods and born of mortal mothers. There are also Romans, such as Romulus, Alexander the Great, Ptolemy, King Cyrus of Persia, Plato, Pythagorus, and others who have the reputation of being born of virgin mothers. So this was nothing new.

The celebration of Christmas is, of course, supposed to commemorate the birth of Jesus. However, historical evidence shows that Jesus was born in the springtime. Some of the early churches observed the birth in April or May, and some in January. Even today the Eastern Church celebrates Christmas on the seventh of January, while the Western Church celebrates it on December 25. Generally, no one is really sure of what day it was. But the birth of Jesus being held on the 25th of December can be traced back to the time of Emperor Commodus (180-192 A.D.), but it is earlier attributed to Telesphorus who had influence during the time of Antonins Pius (138-161 A.D.).

Other cultures also celebrated the 25th of December. The Persians celebrated it as the birthday of Mithras. The Greeks celebrated it as the birth of Bacchus. Egyptians recognized it as the appearance day of Osiris. The Romans also celebrated the Saturnalia festival by feasting, stopping all business, holding public games, and exchanging gifts. The Scandinavians celebrated it as the birthday of Freyr, son of their god Odin and goddess Frigga. Here, too, there was much merry-making and exchanging of presents. The early Germans observed it as part of the Winter solstice, called the Yule feast. They spent time in jovial hospitality, made sacrifices, and worshiped their gods and burned the yule-log on the eve of the 24th. Yule was the old name for the 25th, which came from the word *Jul* used by the Scandinavians, while Noel in French came from the Hebrew word *Nule*.

Actually, the whole affair with the Christmas tree, the use of the mistletoe, hanging wreaths of flowers or evergreens on the doors, giving presents and so on, were all a part of the pagan celebration. The gift-giving we now observe on Christmas is a carry-over from the early pagan celebrations, and is not something that was started by Christianity. In fact, Tertullian, one of the early Fathers of Christianity, called such practices rank idolatry since it was associated with the "customs of the heathen." After all, the use of evergreens, Christmas trees, wreaths, etc., have nothing to do with Christianity, but they were used in the old traditions to signify the return of the sun, the longer days, and the regenerative power that was sure to follow the winter solstice. Thus, the 25th of December was a day of celebration and for showing respect to the gods long before the Christians adopted it for their purposes.

Historically, it is known that Jesus was not even born in the winter. So why is the celebration placed on December 25th? *The New Schaff-Herzog Encyclopaedia of Religious Knowledge* explains that, "the date of the festival depended upon the Pagan Brumalia (December 25) following the Saturnalia (December 17-24), and celebrating the shortest day of the year and the 'New Sun'. . . The Pagan Saturnalia and Brumalia were too deeply entrenched in popular custom to be set aside by Christian influence."

The same Encyclopedia also reveals that emperor Constantine incorporated Sunday as a day of Christian rest and holiday because Sunday was the pre-Christian Pagan day of worship.

December is also the time of year when the celebration takes place of Lord Krishna speaking the *Bhagavad-gita* at Kuruksetra. This could mean that Christ's "Sermon on the Mount" is none other than a reference or similarity to Krishna's sermon delivered to Arjuna while Krishna was mounted on His chariot. The *Bhagavad-gita* is a sermon, given 5,000 years ago, that provides indispensable spiritual guidance to all people, which is also said about Christ's sermon, said to have taken place on the Mount of Olives.

Ultimately, there is nothing Christian about the Christmas celebrations. Even Christians admit this pagan influence, as pointed out in numerous Christian publications. One such publication is *The Plain Truth About Christmas*, by the staunch Christian Worldwide Church of God (P. O. Box 6727, Mumbai, 400 052, India). The booklet seems to plead to rid Christianity of its non-Christian content. It says that Christians tend to "follow the crowd" and assume things about Christmas that are not true. Christmas came not from the New Testament or the Bible, nor from the original apostles. "It gravitated in the fourth century into the Roman church from Paganism."

The conclusion is that if we took everything non-Christian out of Christmas, you would have almost nothing left. In fact, some of the most orthodox Christian countries went so far as to place a statute to ban Christmas. In *World Vedic Heritage* (p. 975-6) we find that: "A statute passed in 1660 A.D. by the Massachusetts Bay Colony in New England, USA, prohibiting the observance of Christmas, declared: 'Public Notice--the observation of Christmas having been deemed a sacrilege, the exchanging of gifts and greetings, dressing in fine clothing, feasting and similar Satanical practices are hereby forbidden with the offender liable to a fine of five shillings.'

"Similarly in 17th century England, Christmas celebrations were banned as 'Pagan and Papish, Saturnalian and Satanic, idolatrous and leading to idleness.' That term Pagan and Papish is again a clear admission that the Papacy is a pre-Christian Pagan i.e. Vedic institution.

"Jehovah's Witnesses has declared in the article 'Is Christmas Really Pagan?' in its journal titled *Awake* (December 22, 1981) that 'All the standard Encyclopedias and reference-works agree that the date of Jesus's birth is unknown and that the church borrowed the date of December 25 from the Romans, along with their customs and festivals.'

"Encyclopedia Americana records: 'It is usually held that the day (December 25) was chosen to correspond to Pagan festivals that took place around the time of the winter Solstice, when the days begin to lengthen, to celebrate the rebirth of the Sun.'

"The New Catholic Encyclopaedia notes that 'On this day (December 25) as the Sun began its return to northern skies the Pagan devotees of Mithra celebrated the birthday of the invincible Sun.'"

From the above references it is obvious that Christmas is being celebrated all over the world on December 25th not because of Christians but in spite of Christians. It would, therefore, be more truthful on their part to admit their participation in pre-Christian customs.

One of the purposes of the Christians in using the 25th of December was to change the pagan festivals into Christian holidays, and, hopefully, to attract the heathens to Christianity. For example, everyone knows that December twenty-first is the winter solstice, the shortest day of the year. For the next three days the length remains the same. But then on December twenty-fifth the day begins to get longer. So on this day the people celebrated in a very raucous manner. They took it that the sun-god was the redeemer and that on account of his birth there was the hope that everyone would be saved. Therefore, when the Christians wanted to establish their Christendom everywhere, they found some opposition to eliminate the birthday of the sun. People had become accustomed to enjoying themselves on that day. Of course, the Christians could not go on celebrating the birthday of the sun-god; so they simply replaced it with the celebration of the birth of Jesus. In this way, the Christians calculated that the pagans could go on with their celebrations but would simply change the meaning of it. So, Christianity incorporated and helped preserve many of the pagan traditions that were observed on the 25th.

Nowadays, the Christians are supposed to be religious people observing the day of Christ's birth, but they still celebrate in a very paganish way. They have kept many of the aspects of the pagan celebration that earmarks Christmas day; namely, drunkenness, revelry, spectator events like football, and feasting on slain animals. Each year so many advertisements go up claiming that amongst the best gifts on Christmas include a fifth of liquor or other useless items. So gradually, Christmas has deteriorated from what was meant to be an observance of a holy day to a mere display of devotion to commercialism.

After all is said and done, anyone can practically see that what is present-day Christianity is a modern adaptation of pre-existing, pagan beliefs and philosophy. Centuries before the time of Jesus, among the "heathen" are beliefs in an incarnate God born of a virgin; his descent from heaven or the spiritual domain; astronomical signs indicating his birth; the rejoicing of the angels or *devas*; the adoration of the magi, shepherds, or local devotees; offerings of precious gifts to the divine child; the slaughter or terrorization of the innocents; temptation by the devil or tests by demons; the performance of miracles; and the death and resurrection or ascension into heaven. These elements can all be found in cultures prior to Christianity.

So what does this mean? From Robert Taylor's *Diegesis* (p. 329), Ammonius Saccus, the Greek philosopher and founder of the Neoplatonic school, expressed, "Christianity and Paganism, when rightly understood, differ in no essential points, but had a common origin, and are really one and the same thing." This is concurred by the historian Mosheim, who speaks of the Christian church during the second century in the book, *Ecclesiastical History* (volume One, p. 199), as follows: "The profound respect that was paid to the Greek and Roman mysteries, and the extraordinary sanctity that was attributed to them, induced the Christians to give their religion a mystic air, in order to put it upon an equal footing, in point of dignity, with that of the Pagans. For this purpose they gave the name of *mysteries* to the institutions of the gospel, and decorated, particularly the holy sacrament, with that solemn title. They used, in that sacred institution, as also in that of baptism, several of the terms employed in the heathen mysteries, and proceeded so far at length, as even to adopt some of the rites and ceremonies of which those renowned mysteries consisted." Herein we can understand that various terms used in Christian rituals are merely adaptations of those rites from earlier religions.

So, in summary, let me say that it has been recognized by many men of the past, such as Bishop Faustas when writing to St. Augustine, Ammonius Saccus the Greek philosopher, the Epicurean philosopher Celsus, Eusebius the historian, and the early Christian writer Justin Martyr, that Christianity does not differ from the old traditions and customs that were called paganism, nor does Christianity hold anything that was not previously known to the ancients. If anything, through its attitude of exclusivity and general feelings of proud superiority, Christianity has lost the elaborate explanations of the once well known truths and now merely holds hazy reflections of the ancient wisdom. So many Bible stories are interwoven with tales borrowed from neighboring cultures, and numerous Christian rituals and symbols have been taken from previous ancient customs and traditions. So, Christians should look beyond the superficialities of modern Christianity to try and see the real religions and cultures from which it came. As Saint Augustine said hundreds of years ago: "The same thing which is now called Christian Religion existed among the ancients. They have begun to call Christian the true religion which existed before." And to quote T. W. Doane from his book, *Bible Myths and Their Parallels in Other Religions*, (page 413), he sums it up as follows:

> We have seen, then, that the only difference between Christianity and Paganism is that Brahma, Ormuzd (Ahura Mazda), Zeus, Jupiter, etc., are called by another name; Krishna, Buddha, Bacchus, Adonis, Mithras, etc., have been turned into Christ Jesus: Venus' pigeon into the Holy Ghost; Diana, Isis, Devaki, etc., into the Virgin Mary; and the demigods and heroes into saints. The exploits of the one were represented as the miracles of the other. Pagan festivals became Christian holidays, and Pagan temples became Christian Churches.

THE SECTARIAN DEVELOPMENT
OF THE CHRISTIAN SCRIPTURES

Just as which day Jesus was born is not clear, neither is the year known for sure. Some say he was born in 4 B.C., or 5 B.C., or even 15 B.C. According to statements made in the gospel of St. Luke, Jesus was born about 10 B.C. This is also verified by Eusebius, the first ecclesiastical historian. Both say that Jesus was born while Cyrenius was governor of Syria, and it is known that he was not governor until about 10 years after King Herod's death. Only the gospel of St. Matthew states that Jesus was born during the time of Herod. But this statement has been discovered to be due to the ignorance of Jewish history by the narrator because the gospel of *Matthew* also mentions the taxing of Cyrenius taking place during Herod's time. This is not true because Cyrenius could not impose taxation until he was governor. And let us not forget that, according to *Luke*, Joseph and Mary went to Bethlehem to be taxed when Jesus was born. In this way, we can see how contradictory statements exist in the New Testament books about important points of Christian theology and history. This also indicates that everything the book of *Matthew* describes regarding Herod is false and that there was no killing of the children by Herod in his hopes of killing baby Jesus because Herod had been dead before Jesus was ever born. Therefore, this concept of the king killing all the children must have come from some other source, as mentioned earlier, and was included in the story of Jesus.

Another point about the birth of Jesus is that, historically, there was no direct account of it. Factually, all the gospels were written several decades after his death and there were no eye witnesses who had actually seen the birth. Traditionally, it is said that he was born in a stable with a few shepherds around, and supposedly some wise men also came from India, although in *Matthew* we find that Herod had sent them. However, the Christian Church never really agreed on how many wise men there were or where they came from. The Christian Church became divided in the 5th century into the Eastern division and Western division. The Eastern Church said there were sixteen wise men who came to see the birth of Jesus, and the Western Church said there were only three. They could never agree on where the wise men came from; so, they simply said from the East. Historically, however, there was never any record that any wise men came from anywhere to see the birth of Jesus. So, basically, no one really knows when or where the birth took place.

Even the Bible is not clear on Jesus' birth. In *Matthew* (2.11) we find that Jesus was born in a house, but *Luke* (2.7, 12, 16) describes that Jesus was lying in a manger, or born in a stable. However, in *Protevangelion*, the apocryphal gospel that is said to be written by James, the brother of Jesus, we find it described that Jesus was born in a cave near Bethlehem. This is also upheld by such early fathers of the Church as Tertullian (200 A.D.) and Jerome (375 A.D.). Furthermore, only in *Matthew* do we find Herod killing all the first-born sons in an attempt to kill Jesus; yet, the other gospels make no mention of such an atrocious crime, neither is it substantiated by any Roman or Jewish historical accounts. Also, there were many histories of that period, written by the contemporary historians of that time, and there is no record whatsoever of such a brutal killing of all the infants, except for one report made by the Essenes during Jesus' lifetime referring to the King as having killed both young and old. Although most Christians will naturally refer to the four gospels of the New Testament, namely, *Matthew*, *Mark*, *Luke*, and *John*, as the truth regarding Christ and the primary basis of Christianity, still it is not possible to determine accurately when these texts were written. It has been estimated that they were written between 50 and 100 A.D. in Greek or Aramaic, no earlier than several decades after the death of Christ. This means that there is no sure way of knowing who the authors were, and it is obvious that by the time they were written most of the data on Christ's life had already been lost.

Therefore, the facts of the matter are that Jesus' year of birth is unknown. Though Jesus was supposed to be a very popular person and followed by many hundreds of people, where he actually grew up is also unknown. As unlike the history of Buddha, Mohammed, and other prophets or incarnations, there is no big compilation of recorded sermons. Even descriptions of his life as found in the Bible offer various versions. And Bibles themselves are of different persuasions as used by the Catholics, Protestants, Church of England, etc. Even the way he looked was never known for certain. The first portrait of Jesus did not come to light until several generations after the death of Jesus. There were also no descriptions of his facial appearance in the Gospels. So how could there be any accuracy in any portraits of Jesus? The most glaring deficiency is the 30 years of his life of which there is no record, except those found in India. Jesus' grave is also not known for sure. Some say Jerusalem, others say Srinagar, India. Of course, he was supposed to have risen to heaven. Thus, many questions regarding Jesus have no answers. Nonetheless, at least the day of his birth should have been known for certain, but December 25th is also far from being the real date.

It is also interesting to note that outside the New Testament there is no evidence that Jesus was crucified by the dictates of Pontius Pilate, nor do any of the historians of that time mention it. However, the Jewish *Talmud* refers to Jesus as having been a student of Joshua Ben Perachiah. The two of them went to Egypt where Jesus became learned in magic, and there died by being stoned, and then hung because of his blaspheming amongst the people.

Whether this is true or not cannot be verified, and many people may not want to try, but it is interesting to note that early historians and writers in Rome, such as Celsus, Lucian, Suetonius, and Tacitus, called Christianity a cult that was based on the principles of magic as taught by Jesus. The Christians were said to hate all outsiders as enemies. It has also been recorded that Jesus performed miracles by the use of magic and powers of the demons. Jesus was often considered a magician, one who had been initiated into the magical art while in Egypt. Thus, some accused him of performing miracles not as a Jewish prophet, but as a magician or necromancer, especially in the way he would cast out devils and his raising Lazarus from the grave. He was also supposed to have had special association with the powerful devil Beelzebul, and was even suspected of being possessed by demons. Some of these writers also asserted that Jesus took portions from the Jewish tradition, such as the idea that the Jewish messiah would appear from a virgin birth, and applied them to himself, thus misleading many Jewish people and directing them to worship foreign gods.

With all this historical confusion, it is not unlikely that some people would even question whether there ever was a real Jesus? Mr. P. N. Oak points out on page 995-6 in his book *World Vedic Heritage*, that through the years there have been Christian scholars who have actually questioned this. "Eminent and learned Christians of numerous nationalities have through the ages doubted the existence of Christ. An eminent American author, William Durant, has in his multi-volume work *The Story of Civilization* (page 553, Vol. III), summarized the issue thus: 'Jesus 4 B.C.--A.D. 30. Did Christ exist? Is the life story of the founder of Christianity. . . a myth? Early in the 18th century the circle of Bolingbroke, shocking even Voltaire, privately discussed the possibility that Jesus had never lived. Volney propounded the same doubt in his *Ruins of Empire* in 1791. Napoleon, meeting the German scholar Wieland in 1808, asked him (whether) he believed in the historicity of Christ'

"'The first engagement in this 200-years war,' adds Durant, 'was fought in silence by Hermann Reimarus, professor of Oriental languages at Hamburg; on his death in 1768 he left, cautiously unpublished, a 1400-page manuscript on the life of Christ. Six years later Gothhold Lessing, over the protests of his friends, published portions of it as the *Wolfnbuettel Fragments*. In 1796 Herder pointed out the irreconcilable differences between the Christ of *Matthew*, *Mark* and *Luke*, and the Christ of the Gospel of *St. John*.'

"'In 1828 Heinrich Paulus examining the life of Jesus ascribed the so-called miracles to natural causes--in his 1192-page book. But David Strauss in his bold and original book, *Life of Jesus*, expressed the view that the supernatural element should be classed as myths. That massive volume published in 1835-1836 led to a furious debate.'

"'In 1840 Bruno Baur began a series of works aiming to show that Jesus was a myth, the personifying of a cult evolved in the 2nd century from a fusion of Jewish, Greek and Roman theology. In 1863 Ernest Revan's *Life of Jesus* with convincing logic and a charming style showed the unreliability of the Gospels. Towards the end of that century a French author Abbe Loisy subjected the New Testament to such a close analysis that the Catholic Church angrily excommunicated him and many others who held similar views.

"'In Holland, Pierson, Naber and Mathas led the movement denying the historicity of Jesus. In Germany, Arthur Drews also expressed similar disbelief. In England scholars like W. B. South, J. M. Robertson, and G. A. Wells have likewise questioned the existence of any Jesus Christ.'" Thus, this debate has been going on for years and still goes on today.

In any case, debating whether or not Jesus actually existed is not our purpose in this book. But the information in the above paragraphs does show the confusion that has existed from the limited and contradictory information that has been provided in Christian theology. We have to admit that further examination does provoke reasonable questions about the existence of Jesus. After all, most of what was known and preached about Jesus first came from Paul, who historically never met Jesus. Other than that, there is no genuinely historical reference to Jesus until almost a century after he was supposed to have lived when Josephus, the Jew historian, wrote his famous volume *Antiquities* (of the Jews) around 93 A.D. Therein he records only what the Christian leaders of his time had started publicizing, that there had been a Jesus, a holy man who performed good works, taught men, and had many Jewish and Greek followers, who was the Messiah. The quote does not provide much information other than what Christians were saying.

When the New Testament was compiled, there were as many as 50 gospels in circulation at the time, but the selection was limited to the ones we find today. These were chosen on the basis that they all maintained the conclusions the early Christians wanted to establish. One book that was left out was the *Gospel of Peter* because it did not accept the crucifixion as an act of atonement by Jesus for the sins of humanity, or at least the believers. And the *Acts of John* was also excluded because it denied that Jesus had a physical body, which is a concept subversive to the traditional Christian doctrine. This means that as the Christian religion developed, it was not necessarily based on the Bible as we find it today, but the Bible is based on the prevailing religion and ideas at the time the books of the Bible were sorted and compiled. Anything that did not meet the proper standard was thrown out. This also means that there was a wide range of views and conflicting opinions about who and what Jesus was, which means they really did not know that much about him. Therefore, we have to ask, how really important was he at the time if so few people knew anything factual about him?

Another point we should consider is that the gospels of the New Testament are not likely to have been written by those whose names are attached to them. Although several of them are written by Paul, the authorship of most of the books in the New Testament is unknown or highly questionable. Therefore, the authenticity of the information in these gospels is just as questionable. In other words, it is neither an authentic account of Christian beginnings nor of the history of the church. Because of this, *historians of religion would call it a myth*. Why is this so? Let us take a closer look.

What we can recognize with enough insight is that each group of early Christians created the image of Jesus in the way that the founder of that school wanted Jesus to be. Through this form of mythmaking, the early Jesus people attracted others to join their ranks based on the idea of becoming a part of the Kingdom of God on earth. It was this that attracted Jews in the cities of Syria, Asia Minor, and Greece where they formed small groups who regularly met together at people's homes to discuss being a part of this Kingdom of God. Gathering together for a meal was a common custom in these groups, which also provided a sense of belonging and fellowship beyond all social identities. Thus, they felt a shared social vision to the point wherein they considered themselves already to be a part of the Kingdom of God on earth.

This is what attracted Paul, which caused his conversion to faith in Jesus, for, as he later said in *Galations* (3:28), they were all one in Jesus. What could provide more of a feeling of fellowship than that? And this is also what Paul later wrote about in some of his letters.

Much of the evidence on this sort of cult based on Jesus can be found in the letters of Paul, written in the 50s. Paul was at first greatly opposed to the early Christians, and took pride in persecuting them. He was a Jew, and proud of it. He admits in *Galations* (1:13) that he viewed Christians as a threat to his own religious convictions and was actively trying to destroy them. It is interesting because later he seemed to view his own earlier religious views, and those who followed them, as a threat to his new religion of Christianity.

Later, he explains in *Galations* (1:12, 15-16) that he had a revelation that Jesus was God's son. Thus, his mind was changed. This has been a prominent point in Christian theology: That Jesus is the son of God. This is the basis of all of Paul's teachings. However, this foundation is perpetuated by an inaccurate translation of Paul's statement. This is explained by Burton Mack on page 102 of his book, *Who Wrote the New Testament?*: "Unfortunately, the New Revised Standard Version [of the Bible] continues a long tradition of sloppy translation by suggesting that God 'was pleased to reveal his Son *to* me' (*Gal*. 1:15-16, emphasis added). The Greek term *en* means 'in' or 'by means of,' not 'to.' Instead, Paul was saying that God 'was pleased to make his own son known by means of me.' He was not claiming a personal, private experience or encounter with God's son. He was reporting a sense of divine commission resulting from his insight (or 'revelation') that the Christians' claim about Jesus had significance for Israel's mission and that he, Paul, would have to lead the way."

So just as firmly as he had once persecuted the Jesus people, he was now just as firmly supporting them. From this story, it was embellished into the version that appears in *Acts* (22:6-11) in which Paul encounters a blinding light that knocks him down on the road to Damascus. Although this was written some eighty years after the event, the idea that Paul had a personal encounter with the resurrected Jesus has become the traditional view of Paul's conversion to Christianity.

Thereafter, beginning from the time of Paul's first letter to the Thessalonians, he had succeeded in changing the message of Jesus into a cult in which the followers had been "called" into God's kingdom, had been "chosen" to follow, "turned" away from idols to God, were inspired by the spirit, and looked on one another as brothers and sisters in the new family of God. So even if the people of the area already had some appreciation for Jesus, Paul came in and turned it into something else, and enthused them into believing they were a special people. This plan of his succeeded, and he was able to form a congregation by turning the figure of Christ into a superhuman, a myth that became a proclamation, the basis of which could be used for an organization or a new religion. This was the first of what was to become Paul's mission of spreading the Christ myth to form a new social arrangement

As Paul preached, he continued to develop his philosophy. It is not that he had everything together from the start. There were still issues about which people approached him, especially regarding what happened after people died in Christianity. This required that he work out how they would have eternal life in Christ. So he kept changing and forming his ideals in order to solve all of the issues and have answers to the questions. In this case, he worked out or imagined an apocalyptic view as the way to answer this concern. Thus, the Christian concept of eternal life was born: that all believers would attain everlasting life at the end of time when they would rise up from the grave and go to heaven, or some other-worldly place, to be together again "in Christ." And as Paul explained in *I Thessalonians* (4:18), "encourage one another with these words," which is what hopeful Christians have been doing ever since. This is just one example of how Paul continued to invent his philosophy to fit whatever need was required.

Anyone, however, who has any real understanding about the soul knows that this idea that after death the soul waits for the end of time to rise again in the rejuvenated body in which he had died, and then achieves everlasting life, is absurd. What happens if the buried body is stolen? Or disintegrates? Or is buried at sea? Or cremated? Or when its organs are donated to benefit the lives of others? In spite of the fact that Paul worked so hard to develop this philosophy, so many questions remain and go unanswered. How can anyone accept it? Yet, due to spiritual ignorance, millions of people did, and millions more still do today.

After the teaching and writings of Paul, the gospels appeared. The gospel of *Mark* is the first, written 40 years after Jesus' time. The only reason it was called

Mark is because Papias, Bishop of Hieropolis in Asia Minor (ca. 130), named Mark as the author. In spite of all the writings of Paul, before the description of the life of Jesus as we find it in *Mark*, there were no references to the death of Jesus as a crucifixion. Other than this, there is no historical way of knowing the real circumstances of Jesus' death. In fact, before *Mark* there was no such description of the life of Jesus anywhere. Even though the author of the gospel of *Mark* is unknown, whoever it was used the recent history of the destruction of Jerusalem in 70 C.E., along with earlier traditions, and crafted a plot to help create the story of Jesus, which has since become the "gospel truth" for Christians. This story is what made Jesus the Christ, Son of God. Without this story, it is likely that the emergence of Christianity as we know it would never have happened.

The gospel of *Matthew* does not seem to have existed in its present form until 173 A.D., when Apollinaris, Bishop of Hierapolis at the time, accredits the book to Matthew. But earlier editions are said to have originally been composed in the late 80s. The surprise of this gospel is that after the descriptions of Jesus in *Mark*, we now find the descriptions given more to everyday proportions, although Matthew did use the previous traditions and information, used much of the material from *Mark*, and added some new stories of his own. This gospel became the preferred gospel and won first place in the New Testament.

The gospel of *Matthew* seems to have been primarily taken from a previous text called *The Gospel of the Hebrews*, which gave the genealogy of Jesus back to David, yet did not contain a description of Jesus' virgin birth. Thus, some say the story of Jesus' birth was added later after the idea had been taken from other stories of significant personalities being born from pure virgins.

The gospel of *Luke* and its sequel, the *Acts of the Apostles*, were written in the early second century, around the year 120 C.E., 75 or more years after the time of Jesus. Again the author is unknown. Only in the second century was the work attributed to Luke, similar to the way other earlier anonymous writings were attributed to the apostles or their companions to give them some credibility.

At the time of *Luke* what we find is more emphasis on the apostles, along with their link to the bishops, the instructors of Christian society, which was a powerful position. We also find a different view of Jesus, one that is more casual and relaxed compared to the more confrontational tone in *Mark* or the serious teachings in *Matthew*. Again some of the previous information and stories were used, but additional ones came from somewhere or were imagined and included.

Then we have the gospel of *John* which was written in the 90s, and provides evidence to indicate that it was developed by a completely separate and independent Christian community that had its own ideas on Jesus. This is why it starts from a view of the cosmic powers before the time of creation. Then we read of God's word creating life and moving the worlds, and then later are told that Jesus is that word. So in *John* we have a completely different kind of Jesus who appears from heaven. In this gospel, some of the stories found in the other three are left out and new ones installed. Others are rearranged in their order and changed in their content, and the miracles provide opportunity for discourses in which Jesus emphasizes that he is the son of the Father. In this way, the community from which this book came certainly put its own stamp and interpretation on the material and traditions regarding Jesus.

Many people feel that the gospels of the New Testament are written by the 12 apostles, so who could have been more authorized to write them? But the 12 apostles were Andrew, John, Bartholomew, Judas, Jude, James, another James, Matthew, Peter, Phillip, Simon, and Thomas. After Judas committed suicide, he was replaced with Matthias. So Mark, Luke, and Paul, who are supposed to be authors of several of the New Testament books, were not apostles. And Paul never even met Jesus and only became a Christian several years after Jesus had disappeared. Even *Revelations* is accepted by many scholars to be merely a collection of works by unknown authors.

By careful study one can find many discrepancies between the gospels, which questions their validity. The authors, whoever they were, wrote of things of which they had little knowledge, and ascribed sayings to Jesus that do not conform to his faith. Thus, they obviously wrote their tales as they heard them from other reports or previously existing texts, and in this way included various inaccurate statements.

For example, *St. Mark* (7.31) states: "And again, departing from the [Mediterranean] coasts of Tyre and Sidon, he came unto the Sea of Galilee, through the midst of the coasts of Decapolis." What is wrong here is that it is known that Decapolis was on the southeast side of the Sea of Galilee, and northeast of Judea. So there were no coasts of Decapolis, which is a name that was not known prior to the time of Emperor Nero, who reigned 54-68 A.D. This indicates that the narrators knew little of what they were writing about, at least in regard to the local geography, not to mention other things. Many other such examples are also available, which we will not include here.

We also find where the narrator of *Matthew* has Jesus explain in chapter 24 the signs that will indicate the second coming of Christ. These include false Christs and false prophets, pestilences, earthquakes, famine, wars, nation against nation, the darkening of the sun and moon, the stars falling from the sky, etc., all described in verses that are often referred to by many. But finally in verse 34, Jesus specifically says: "Verily I say unto you, This generation shall not pass, till all these things be fulfilled." But we can plainly see that many, many generations have passed since the time this was said. Years later, the fact that the return of Jesus had still not taken place was attempted to be justified in *II Peter*, Chapter Three, where it says that the Lord is not slack in His promise and the day of Jesus' return will come like a thief in the night. This is a prime example of how one book of the Bible tries to justify mistakes made in another, and shows how convinced the early Christians were that Christ was expected to appear again very soon. Well, they are still waiting. However, many Christians use these same descriptions today to preach that we should have faith that Christ will come again at any time.

Nonetheless, Christianity became stronger a few hundred years after the time Jesus is said to have died. Constantine and the Pope, with the intention of suppressing all contradictory views of Jesus' divinity, commanded that all such "heretical" books should be found and completely destroyed. The authors of these works and their followers were all automatically excommunicated and declared eternally damned. Emperor Theodosius convened the second General Council at Constantinople in 381 and severely persecuted as heretics all those who did not accept the resolutions. Thus, the standard was set and was spread by force. Nearly 50 years after the death of King Constantine, the Church became the official religion of the Roman Empire and the position of the Church was then fixed. Nonetheless, many philosophical debates continued, as one did between Nestorius of Constantinople and Cyril of Alexandria in the fifth century. Nestorius accepted the humanity of Jesus and described Mary as the mother of Christ rather than the mother of God. Cyril, taking the view the Church propagated that Christ was God, greatly opposed Nestorius. The third council of the Church at Ephesus, in 431, condemned the ideas of Nestorius and exiled him to the desert of Egypt in 435, but his theories continued to spread into Persia, India, and on into Central Asia and China. Such controversies in the Church continued and lead to different conclusions and the formation of different sects. Even today we can see the almost unlimited variance of Christian sects and churches, each of which has its own ideas as to what is the nature of Christ, what is the soul, what is heaven, and so on. And each one thinking they are superior than all of the others.

In light of these disputes over Christian philosophy, it has been found that more theologians and biblical scholars who understand the actual history of the biblical texts are less likely to blindly accept such concepts as the immaculate conception of Jesus or his death on the cross. It is this that forces the Church to continue to re-examine the foundations of the Christian religion and the idea that the Bible is "the word of God," written by men who were "inspired" by the Holy Spirit. Not to be sure about such matters and yet preach as though the Bible is infallible is certainly a grave error, especially when the high-living preachers pose as the most righteous and truthful, concerned for the souls of all men, while demanding their followers to be righteous believers as well, and to show their faith by giving lots of money and time for the cause.

What all this means can be summarized in the words of Burton L. Mack, author of *Who Wrote the New Testament?* (page 308), one of the most scholarly and intriguing books on the formation of the New Testament I have ever read: "The writings in the New testament were not written by eyewitnesses of an overpowering divine appearance in the midst of human history. This is the impression created by the final formation of the New Testament. Dismantled and given back to the people who produced them, the writings of the New Testament are the record of three hundred years of intellectual labor in the interest of a thoroughly human construction. . . When combined with the Jewish scriptures, moreover, for the reasons we have been able to identify, the Christian Bible turns out to be a masterpiece of invention. It is charged with the intellectual battles and resolutions of untold numbers of persons who invested in a grand project three centuries in the making. It finally reads as the epic they imagined to sustain them, the history of God's plan to establish His kingdom on earth. To be quite frank about it, the Bible is the product of very energetic and successful mythmaking on the part of those early Christians."

The Bible is the Christian epic and holy book. Thus, it can be difficult to be critical of it. And Christians especially will be hesitant to look at whatever discrepancies are found and apprehensive to view its faults. Some feel that it is a book that should not be questioned in such a way. However, the Christian mind-set can often be recognized by the way they look over this world and criticize others on the basis of what the Bible says, all the while thinking the Bible is beyond reproach. As soon as someone wants to question the authenticity of the Bible, Christians generally quickly lose the ability for calm analysis, introspection, or cultural critique. However, since they have interpreted the course of history by the stories the Bible contains, and the fact that the Bible's development spans more than a thousand years in a time when other histories have been recorded, scholars will expect that what it says should be verified. What has happened is that much of this history and the stories found in the Bible often do not corroborate other recorded histories. Then how truthful is the Bible? We cannot keep pressing forward the premise of the Bible if it does not lead to the truth, or if we are all merely believing in the hope that it is the truth. It may turn out that belief in the Bible and faith in Jesus are two entirely different things. It seems to be turning out that the man Jesus is different than the myths in the New Testament that have been built up around him. There may, indeed, be a difference between what he actually taught and what the Bible says he taught. And if there is a difference, then from where did these traditions, teachings, and cultural traits really come? That's what we should really try to understand, which is what this book is all about. That's what we will continue to investigate in the following sections.

THE VEDIC INFLUENCE ON CHRISTIANITY

When we consider the story of how baby Jesus appeared in the heart of Mary by immaculate conception, as well as the bright star appearing in the night sky, we can discern a direct parallel to Lord Krishna's birth three thousand years earlier in Vrindavana, India, as recorded in the Vedic literature. It is described in the ancient Vedic texts how Krishna appeared in the mind of Vasudeva, Krishna's father, and was then transferred into the heart of His mother, Devaki. During Krishna's birth, the bright star Rohini was high in the sky, and the king at the time, Kamsa, actually ordered the killing of all the infants in an attempt to kill Krishna, similar to the way Herod was supposed to have done as described in the gospel of *Matthew*. And just as a multitude appeared among the shepherds in the hills praising God at the time of Jesus' birth, there were also many demigods who came and danced and sang about the glories of Krishna when He was ready to appear in this world. Krishna was born in a cave-like dungeon, while Jesus was also born in a cave, although some say a manger in a barn. Rays of light illuminated the area after they had taken birth. While newly born, they both spoke of why they had come to this world. And as wise men were supposed to have presented Jesus with frankincense and myrrh, baby Krishna was also presented with gifts that included sandalwood and perfumes.

At the time when Krishna left this planet, His foot was pierced with an arrow, while Jesus' side was pierced with a spear. There was a darkness that descended when Jesus is said to have been crucified, just as there was a darkness and many calamities taking place when Krishna left this world. And as there is a description of many ominous signs that are to signify the second coming of Christ, there are even more symptoms of the terrible age of Kali that we are going through that indicates the time before the coming of Krishna's next incarnation as Kalki. Many of these I have included in my book, *The Vedic Prophecies*. There arc many other parallels that we could refer to that are disclosed in the *Vedas*, which were written many hundreds of years before the Bible.

Jesus preached in a way that can also be compared to the sayings of Krishna. For example, in *Bhagavad-gita* (7.6-7) Krishna said, "I am the cause of the whole universe, through Me it is created and dissolved, all things are dependant on Me as pearls are strung on a thread." Jesus said, "Of Him and through Him, and unto Him, arc all things. All things were made by Him; and without Him was not anything made that was madc." (*John* 1.3) Krishna had said (*Bg*.4.7), "For the establishment of righteousness I am born from time to time." This compares to Jesus in *John* 18:37, wherein he says, "Thou sayest that I am a king. To this end was I born, and for this cause came I into the world, that I should bear witness unto the truth. Every one that is of the truth heareth my voice." These and many other comparisons can be made. Nonetheless, the fact is that the history of Krishna is thousands of years older than that of Jesus.

In this way, practically speaking, what we find in the Bible regarding Jesus' birth is a description of the appearance of Lord Krishna, but only the names have been changed. Of course, there are different theories about how this happened. One theory is that when the Christians went to India, they found out that this story was there in the *Bhagavat-Purana*; so, they immediately had to change the date of when the *Bhagavat-Purana* was supposed to have been written. So now the historians generally say that it was written about 1400 years ago. Otherwise, how could they explain the story of Krishna's birth being so similar to the story of Christ's birth? They thought that the Vedic pundits must have heard about the story of Jesus and adapted the story to their own incarnation, as if the Vedic scholars would demean themselves by putting a story into their scripture that was heard from people who were considered low-born foreigners. Actually, what happened was just the opposite.

    Since both the *Bhagavad-gita* and the *Srimad-Bhagavatam* contain many
similar sentiments and descriptions to Christianity, numerous Christian scholars
have tried to prove that the stories therein had been borrowed from the Bible.
However, this has been proved to be quite the reverse. This is has been accepted
by Reverend J. B. S. Carwithen, known as one of the "Brampton Lecturers," who
says, as quoted in Reverend J. P. Lundy's *Monumental Christianity* (pp. 151-2),
"Both the name Crishna and the general outline of his story are long anterior to
the birth of our Savior [Jesus Christ]; and this we know, not on the presumed
antiquity of the Hindoo records alone. Both Arrian and Strabo assert that the God
Crishna was anciently worshiped at Mathura, on the river Jumna, where he is
worshiped at this day. But the emblems and attributes essential to this deity are
also transplanted into the mythology of the West."

    Monier Williams, one of the accepted early Western authorities on Hinduism,
Professor at Oxford in London and a devout Christian, also focused on this issue
when writing for the "Society for Promoting Christian Knowledge" in his book,
Indian Wisdom. Therein he states: "To any one who has followed me in tracing the
outline of this remarkable philosophical dialogue, and has noted the numerous
parallels it offers to passages in our Sacred Scriptures, it may seem strange that I
hesitate to concur to any theory which explains these coincidences by supposing
the author [of such Vedic books as the *Bhagavad-gita* and the *Srimad-
Bhagavatam*] had access to the New Testament, or that he derived some of his
ideas from the first propagators of Christianity. Surely it will be conceded that the
probability of contact and interaction between Gentile systems and the Christian
religion of the first two centuries of our era must have been greater in Italy than
in India. Yet, if we take the writings and sayings of those great Roman
philosophers, Seneca, Epictetus, and Marcus Aurelius, we shall find them full of
resemblances to passages in our Scriptures, while there appears to be no ground
whatever for supposing that these eminent Pagan writers and thinkers derived any
of their ideas from either Jewish or Christian sources. In fact, the Reverend F. W.
Farrar, in his interesting and valuable work, *Seekers After God*, has clearly shown
that 'to say that Pagan morality kindled its faded taper at the Gospel light, whether
furtively or unconsciously, that it dissembled the obligation and made a boast of
the splendor, as if it were originally her own, is to make an assertion wholly
untenable.' He points out that the attempts of the Christian Fathers to make out
Pythagoras a debtor to Hebraic wisdom, Plato an 'Atticizing Moses,' Aristotle a
picker-up of ethics from a Jew, Seneca a correspondent of St. Paul, were due in
some cases to ignorance, in some to a want of perfect honesty in controversial
dealing. . . It must indeed be admitted that the flames of true light which emerge
from the mists of pantheism in the writings of the Indian philosophers, must
spring from the same source of light as the Gospel itself; but it may reasonably be
questioned whether there could have been any actual contact of the Hindoo
systems with Christianity without a more satisfying result in the modification of
pantheistic and anti-Christian ideas."

Again, Monier points out the antiquity of the Vedic culture, practically over and beyond all others, when he explains on page iv of his book: "It should not be forgotten that although the nations of Europe have changed their religions during the past eighteen centuries, *the Hindu has not done so, except very partially*. Islam converted a certain number by force of arms in the eighth and following centuries, and Christian truth is at last slowly creeping onwards and winning its way by its own inherent energy in the nineteenth; *but the religious creeds, rites, customs, and habits of thought of the Hindus generally have altered little since the days of Manu. . ."*

In light of all this research, by myself and others, we can conclude with the words of T. W. Doane in his book, *Bible Myths and Their Parallels in Other Religions*. Therein he goes so far as to say at the beginning of Chapter Twenty-Eight, ". . . the mythological portion of the history of Jesus of Nazareth, contained in the books forming the Canon of the New Testament, is nothing more or less than a copy of the mythological histories of the Hindoo Savior Crishna, and the Buddhist Savior Buddha, with a mixture of mythology borrowed from the Persians and other nations. . ."

One archeological find that proved that knowledge of Krishna antedated Christianity by at least 200 years was the Heliodorus column, built in 113 B.C. in central India by the Greek ambassador to India, Heliodorus. On it is an inscription commenting on the ambassador's devotion to Lord Vishnu (Krishna) and mentioning when the column had been erected. The column still stands near the town of Vidisha.

We must remember that when the Christians first came to India to preach, they were not very well received by the local people. There was very little penetration because the Christian priests and missionaries were seen for what they were: *mlecchas* and *yavanas*, more or less unclean cow-killers or untouchables in local terminology. So it is doubtful that the Vedic pandits spent much time even listening to them, what to speak of writing scripture or changing the story of Krishna's birth on account of hearing these missionaries. Of course, now as Indian society has deteriorated and become more attracted to Western values (partly due to being indoctrinated by the British rule years ago), Christianity is more easily accepted.

So, the conclusion we must arrive at is that the story of Lord Krishna's birth, along with numerous other parts of the Vedic philosophy, must have come to the mid-eastern part of the world because of the many trade caravans going back and forth at that time from India to the region of Palestine. Since there were no real witnesses of Christ's birth and hardly any history in the gospels of the life of Christ up to the age of thirty, it is likely they applied the story of Krishna to Jesus' life. Otherwise, there is little historical evidence that any of it is factual.

There is evidence, however, as more facts are being uncovered, that contends that Jesus may have been nailed to the cross but did not die on it. After having been taken from the cross, he later recovered from the ordeal rather than rose from the dead. The Shroud of Turin, if it is authentic (which has been a great debate by itself), seems to provide some evidence that Christ was not dead when taken from the cross since his body was still bleeding while wrapped in the cloth. Even if Christ did appear to die on the cross, being a yogic master, he could have put himself into trance to be revived later. This goes on even today with yogis in India or fakirs in Egypt who can appear to die, be buried for hours, days, months, or sometimes years, and then be uncovered and resurrected from their apparent death. Even the Koran (4.157) claims that Jesus did not die on the cross.

There is also evidence that after the crucifixion Jesus traveled through Turkey, Persia, and then India. The Russian scholar Nicolas Notovitch discovered in 1887 Buddhist documents at the Hemis monastery in Ladakh that describe the life of Issa. Issa is the Tibetan spelling while Isa is the Arabic spelling of the name Jesus, and the name commonly used in Islam. The manuscript was originally from Lhasa, translated into Tibetan from the Pali language. Jesus' ascension into heaven may have referred to his entrance into Kashmir, an area considered by many to have been like heaven or the promised land.

Furthermore, the *Bhavishya Purana*, dating back to 3000 B.C. and compiled by Srila Vyasadeva, also described the future coming of Jesus and his activities. Dr. Vedavyas, a research scholar who holds a doctorate in Sanskrit, said that the *Purana* tells of how Jesus would visit the Himalayas and do penance to acquire spiritual maturity under the guidance of the sages and *siddha-yogis* of India. Dr. Vedavyas says that besides describing the future events of Kali-yuga, the *Purana* predicted that Jesus would be born of an unmarried woman, Kumari (Mari or Mary) Garbha Sambhava, and would first go to India when he was 13 years old and visit many Hindu and Buddhist holy places. This was his spiritual training in a time of his life of which the gospels are totally ignorant. Furthermore, the actual burial place of Jesus is believed to be in Anzimar or Khanyar, Srinagar's old town in Kashmir, where thousands of pious pay homage to the tomb of Issa each year. There is where he settled and died sometime after the crucifixion.

In any case, the Christian Church began with what Paul said about the resurrection of Jesus. Whether the resurrection actually happened or not cannot be proved. Nonetheless, a new faith was born. But through the years there has been much controversy about the nature of Jesus and whether he was actually God as some Christians seem to believe. None of his direct disciples believed that he was, and, indeed, there are many Bible verses which state directly that he was the son of God, such as *Luke* 1.35, *Matthew* 17.5, *John* 4.15, 8.28, 14.28, and others. Only Paul put forward the idea that Jesus was God. But historically it is said that Paul never met Jesus personally, and was converted to Christianity several years after Jesus' disappearance. Other than that, most of Jesus' followers thought that perhaps he was the Jewish Messiah. But the Jewish Messiah, according to their prophecies, was not God but rather a Jew who was empowered by God. This actually fits into the Vedic view because there are many empowered living beings who appear from time to time who are sent by God to represent and disseminate

His law. Furthermore, Bhaktisiddhanta Sarasvati, one of the great Vaishnava spiritual masters in the Madhava-Gaudiya line of disciplic succession, has stated that Jesus was a *shaktyavesha avatar*, or an empowered living entity meant to preach the glories of God.

People may say that Jesus walked on water, healed the sick, raised the dead, so he must have been God. But even today in India there are *yogis* who can walk on water or do other amazing things, like walking over hot coals. This is not like the Hollywood fad of fire walking, but the *yogis* let the coals burn for days and get so hot that you cannot even get near them without burning your clothes. Then, after spending one month in penance, praying to Durga, they walk across the fire and do not even burn their feet. But some people will say this is the work of the devil. However, is this not peculiar logic to say that walking across fire is of the devil, but if one walks across water he is God? This kind of thinking that is usually found amongst fundamentalists simply shows a great ignorance of yogic powers, which is all walking across fire or water is. Therefore, the miracles of Jesus are a sign of his knowledge of the mystical powers that come from practicing yoga. But it is not a proof that someone is God. In fact, the Dead Sea Scrolls prove more or less conclusively that the whole concept of Jesus Christ's divinity is a later addition.

One important part of Eastern knowledge that was present in early Christianity was the understanding of *karma* and reincarnation. I have already discussed this and pointed out some of the verses that showed the acceptance of reincarnation in the Bible in *The Secret Teachings of the Vedas*; so, I will not go into it so deeply here. But it is known that the Second Council of Constantinople in 553 A.D. threw out all references to reincarnation and stated that the idea of it was a myth, and anyone who believed in it would be excommunicated. Of course, this action would not be unexpected in light of the other things the Church has done throughout history in order to place itself as the only way to reach heaven and attain the mercy of God. By eliminating the possibility of reincarnation and the soul's existence prior to this life, there could be no chance for the soul to reach the state of spiritual perfection over a period of several lifetimes. There would only be this one lifetime in which the soul came into existence, and one chance for a person to reach either heaven or eternal hell, which would be determined by the intervention of the Church. In other words, the Church felt threatened by the fact that the soul has an eternal and personal relationship with God that must be rekindled either in one, two, or however many lifetimes it takes, and this relationship does not necessarily depend on one's good standing in any religious organization. Thus, people could try to re-establish their relationship with God by other means than the dictates of the Church, which is what the Church could not tolerate.

Unfortunately, by taking out the knowledge of reincarnation and *karma*, the Church has created huge gaps in its philosophy which leave questions it cannot answer. For example, the Christians cannot explain why one person may be born blind, poor, deformed, or sickly, while another may be born healthy and rich. They do not understand why reversals in life may happen to some, and others seem to have a life of ease. They cannot explain why these differences take place and, in fact, they sometimes blame God for such things, which only shows their ignorance of spiritual knowledge. Furthermore, they do not understand the science of the soul and our spiritual identity, the nature of the spiritual realm, the characteristics of the personality of God, nor the pastimes and incarnations of God, and so on. Thus, the spiritual knowledge that the Christians utilize in their philosophy is very elementary and incomplete. And as we have already established in our previous writings, reaching complete spiritual perfection is not possible in such an incomplete spiritual process. At best, it promotes good moral values, detachment toward worldly life, attachment and devotion to God, and the possibility of reaching the heavenly planets. However, the heavenly planets are still within the material cosmic manifestation and not in the spiritual realm. A real religionist or transcendentalist is interested only in reaching the level of spiritual realization that enables him to directly perceive his spiritual identity and enter the spiritual strata far beyond this material creation.

Actually, Christians still must accept the understanding of *karma* and reincarnation to some extent in order to explain logically how one can have a life after death in heaven or hell. According to the Christian doctrine, qualifying for heaven or hell depends on one's actions in this life. That is called *karma* in Vedic literature. And as one enters heaven or hell in his next life, he takes on or incarnates in a different form. This is reincarnation. So Christians must, at least to this degree, accept *karma* and reincarnation whether they fully understand it or not. But to understand it more completely, as explained in the philosophy of the Vedic literature, allows us to realize that our good or unpleasant situations in this life depends on our activities from past lives. And by our activities in this life we can cause our future existence to be good or bad, or we can reach the heavenly or hellish planetary systems to work out our *karma*. This understanding is accepted by many cultures throughout the world. In fact, the scholar Max Muller remarked that the greatest minds humanity has produced have accepted reincarnation.

More connections between Christianity and the Vedic culture can be recognized as follows:

The ancient Vedic custom of applying ash or sandalwood paste to the body is still retained by Christianity in the observance of Ash Wednesday. The so-called "All Soul's Day" is an exact translation of the Vedic observance of *Sarva Pitri Amavasya*, the day fixed by tradition for the worship of all deceased ancestors.

Another Christian tradition derived from Vedic origins is that of having and ringing bells in the churches, especially before or during worship. In Vedic temples it is often seen where bells are rung during worship and when pilgrims enter the temple, announcing their entrance. Christian churches also ring bells to announce the beginning of worship. The word "bell" comes from the Sanskrit *bal* which means strength. This is in reference to the idea that ringing a bell adds force to the voice of prayer in invoking divinity.

When the Christians say "Amen" at the end of their hymns or to emphasize something, what they are saying is a corrupted form of "Aum" or "Om," which is a standard form of Vedic meditation and name of the Supreme Being.

While we are on the topic of words used in Christianity that are derived from Sanskrit, the Catholic term "Madonna," another name for Mother Mary, comes from the Sanskrit *Mata Nah*, meaning "Our Mother." This is also derived from the great Vedic Mother Goddess. Thus, Mother Mary was a reference not only to the mother of Jesus alone, but a reference to the Goddess, mother of all humanity. Furthermore, the European term of "Madam" is a soft pronunciation of the Hindu term *mata* or *mataji*, which also means "Mother."

The term "vestry" in referring to the room in churches in which holy clothes are kept comes from the Sanskrit word *vestra*, meaning clothes. Even the word "psalm" with a silent "P" comes from the Sanskrit word *sam* or *sama* which means holy and serious sacred songs, hymns or chants, as found in the *Sama-veda*.

Other Christian links with Sanskrit words can be found in the name Bethlehem, which is the English mispronunciation of the Sanskrit *Vatsaldham*, which means "the home (town) of the darling child." The Sanskrit term *Nandarath* is linguistically connected with Nazareth. *Nandarath* means Nanda's chariot, and King Nanda was the guardian at whose village he nurtured Lord Krishna (sometimes pronounced as Chrisn, and later Christ in some regions).

The Christian term "Satan" and the Islamic term "Shaitan" both are derived from the Sanskrit term *Sat-na*, which means non-truth, falsehood, or fraudulence. The Christians who explain the term "Devil" as a fallen angel should realize that the word is derived from the Sanskrit terminology which signifies a fallen *Deva*.

At the beginning of the book of *John* in the New Testament, it states, "In the beginning was the Word, and the Word was with God, and the Word was God." This is actually a verbatim translation of the Vedic Sanskrit *mantra*: "*Prajapatirvai idamagraasit, tasya vag dvitiyaa asit, vag vai paramam Brahma.*"

The Holy Spirit in Christianity is called *Paramatma* in Sanskrit, or *Parakalate*. In Greek the word is *Paraclete*. This is the God of that spiritual knowledge which is revealed or descended, or the *Veda*, which is spoken through the prophets (Sanskrit *purohitas*). *Veda* is *Yeda* in Hebrew, the word God uses for His Self-revelation in *Exodus* of the Old Testament. *Veda* in Greek is *Oida*, and *Aidos*, from which the English word *idea* is derived. The term *oida* is used for God's/Christ's Sel-revelation in the New Testament. Thus, the *Vedas*, the Old and New Testament, and the related scriptures are but part of one continuous revelation of God.

Dr. Venu Gopalacharya also points out in his book, *World-Wide Hindu Culture* (pp. 158-9), that in the book of *Genesis*, Chapter 22, God told Abraham that he and his wife, Sarah, would be blessed and God would, "make your descendants as numerous as the stars in the sky and as the sand on the seashore. . . and through thy seed, shall all nations be blessed because thou hast obeyed my voice." Dr. Venu Gopalacharya explains, "Abraham and Sarah [Sarai] refer to [or was derived from] the Indian version of Brahma and Sarasvati. This indicates that this is an abridgement of some of the versions in the Indian *Puranas* referring to 'Brahma and his consort as the first aspects of the Supreme Lord or His agents of creation and offering sacrifices [or performing austerities].' In the commencement of the book of *Genesis*, the sentence, 'In the Beginning, God created the heaven and the earth, and the earth was formless and empty, darkness was over the surface of the deep, and the Spirit of God moved upon the waters.' This is similar to the Vedic *Puranas* stating that MahaVishnu or Narayana was lying on Adisesha in the ocean, [who is] the original source from which Brahma comes into being. The killing of Abel by his brother for the sacrifice of animals refers to the slaying of *Asuras* by the *Devas*, their own brothers, due to the difference of opinion about the mode of offering sacrifices or worshiping God.

"Just as Indian *Puranas* were compiled to glorify a particular aspect of the Supreme Lord as Vishnu, or of Shiva, Durga, Ganesha, etc., the Old Testament deals with 'Yahwe,' an aspect of the angry god Rudra. As the word 'Rudra' means a weeping god, the Jews for worship use weeping before the wailing wall of the 'Dome of the Rock' within the temple of Harmahesh Sri (called by Judaic religionists as *Haram Esh Sheriff*) in the old city of Jerusalem, i.e., Yadusailam. The Jews spell the name of the city as 'Yerushalayim,' of which the Sanskrit synonym is *Yadu Ishalayam*, which means the temple of the Lord of the Yadus [the descendants of Lord Krishna's clan].

"Dr. S. Radhakrishnan has informed in his book, *Pracya Mattu Paschatya Sanskriti*, that the Greeks asserted that the Jews were Indians whom the Syrians called Judea, the Sanskrit synonym of which is *Yadava* or *Yaudheya*, and the Indians called them Kalanis, meaning orthodox followers of the scripture."

This information certainly provides serious insights into the relationship between the early Jews, Christians, the Bible, and the Vedic culture. I could go on pointing out more Eastern traditions that influenced or were adopted and preserved in various levels of Christianity, but there are other topics that should be covered.

THE DARK SIDE OF CHRISTIANITY

Let us not forget how many of the pagan or Vedic festivals and temples were forced to become Christian. The Church has a long and bloody history in its concern for the souls of all men. In the fourth and fifth centuries, the Church began to burn the huge libraries and close the schools of free thought in places like Alexandria, Athens, and elsewhere. To push on Christian thought and control the philosophical views of people, it was Christianity, especially the rules established by the wicked King Constantine, that began what is called the Dark Ages. This was a time of intense prejudice, cruelty, and persecution against all who may not have been in complete agreement with the Christian doctrine. The early Christian leaders were cruel and looked on anything other than their own faith as heresy, just as we see today some modern fundamentalist Christians who view anything other than Christianity as being associated with the devil and worthy of being stamped out. This is the same kind of logic they use to say that it is the wrath of God on the heathen if a Hindu temple is damaged by a storm or something, but it is the work of the devil if a bolt of lightning strikes a church.

Once Christianity began to spread through Europe, it was often met with resistance, but the "heretics" were treated with torture and death. Christianity was a religion of the sword that compares with the organized terror of the Nazis. Anything the Christians did not like they destroyed, including academies and the books by the Greek poets and philosophers of the time. They went so far as to kill Hypatia, the great woman who was head of the School of Philosophy at Alexandria. This was accomplished by a mob attack on her in which they tore off her clothes, and then dragged her into a church and killed her. Then they cut her body up into pieces with oyster shells, and burned her piece by piece. Thus, came the end of Greek philosophy in Alexandria. This was simply because Hypatia was a woman known to teach men in her lectures, and because Cyril, the Christian bishop of Alexandria, wanted to ruin her. Cyril hated her because of her many accomplishments and because she was a symbol of individual freedom, and freedom from the fanatical and growing power of the Christian Church. Quite obviously, the Church had no respect for women and, like barbarians that many of the men seemed to be, treated them so.

Later, in 1233, the Roman Catholic Church established the Inquisition as the forceful aspect of the Vatican for the purpose of eliminating heresy. In the thirteenth century it began its slaughter of heretics throughout Europe. In the cases of heresy that the Inquisition dealt with, charges could be brought up on anyone, and the offenders would not have to be told who accused them or what specifically were the accusations. If a neighbor simply did not like you, they could start rumors that would force you to be subjected to the torture of the Inquisition. If you were found guilty of any kind of heresy, you could face punishment of heavy fines or even death by being burned alive. In 1252, Pope Innocent IV authorized the use of torture while the accused was being interrogated. Once the torture started, it usually did not stop unless the victim confessed to whatever the charges were. The Spanish Inquisition was established in 1480 and was much more severe in the way it meted out punishment.

As this madness swept across Europe, things became totally barbaric and the Inquisition, which sometimes held its trials in secret, struck fear into the hearts of everyone. Thousands upon thousands were killed and burned alive as the Church and authorities grew rich by confiscating the property of the victims, all in the name of Christianity. Unfortunately, many of these so-called heretics were people or clerics who simply wanted to return to the basic piety and message of Jesus and distance themselves from the intrigues and excesses found in the Roman Church.

In time, the interest in the condemning eyes of the Church and Inquisition included not only wiping out heretics but also finding witches. In many cases, the charge of being a witch or heretic was the same. The witch hunts started in the 14th century and lasted more than 300 years and affected all of Europe. By the 17th century, as many as 200,000 or more people had been killed by the Christian-controlled courts.

For many years being a witch was nothing extraordinary. It merely meant that someone was familiar with the use of herbs and the old folk traditions of healing. It may also mean that one followed the old nature religions, or respected the early demigods and goddesses, like Thor, Wotan, Herne, Mithra, etc., that were popular in various regions prior to Christianity. There may have been a few who could cast spells, but that was not the primary objective.

Over the years as the Roman Empire declined, the power of the Church rose. As it did, it began to incorporate the days of pagan celebrations into its holy days, like Christmas, as previously explained. As this did not always work to distract the people's attention from these pagan practices, the Church declared that these pagan gods were all demons. Thus, these demigods, along with the creatures of the subtle realm, like elves, gnomes, fairies, etc., and anyone recognizing or respecting them, were considered enemies of the Church and all true Christians.

Later, the Church went so far as to say that witches were not merely practitioners of paganism, but were servants of the devil. This made them even more despised in the eyes of the Church. Thus, everything from reciting prayers to heal the sick, casting horoscopes, preparing charms, or wearing amulets, to using folk remedies for disease, was condemned as being the practice of a witch.

Large gatherings of witches performing their rites were called sabbats. The Church made up many disgusting activities that the witches were supposed to have performed at these sabbats. These included such things as riding to them on a broomstick, worshiping the devil, kissing his genitals or anus, copulating with the devil, forming a pact with the devil, sacrificing babies and then roasting and eating them, engaging in wild orgies, or announcing to the other witches all the evil deeds they had recently done. Anyone accused of being a witch would be charged with performing any or all of these activities, making them extremely wicked in the eyes of the Christians. And under enough torture, these poor men and women would confess to anything in hopes of having the torture end. Any people the Church did not like could be accused of being a witch: servants of the devil. Thus, their fate would be sealed.

Let us remember that in Christianity the concept of a devil or Satan, the ultimate god of evil and enemy of God, was carried over from Judaism, which had taken it from Zoroastrianism where it originated. Before Zoroastrianism, the existence of a mighty god of evil was not a concept that had been present in the early religions, though there may have been some demons or spirits of an evil nature. Even other religions at the time did not recognize a Satan, or any such god of evil or Prince of Darkness. So, if there really is no Satan, in which many people in Christianity and Islam still believe, this would indicate that all of the charges against witches and their connection with the devil were false from the start. They had simply been fabrications, a pretext for the Church to use in order to maintain power and control and to instill fear in the hearts of its subjects. The propaganda was that the Church was one's only salvation from the power of the devil and eternal damnation.

Unfortunately, a single person accused of being a witch could implicate dozens of others since victims under torture would often confess to anything or accuse anyone else who the torturers suggested. The torturers would demand that accomplices be named, otherwise the torture would become more severe. Many times the accused women would be raped before being tortured. The instruments of torture would be blessed by a priest before being used so that they would more efficiently perform the will of God. Some instruments were the rack, which could stretch and dislocate the joints of the body, pulling arms, knees, and hips from their sockets and increasing the body's length by a foot; the knee splitter, a vise that could crush joints, shins, etc.; thumbscrews; the head crusher, which could put enough pressure on the skull to shatter it or make eyeballs pop out; a metal spiked chair; and other instruments used in much more sadistic ways, such as a simple wagon wheel. This would be used to hit and break all the major bones of the victim's body as he lay helplessly tied to the ground. Then the executioner would thread the victim's broken arms and legs between the spokes of the wheel. The wheel would then be raised up on top of a pole, under which a fire would be made to slowly roast the victim to death, or he would just be left for the vultures.

Obviously, a religion that can resort to such tactics of torture is no religion at all. It is an abominable and vengeful institution that is merely interested in maintaining political power and control rather than saving souls. Such an institution hardly has any understanding of mercy, compassion, kindness, or the law of *karma*, what to speak of the higher principles of real spiritual knowledge.

As the witch burnings increased, sometimes whole villages simply disappeared. And few individuals were bold enough to object to the proceedings since the Inquisition made it plain that only another witch would find fault with it. And those who tried to justify what the Inquisition did would cite the Bible verse, "thou shalt not suffer a witch to live," from *Exodus* (22.18). But it was not only the Roman Catholic Church who actively tried to kill anyone accused of witchcraft, the Protestants did so as well. Martin Luther shared the same view of witches as the Roman Church, and went so far as to say that he would burn them all. Oddly enough, the Catholics and Protestants were engaged in much fighting between each other. To help destroy the Protestants, Catholics would start rumors about Protestant people being engaged in witchcraft, who would then soon be facing the Inquisition, and then death at the stake.

In time, there were the most deceitful men known as the witch hunters who would be paid for discovering and obtaining confessions from heretical witches. One technique the witch hunters would use to discover who was really a witch was to find a patch of skin that would have no feeling, which was said to be the mark of the devil. The accused women would be forced to go to the quarters of the witch hunter and take off her clothes while he would search her body for the devil's mark. To help find such a mark they would use instruments resembling ice picks to poke the skin. Some of these allowed the blade to easily withdraw into the handle so the victim would feel nothing while it would look like it was poking the skin. Thus, an innocent woman would be implicated and tortured until she confessed and named others of being witches. In this way, a profitable career would be made by the witch hunters for finding so-called witches amongst innocent villagers.

Once a woman was accused of being a witch, her death was certain. During one period of 150 years, a total of 30,000 women had been burned at the stake, all in the name of Christianity. Gradually, enough people began to speak out against the prosecutions and witch burnings that they began to subside. But for many years after they had ended, the prejudice, suspicion, and fear that the Church fostered about witches or witchcraft continued, even to the present day.

One of the reasons for this terribly callous attitude toward women was that the leaders of early Christianity were Jews, and in the Hebraic tradition they had little regard for women. Saint Augustine of Hippo went so far as to say women had no souls. This is certainly a ridiculous statement, but the real absurdity is that enough men thought it a serious possibility that it became an issue that was actually debated at a Council at Macon in the sixth century. Whether this attitude toward women helped explain the killing and cruel treatment of so many women who were labeled as witches later on, it is hard to say, but it probably contributed to it. This shows how spiritually underdeveloped the Christian philosophy was.

Even Paul taught that women should be silent and simply serve their husbands. After Paul, King Constantine was the chief exponent of male supremacy and women's inferiority. It was also Constantine, the first Christian Emperor, who slowly boiled alive his first wife under the suspicion of committing adultery. He also murdered his son Crispus and killed his brother-in-law Licinius, who had been more broad-minded about the pagans at the time. Constantine also had Licinius' son whipped to death for no reason. This paved the way for the cruel habits and attitudes of other rulers that followed over the next 14 centuries to murder their wives or those they did not like. Even Saint Thomas Aquinas in the Middle Ages placed women lower than slaves.

This type of ideology comes from nothing more than an almost total lack of any kind of spiritual understanding. As we have explained in *The Secret Teachings of the Vedas*, consciousness in any living body is a symptom of the soul within. On the eternal, spiritual platform everything is absolute. So, even though there may be any number of differences between one material body and another, how can one soul be superior to another, regardless of whether the body is male or female? Spiritually the only difference between any of us is the level of spiritual realization we have attained. Otherwise, to question whether women have souls or not is completely preposterous. Of course, let us remember that this form of ignorance is the same ignorance that causes many followers of these fundamental religions to remain convinced that animals have no souls and are meant simply to serve man in any way we choose, or to be bred only to be eaten. And, as we can see, this exploitation of animals spills over to the exploitation of women and the callous or cruel attitudes people have toward each other.

The dominating nature of the Church can also be seen in the early history of the Americas. In 1492 Columbus landed in America and many Christian missionaries soon followed. In many cases, the Europeans arrived hungry and in need of assistance. The native American Indians helped them at first, only to be treated later as any other pagan and heathen culture in the view of the Christian Church, which was that all non-Christian civilizations should either be converted or conquered and dominated in any way it saw fit. Rather than coming to the New World to understand a new culture and share in its knowledge and resources, the European conquerors preferred to take control of the land and dominate the native people. It was the Church that implemented campaigns to destroy all religions, languages, and histories of the native American Indians. With the condescending Christian attitudes toward the American natives, many Christian conquerors felt no pity for killing hundreds of thousands of American Indians in order to claim the territory and do their will with it. In addition, as many as 50 million Indians died from the diseases that the Christian Europeans brought with them, such as smallpox, measles, etc.

To justify their conquering of the American land and natives, the Christians adopted the concept of "Manifest Destiny," which proclaimed that the land was allotted to them by God to do as they wished. This is in accord with their ethnocentric philosophy that justifies their feelings that they are superior to every other race and culture, and should rule over or convert them.

The Christian Spaniards are known for their most bloody conquests in the 16th century of the Taino Indians of Hispaniola (present day Haiti and the Dominican Republic), Mexico's Aztec Indians, the natives of Panama, as well as the Inca Empire along the Andes Mountains in South America. Once again it was all in the name of Christianity and their desire to find gold and riches. "Santiago" was the battle cry, and the name would often be shouted out by the soldiers in their massacres of the Indians. Santiago Matamoros, St. James the Slayer of Muslims, was the patron saint of the Christian armies of King Ferdinand and Queen Isabella when they crushed Granada, the last Muslim community that was left in Spain in 1492. The cry "Santiago" became a call for the heavenly power to purge the earth of all non-Christian infidels, no matter if they were Muslims or Jews in Europe, or natives of the Americas.

Much of the money that Spain used for the military conquests in the New World had been obtained from the property and wealth confiscated from the Jews during the Inquisition. Although many of the civilians who came to America had hopes of finding religious freedom, the same bigotry they were fleeing they now directed toward the American Indians.

In order to find treasures, the Spaniards would torture the Indian chiefs for information, and both men and women were forced to carry heavy loads of valuables to the Spanish towns. And no pretty woman, married or not, was free from being raped as long as these Spanish barbarians were present. Thus, the Indians were forced to serve the new masters in the most demeaning ways. In this process, most of the Indian culture was gradually wiped out, primarily because of the disrespect the Christians had for any culture but their own.

Columbus originally came to America looking for a way to make money by finding a new route to India and an easy source of gold. After he arrived in America and learned that he would not be able to make his fortune from gold, he decided to try making a profit by capturing the local Indians to be sold as slaves in Europe. Most of the captives in his first load died on the way, so his venture of trading Indian slaves did not work. But his idea of slave trade was quickly picked up by others. In fact, it was the Spanish Catholic priest Bartolome de Las Casas who encouraged the enslavement of Africans instead of the native Americans who were dying in great numbers. In 1505 the first African slaves were shipped to the Americas by the Spanish Conquistadors, and as many as ten million slaves were brought during the next four centuries. The high point of the slave trade was in the 1700s and was primarily done by the British, French, Dutch, and Portuguese, who were all of the Christian persuasion. Most of the slaves went to the Caribbean and Brazil, and the rest went to North America. After slavery was abolished (1834-38), the trade continued under the name of Indentureship. This is when the Europeans tricked many people from India to relocate with the promise of making money. Unfortunately, and unknowingly to the Indians until it was too late, they were brought all the way to places like Trinidad, Guyana, and Suriname in order to provide plantation owners with cheap labor for working in the sugar cane fields. Once the Indians arrived in these colonies, they were often treated worse than the previous slaves. From 1838 to 1917, over half a million Indian people were brought to the Caribbean alone, not to mention other places. This is how the Christian tendency and desire for domination swept through the Americas and redistributed major portions of the world's population.

THE PRISON OF RELIGION

One of the reasons I have included this information on the dark history of Christianity is to show how inflexible the Church became in considering other paths of understanding universal truths. It did not matter whether it was the religions that had existed before Christianity, or folk healing, astrology, Roman demigod worship, Greek philosophy, Celtic mythology, Judaism, Hinduism, Islam, Buddhism, or whatever. They were all heretical in the eyes of the Christians. This not only meant that these practices were not worth considering, but also that those who practiced them were automatically labeled as the lowest of mankind, heathens, pagans, idol worshipers, enemies of the Church who should be tortured and killed in the most sadistic ways, or at least thoroughly dominated. This is what can happen when a group or institution has such a divisive vision. Rather than increasing harmony, understanding, and God consciousness, the institution turns the land into a battlefield leaving scores of senseless deaths, torture, and mistreatment in its wake. So, after reading this history, we have to ask ourselves, who were the real barbarians? Who were the real enemies of all forms of understanding and philosophy? Who were the ones afraid of losing power and control to the point where they killed anyone who might be a threat? And did the devil really exist amongst all those so-called witches who were executed, or was he actually located in the hatred the Church exhibited toward hundreds of thousands of fellow human beings, unless they became converts? And where was the mercy and forgiveness that the Church proclaimed to be a necessary quality to reach heaven? And though great reforms have been made, has the beast of such fanaticism and narrow-mindedness been vanquished, or is it only sleeping?

In the present times, we might not have witch hunts, but we still find what is called "the fear of cults." This fear is nothing more than irrational prejudice based on the ignorance of foreign customs by fundamentalists who feel that anything other than their own conventional religion or viewpoint is bad, is a cult, and should be viewed with suspicion. This prejudice and persecution can presently be seen in the courts of government that force different groups or less conventional religions to prove to a jury the legitimacy of their religious beliefs, and their constitutional right to practice freely the legal traditions of their religion. This cuts away at the religious and legal freedoms on which this country of the United States was founded, and the freedoms that many other countries claim to have. This is nothing more than a repeat of history in which fundamentalists try to enforce their own dogma on everyone else, some of whom, like Hindus or Buddhists, have far more experience and history in their culture, and a much further developed philosophy of spiritual topics than Christianity.

Of course, there may be some cults that are very secretive about what they do. These should be carefully analyzed to see if they practice something unlawful. But many so-called cults are nothing more than groups of people practicing spiritual customs that have been in existence for thousands of years. Let us not forget that Christianity was viewed as nothing more than a small cult of eccentric people in the beginning. And if it was not for cults like the Essenes, of which Jesus was a member and in which he first began his spiritual training, there may never have been any Christian religion. Even the Christians were known as nothing more than a radical cult in the beginning.

Let us also remember that the founding fathers of the United States did not start this country on the basis of any one philosophy or religion, Christian or otherwise. Ben Franklin, John Hancock, Joseph Hewes, Robert Payne, and 28 of the other 56 men who signed the Declaration of Independence were Masons, men interested in pursuing metaphysical understanding that might not necessarily be completely in line with Christianity. Even the date of July 4, 1776 was astrologically calculated as being a favorable time for initiating activities for the future well-being of this country. Also, when George Washington laid the cornerstone of the White House, he did so in full Masonic uniform, thus utilizing a 3,000 year old Egyptian ritual. In this way, you could say this country was founded on freedom of choice: the freedom for one to choose the philosophy and idealism most suited for him or her while living peacefully with others, and without forcing that idealism on those who may not feel the same. But any form of tyranny, whether religious or political, that works unjustly to force its views on others, will work against such freedom and will stifle the growth and development of the individuals who make up that country. When this is noticed, it must be corrected immediately.

The reason why I have called this section *The Prison of Religion* is that religion can also be a way of confining and restricting people of their understanding of the universe and themselves through the use of fear, guilt, violence, and the oppression of anything that shows a different view than what is being indoctrinated into society. It has been the most militant of religions that has suppressed the ancient avenues of reaching higher levels of understanding our multidimensional nature. Thus, by mere blind faith in whatever the church or priests are giving us, or allowing us to know, we are kept in a lower consciousness than what is really possible. In this way, higher realms of thought, wisdom, love, and knowledge are kept away from the masses. After all, knowledge is power, and your ignorance is my strength. To keep power over others, the church has systematically abolished a wide range of spiritual and esoteric knowledge that would, otherwise, give mankind the ultimate freedom. And because people who understand their true spiritual nature and the power that lies within themselves become impossible to manipulate, it is necessary to keep this knowledge hidden. So the idea would be to keep the truly spiritual knowledge concealed while creating and perpetuating a religion, or a standard of "science," that keeps people bound by the above mentioned factors: fear, guilt, violence, and intimidation. To tread outside the accepted jurisdiction of knowledge or understanding, or outside the rules of the institution, will bring fear. Questioning the present system, or doubting its effectiveness, or desiring to know more about God or whatever else you would like to understand, will bring guilt. In this way, such ancient sciences as astrology, yoga, meditation, or the deepest understandings of the soul, and much more, have been made to look evil or even absurd, and thus be dismissed, or preferably even outlawed.

In this regard, reports have been given about how the Vatican has sealed vaults that contain thousands of ancient esoteric books, all of which are kept out of circulation from the public. This indicates the methodical removal of various levels of spiritual and metaphysical knowledge from society, while claiming that anything other than the established doctrine of the church is satanic, evil, and hellbound. The Inquisition was a wonderful method of producing this effect. Even today we can see how some people are so affected by this tyrannical tendency that they still are afraid of looking at anything other than what the Church condones. However, most of these people are totally unaware of the "pagan" heritage found in Christianity or Judaism, which makes it very similar but with a different name. It is practically the same medicine but in a different bottle. To remove this understanding from public knowledge, it became necessary that whenever Christianity or other militant religions conquered a country or culture, the first thing that was done was to capture or destroy all of the ancient sacred texts. Any organization that destroys the ancient knowledge and historical records of a civilization is never going to present the true history of the world, or the spiritual wisdom of its culture. Thus, the view of history is controlled and the population is kept in ignorance and under subtle restraint. And the people who are allowed to understand any of the truth are those of the elite or who are already in power.

By discussing the history of the Christian Church, we are showing to what extent a religion will go to maintain power and control, especially when it feels threatened by what it does not understand. Furthermore, the dark history of Christianity represents the fanatically narrow-minded side of it that has continued to the present day in the form of fundamentalists thinking that if a religion or culture is not Christian, then it must be of the devil. Or then at least they will not go to heaven. Christians are often ready to dismiss or criticize other religions and cultures without understanding them. They may see a ceremony or ritual of another religion and immediately say it is heathen or devil worship, without realizing that it is the worship of the same Supreme Being that they worship. But a similar misunderstanding can happen in Christianity. For example, in the Eucharist ritual they partake of drinking the blood and eating the body of Christ. Does this mean that Christians are cannibals, or have a cannibalistic mentality to eat the body and drink the blood of their savior? Not if you understand that the blood and body of Christ is distributed *symbolically* in the form of wine and wafers. So proper understanding is needed in any religion.

Actually, it does not matter whether the previous segment is about Christianity or some other religious or political institution. The point is that all people have to have the freedom to find themselves to the fullest extent on whatever path it takes, providing it is a bona fide path. So how do we make sure we can continue to have this freedom? By understanding each other and other cultures of the world and other paths of self-discovery, and by recognizing the value that they have to offer. We must also bury our preconceived prejudices that are based on our immature feelings of superiority because, spiritually speaking, we are all the same. We just have to attain that spiritual vision to see the reality of it. And the path we take to do that is the only difference among us.

A true religion paves the way for everyone to become spiritually aware, and to establish his or her own relationship with the Supreme. If a religion is not based on the higher principles of self-realization, but is merely based on dogmatic rules and regulations that it forces on others, then it becomes a trap based on fear, guilt, and intimidation. One must not be afraid to break free from such a trap.

In light of this it is interesting to point out that in 1991a letter was released from the Vatican to the Bishops which criticized zen and such spiritual practices as yoga and meditation. The letter was written by Cardinal Ratzinger but was also approved by Pope John Paul II. The letter warned against the sensations of spiritual well-being that one gets from practicing yoga or meditation, and said that this could lead to schizophrenia, moral deviations, or even psychic disorders, and degenerate to a cult of the body. Now on what basis do they make these claims? Of course, if one improperly practices a complicated form of yoga, such as *kundalini-yoga*, there may be some adverse results. But for the most part, yoga and real transcendental meditation means to fix the mind and become absorbed, at least for certain lengths of time, on that which is transcendent, which is God. This is real spirituality, as well as the original mystical tradition in Christianity. So what is wrong with this when this is the goal of any spiritual path? Why would they issue such a letter, unless they are once again simply trying to condemn every other form of religion? If this is the case, this signifies that they are not really interested in true spirituality or in helping people with spiritual advancement. Yoga and meditation have existed for thousands of years before Christianity ever came along. Why should people not look at other cultures to get answers and experiences that are not found in conventional Western religions? The reluctance to do so is merely a reflection of the fear and misunderstanding that people have. Many Christians have risen to new levels of understanding biblical teachings by practicing various aspects of the Vedic path.

Another example of this fear and apprehension is the prayer book that was issued by the International Mission Board of the Southern Baptist Convention, the USA's largest Christian Protestant church, in October of 1999. The book asked its members for the conversion of Hindus. In it was found such derogatory and slighting statements as: "More than 900 million people are lost in the hopeless darkness of Hinduism." Therefore, it advised Christians to, "Pray that Hindus who celebrate the festival of lights [Diwali] would become aware of the darkness in their hearts that no lamp can dispel." It further said that, "Satan has retained his hold on Calcutta through Kali and other gods and goddesses of Hinduism. It's time for Christ's salvation to come to Calcutta."

This statement clearly shows the lack of understanding of the Vedic and even pagan heritage that is still found in the many practices of Christianity, as I have previously explained in this chapter. It also shows quite clearly the narrow view of spirituality that the publishers of such a prayer book and its followers have. Fortunately, not every Christian felt that the book was proper or justified in what it said. However, when Don Kammerdiener of the Southern Baptist Convention's International Mission Board was asked about the prayer book's demeaning statement that Hindus are lost in darkness, he told the Statesman, "Anyone who does not walk in the light of Christ is lost in darkness." This is exactly the effects

I am talking about in this section called *The Prison of Religion*. This person is locked into the misgiving that anything other than what he believes, or anything alien to his own perception, is of the devil or leads to darkness. This is the seed of religious bigotry that is found in so many religions, especially those who have been the most violent and warlike. It also is what keeps people from reaching the highest levels of spiritual perception and godly love, and from seeing the unity between us all. It keeps them bound by fear, guilt, apprehension, and suspicion of anything new or different. It is a pathetic state, but into which millions are locked.

Another point in regard to the Christian attitude against Hinduism took place in December of 1999 when the Pope visited India. While there, the Pope guided a meeting with the Catholic Bishops in Delhi. From that was produced a 140-page document, which stated the purpose and hopes of the Catholic Church in India: "Just as in the first millennium the Cross was planted on the soil of Europe and in the second on that of the Americas and Africa, we can pray that in the third Christian millennium a great harvest of faith will be reaped in this vast and vital continent of Asia."

Again we find that the Church has, regardless of what else it says, the main interest of converting anyone outside Christianity. However, what has this Christian religion accomplished in Europe that makes it think it is the sole factor in saving everyone's soul? We should remind the Pope and the Bishops that two of the bloodiest world wars in history were started by the European Christians. And how was it that a Christian Germany sent over 5 million Jews to the gas chambers? Was it Christian Spain that drove the many Muslims out of the country years ago? And today we see that the Christian Catholics and Christian Protestants are fighting each other to death in Ireland. The Pope himself has described the Protestant affects on Catholics as the attack of wolves. Where is the spirit of Christian brotherhood and love if things like this happen on such a regular basis throughout history?

So we need to ask, how do they expect their preaching work in Asia to be taken seriously amongst religions that have been flourishing for far longer than Christianity when Christian Catholics and Protestants hate each other? The fact is that the Church allots to itself a role that so far does not fit. If the Church sees other non-Christians merely as targets to bring into its fold, this is hardly the way to show peace and amity among the other religions of Asia. The fact is that the claims to spiritualism made by Christianity hardly stand up to the tests of reason and philosophy that are shown by the Vedic culture (Hinduism), Buddhism, and other religions in Asia. The Church of Christianity needs to clean its own house before taking on any more adventures of greed and violence in the name of Christ that would only disturb the world and cause more social unrest and war.

In any case, it does not take much study to understand that there was a great difference between the ways and teachings that are credited to Jesus and the methods and theocracy of the Church. Jesus was obviously an empowered preacher for spreading theism and spiritual love. But people should recognize Jesus for what he was, which was a Vaishnava, a devotee of the Lord. And those who call themselves Christians should worship him by following in his footsteps and take the time to understand the many aspects of God consciousness exactly as Jesus did in his travels through India and Persia before he took up his work of preaching to his people. This does not mean that one must necessarily travel to the East, but the point is that if one looks closely, he can understand that the teachings of Christ are based on the same essential spiritual truths as found in the Vedic literature. Therefore, by understanding the essential spiritual teachings in the Vedic precepts, one can more easily understand the teachings in the Bible and the real teachings of Jesus, which every Christian should do. So, let us take a closer look at what Jesus is said to have taught.

JESUS TAUGHT BHAKTI-YOGA

Another aspect of understanding the Vedic teachings in Christianity is to simply look at what is written regarding the teachings of Jesus. By studying the teachings that are ascribed to Jesus, we can easily recognize that the essence of what Jesus taught was an elementary level of *bhakti-yoga* and *karma-yoga*. He taught that everyone should love God with their whole heart and mind, which is the quintessence of *bhakti-yoga*. *Bhakti* means devotion and surrender to God. As stated in *Matthew* (22.36-40): "Master, which is the greatest commandment in the law? He answered, Love the Lord thy God with all your heart, with all your soul, with all your mind. That is the greatest commandment. It comes first. The second is like it: Love your neighbor as yourself. Everything in the Law and the prophets hangs on these two commandments." These two rules are the heart of the processes of *bhakti* and *karma-yoga*.

In this way, Jesus taught people the most basic portions of God's law and gave the most simple commandments, such as, "Thou shalt not kill," and "Thou shall not steal," and so on. These rules deal only with moral standards. They do not deal with the higher principles of spiritual discipline or transcendental realization. This is a sign of the kind of people Jesus was dealing with. They were very primitive and had to be taught the most basic of spiritual knowledge. Obviously, one cannot comprehend advanced spiritual topics if he or she does not have any understanding of simple moral values. Therefore, Jesus was very limited in what he could teach the people of that era. As Jesus said, (*St. John* 16.12-13, 25):

I have yet many things to say unto you, but ye cannot bear them now. Howbeit when he, the Spirit of truth, is come, he will guide you into the truth: for he shall not speak of himself: but whatsoever he shall hear, that shall he speak: and he will shew you things to come. . . These things have I spoken unto you in proverbs: but the time cometh, when I shall no more speak unto you in proverbs, but I shall show you plainly of the Father.

Thus, Jesus could not reveal the whole truth to the people of that era, but promised that there would be a time when the whole truth would be open to everyone. But whether the people accept it or not is another thing.

Jesus also taught that one is judged by his works and the way they behave. This is also the same process as found in *bhakti* and *karma-yoga*. Without good works and sincere devotion, one cannot enter into the kingdom of God. Yet, we find in modern Christianity an emphasis on faith, not on works. But this is not upheld in the Bible, as we can see in this verse: "But wilt thou know, O vain man, that faith without works is dead." (*James* 2.20) Jesus never said that faith alone was all it took to enter the promised land. The way one works is a sign of his faith. And those that do claim allegiance to the faith and preach in the name of Christ yet do various duplicitous activities in private are still bereft of attaining the favor of Christ, as stated in *Matthew* (7.21-23):

> Not everyone that saith unto me, Lord, Lord, shall enter into the kingdom of heaven, but he that doeth the will of my Father which is in heaven. Many will say to me that day, Lord, Lord, have we not prophesied in thy name? And in thy name have cast out devils? And in thy name done many wonderful works? And then will I profess unto them, I never knew you; depart from me, ye that work iniquity.

This, therefore, is the essence of Jesus' teachings that, as we can see, include the same basic principles of *bhakti-yoga* and *karma yoga* (loving God, upholding God's law in all our actions, and doing good for others), which is fully explained in the Vedic literature. Jesus never presented anything new or invented, but taught what God had taught and gave all credit to God, as verified as follows:

> The son can do nothing of himself, but what he seeth the Father do. (*John* 5.19). . . When ye have lifted up the son of man, then shall ye know that I am he, and that I do nothing of myself; but as my Father hath taught me, I speak these things. (*John* 8.28). . . I go unto the Father, for my Father is greater than I. (*John* 14.28)

In these verses we have the words of Jesus from the Bible that explain that he taught only what God had spoken and was not himself God, but was the son of God the Father. Furthermore, in *Bhagavad-gita* (9.17), Krishna specifically explains that He is the Father of all living entities, and (*Bg*.7.6, 10.8) is the origin of all that is material and spiritual. Therefore, no contradiction exists in the understanding that Jesus was a son of God, and Krishna is the supreme Father and Creator of all. In this way, we can see that the essence of Christianity is the basic teachings of the Vedic philosophy.

DO ALL CHRISTIANS GO TO HEAVEN?

Regardless of whether or not Christianity is a complete spiritual process that can bring one to spiritual perfection, most Christians feel that they are bound to go to heaven because, as they say, Christ died for their sins. So even if they cannot give up their sinful habits, all they have to do is have faith and they will be saved. Yet this is a controversial point. Not all of the gospels that were in circulation when the New Testament was compiled agreed that the crucifixion was an act of atonement. Even the divinity of Jesus was added later, after he had already died, as the Dead Sea Scrolls indicate. And the Jews completely rejected him as a divine person or Messiah. And if Jesus is really not the messiah or of divine nature, that practically cancels the basis of Christianity, which is what Jewish people think.

Jesus was, however, a Jew whose message was primarily for the Jewish people. In *Matthew* (10.5-6), Jesus tells his twelve disciples to go and preach, but not to the Gentiles (non-Jews), nor to the Samaritans, but go to the lost sheep of the house of Israel. Again in *Matthew* (15.22-24), a woman besought Jesus and asked for mercy because her daughter was vexed with a devil. But Jesus said nothing to her. Even his disciples, who were Jews, asked him to send her away because she cried after them. Yet his answer was that he had come to this world only for the lost sheep of Israel. His intention was to help only the Jewish people. Only after much pleading from the woman did Jesus finally cure her daughter. So this seems to indicate that Jesus' main interest was with the Jews; yet, they completely rejected him. And when he was crucified by the Romans, this was taken as further indication that he was not the messiah that was described in the Jewish prophecies. Nonetheless, the Gentiles and non-Jewish people accepted the doctrine of Christianity and now believe they are saved by the blood of Christ, which is a concept that came primarily from Paul.

So do all Christians go to heaven? Not when you consider all the rules for exclusion. According to the books in the New Testament, Jesus left specific instructions that have to be followed or entrance into heaven may not be as sure as many Christians think. In *Matthew* (10.37), Jesus says that if anyone loves his or her father, mother, son, or daughter more than him is not worthy of him. But also in *Matthew* (15.4), God commands that a person must honor his father and mother, and he that curseth his father or mother must die the death. So you must honor your parents, but not more than you love Jesus or you will not get to heaven.

Jesus also explains in *Matthew* (12.36) that any idle words a man speaks will have to be accounted for on the judgement day. So you must also avoid idle words and gossip. That is not an easy task for many people. Many so-called Christians I see do not even make the attempt. Jesus further explains in *Matthew* (16.23-28) that a person must deny himself the interests or pleasures of men and take up the cross and follow him if he expects to reach the kingdom of God. This certainly indicates that more than mere faith is expected of a Christian, but how many can deny themselves of the common pleasures of men and take up the cross?

In *Matthew* (18.34-35), Jesus says that the Lord will punish you if you do not forgive everybody of their trespasses against you. And again in *Matthew* (25.35-46) we find that it is expected that a good Christian must feed and clothe the poor, and take in the homeless, though they be strangers, for as much as you do this for them, you do it also for Jesus. And if you ignore such people, it is as if you ignore Jesus, and you will go into everlasting punishment.

Now we can see that the requirements for getting into heaven are getting more demanding. But wait, there is more. In *Matthew* (19.20-30), a man comes to Jesus and wants to follow him, but Jesus tells him to first sell everything he has and give the money to the poor. However, the man could not bring himself to do that and sadly went away. Jesus explained to his disciples that hardly any rich man can enter heaven; it is easier for a camel to go through the eye of a needle. Then his disciples were amazed and questioned, if this was the case, who could be saved? Jesus replied that all things are possible with God, but those who have forsaken houses, father, mother, wife, children, or property for his name's sake shall inherit everlasting life. So if you cannot become renounced, you miss everlasting life.

Similarly, in *Luke* (6.20, 24-30), Jesus says blessed are the poor, for they shall reach the kingdom of God, and woe to the rich, woe to those who are full for they will be hungry, and woe to those who laugh now for they will know sorrow. Plus, you must love and do good to your enemies and those that hate you, give the other cheek for those that hit you, do not forbid anyone to take your coat, and do not ask that your goods be returned from one who takes them. (This is all a huge difference compared to the time and tactics of the Inquisition.)

In *Luke* (9.61-62), there is the story of a man who came to Jesus and asked to follow him, but first simply wanted to bid farewell to his family. But Jesus rejected him and said that no man, having once put his head to the plough and looks back, is fit for the kingdom of God. In another place in *Luke* (9.59-60), Jesus orders a man to follow him, but the man requests that Jesus first allow him to bury his father. Jesus, however, says to let the dead bury their dead, and go preach the kingdom of God. In *Matthew* (5.21-22), Jesus explains that if a person kills another he shall be in danger of the judgement. But he further explains that simply getting angry at another without just cause shall also put one in danger of the judgement. And (*Matthew* 5.20) unless your own righteousness exceeds that of the scribes and Pharisees, you shall in no case enter the kingdom of God.

What all this seems to indicate is that anyone who wants to follow Jesus has to display a high degree of detachment and renunciation from the world and its material attractions and pleasures, and take up the cross. Otherwise, they are not true followers of Jesus, nor are they fit for the kingdom of God. Many Christians may feel that faith alone is all they need to be saved, but these biblical quotes of Jesus certainly indicate that he expected and required much more than that.

So what happens to all those who cannot measure up to the proper standard? In *Matthew* (13.41-42), Jesus says that the Son of man will send his angels who will gather out all the things that offend and the people who do iniquity and cast them into a furnace of fire where there will be great wailing and gnashing of teeth. If all these rules that Jesus explains must be followed perfectly, along with all the commandments, etc., in order for Christians to get to heaven, then that furnace must be a mighty big place. But what kind of God would create a hell where people eternally suffer? Especially if, according to Christian theology, they are given only one lifetime to have one chance at either becoming perfect and righteous or go to eternal hell. What is the value of eternal punishment if it never ends and the soul does not get the chance to rectify himself? Why would God create living beings who have a fallen tendency and then send them to suffer eternally if they cannot measure up to the proper standard? Threatening someone with eternal damnation is hardly an expression of love and mercy. Therefore, this Christian concept of God and hell makes little sense because this form of punishment is not a matter of rehabilitation, but is based on an attitude of anger and vengeance. What need does God have for this if He is a God of love, mercy, and compassion? Why would God spend His time acting like an angry tyrant? He certainly has better things to do.

The Christian concept of God is that He is a God we must fear. To verify this some people, of course, will point out that in *Exodus* (20.5) it is written that God says He is a jealous God. But a person exhibits jealousy or anger when he is afraid of losing something, feels insecure, is competing with another, or does not get what he wants. So why would God, who is the creator and controller of everything, feel insecure or fearful? Qualities such as jealousy, insecurity, anger, or vengeance are qualities found in the modes of passion and ignorance. And these modes do not touch the Supreme. But God is perceived differently by different cultures.

In the *Bhagavad-gita* (9.18), Lord Krishna says that He is the creation, the basis of everything, the sustainer, the goal, the refuge, the master, and the most dear friend. This is a much more appropriate understanding of God. Naturally, He must be our friend since we are all parts of His spiritual energy. The only thing that gives the appearance of our being in opposition with God, or being fearful of Him, is our ignorance of spiritual reality. This ignorance must be overcome with spiritual knowledge, not compounded by the inadequacies of a religion that is lacking in spiritual awareness and provides a deficient understanding of God. The goal of any complete spiritual path is to attain enlightenment of God, our spiritual identity, and our relationship with God. The goal of the Vedic path of *bhakti* is to develop love and devotion for God, but you cannot love someone when you are afraid of them. Love and fear are incompatible. Therefore, a spiritually realized person will find it difficult to accept that God is angry, jealous, or vengeful. Why should God be angry or vengeful with us when the universal laws that have been established by God automatically take care of whatever good or bad things we deserve? One who is spiritually realized knows that God allows us the freedom to do what we want within the confines of the universal laws, such as the law of *karma*, and is always waiting for us to turn toward Him, and that He is a God of love, mercy, compassion, and unfathomable understanding. This is God as He really is and is the God we will know in our state of spiritual enlightenment. This is the benevolent God we learn of in the Vedic literature. This is the Supreme Being who cares more about us than we do Him, but who is always waiting for us to turn toward Him and is always with us as Supersoul, *Paramatma*. This is what the Christians do not know.

THE BIBLE TEACHES THE CHANTING OF GOD'S NAMES

The Old Testament, which is also extremely important in Christianity, also teaches many of the same principles of spiritual development as found in the Vedic process. We can especially find these similarities in the process of *bhakti-yoga, mantra-yoga*, and *sankirtana* (the congregational singing of the holy names of the Lord). The teachings in the Bible about the holiness of the name of God and the need to congregationally sing God's name and praises are quite evident. This applies as much to the essential Jewish forms of worship and meditation as it does to the Christian, and almost every other religious tradition.

In one of the foremost prayers spoken by Jesus, it is said, "Our Father, who art in heaven, hallowed be Thy name." The value and holiness of the name of God, as well as being the primary way to meditate on Him, is stressed throughout the Bible. This is also taught in the Vedic literature. Many verses instructing people to sing praises to God and sing His holy name are found. Even in the books of Moses we find evidence of this: "Then sang Moses and the children of Israel this song unto the Lord, and spake, saying, I will sing unto the Lord, for He hath triumphed gloriously." (*Exodus* 15.1)

Furthermore, after delivering the ten commandments, Moses told his people:

Hear, O Israel: the Lord our God is one Lord: And thou shalt love the Lord thy God with all thy heart, and with all thy soul, and with all thy might... Thou shalt fear the Lord thy God; Him shalt thou serve, and to Him shalt thou cleave, and swear by His name. He is thy praise, and He is thy God, that hath done for thee these great and terrible things, which thine eyes have seen. (*Deuteronomy* 6.4-5, 10.20-21)

Thus, we find that the Bible also sets forth the basic principles for people to follow that were the same as those found in *bhakti-yoga* and *mantra-yoga* of the Vedic tradition: that one should love and serve God completely and take shelter of Him through the process of singing praises to Him.

The fact of the matter is that the Old Testament, although describing the process within the context of Judaism, is full of the same essential teachings as found in the Vedic literature. Therefore, there is no surprise to find, in the midst of all the various stories, the following verses from various parts of the Bible which state that one should sing songs unto the Lord and praise His holy name: "Hear, O ye kings; give ear, O ye princes; I, even I, will sing unto the Lord; I will sing praise unto the Lord God of Israel." (*Book of Judges*)

"Thus all Israel brought up the ark of the covenant of the Lord with shouting, and with sound of the cornet, and with trumpets, and with cymbals, making a noise with psalteries and harps." (*I Chronicles* 15.28) This description certainly sounds like a typical chanting (*sankirtana*) party as you would find in the temples of holy cities in India and elsewhere. And the following verses sound exactly like some of the Vedic quotes that describe *mantra-yoga*. This indicates that chanting the holy names of the Supreme is definitely the spiritual process for this age, regardless of what culture or tradition with which you affiliate:

> Then on that day David delivered first this psalm, to thank the Lord, into the hand of Asaph and his brethren. Give thanks unto the Lord, call upon His name, make known His deeds among the people. Sing unto Him, sing psalms unto Him, talk yet of all His wondrous works. Glory ye in His holy name; let the heart of them rejoice that seek the Lord. Seek the Lord and His strength, seek His face continually. (*I Chronicles* 16.7-11)

Another quote given in *Isaiah* (42.10-12) concerning the fact that everyone in the world should declare the Lord's glories is the following:

> Sing unto the Lord a new song, and His praise from the end of the earth, ye that go to the sea, and all that is therein: the isles, and the inhabitants thereof. Let the wilderness and the cities thereof lift up their voice, the villages that Kedar doth inhabit: let the inhabitants of the rock sing, let them shout from the top of the mountains. Let them give glory unto the Lord, and declare His praise in the islands.

An interesting point about the above quote is the name Kedar. In the Vedic tradition this is a name for Lord Shiva. The Psalms of David also put special attention on chanting the holy names of God, and practically instructs how congregational chanting should be performed. Anyone familiar with the congregational chanting and singing of the Lord's names and praises as seen in the temples and religious festivals of India will know that the following verses are practically eyewitness descriptions of how they practice this method.

> Make a joyful noise unto the Lord, all the earth: make a loud noise and rejoice, and sing praise. Sing unto the Lord with the harp, and the voice of a psalm. With trumpets and sound of cornet make a joyful noise before the Lord, the King. . . O clap your hands, all ye people; shout unto God with the voice of triumph. (*Psalms* 98.4-6, 47.1)

Praise ye the Lord. Praise God in His sanctuary: praise Him in the firmament of His power. Praise Him for His mighty acts: praise Him according to His excellent greatness. Praise Him with the sound of the trumpet: praise Him with the psaltery and harp. Praise Him with the timbrel and dance: praise Him with stringed instruments and organs. Praise Him upon the loud cymbals: praise Him upon the high sounding cymbals. Let everything that breath praise the Lord. Praise ye the Lord. (*Psalms* 150.1-6)

The Bible also indicates that as one continues to engage in this process, one becomes more and more fixed in understanding God; one's faith continually increases, as mentioned:

My heart is fixed, O God, my heart is fixed: I will sing and give praise. Awake up, my glory; awake, psaltery and harp: I myself will awake early. I will praise thee, O Lord, among the people: I will sing unto Thee among the nations. For Thy mercy is great unto the heavens, and Thy truth unto the clouds. Be thou exalted, O God, above the heavens: let Thy glory be above all the earth. (*Psalms* 57.7-11)

It is also established that if one expects to be successful in one's search for God, the Absolute Truth, one must relentlessly engage in chanting God's names and glories: "O give thanks unto the Lord; call upon His names: make known His deeds among the people. Sing unto Him, sing psalms unto Him: talk ye of all His wondrous works. Glory ye in His holy name: let the heart of them rejoice that seek the Lord. Seek the Lord, and His strength: seek His face evermore." (*Psalms* 105.1-4) And also the following: "Praise the Lord, O my soul. While I live I will praise the Lord: I will sing praises unto my God while I have any being. (*Psalms* 146.1). . . And they that know Thy name will put their trust in Thee: for thou, Lord, hast not forsaken them that seek Thee." (*Psalms* 9.10)

As one advances in one's self-realization and in one's faith in praising God, one will naturally feel much happiness and joy in doing so, according to the *Psalms* in such verses as, 100.1-2; 104.33-34; 147.1; 92.1; 113.1-3, as exemplified in the following: "Sing unto the Lord, O ye saints of His, and give thanks at the remembrance of His holiness. Thou hast turned for me my mourning into dancing: thou hast put off my sackcloth and girded me with gladness: To the end that my glory may sing praise to Thee, and not be silent. O my God, I will give thanks unto Thee forever." (*Psalms* 30.4,11-12)

In this way, many verses throughout the Bible, only a few of which are presented here, establish the chanting of the Lord's names as an integral part of the early Judaic and Christian traditions. This is all very much in line with the ancient Vedic process of *bhakti-yoga* and *mantra-yoga*, which the Vedic texts fully describe in numerous verses. In fact, that is all that has been explained in this segment, using only the evidence as presented in the form of biblical references.

Obviously, this means that, according to both the Eastern Vedic or Western Christian traditions, everyone should sing or chant the name of God as often as possible. However, the Bible does not clarify which name, so what name do we use? Here is an example of what we can learn by looking at other cultures, such as the Vedic culture, that are more complete in their philosophy and spiritual understanding.

THE NAMES OF GOD

God is called by many names, such as Jehovah, Allah, El Shaddai, Elohim, Adonai, Yahweh, Krishna, Govinda, Vishnu, and so on, according to particular traditions. Any bona fide name of God that one chants sincerely will help one attain spiritual emancipation, if for no other reason than it focuses one's mind on the Supreme to some degree, depending on how clearly you focus your attention. However, some names of God are more direct in their descriptive power and in their relationship with the Supreme, while other names are nothing more than titles. For example, Allah simply means "Great One," Adonai means "Lord," Elohim means "The Almighty," and some say that Jehovah is not a name at all but merely refers to the name. The word "God," which can be traced back to the Sanskrit through the Old Teutonic language, simply means "to invoke" or "the object of worship." We all know God is great and is the supreme object of worship, but the above names really do not explain much about God.

Some people call upon the name of Jesus Christ in their prayers. This is also very effective because the name Christ comes from the Greek word *christos*, which means the anointed one or messiah, and *christos* is the Greek version of the Sanskrit name Krista or Krishna, which is a direct name of God, which means the one who is all-attractive and who gives the greatest pleasure.

Also, the name Jesus is spelled Isus or Iesus in Latin, and Isa in Arabic. H. Spencer Lewis, in *The Mystical Life of Jesus* (p. 220), explains, "The i and j in the early Latin language were identical in form." This means they were also interchangeable, so *iesus* can become Jesus. These names are linguistically connected with *Isha*, the Sanskrit root for *Ishvara*, which is the Vedic name for God meaning the Supreme Controller. Thus, even the name of Jesus has a Sanskrit derivative. And the name Krishna in some parts of India is pronounced as Krisn or Chrisn, or even Christ as in Bengal and Karnataka. Thus, the "n" and "t" are interchangeable according to region. Put the two words together and you have the name "Jesus Christ." So no matter whether we call on "Jesus," "Christ," "Krista," or "Krishna," we are referring to the same Supreme Being.

As we learn in the Vedic texts, some names like Krishna, Vishnu, Govinda, or Rama are more direct and potent in addressing God and His energies and in reawakening our spiritual awareness. These names address the various qualities and pastimes of God, which are eternal and transcendental to material nature. In other words, these names are spiritual vibrations which exist on the same spiritual platform as the Supreme. Thus, by always invoking the transcendental energy of God through the chanting of His holy names, one comes in contact with this eternal energy which works to spiritualize our consciousness. As our consciousness becomes more and more purified, we actually become more in tune with God and His spiritual energy. This continues to the point in which we actually reawaken our spiritual vision that allows us to understand exactly who and what we are. This is called spiritual or self-realization. Thus, as it is instructed in the Vedic literature and also in the Bible, people should systematically chant and meditate on the spiritual names of God for spiritual perfection and liberation from material life and the repeated cycles of birth and death.

I have supplied much more information about the goals and methods of the Vedic process for spiritual development that are the most beneficial for this day and age in my book, *The Universal Path to Enlightenment.*

CHAPTER TWELVE

The Vedic Influence in the Orient

The Orient was also influenced by the Vedic Aryan culture. This happened because the Vedic Aryans had a philosophy which had been given to humanity by the Supreme, and they wanted to take their dynamic culture and disseminate their knowledge to all parts of the world. With that aim they established centers of learning, military posts, trade routes, government and administrators, and a priestly class, all of which contributed to organizing a peaceful coexistence, a spiritually oriented way of life, with liberty and justice for all. To do this, the Vedic Aryans also traveled to the East, sailing over the seas to the Pacific islands. Only after the *Mahabharata* war did the Vedic culture begin to fade from its prominence and high standards. So how did the Vedic influence reach the Orient?

The *Mahabharata* and the *Puranas* describe many kings who had dominance over the whole world. Among some of the greatest colonizing Aryans were the sea-faring branches from the Gangetic region that had a great effect on the Indo-China area. T. de Lacouperie explains in his book, *The Western Origin of Chinese Civilization*, that on the China coast, in the Gulf of Kia-tchou, Hindu leaders established trading centers; one at Lang-ga to the south, and Tsih-miah or Tsih-moh to the north. These traders also established the system of coinage in China near 675 B.C., and made coins imprinted with their names and the names of various Chinese cities on them.

These Aryans controlled the Chinese sea-trade for many years and established many other centers and ports in Myanmar (Burma), Malaya, Siam, Cambodia, and islands such as Sumatra, Java, Borneo, and the Philippines. To this day in these areas most of the writing is in alphabetic letters derived from the Indo-Aryan version, and the popular religion is the old form of Buddhism from India. Anyone can recognize many similarities between the art, architecture, sculptures, and traditional dress of these areas and that of India. Even today, the Chinese habits of circumambulating temples is a Vedic carryover. You can see Chinese goddesses standing on a lotus flower, styled after the Vedic goddess Lakshmi. And as in India, Chinese still think it is fortuitous to offer pilgrims water from sacred wells.

Additional evidence of how the Vedic Indians traveled through the islands of the South Pacific is described on page 265 of Mr. Oak's book, *Some Blunders of Indian Historical Research*:

"An issue of the *Dharma* quarterly, published by the Pure Life Society, Petaling in Malaya, had a couple of years back carried an article in one of the issues describing how a bell with a Tamil inscription had been found with an Australian tribal--a Maori. The bell was obviously used by an Indian ship which got wrecked near the Australian shore. Some Maori fishermen happened to find it in their haul. That is how they came by that bell which has survived as a rare relic of the age when Indian ships sailed the high sees carrying Indian armies, merchants and scholars to all parts of the globe, then known as Bharata Varsha."

From the evidence that follows we will see that the Vedic civilization was the pre-eminent culture and faith of the entire world in ancient times. It was prevalent throughout the Pacific region from India to Malaysia, Indonesia, Borneo, Korea, Indochina, the Philippines, Japan, Australia, New Zealand, and farther east and up to Mexico. (More information about this is included in the next chapter, *The Vedic Influence in the Ancient Americas*.) This phenomenon, unique in world history, also bears testimony not only of the spiritual but also the great material advancement achieved by the ancient Indians in every walk of life. So now let us take a look at specific areas of the orient to see what evidence we find of Vedic influence.

JAVA

The name Java came from the Sanskrit *Jawadvip*, which means a (*dvip*) island (*yawa*) shaped like a barley corn. *Yawa* later became pronounced as Java, and the word *dvipa* was dropped. This shows the mastery the ancient Indians had in charting and mapping the world. Otherwise how could they have noticed it was shaped like a barley corn? The Vedic Indians must have charted Java, *Yawadvip*, thousands of years ago because *Yawadvip* is mentioned in India's earliest epic, the *Ramayana*. Old Javanese songs describe episodes from the Indian *Ramayana* and *Mahabharata*. Shadow-plays are often woven around these epic tales, especially of Krishna and Rama. Even today the ruins of Shiva and Vishnu temples can be seen all over Pantarin of Eastern Java. Therefore, although Java and Sumatra are today prominently Muslim, we can safely say that before the 14th century when Arab marauders engaged in their terror raids upon this region, Java and Sumatra were a part of, and practiced, the Vedic culture.

One of the areas where the Vedic culture still survives is nearby Bali. It was here where the last of the Hindu princes in the region withdrew and luckily remained insulated from Islam. In the fifteenth century under the Muslim rule in Java, the emperor there emigrated to Bali with his entourage, priests, scholars, and artists, with a view to protect the ancient traditions of the Vedic culture. Even to this day the royal families of Jogjakarta and Surakarta encourage traditional music, arts, dances, and displays of plays based on the Vedic epics, *Ramayana* and *Mahabharata*. In this way, Bali has survived as the only Hindu territory outside India where the people remained Vedic without having been sucked into any other of the more modern religions.

INDONESIA

Java, Bali, and Sumatra are all Sanskrit names. All of the most ancient of Indonesian shrines are dedicated to Indian Vedic deities and depict scenes from Indian epics. Indonesian dance and music are of Indian origin. All its ancient cities, villages and towns bear Sanskrit names, as are most personal names. They still hold the fourfold Brahmin, Kshatriya, Vaishya, and Shudra classifications of society. And they still recite the *Bhagavad-gita* and observe various Vedic customs. Their language is a dialect of Sanskrit known as Basha, a Sanskrit term. The Indonesian flag, being of two colors, bears the Sanskrit name *Dwivarna*. The five cardinal points of the Indonesian constitution are also designated by the Sanskrit word *Panchashila*. Its airline is called *Garuda*, the Sanskrit name for the eagle carrier of Lord Vishnu. The old Javanese alphabet derives from the Pallava script of South India. One such inscription was found in the south-eastern region of Borneo on four octagonal stone pillars, written in Sanskrit in a 4th century Indian script. Indonesians still follow the Vedic year and call it *Sakh-Samvat*.

It is not generally understood that the name "Indonesia" does not refer to Asia. The term "Nesia" signifies a group of islands, and "Indo" of course means India. Thus, Indonesia means Indian Islands.

On the outskirts of the city Jogjakarta (or Yogyakarta), is a famous ancient Vedic temple complex known as Borobudur, displaying the majestic Vedic architecture, and now containing hundreds of statues of the Buddha. The late Dr. Raghuvira, a great Indologist, relates that the Indonesian islands are strewn with temples. As described on page 169 in *Some Missing Chapters of World History*, Borobudur in particular is unique. "Every terrace marks a spiritual stage upward. There are five kilometres or three miles of sculptures. There artists must have trained by master craftsmen from India. Faces are Indian, dresses are Indian, and the stories are from Jatakas. The scene of King Shibi, cutting off his own flesh and weighing it against the pigeon in order to offer an equal amount of flesh to the hawk, is depicted with a sensitiveness which is rare even in India. Scenes of the Indian merchant marines are most valuable for reconstructing a correct picture of Indian adventures.

"Not very far from Borobudur is the complex of Prambanam, the like of which is known neither to India or to any other neighboring or distant land. . . Here are the life-cycles of Lord Krishna known as *Krishnayana* parallel to the *Ramayana*, the powerful dragon being torn asunder by the superb arms of the Divine boy Krishna. In another place is the scene of Kumbhakarna being awakened by conches and screeches of elephants, a portrayal of the highest order. . . The central triad of temples devoted to the Trimurti [Vishnu, Brahma, and Shiva] was originally surrounded by smaller shrines in four encircling rows. . . "

Vedic culture began to lose its ground here in the 13th century. Most of the inhabitants, terrorized by invading Arabs, were forced to accept Islam in the 15th century, after many of their men were massacred, women raped, and homes looted.

BORNEO

As described by Mr. Oak on page 166 of *Some Missing Chapters of World History*, he relates, "If the dense forests of nearby Borneo are thoroughly explored they will reveal many historic relics of the sway that the ancient Hindus held there. The sultan of Brunei (in Borneo) bore the title of Seri Bhagwan, meaning Shree Bhagavan (Lord Almighty). Recently because of the sultanate's long alienation from the Sanskrit, that term is being wrongly interpreted as 'the royal advisor.'

The ancient Indian name by which Indonesians call Borneo is Kalimanthan. Kali is the popular Indian goddess who is devoutly worshiped by the general masses of Vedic followers and Indian rulers alike. Furthermore, part of Borneo is Sarawak. Till recently the Sarawak region was ruled by an Englishman. However, he also bore the title of *raja*, which shows that Borneo was a part of the Indian empire in East Asia.

MALAYSIA AND SINGAPORE

Singapore is a standard Sanskrit name, "pore" being derived from the Sanskrit *pur* for place, and "Singa" derived from *Nrsingha* for lion, as in the name of Narasinghadeva, the half-man/half-lion incarnation of Lord Vishnu. So Singapore is the "Lion City." It was a major port on the routes between India and the Pacific Islands and on to Mexico. The British explorer Raffles recorded in his Memoirs near the close of the 15th century of seeing a fortress built by King Parameshwara near what is now Stamford Road.

Malaya also is a Sanskrit word, and Malayan towns bear Sanskrit names. Even though it is an Islamic country, the rulers in the native states continue to bear Sanskrit titles. Royal princesses are called Putri, Mahadevi, Vidyadhari, while the men have names such as Rama and Lakshmana. Even their palaces are known as *Asthana*, which is a Sanskrit word. Two generations ago the ruler of Johore Bahru was known as the Maharaja. That title still appears embroidered or embossed on their table-spreads.

All excavations in Malaya yield nothing but Vedic images and temples. A Shiva temple was excavated in Sungei Pattani only a few years ago. Another Shiva temple was discovered at Petaling Jaya, the name of which means "the Great

Crystal Emblem of Lord Shiva," indicating that there could have been a great crystal Shiva-*linga* there. Also, the ancient Sanskrit text known as the *Pundarika Statra* was found a few miles from the city of Ipoh at the hot water stream. That spot has an extract inscribed on a framed marble slab hung on a post.

An Indian monk, Brahmachari Kailasam (Swami Satyanand) who has settled in Malaya has written a book called *Glimpses of Malayan History*. In it he describes sites of Indian historic and archeological interest found in the region of Malaya to Korea.

The name of the Malayan capital of Kuala Lumpur is also Sanskrit. The original Sanskrit name was Cholanampuram, which means "the city of the Cholas." The town of Seramban comes from the Sanskrit *Shree Ram Van*, meaning the bower of Lord Rama. The name of Sungei Pattani comes from the Sanskrit *Shringa Pattan*, meaning "mountain city."

Other Malayan words with Sanskrit connections include the following:

MALAYAN	SANSKRIT
Seri	Shree (beauty and charm)
Sari-mukha	Shree-Mukha (light of the countenance)
Santeza	Santosh (peace, tranquility)
Senja	Sandhya (twilight)
Seloka (satirical poetry)	Sloka (stanza)
Seksa	Shiksha (suffering, hardship)
Saudara	Saho-dara (of the same womb, brother or sister)
Roma	Roma (downy body hair)
Rona	Warna (color)
Ancharona	Panchawarna (five-colored)
Resi	Rishi (sage of great respect)
Rata	Ratha (chariot)
Setiya	Satya (truth)
Setiawan	Satyawan (faith, loyalty, fidelity)
Ranjuna	Arjuna (Krishna's devotee in the *Bhagavad-Gita*)
Puji-Pujian	Param Pujaneeya (respected elder)
Puja	Puja (worship)

Many Sanskrit words remain in the Malayan religious terminology. We could go on with many more examples in the chart above, but this should provide enough evidence to show the overpowering influence that Sanskrit still yields in this region.

THAILAND

Thailand, alias Siam, also has a great Vedic heritage. In spite of the Chinese twang, its language is almost totally Sanskrit. Every sovereign is still called Rama, in memory of the greatest monarch, Lord Ramachandra. Before they made Bangkok their capital, their traditional capital was also called Ayodhya, before the Burmese invaded it. The coronation of sovereigns and other rituals are still performed according to Vedic tradition. This makes sense seeing how the royal priest of Thailand is a Vedic Brahmin.

The King of Thailand still observes the festival known as the Royal Plowing ceremony. It is an old Vedic ritual for honoring the cows and bulls. The national and royal symbol for Thailand is Garuda, the celestial eagle carrier of Lord Vishnu. Thailand's king, Bhumibol Adulyadej, gets his name from Sanskrit, which means "the strength of the land of immeasurable splendor."

In the royal temple in Bangkok is the Emerald Buddha. However, on the interior walls of the temple yard you will see paintings of the *Ramayana*, indicating that this was once a Vedic temple of Lord Rama. All temples bear Sanskrit names, such as Wat Arun, and Wat Dev Sri Indra. *Wat* means a banyan tree in Sanskrit, which would almost always be planted near a temple or holy shrine in the Vedic tradition. Even the name of hotels and other businesses have Sanskritized names. The common greeting is Namaskar, and also "Sabaddi," which refers to *Swasti* in Sanskrit, meaning be well or all is well. There are also cities with the Indian names of Ayodhya, Cholpuri, Rajpuri, Fatepur, and so on. Styles of dance, music, and costumes can all be traced to their Indian origin. Excavations have also yielded Vedic images and inscriptions.

NORTH AND SOUTH VIETNAM, CAMBODIA AND LAOS

This area was also once a part of the great Vedic empire. The port of Saigon, for example, was named using a Sanskrit word, *Gaon*, which means a town, and the suffix means many, so it means "many townships." The Mekong River was named after "Ma Ganga," or Mother Ganga (the Ganges).

The name Laos is pronounced as Lava by the local people in memory of Lava, the son of Lord Ramachandra. The capital of Laos is Vientiane, pronounced as Van Chan by the local people, which is a corrupt form of the Sanskrit word *Vana Chandan*, meaning a forest of sandalwood trees.

A more obvious form of Vedic influence in the Far East can also be seen. There were those who converted from the Far Eastern doctrines and directly engaged in the Vedic tradition. As far east as Kampuchea, we can find temples built by the kings of ancient Cambodia, such as Angkor Wat, a large and well known temple complex devoted to Lord Vishnu and the Vedic demigods. Here *Wat* means banyan tree and *Angkor* means its sprout. The surrounding area is still called by the Indian name of *Aranya Pradesh*.

The area of northwestern Cambodia was called Angkor, where the capital of the ancient Khmer Empire was located through the 9th to 15th centuries A.D. The empire was one of the largest in the history of the area and had expanded to include all of Cambodia and most of Vietnam, Laos, and Thailand. It was Jayavarman II, the first great king of Angkor, who introduced the Indian Vedic system of philosophy to that area. Since his reign, it became a tradition that every king of the region would build a large temple which was dedicated to either Vishnu or Shiva. After the king's death, the structure would also serve in memory of the king who had built it. Over the years, more than 70 large and magnificently carved temples were built. Ruins of the temples are spread over an area of 100 kilometers. Images of the Vedic deities of Brahma, Vishnu, and Shiva intersperse the surrounding walls. One most noteworthy sculpture is that showing the demigods and demons churning the ocean using the Vasuki serpent and the Mandara mountain as the turning rod.

Among the ruins have been found numerous images of the Vedic deities and inscriptions mentioning the names of the Indian kings who once ruled over the kingdom. Some of the names include Jayavarma and Suryavarma. The museum at Pnom Penh is full of Vedic images and inscriptions.

Hundreds of architects and thousands of laborers were required for years to build each of these temples. Angkor Wat ("temple of the capital"), the greatest and best known of these temples, was built by Suryavarman II in the early 12th century, taking thirty years to complete. The temple complex was designed to represent the Vedic descriptions of the cosmological arrangement of the universe. Thus, the Vedic knowledge had been known and respected in the orient for many years.

One interesting point to consider is that though the main temples at Angkor Wat were built less than 1000 years ago, the ground plans for these temples match the constellation of Draco as it would have appeared in the sky in 10,500 B.C. This means that the sire itself is much older than the buildings on it. Furthermore, Draco is directly opposite the constellation of Orion in the sky, which has been connected with the ancient Egyptian pyramids. This may lead one to consider that the sites of Angkor Wat, the Egyptian pyramids, along with many other ancient places around the world, were once connected to a vast, global culture that was highly knowledgeable about astronomy, and used it in its architecture and mystical constructions, amongst other things.

The word Cambodia itself has Sanskrit roots from the name Khambu, the ancestor of those called Khambu-ja or Kambhoj, his descendants. Thus, we have the name Cambodia. Also, remnants of the Hindu traditions and rituals remain in the coronation custom. And traditional cultural entertainment is based on stories of the Indian epics rendered in song and dance.

There have also been the discovery of ancient 6th century cave temples that show influence from India and were possibly built by Indian settlers. They are located in Kampot province on Cambodia's southern coast. The undersecretary of state, Michael Tranet, said that it appears that Indians probably arrived here by sea. Six German cave specialists and two officials from Cambodia's ministry of culture concluded a four-week survey of 37 caves in Kampot and Kratic provinces.

One of the main discoveries was an outstanding temple covered by mineral deposits inside Kampot's Kehong mountain. Ancient pottery pieces were discovered in the cave called Roung Prasat that were of solely Indian influence. All of this information provides evidence that the entire region was inhabited by Indians and ruled by Vedic administrators. (More information on Cambodia is provided in the next chapter on the Vedic influence in the Americas).

KOREA

The name Korea is derived from the Sanskrit *Gauriya*, which became Goriya before it was changed to Korea. Changing the "G" sound to the "K" or "C" sound can also be recognized in the Sanskrit word *Gau* which changes in English to "Cow." Gouri is the Vedic goddess and consort of the demigod Lord Shiva. She was the principal deity of this region, so consequently the country was named after her.

MYANMAR (BURMA)

Burma is an abbreviation of the Sanskrit name *Brahmadesh*, or the region of Brahma. The names of its rivers are Sanskrit names, such as Irrawati, Brahmaputra, and Chindwin (from Chintanvan--a region of forests for meditative seclusion). Its cities also have Sanskrit names, such as Rangoon, Prome, Mandalay, Meiktila (Mithila), and the ancient Prangan (city of exquisite temples) all remind one of Burma's Vedic past. Its head of state is also known as Adipadi, which is the Sanskrit Adhipati, referring to the chief executive. The kings also bore Sanskrit names. Plus, the people enjoy the annual Indian festival of Holi, and throwing colored water and dyes on one and all.

CHINA

In China, Manchuria derives its name from the Vedic goddess Manjushri. In time, the "ju" was pronounced as "chu" and became known as Manchuria. Also, as mentioned in a footnote on page eight of Volume II of *Aryatarangini* by A. Kalyanraman (Asia Publishing House, Mumbai), China is also mentioned in the *Ramayana* as the land of *Kosa-Karas* (silk worms).

How China was part of the Indian Vedic empire is explained by Professor G. Phillips on page 585 in the 1965 edition of the *Journal of the Royal Asiatic Society*. He remarks, "The maritime intercourse of India with China dates from a much earlier period, from about 680 B.C. when the sea traders of the Indian Ocean whose chiefs were Hindus founded a colony called Lang-ga, after the Indian named Lanka of Ceylon, about the present gulf of Kias-Tehoa, where they arrived in vessels having prows shaped like the heads of birds or animals after the patterns specified in the *Yukti Kalpataru* (an ancient Sanskrit technological text) and exemplified in the ships and boats of old Indian arts."

It is also recorded that India exported beautiful printed fabrics to China as far back as the fourth century B.C. The Chinese explorer Chau Ju-kua documents in the thirteenth century that Gujarat was the source of cotton textiles of every color, and from where they would be shipped for sale to the Arabian countries each year. The thirteenth century is also when Marco Polo witnessed the export of Indian cloth to China and Southeast Asia in the largest ships then known. These would sail from the Andhra and Tamil coasts.

More evidence of the Vedic influence in China is provided on pages 564-566 of *World Vedic Heritage* by P. N. Oak. Therein he gives a most interesting analysis, which I include in its entirety:

"A Chinese coin of the second century found in Mysore also indicates that China was a part of the ancient world. *Uttaraptha* was the Sanskrit name of the ancient international highway which connected India with China, Russia and Iran. Correspondingly, the Sapta Sindhu region comprised the Pamir Plateau, Western and Eastern Turkistan and Afghanistan. Khotan is a mispronunciation of the Sanskrit name Gosthana, while Prakanva was the original Sanskrit name of Ferghana.

"Auriel Stein found evidence of Indian rule in Turkistan and Khotan in the form of coins and inscriptions and the use of an Indian language in its administration up to the 3rd century A.D. Officials bore Indian names as Nandsena and Bheem. The offices they held also bore Sanskrit names. The person gathering and delivering mail was known as *Lekhaharak*. It is this word which led to the English word 'Clerk.' A messenger was known as *doota*, and the spy was known as *Chara*. In the upper Pamirs and in Tibet too, the Vedic civilization was to be seen everywhere.

"The Kucheans (on the border of the Gobi desert) and the Khotanese, though a thousand miles to the north of Punjab, had the same culture as Punjab.

"It may thus be seen that the entire region surrounding China was steeped in Vedic culture. Consequently, China too was pervaded with the same culture. Chinese history too, like that of other countries, begins from the legendary Flood.

"The father of Chinese history, Su Ma Chien (who lived around 149 B.C.) refers to a tradition that the swamps of Central China were reclaimed by a legendary hero called 'Yu the Great.' Obviously, this 'Yu' is none else than Manu of the Vedic tradition. Thus, the beginning of Chinese history from the Flood and from Manu also indicates that the Chinese tradition is Vedic. The other clue we get is from the metamorphosis of Vedic, Sanskrit names. The term 'Manu' has been robbed of its first syllable while only the last is retained as 'Yu.' But its association with the Flood enables us to identify the name as Manu.

"According to current thinking, Chinese culture starts with the Shang dynasty (about 1700 B.C.). But the metal industry of that age is so advanced that historians surmise a long stretch of history to lie behind it. All such theories and counter-theories and the trial and rejection method in the reconstruction of the ancient history of China serve to highlight their basic mistake. China, like every other region of the world, had a Vedic civilization with Sanskrit as its language. The name of the earliest dynasty, Shang, is none other than the Sanskrit word *Simha* [with the Chinese twang] which came to be pronounced as Singh in North India, as Cing alias King in England, and as Shang in China. The Chinese switch to ideaographs was caused by some historical upheaval which cut off the Chinese region for a long stretch of time from its educational links with India.

"The Chinese also refer to an earlier Hsia dynasty of 17 or 18 kings supposed to have ruled China from 2205 B.C. to 1765 B.C. when it was overthrown by 'Tang the Successful' founder of the Shang Dynasty.

"Here again we bump against the same 5000-year barrier. The 1983 years of the Christian era added to the 2205 B.C. years mentioned above takes us almost to the early years after the *Mahabharata* war. Thus, as observed by us elsewhere, no matter which thread of history we pick up, viz. whether Indian, Chinese, Japanese, Roman, Egyptian, or any other, we reach a dead end at circa 3138 B.C., the date of the *Mahabharata* war. Therefore, it would be right to assume that until the *Mahabharata* war, like the rest of the world, China too spoke Sanskrit and practiced Vedic Culture. After the war it gradually lapsed into a state of segregation and isolation developing a distinct identity in script, pronunciation, language and art. The name of the earliest known ruling dynasty Hsia [Xia] could be Ikshwaku, Hehaya, or some well-known Vedic Kshatriya dynasty of the past.

"This conclusion is reinforced by the observation of Chinese historian Dr. Li-Chi who discovered an astonishing resemblance between the Chinese clay pottery and the pottery discovered at Mohenjadaro on the Indian continent, and at Jamadat Nasr in Mesopotamia. This pottery link-up corroborates our thesis of an ancient worldwide Vedic culture.

"Both Sir L. Wooley and Arnold Toynbee speak of an earlier ready-made culture coming to China. They are right. That was the Vedic, Hindu culture from India with its Sanskrit language and sacred scripts. The contemporary astronomical expertise of the Chinese, as evidenced by their record of eclipses; the organizing of sacrifices to propitiate the deities of these astral phenomena, the philosophy of the Chinese and their statecraft, all point to a Vedic origin. That is why from the earliest of times we find Chinese travelers visiting India very often to renew their educational and spiritual links.

"Taoism is *Deva*-ism. The Chinese philosopher Lao Tzu propagated the Advaita (non-dual) philosophy of the Vedic tradition. The name of his 'Toa' philosophy has been completely misunderstood by all scholars who have written on China so far. The Chinese word 'Tao' [the 'T' pronounced as a 'D'] is nothing but the Sanskrit word *Deva*. Consequently Taoism is Chinese Vedic Theism."

In this same line of thought, Count Biornstierna observes on page 85 of his book *The Theogony of the Hindus*: "What may be said with certainty is that the religion of China came from India."

China was influenced by India in other ways as well. For example, the alternative form of medicine known as acupuncture is believed to have originated in China. In Korean academies, students are correctly told that acupuncture originated in India. An ancient Sanskrit text on acupuncture is also said to be preserved in the Ceylonese National Museum at Columbo in Sri Lanka.

Further evidence of the influence of Vedic culture is recognized by the popularity of the Chinese dragon, which comes from the importance of the great serpent Seshanaga on which Lord Vishnu reclines. Such popularity of the dragon came from the images of Vishnu that had been found in the Vedic temples that were once in China. One such temple is the Brahma temple in the city of Hang Chau, as described and mapped on page 212 of Marco Polo's memoirs. The temple, now long destroyed by invaders, is still marked by two columns which bear Buddhist inscriptions. They still retain the name and mark the site of the temple, and date it from the 6th century.

In Fjiyan province at Quanzhou, on the southeastern coast of China, there are the remains of a Shiva temple. It still has a Shiva-*linga* over five meters tall and numerous Tamil inscriptions. Even as late as 1950, childless Chinese women would go to invoke the blessings of the deity for motherhood. You can still find numerous carvings on the walls of the Vedic legends. Such carvings include an elephant placing a flower on the Shiva-*linga*, a cow pouring its milk on the Shiva-*linga*, God's incarnation of Narasimha tearing out the entrails of the demon Hiranyakasipu, Vishnu mounted on the airborne eagle Garuda, Krishna playing the flute in Vrindavan, a prankish Krishna taking the apparel away from the bathing cowherd girls of Vrindavan, Krishna dancing on the multi-hooded cobra Kaliya, Shiva bearing the Ganges River pouring down from heaven, Hanuman on his flight to Lanka, and many others.

Also, discovered by Professor Dr. Raghu Vira, there is a pillar erected in 1104 A.D. in the village of Hsuan-wu, Lo-yang district, with a Sanskrit text written from top to bottom and right to left. Furthermore, in the rock-cut temple at Tun-huang, and another in Kung-hsien, you can find carved images of Ganesh with other Vedic deities, such as the sun, moon, Cupid, and the nine planetary divinities. These discoveries must have been there for many hundreds of years.

As explained on page 1285 of *World Vedic Heritage*, all this evidence is corroborated by a Chinese dignitary, Yuag Xianji, member of the Chinese People's Political Consultative Conference, speaking at the C. P. Ramaswamy Aiyar Foundation, Madras, March 27, 1984. He said, "Recent discoveries of ruins of Hindu temples in Southeast China provided further evidence of Hinduism in China. Both Buddhism and Hinduism were patronized by the rulers. In the 6th century A.D. the royal family was Hindu for two generations. The following Tang dynasty (7th to the 9th century A.D.) also patronized both Hinduism and Buddhism because the latter was but a branch of Hinduism. Religious wars were unknown in ancient China. The Chinese worshiped Shivambu--the Chinese name for Durga. The resurgence of Hinduism and the decline of Buddhism in India after the 7th century had its echo in China with temples of Mahadeva coming up. The temples had Hindu priests. In the 6th century members of a Chinese ruling family were known by their Hindu pet names as Narayan and Shiva Dasa respectively. Hinduism still exists in China in the guise of Buddhism. Buddhist monasteries have a Hindu touch and many of them could be mistaken for Hindu temples as they are full of idols similar to the Hindu pantheon."

We find additional insights into the connection between China and India in *World-Wide Hindu Culture* (p. 110) by Dr. S. Venu Gopalacharya. The Vedic influence in China can be seen many years ago in the similarities in the philosophies. The general principles and codes for living like those in the Vedic lifestyle and the spiritual path of *Sanatana-Dharma* are also found in the ways of Taoism, the moral principles of Confucius, and Mahayana Buddhism. The Chinese also worship gods, goddesses, and ancestors with *mantras, tantras,* and ritual. Their beliefs in the creation of the universe, rebirth, *karma,* and the usefulness of rituals and the assistance of divine powers to humanity are also similar to the Vedic customs.

For example, in the Chinese tradition we find the description of the creation to be very similar, in a general sense, to that found in the Vedic literature. They believe that in the beginning everything was once like a single ocean having the divine powers of nature and spirit in subtle form. These mixed and became converted to the male principle Yang and the female principle Yin, as well as heaven and earth. This is similar to the Shiva/Shakti principle in the Vedic tradition. Then the Yin and Yang gave rise to the universal man, Pangu. The organs of Pangu became converted to the various divisions of the universe. His breath became clouds and winds. His eyes gave rise to the sun and moon. His hands and legs became the directions. His body, flesh, nerves, and veins changed into hills, earth, plants, trees, grass, etc. This description is very similar to that of the Lord's manifestation of His universal form as described in the *Puranas*.

On page 108-9 of *World-Wide Hindu Culture* we find additional information. According to *China and Her Neighbors*, published by Progress Publications in Moscow, the earliest forms of contact between India and China go back thousands of years. This connection is mentioned in the ancient Vedic literature, such as the *Ramayana, Mahabharata,* as well as later texts like the *Arthashashtra* and the *Manudharmashashtra*. A Chinese language Buddhist document refers to a merchant by the name of Sribandhu, an Indian Buddhist sent by Ashoka to China in 218 B.C. Furthermore, even as far back as 138 B.C. when Zhangquin, the head of the Chinese embassy, went to Bactria, he found that the Indian merchants supplied cloth and Indian goods to Bactria. However, Sino-Indian trade links had existed long before that period through upper Burma and Assam and through Sichuan in Southern China.

Dr. Venu Gopalacharya goes on to explain, "As per the Chinese book *Hanshu,*

Wang Mang was trying to persuade Kanchipur [India] and Ceylon to maintain diplomatic relations with China and succeeded in that by the turn of the second century B.C. It states that the following were some of India's produce--elephants, rhinoceroses, tortoises, gold, silver, copper, iron, lead, fabrics, tin, woolen carpets, perfumes, loaf sugar, black pepper, ginger, and black salt. By the first century A.D., considerable mutual benefit had been gained in medicines, mathematics, astronomy, metallurgy, and Indian chemistry. Alchemy owed much to Chinese scholarship. India received silk and paper from China. Indian chess also became popular in China. While Fahian was in India, Buddabhadra, an Indian Buddhist, arrived by sea in 389 A.D., remained in China for 30 years and translated many [Sanskrit] Buddhist texts to Chinese in collaboration with Fahian. Movement of missionaries and pilgrims between India and China left palpable Indian traces on Chinese architecture, plastic art, literature and language, as well as many branches of science, such as astronomy, mathematics, and medicine, besides purely religious and philosophical impact. The Chinese pagodas, *stupas*, and Danhuang cave temples were in imitation of Indian counterparts. The Chinese emperors maintained Indian musicians, dancers and acrobats. Thus, the development of Chinese theatrical tradition owes much to India.

"One tentative assessment suggests that 35,000 new words and expressions were introduced into the Chinese language by the tenth century. Certain of the most ancient Chinese printed books are in Sanskrit. An outstanding example of this linguistic interaction is a Sanskrit-Tibetan-Chinese dictionary of technical terms dating to the ninth century A.D. One of the Chinese emperors became a disciple of Shivagupta, an Indian missionary. There were 3000 Indian monks in Luoyang region alone during the sixth century A.D. By the eighth century A.D., the Chinese had precise and detailed knowledge of the sea route from Guangzhou to Baghdad. Ziadan writes that it took 90 days to reach Baghdad by that route. More Indian embassies went to China than vice versa up to 750 A.D. through Central Asia as Islam spread in North India. However, missionaries and pilgrims, to collect Buddhist texts, continued up to the tenth century A.D."

Another point regarding the advancements and innovations of Chinese culture is made by Joseph Needham. In the book, *The Genius of China: 3000 Years of Science, Discovery and Invention*, Robert Temple reviews the findings of Joseph Needham at Cambridge University. He says that the Chinese knew and used poison gas and tear gas in the fourth century B.C. They manufactured steel from cast iron in the second century B.C. They built the first suspension bridge in the first century A.D. They were making cast iron in the fourth century B.C. And they invented matches in 577 A.D. This was respectively 2300, 2000, 1800, 1700, and 1000 years before the West. So, as Needham asks, how could the Chinese have been so far in advance of other civilizations? And if the Chinese mentality was so innovative, then why aren't they now?

As some historians suggest, it is because China inherited its knowledge from a previous advanced society. Thus, they merely used the earlier established knowledge the ancients already knew. And, as already discussed, all arrows point in the direction to the Vedic culture of India as being the preceding advanced civilization which shared its knowledge with the world, of which China was aware. Thus, China owed much to India for its early achievements.

Dr. Venu Gopalacharya sheds more light on this fact on page 180 of *World-Wide Hindu Culture*. "Twenty Indian works on Astronomy were available in China by the end of the sixth century. Indian methods of calendar computation were translated into Chinese and developed. Indian mathematics, a compendium translation produced then, was followed by several mathematical works under the general title of the Mathematical Sutras. Indian medical books, numbering hundreds, were translated into Chinese. Indian doctors were employed by the Tang emperors. . . Chinese exported [to India] silk, copperware, medicines, earthenware or ceramics and porcelain, and [in exchange] bought spices, pearls, precious stones, ivory, and fine examples of Indian craftsmanship."

This explains the advancement of Chinese medicine and mathematics through the help of Indian doctors and books. It had obviously been a mutually beneficial trade arrangement. Unfortunately, from 1440 onwards, diplomatic contacts between India, China, and other south eastern countries declined as the control of the sea routes to China was seized by the Europeans. Nonetheless, this shows how there was a strong Vedic influence in China from thousands of years ago.

BUDDHISM

Besides the Vedic similarities in Buddhism already mentioned, there are many additional correlations between the Vedic literature and the Buddhist religion of the Far East. For example, the word *Ch'an* of the Ch'an school of Chinese Buddhism is Chinese for the Sanskrit word *dhyana*, which means meditation, as does the word *zen* in Japanese. Furthermore, the deity Amitayus is the origin of all other Lokesvara forms of Buddha and is considered the original spiritual master, just as Balarama in the Vedic literature is the source of all the Vishnu incarnations and is the original spiritual teacher. Also, the trinity doctrine of Mahayana Buddhism explains the three realms of manifestations of Buddha, which are the *dharmakaya* realm of Amitabha (the original two-armed form is Amitayus), the *sambhogakaya* realm of the spiritual manifestation (in which the undescended form of Lokesvara or Amitayus reigns), and the *rupakaya* realm, the material manifestation (which is where Lokesvara incarnates in so many different forms). This is a derivative of the Vedic philosophy. Thus, Lokesvara is actually a representation of Vishnu to the Mahayana Buddhists.

All the different incarnations of Vishnu appear as different forms of Lokesvara in Buddhism. For example, Makendanatha Lokesvara is Matsya, Badravaraha Lokesvara is Varaha, Hayagriva is the horse-necked one as described in the *Vedas*, and so on. And the different forms of Lakshmi, Vishnu's spouse as the Goddess of Fortune, appear as the different forms of Tara in the White Tara, the Green Tara, etc. Even the fearful forms of Lokesvara are simply the fearful aspects of Lord Vishnu, as in the case of the threatening image of Yamantaka, who is simply the form of the Lord as death personified. The name is simply taken from Yamaraja, the Vedic lord of death.

Many times you will also see Buddhist paintings depicting a threefold bending form of Bodhisattvas and Lokesvaras much the same way Krishna is depicted. This is because the Bodhisattvas were originally styled after paintings from India, which were prints of Krishna. Most images of Tara are also similar to paintings of Lakshmi in that one hand is held in benediction. And Vajrayogini, the Buddha in female aspect, is certainly styled after goddess Kali or Durga. Kuvera, the lord of wealth in the Vedic culture, is Kuvera Vaishravana in Buddhism. There are many other carry-overs from the Vedic tradition into Buddhism that can be recognized, such as the use of ghee lamps and kusha grass, and the offerings of barley and ghee in rituals that resemble Vedic ceremonies.

JAPAN

The Vedic influence in Japan can also be recognized by the way its people once worshiped the deities of the Hindu pantheon. On page 940 of *World Vedic Heritage*, we find that it is described how the Vedic demigod Ganesh, "Used to be consecrated and worshiped on a special altar in the royal palace in Japan in July/August on the Ganesh Chaturthi days as per Vedic tradition since time immemorial. Even now Ganesh (alias Shoten) is invoked and worshiped by the Japanese in the Vedic tradition when seeking good luck, fortune or success in professional endeavors. Merchants of Kansai worship Shoten in Hoshanji temple on Mount Ikomei in Nara. The biggest Ganesh temple in Japan is in Osaka city where a permanent priest is on duty to conduct ritual worship of the deity."

Actually, Japan has thousands of temples of Vedic deities which are unknown to the outside world because they are called by different names. For example, the Japanese and Chinese pay homage to Ganesh but call him Shoten or Kangijen. The Japanese also worship goddess Durga and make offerings to her of pomegranate juice instead of the traditional goat's blood. However, the Sanskrit name *Kali-devi-ma* gets changed into the Japanese language and is pronounced as 'Kariteimo.'

The main religion in Japan is Shinto or Brahman Okyo. These words appear to be corrupt forms of the Sanskrit Sindhu and Brahma Vakya. [Sindhu indicates those living on the banks of the Sindhu or Indus River.] The Navaratri celebration of paying spiritual homage to the dead ancestors in September/October is traditionally a Vedic custom. Thus, paying respects to the dead ancestors, as found in the Japanese Shinto tradition, originally comes from the Sindhu (Vedic) culture. The following principles of Shintoism are similar to those of the Vedic religion:

1. The divine will and laws should not be broken.
2. Devotion to God helps to get over hardships and diseases.
3. As the whole world is like a single family, anger should be avoided under all circumstances.
4. Everyone should render his or her duties to the ancestors and divine powers.

Thus, Shintoism has many present day carry-overs from Hinduism.

Cremation also points to the Japanese having been adherents to the Vedic culture. Even the Japanese wrestling styles, with the wrestlers wearing nothing but loin cloths, is of Indian origin. Jujitsu is also an art of self-defense with roots in India. Jujitsu, or jujutsu, is a word that derives from the Sanskrit word *yuyutsu*, which appears in the first verse of the *Bhagavad-gita*, which signifies those desirous of fighting. The Sanskrit "Ya" often changes in other languages into "Ja."

The Japanese call their country Nippon which comes from the Sanskrit word *nipun*, which fittingly means dexterous. The name of the sovereign of Japan known as Hurohito also can be traced to the Sanskrit *Sura-Suta*, replacing the "H" with "S." *Sura-Suto* signifies the Son of God. A slight change in this is *Surya-Suta*, which means "descendant of the sun." This is more fitting in that the Japanese do consider their emperor to be a descendant of the sun-goddess. Correspondingly, Manu, the first global ruler by Vedic traditions, was known as Vaivasvat, son of the sun.

The Japanese suffix *San* is equivalent to Mister, but is added after the name. It means a good, kind, helpful, and cultured person. This is the same as the system in India in which the honorifics are added after the person's name. Many other similarities between Sanskrit words and the Japanese language also exist.

As Dr. Venu Gopalacharya further points out in *World-Wide Hindu Culture* (pp. 114-5), according to later historical evidences, the ruler of Korea once sent a golden image of Gautama Buddha and many books of Mahayana Buddhism as a gift to the emperor of Japan. From that time, religious and cultural contacts between Japan and India steadily grew. The Japanese emperors gave patronage to the Buddhist and Brahmin scholars of the famous Nalanda University. In the eighth century, the then emperor of Japan installed a huge bronze image of Gautama Buddha in the city of Nara and got the temple of Horiyuju painted in a fashion similar to the cave temples of Ajanta, which has many murals covering the walls depicting Buddha's life.

Even now you can find images of Gautama Buddha, Bodhisattvas, as well as Vedic gods and goddesses, along with the divine symbols of Shintoism, worshiped in the temples of Japan. You can find such divinities and Vedic gods, or variations of them, as Amitabha, Indra, Rudra, Kartikeya, Kubera, Surya, Yama, Vayu, Brahma, Sarasvati, Shiva, Nagarjuna, and others that are popular in Japan. You can find many of the Vedic gods with Japanese names. For example, the Vedic Kubera is known as the equivalent Bishamon. Varuna is the Suiten, the watergod. Shiva is Daikoko, god of darkness. Visvakarma, the Vedic architect of the demigods, is Bishukatsuma, god of carpenters. Vishnu is Amida or Amitabha.

Brahma-Sarasvati is Temmango-Benton Soma. (Temmango is the god of learning while Benton Soma is goddess of speech.) Indra is Tai Shakuten, and Ganesh is Sho-ten. In short, you could say that the Chinese and Japanese are Hindus as much as Hindus in India are Buddhists. They are all very much related.

REIKI

Reiki is said to have come from Japan. Reiki is a healing art which deals with universal (*rei*) life-force (*ki*). However, it has its roots in the *Ayurveda* and a long history in India. It was rediscovered by a person named Usui from the Sanskrit Buddhist scriptures in the Japanese monasteries. The practitioner transfers *ki* or *prana* to *marma* points on one's body. This creates a more natural flow of *prana* which causes a higher level of balance in the subtle body. This can help cure or prevent disease. *Marma* points are the acupuncture or acupressure points on the skin through which the *nadis*, as we understand from *Ayurveda* and the science of yoga, can be affected or adjusted for a better flow of *prana*, life-force. The *nadis* are the nerve-like channels through which flows the life-force in the subtle body. This knowledge was first explained in the Vedic literature of India and, again, has only recently been rediscovered.

* * *

These are all brief accounts of the historical and cultural similarities between the Oriental countries and that found in the Vedic culture. Many more details could be provided, and new findings are always being discovered. However, the point is that all this evidence makes it clear that wherever we look carefully into the past we come across nothing but the ancient Vedic culture and Sanskrit language worldwide. This is the original, primordial culture from which all other cultures are but descendants.

Why did all of these cultures become distinct or separate from the once global Vedic culture? It seems that after the *Mahabharata* war and the disappearance of Lord Krishna, the Vedic kingdoms declined and the worldwide Vedic cultural centers were depleted of funds along with the support from its knowledgeable scholars, teachers, scientists, and administrators. As India faced its own internal struggles and political upheavals, as did also China, Japan, and other countries, all links with India were strained and became disconnected. Thus, the Vedic culture that once pervaded the world began to recede, leaving the Indian and Vedic cultural centers throughout the planet to be gradually swallowed by the regional characteristics. With time, languages, dress, the arts, etc., all became changed and increasingly distinguished from its Vedic origins, and more influenced by the changing tastes of the people of the region.

CHAPTER THIRTEEN

The Vedic Influence in the Ancient Americas

The traditions of the ancient Americans have numerous similarities with Vedic culture. In the legends of the Sioux Indians, there is the story of how their ancestors were visited by a celestial woman who gave them the religion they follow. She had explained that there are four ages that is symbolized by how a buffalo loses one leg during the advent of each age. This shows that with each age, conditions deteriorate. Presently, the buffalo has only one leg. This symbolism is directly in accordance with the Vedic version. Other tribes of the Indians of North America, especially the Hopi, also have descriptions of the four ages, or four worlds as they call them, that are similar to the deteriorating effects of the four ages in the Vedic tradition; namely Satya-yuga, Treta-yuga, Dvapara-yuga, and Kali-yuga. They also accepted the concepts of reincarnation, respect for nature, the nature spirits or demigods, etc., which are very similar to the concepts found in the Vedic philosophy. In Mexico, ancient paintings were found that showed heads of a rhinoceros, as well as paintings of a man with the head of an elephant, like Ganesh in India. And we all know that the rhinoceros and elephant are not animals found in the Americas.

An obvious point about the Mayan connection with that of the Vedic is, for example, that the word *Maya* is from the Sanskrit language of India, which I will discuss more later. Deities of Ganesh, the same as in India, have been discovered in excavations in Central America and Mexico. Additional Vedic deities that were found by archeologists in ancient America include those of Shiva, Kali, and the sun, though they may have been in slightly varied forms. And forms of Buddha had been found in the jungles of Honduras by Professor F. W. Putnam.

The physical and facial characteristics of the people of Mexico are also similar to the people of northeast India. Even the traditional songs of the Mexican people contain similar sentiments of those of India, such as when a mother bids her newly married daughter farewell. Mexican women's clothes still resemble the long dress and short blouse like an East Indian sari and choli. Women still prepare flat bread made from corn flour like the Indian chapati made from wheat flour.

Studies have concluded that similarities in Mayan, Aztec, Inca, and North

American Indian civilizations have a strong connection with Indian Vedic Aryans and the Southeast Asian countries. For example, the Aztec and Mayan architecture of ancient Mexico and Central America is very similar to the Vedic buildings and temples and pyramids of Egypt. They shared many other things in the areas of customs, art motifs (such as the lotus flower found at Chichen Itza), time measurements, calenders, local gods, styles of dress, and, of course, in architecture, astronomy, and religious symbols. Similarities can be seen in sculptures of the native dress and solar symbolism, rituals of worship, systems of government, and in language and names. In fact, the name Argentina (meaning connected with silver) is related to the name of Arjuna (meaning of silver hue). Arjuna was one of Krishna's closest devotees. Witnesses have also found Sanskrit letters carved in the stone on Sugarloaf Mountain in Brazil.

The remnants of great cities with roads, water tanks, canals, forts, etc., found in South America leads one to accept the fact that it must have been quite a developed civilization. Due to the traces of Vedic architectural design, city planning, mythology, and images of worship found in this area, many researchers consider that this society was originally developed in India. For example, in the book *The Conquest of the Maya* (published by Jarrold's in England), J. Leslie Mitchell explains that the basis of the old Maya empire was not of the work of the ancestors of the present day Maya, but was an import from the same foreigners that built the palaces and temples of the Chams and Khmers in Cambodia, and the temples in Java. [More of this connection will be shown later in the chapter.] He also points out the similarities between the Maya rain-god Chac and the Vedic Indian Indra, and the Maya monkey-god and the Vedic Hanuman. The Vedic origin is further enhanced by the frequency that the elephant motif is found in Maya art, especially the earlier works of the Maya, such as at Copan, although the elephant never existed in the region. Mr. Pococke also says in this regard: "The Peruvians and their ancestors, the Indians, are in this point of view at once seen to be the same people."

One reason for these similarities between the Americas and India is that in ancient Vedic times there were two great architects, Visvakarma of the demigods or Aryans, and Maya of the *asuras*. The Mayan people, also known as technicians, were no doubt named as such because of being connected with this person named Maya, or Mayasura and Maya Danava. They were a part of his clan or tribe. They had fallen away from the Vedic way of life and were sent or escaped to the region of Central America. They also carried with them much of the science of astronomy and navigation for which this Mayasura was known. This will become more apparent as we proceed through this chapter.

Mayasura's knowledge is more fully explained in the classic work of Indian Vedic astronomy known as the *Surya Siddhanta* for which he is given credit. Many people have wondered from where the Mayans acquired their astronomical knowledge. This would explain how the Mayan people had such a high degree of understanding in astronomy, from which they also developed their calendar. The

Mayan calendar was a science they had long developed, carrying it with them from their previous location and civilization. Incidentally, for them, the end of the world, or the way we have known it, is calculated as December 23, 2012. Thus, the calendar was not merely a record of time, but also a prediction of social changes.

The *Surya Siddhanta* is dated back to around 490 A.D. by Rev. Ebenezer Burgess who uses certain descriptions of planetary positions it describes. However, its knowledge and information are said to have originally been known as long as 13,000 years ago. In his book, *Ancient Indian Technologies*, Ravindranath Ramchandra Karnik agrees and dates it back to 13,902 B.C. Others say that some of the star positions it describes date back over 50,000 years. Furthermore, when following a vocal tradition, common to most ancient Vedic texts, much of it is likely to have been known many thousands of years before it was embellished and composed into its present written form. Actually, the text of the *Surya Siddhanta* explains that it was revealed to Mayasura many thousands of years ago.

At the Bolivian site of Tiahuanaco, there is a huge and important astronomical structure that gives credence to the above information. Within this structure is an arch called the Gateway to the Sun, which was used for tracking the rising and setting of the sun throughout the seasons. The corner pillars of the huge courtyard shows the northernmost and southernmost movements of the sun. Though the sun's movements are now outside the jurisdiction of the corner posts, the positioning of the structure would have matched the suns longest and shortest days back in 10,500 B.C. The implications of what this means are enormous. Even at that time the people built structures for use in astrology and observing seasonal changes, and, thus, were quite advanced.

The Nazca lines in southern Peru are huge drawings on the surface of the earth that cannot be properly recognized unless viewed from the air. How they were so accurately drawn, nobody knows. Nonetheless, it has been discovered that these Nazca lines match star constellations in the sky. The great spider, for example, is an exact model of the Orion constellation as it would have appeared over 2000 years ago.

Like the Vedic culture, the Maya had a pantheon of demigods, many of which have similarities to the Vedic deities. Mayan gods like Xiuhtechutli and Xipe Totec have their Vedic counterparts in Indra and Agni. Indra, like Xiuhtechutli, was the rain god and guardian of the Eastern Quadrant, and Agni, similar to Xipe Totec, was the god of sacrificial fire, born in wood and the life force of trees and plants. Then there is the Vedic Ushas, the beautiful goddess of the Dawn or Sky, who is similar to the Mayan view of Venus, goddess of Dawn.

Furthermore, hymn 121 of book ten in the *Rig-veda* is very similar to the description of creation as found in the Popol Vuh. In fact, there are numerous similarities between the Vedic creation legend and that described in the Popol Vuh. (These have been described in my previous book, *How the Universe was Created and Our Purpose In It.*)

The Mayan religious rituals also included attention to and worship of the ancestors, and were often based on astrological dates, similar to the Vedic people. The Mayans were advanced astrologers and able to calculate the length of the year more precisely than the Europeans. This was no doubt based on an earlier system that the Mayans brought with them, as referred to in the *Surya Siddhanta*. Mayans also calculated the Venusian year at 584 days, which modern astronomers have figured to be 583.92. So their system was well established.

These and other similarities in the philosophy and culture of the ancient American people and that of the East show that there must have been a link between the two areas. One geographic connection for this link is the Bering Strait between Russia and the United States. The water of the Bering Sea is still comparably shallow. It is here that the Asiatic tribes may have journeyed over to the Americas many years ago and traveled south, planting their philosophy and religion wherever they went. This was accepted in varying degrees by the people in different localities.

Groliers 1997 CD-ROM Encyclopedia says that the ancient Mayan Indian ancestors are believed to have crossed the Bering Straits from Asia more than 20,000 years ago. Archeologists today also declare that Central America was populated by 20,000 B.C. The Maya kept historical records, but they only go back to 50 B.C. However, the Mayan chronological calendar goes back to a date that correlates to August 13, 3114 B.C. The Olmecs also had a calendar that started from 3113 B.C. [Once again we find another date in the history of society that correlates with the time of the *Mahabharata* war at Kuruksetra, the time when the breakdown of the world Vedic empire began.] These similarities could mean that the most recent Mayans and Olmecs arrived here at this time, fleeing the destruction on the other side of the world after the catastrophic war, and then settling in Central and South America.

Another possibility of how people of the East traveled to the Americas is sailing by way of the Aleutian Islands, or the islands of the South Pacific, some of which had been colonized by the Aryans as noted earlier in this book. This may not have been so difficult when we understand that from the coasts of Peru to India are two westerly ocean currents, south of the equator. They go north of the Philippines and on through Indonesia. Another ocean current from the east of Japan goes east toward Mexico. Knowledge of these currents could have greatly assisted the sailing of any sea-faring traders.

Another book that provides evidence in this regard and opinions on the Vedic influence found in America is the out of print book called *The Sphinx Speaks* by Jwala Prasad Singhal. On page 54 he explains that when the architect Maya Danava was banished from India, he most likely fled to South America by way of the land-bridges that were provided by the Lemurian continent. This would certainly date the event to many thousands of years ago. The signs of his activities and great architecture are still found in the form of magnificent stone temples topping pyramidal structures in Mexico and Peru. Mr. Singhal also feels that it is probable that the Mayan civilization as well as the Inca culture were carried and established there by Maya Danava and his confederates.

Another point of similarity is that the many ancient cultures of the Americas, such as the Maya, Inca, etc., all worshiped the sun. This is because they were all descendants and at one time part of the solar race or dynasty from Ayodhya, India, in line with Lord Ramachandra, and, thus, they gave their tribute to the sun.

On page 112 of *The Sphinx Speaks*, Jwala Prasad Singhal explains that one of the reasons for the spread of the Heliolithic or sun worshiping culture was because of the influence of Maya Danava, the great architect of the Daityas, and his friend Nimuchi, both of whom fled to Patalaloka, or South America. Escaping through Sri Lank, Malaya, Australia and onward, they reached Mexico and founded the Mayan civilization. Nimuchi went on to Mexico and founded the Moche (or Mochica) civilization in Peru, which later developed into the great Inca empire. The proof of these two great Daitya chiefs is the great stone monuments in the islands along their route as well as in the Mayapan regions of Mexico and in the Moche and Inca regions of Peru. Since there are no such pyramids or other huge ancient stone structures in the area of Alaska or the Bering Straits, this indicates that the Alaskan route is most unlikely to have been the popular way these migrating people used.

Another writer, Victor W. Von Hagen, in his book *Realm of the Incas*, first published in March of 1957 by Mentor Books, relates on page 30 that the Mochicas, "are a caste-minded empire; they lord over the northern Peruvian desert and one can still see the remains of their temples, one of which called 'Huaca del Sol' in the Viru Valley is constructed of approximately 130,000,000 sun-dried adobe bricks. This suggests, naturally, a complex social organization to accomplish so effective a construction. Their advanced society is given further emphasis by their skill in gold casting and wood carving. The Mochicas had warriors, messengers, weavers, and doctors; they built roads and organized a courier system, and perfected many a social pattern that appeared later in the political organization of the Inca."

Besides the Huaca del Sol, or Temple of the Sun, there was also the Huaca de la Luna, or Temple of the Moon, both of which are not far from the present city of Trujillo. This means that in the Moche culture both the sun and moon were worshiped. This was also the case in the Sumerian culture. This is in accord with the Post-Rigvedic times, as well as in the Puranic times, when there were two royal dynasties in India. These were the Suryavanshi or the descendants of the Sun, being in the line of Vaivasvata Manu, and the Chandravanshi or the descendants of the Moon in which Lord Krishna appeared. This worship, therefore, could be little more than a carry-over from the Vedic culture.

The Aztecs also had a pantheon of gods. The main Aztec gods are very similar in character to the Vedic demigods, though pictured differently. Tezcatlipoca (Smoking Mirror) is affiliated with obsidian. The dark complexion could be a reference to the darkish complexion of Vishnu or Krishna. Tonatiuh, the sun, is very much revered as the Vedic Surya, source of life. The Aztecs placed importance on the east-west path of the sun in the same way most Vedic temples are built to face the rising sun in the east. Quetzalcoatl, the feather serpent and the inventor of all great things, was fashioned after a combination of air (eagle), earth (snake), and water (clouds). He is depicted as part bird, part snake, and often with human features. This is similar to Garuda, the eagle carrier of Lord Vishnu who is known for eating serpents, and sometimes pictured as carrying a snake with his feet. Garuda is, similarly, often featured with a human face. The Vedic stories relate how Garuda once threatened the multi-hooded Kaliya serpent, who later was subdued by Krishna. Also, like Vishnu who holds a conch shell, the conch shell was the mark of Quetzalcoatl. Tlaloc, the rain deity, is very similar to the Vedic Indra who is in charge of the rain. Tonantzin (Honored Grandmother) is the deity of the earth, the Vedic Bhumi. One major difference between the Aztec and Vedic worship of the deities is that there was no Vedic custom for human sacrifice to all of their demigods. This was one of the results of the Aztecs having fallen away from the true Vedic lifestyle.

The priests of the Aztecs maintained the ritual fires in the temples, similar to the Vedic process of the sacred fires in the Indian temples. Priests were also responsible for rainmaking and performing the sacred rites. Vedic ritual was also known for being important to produce rain. Some Aztec priests specialized in divination, prophecies, astronomy, watching the movements of the planets, calendrical calculations, etc. Others were teachers, counselors, or leaders, all very much like the Vedic Brahmins.

Another point provided by Jwala Prasad Singhal in *The Sphinx Speaks*, (page 115, 117) is that the Incas developed in a territory that was inhabited by people called Keshawas or Quechuas, whose language also was called Quechuas. The Incas later adopted it as their language. Mr. Singhal considered that these Keshawas or Quechuas were evidently the Yakshas of the Puranic tradition, some of whom having fled to America. As explained further by Victor W. Von Hagen, in his book *Realm of the Incas* (page 54, 58), the social customs of the Quechuas also had a strange parallel to that of India. For example, a new baby was not named for the first two years, but was simply called 'wawa,' or baby. Then there was an elaborate hair cutting ceremony, similar to the Vedic custom. At fourteen a boy, having reached puberty, put on his breech cloth and became a man. This could be likened to the sacred thread or Yagyopavit ceremony at this age for Hindu Brahmin boys. For girls at this age there was the hair-combing ceremony. At the age of twenty, a man was expected to marry. If he did not, a woman was chosen for him.

The Quechuas also produced 240 varieties of potatoes and 20 varieties of maize and numerous other things. They also produced cotton. About cotton, Mr. Hagen states on page 68, "Early Peruvian man cultivated cotton--before it was cultivated by the Egyptians. It was known to the Assyrians as 'tree wool,' yet the Greek etymology of the word points to the fact that it came originally from India."

Another strange but interesting link between the Peruvians and the Vedic culture is explained by Henry Gilman in his book *Ancient Man in Michigan*. The Peruvians, among other societies, such as the Mound Builders, Neolithic people of France and the Canary Islands, would bore a small hole in the top of the skulls of the dead so the soul might easily pass out. This is a Vedic understanding that is common among yogis, Tibetans, and others that if the soul passes out of the body through the head, especially the top, then it is a sign of a higher birth in the next life. Boring a hole would be a mechanical means of trying to guarantee this result.

More on the Incas and Peru is supplied by writer S. Y. Narayana Moorthy, in his article *Vedic Studies in the West--Historical Evidence*, published in the November 1987 issue of *Astrological Magazine*. He has pointed out that there have been figurines of Shiva in South American museums. Furthermore, the poetry of Peru contains similarities to the *Ramayana* and *Mahabharata*. Hymns of the Inca rulers of Peru and their caste system also resemble those found in the Vedic culture. Moorthy goes on to relate that Syrian author Zenob says the worship of Krishna was present in America in the second and third centuries before Christ. There were temples with large images of Krishna, and several thousand followers of the Krishna religion in the region of Lake Van.

Regarding images, R. Karnik explains in his book, *Ancient Indian Technologies* (p. 75), high up on a plateau in Peru the Inca people had a 7.5 meter tall image of the elephant-headed Ganesh with his mouse at his feet. The image is made of several large pieces of stone, similar to the construction of a temple nearby. So a connection between the Incas of Peru and India had to have been there.

Another aspect of the Inca carved stone images is that they show facial traits that characterize the five major races from all over the world. This could not have been possible unless the people had already navigated or were familiar with all parts of the globe. Thus, they had to have had the skill of sailing and navigation and could determine longitude. The method for this had been passed down in the form of knowledge presently found in the Vedic *Surya Siddhanta*, which enabled them to figure longitude of any place in the world and, thus, the route to get there.

The La Venta site of the Olmecs has sculptures that show various African and bearded Caucasian features. The bearded ones are usually associated with the feathered or plumed serpent. Nonetheless, it reflects a society of sea-faring people that had been well acquainted with cultures from around the world.

Viracocha, the pale-skinned, bearded god is said to have come to this area on a boat without paddles, and taught the people astronomy and architecture, as well as a philosophy of compassion and love. Thus, knowledge of navigation would be natural, and was passed on to the people of the region.

In an article in the *Atlantis Rising* magazine (Number 17), called *Atlantis in America*, George Erikson presents some additional evidence from his book, *Atlantis in America: Navigators of the Ancient World*. Although the premise of the book is that Atlantis was the forgotten society of Central America, he agrees with the fact that they were navigators of the seas in ancient times, and were a part of a culture that had connections with those of Sumer, Egypt, India, and others.

One example is that traces of cocaine and nicotine have been found in Egyptian mummies, showing the use of this drug and tobacco in Egypt many years ago, at least among the higher classes of people. The cocoa and tobacco plants are genetically solely American. Furthermore, by 12,000 B.C. there was a diffusion through the Pacific region of the American sweet potato, and the spread of the American coconut and cotton plant. This could not have happened unless there had been trading going on among the people of these areas, thus proving they were navigating the oceans. This theory is further verified by the ancient Peruvian name of the sweet potato, which is *kumara*. This is identical with its pronunciation in Polynesia, from Easter Island to New Zealand. And as anyone familiar with Vedic culture knows, *kumara* is directly a Sanskrit word still used throughout the Vedic literature.

Another example is the parrot, which is a bird that some feel is genetically solely American, yet appears not only in South America, but throughout Polynesia and India from as far back as 15,000 years ago. The bird is too poor a flyer to traverse to these areas on its own. Thus, it had to have reached these locations through the assistance of sea-faring navigators.

As further related in *The Sphinx Speaks,* Mr. J. Alden Mason, who spent most of his life from 1917 to 1957 in the study of research in archeology, anthropology, ethnology, and folklore of American Indians, wrote an important book named *The Ancient Civilizations of Peru* in 1957, published by Pelican Books. In the section of "Origins" on page 20, he comments on the similarities and connections between the American civilizations and that of Asia. He explains that, "The American Indian physique type is fundamentally similar to the Asiatic and obviously a subgroup of the latter.

"Trans-oceanic migrations to America have always been a favorite creed of those with the will to believe, but until quite recently anathema to all reputable American anthropologists. However, ignoring the mythical 'Lost Continent of Mu,' evidence of trans-Pacific contacts are strong enough to be almost convincing to many good anthropologists. Their time, extent, route, nature, and effect are still so little known that no cogent, comprehensive picture of them has yet been proposed. But there are many curious and close resemblances in cultural elements between several regions in mainland America and Polynesia, Melanesia, and South-eastern Asia that are difficult to account for on other grounds than historical contact.

"There are many cultural resemblances between Polynesia and America, though others seem to by-pass the islands and directly connect Cambodia and Middle America, or Melanesia and Alaska, for instance. However, the physical type of Polynesians, their language, and the fundamentals of their culture connect them with South-eastern Asia rather than with America, and there is little doubt that they originally came from the Malayan region at no very remote period. In fact, they still retain very detailed legends of their migrations, at least the later ones--it has been conservatively estimated that they did not reach Easter Island until the fourteenth century A.D., at which the Peruvian civilization were at their apogee. Pre-Polynesian occupations of the eastern Pacific islands are not indicated, much less proved, and we know of no other Oceanic people who had the skill and the equipment in navigation to be able to make such voyages.

"In fine, the resemblances between certain cultural features in America and in Polynesia, Melanesia, Indonesia or South-eastern Asia are too great and too close to be explained away as parallel developments."

One other piece of the puzzle that is quite fascinating is that on Easter Island, 2600 miles off the coast of Chile in the middle of the Pacific Ocean, undeciphered hieroglyphics have been found that match those of Mohenjo-daro, the ancient Aryan city of the Indus Valley region. That is not possible unless the Vedic Aryans had been there nearly five thousand years ago, or if it had been a part of the Vedic empire in ancient times.

A new development is the similarities found between the petroglyphs of the Hawaiian Islands and those symbols on the Harappan seals, both of which resemble the old Brahmi script, as related by the Indian scholar B. C. Chandra in his *Vestiges of Indian Culture in Hawaii.*

Even in Brazil the paintings at Pedra Furada depict animals that include camels, the same as those of India and the Middle East. George Erikson explains that these were abundant in the Brazilian region and became victims of a mass extermination or cataclysm 12,500 years ago. However, if that was not the case, then knowledge of the camel had to have come through the means of sea-faring traders from the area of India. In any case, the above evidence shows a connection between these two parts of the world from many thousands of years ago.

In his book, *Hindu America,* Bhikshu Chamanlal has made a thorough research and has established that the pre-Spanish rulers of the Americas were of Vedic origin, especially from South India. He compares the cultural, social, political, and economic structures of the Aryans of India with those of pre-Spanish America. He also compares the similarities of their religions through illustrations and scores of photos of art pieces relating to the images of gods and goddesses and temples of ancient India and Central and South America. In the photos are stone-carved images from the ruined temples that depict Narasimha (the lion incarnation of Vishnu) of Copan (Sopan), Chacmool (or Sakramula–Indra or Vishnu) of Tula, Kalpavriksha of Palanque (or Patala Lanke), a carved image of a turtle (Kurmavatara) of Guatemala, and others. There are also three pictures which show: A) Vamanadeva in Mexico, B) A god wearing a turban from Quir Ugua (Chiragaw), and C) A Buddhist Sangha in America from Guatemala. The peculiar thing about these three images is that they all have inscriptions of their titles in Kannada-Telugu script. The third image has the inscription in Mexican script as well. Now how is this possible without an Indian connection?

In another photo of the Inca ruler Atahuallpa, you can see a red *kumkum* mark on his forehead, along with facial features common of a person of Indian origin. This photo was from the December, 1973 issue of *National Geographic*, page 729.

In a photo relating to a receptacle for offerings with an image of the sun-god kept in the Museo National in Mexico City, one can see the image of Rudra, one of the forms of Shiva, with Vibhuti (sacred ash), matted hair, holding the Ganges and a crescent moon.

Research has uncovered how the Kannada-Telugu and Sanskrit speaking Aryans came to America, and how America was a colony of Greater India. As the Inca rulers were proud to belong to the Solar race stemming back to Ayodhya and the family of Lord Ramachandra, their titles are clearly referred to as Angaka Rajas in the Kannada-Telugu inscription of Guatemala. This is one of the means by which their origin can be traced.

More confirming evidence about the connection between the cultures of Central and South America was reported in the June, 1995 edition of *Hinduism Today*. Therein, Sri V. Ganapati Sthapati, one of India's foremost temple architects and an expert in sculpture and stone construction, reported his examinations of the ancient temples and stone buildings at the Mayan sites in Central and South America. One of the residential buildings at Machu Picchu was immediately recognized as having a thickness of 33 inches, a standard measure in South India, which was first expounded by Maya Danava. The buildings were also built on a module based plan, and their lengths were never more than twice their width. This is according to the standard rules of the *Vastu Shastras*, or the group of texts on architecture, art, and town planning, of which belongs the ancient manuscript *Mayamatam*, or "Concepts of Mayan," said to be authored by Maya Danava.

At Saqsayhuman, the rocks weighing up to 160 tons in the stone walls are fit together so tightly at this ancient site, dating from 400 B.C. to 1400 A.D., that no one knows how they were made. However, Sthapati immediately recognized the small knobs on the base of the rocks which are used as levers and is the exact system still used in India to move large rocks with the help of 30 to 40 men.

Further similarities between the Inca and Indian traditions include the way stones are quarried by splitting off slabs, along with the methods of joining and fitting stones, leveling the stones with a plumb line, the use of lime mortar, etc. The use of mortar can be seen in many areas of India, including the stone and brick buildings at Mahabalipuram, Tanjore, and practically all over India, especially in the south.

At the Mayan Pyramid of the Castle at Chichen Itza, the structure again conformed to principles of the *Vastu Shastra*. The top temple structure was one-quarter of the base dimensions, and the stepped design was based on the eight-by-eight grid system. Along with other things, such as the wall thickness, location and thickness of the columns, etc., all of which are similar to Vedic standards.

This helps further the conclusion that these cultures, although developing their own ideas later on, based many of their original values and methods of artistic, architectural, social, and religious orientation on the Vedic Indian system. They were no doubt quite influenced by, and utilized, the principles that they directly inherited or which were carry-overs from the original Vedic culture.

We have to remember from other portions of this volume that the Vedic Aryans were well aware of the geography of the world and the sea routes for reaching the other continents from India. So the continents of North and South America were not unknown to them. In fact, the name America comes from the Sanskrit word *amaraka*, meaning land of the immortals. *Mara* means death, *amara* means no death or beyond it. Furthermore, though Patala is often referred to be a planet many thousands of miles below the earth, many people feel that the name Patalaloka--land below India--in such Vedic texts as the *Ramayana* also refers to the Americas, specifically South America, meaning the island continent on the other side of the globe from India. The *Puranas* have described that there is a connection between India and the Americas since time immemorial. For example, the *Puranas* explain that after Durga fights with the demons, they were sent to live in Patalaloka. In the *Matsya Purana*, it is described that Mayasura, the speaker of the *Surya Siddhanta*, and his followers escaped to Patala by the western sea after Tripura Dahana. It is also said that he built beautiful cities and buildings in the Patala region. Furthermore, it is considered that the clan of people known as the Nagas, as mentioned in the *Ramayana*, were also known as the Maya. The Nagas are generally considered a class of serpents. However, they are also considered devotees of the serpent cult, or a war-like race of *asuras* or demons. So, they may have been people who were regarded as having a snake-like mentality or consciousness. The Nagas were also known to be expert navigators whose ships sailed from the eastern to the western oceans in remote ages, and for being learned architects who built great cities.

In this regard, the *Mahabharata*, written 5,000 years ago, also explains that the Mayans had constructed a magnificent palace for performing a great Rajasuya ceremony. Additionally, the *Mayasilpasastra*, a text on the science of Vedic architecture, is also a well known book in Sanskrit. So these references in such ancient books as the *Puranas*, *Mahabharata*, and *Ramayana* show that there was a connection between the ancient Aryans of India and the Maya in the land we now know as the Americas from at least 5,000 years ago if not much earlier. Thus, we can fairly safely conclude that these Mayan people were the ones who colonized parts of Central America thousands of years ago. It was many years later that the descendants of these same rulers, who were known as the Angakas, ruled over the states of Anga (Bihar) to Karnataka in the second to seventh centuries. They used the Kannada-Telugu and Oriya languages.

Furthermore, the father-in-law of Ravana, the chief demon in the *Ramayana*, was known as a Mayan ruler according to the *Mahabharata*. It is also said that he was married to a daughter of Mayasura. In relation to this, there are legends of a tunnel system that connected India and Sri Lanka with South America that Ravana was supposed to have used for travel and for storing his vast riches of gold and jewels. Ancient caves throughout India, such as at Ellora, Ajanta, the Elephanta Caves at Mumbai, and other ancient ruined cities, were said to have hidden entrances that opened into a network of subterranean tunnels. I personally visited an ancient temple in Ujjain, in central India, which had an entrance to a tunnel system that was said to lead to any part of India, even as far away as Badrinatha in the Himalayas. However, it had been sealed with a big steal plate by the Indian government during Nehru's time to prevent people from entering it.

It has also been recorded how Tibetan Lamas assert that a vast network of underground tunnels do in fact exist in America. Through these tunnels a person is supposed to be able to reach other portions of the world. Legends have it that in this underworld lives an ancient society that escaped a tremendous cataclysm. The fact is that there is a cave system in the Andes of Peru. However, the Peruvian government has closed many of the entrances. The tunnels are collectively known as the Tunnel of the Incas. It has been reported that they run hundreds of miles through Peru, from Lima to Cuzco and farther west, and then on to the Atacama desert in Chile. Some of these tunnels are believed to still house the remaining treasures of the Incas. However, some people believe that the Incas did not have the technology to build such elaborate and deep tunnels. Thus, the tunnels must have already been there, built previous to the Incas. Some of these tunnels are estimated to date back from ten to fifteen thousand years prior to the Incas. This really means that the tunnels could be so old that it is impossible to know how ancient they are. Thus, they certainly could have been built during the times of the *Mahabharata* or even the *Ramayana*, and used by the likes of Ravana. One story I have heard from others is that there was once a half-crazy man who emerged out of a tunnel in Brazil, who held in his hand an ear of corn made of solid gold. Could this have been a remnant of the lost treasure of Ravana?

One example of the *Ramayana* referring to the region of Patala is found in the *Uttara Kandam* section. In Chapter One, there is the story of how the Rakshasas came to live in Sri Lanka. Malyavan, Sumali and Mali were three demon brothers who headed the Rakshasas at the time. When they grew too aggressive, they fought with the gods, and even with Lord Vishnu, who easily defeated and killed Mali. After this, Sumali and Malyavan retreated back to Lanka, but later attacked Lord Vishnu again. Being defeated numerous times, they finally left Lanka and took up residence in the Patala region. This could mean that they traveled through the tunnel system to reach America.

Another example is of how Ravana crossed the ocean to reach Patala. Patalaloka is often considered a separate planet many, many miles below the earth. However, in this description, found in the *Ramayana*, *Uttara Kandam*, Chapter Six, it describes how Ravana was on his conquering tour. He had got on his Puspaka chariot, which was a powerful *vimana*, and entered the ocean in order to reach the Patala region, the abode of the Uragas. Ravana then entered Bhogavati, the city of Vasuki and reduced the Nagas to submission.

This example involves a few things that we need to remember. Firstly, Ravana had a *vimana* which, as discussed elsewhere, is a craft that can fly, sail, or even travel under the water. In this case, entering the ocean water is the way Ravana reached Patala. The ocean had to have been what is now the Pacific Ocean, not outer space. Secondly, as previously mentioned, some people feel that the Nagas are in fact the same as the Mayans, or a race of war-like people. Ravana's father was a Mayan ruler. Bhogavati is the magnificent capital of the Nagas, guarded by serpents, or serpent-like people (sometimes meaning people with the consciousness like a serpent), and dedicated to Vasuki, the king of serpents. Vasuki is described as the eldest son of Kasyapa and his wife Kadru, and who started the clan of Nagas. Uragas are also considered a class of serpents, but often represented with human faces. Thus, Ravana knew of this region and conquered the people there.

In this way, we can see that Vedic civilization had been an influence on pre-historic America, and that those connected with the ancient Vedic culture, or were offshoots of it, had been settlers in America many thousands of years ago. More recent evidence of the Indian influence in the Americas, as discussed below, is explained on pages 123-130 of *World-Wide Hindu Culture*, by Dr. Venu Gopalacharya, which shows pre-Spanish rulers in the Americas were from India.

He explains how descendants of the Vedic Aryans again reached and colonized the Americas more recently than the ancient *Mahabharata* times. After the fall of the Kanva and Sunga dynasties of Magadha, India, the royal families established several kingdoms in South India and South East Asia. They also ruled in Kambhoj (Cambodia) from 650 to 1350, Champa (250 to 1000), Srivijaya (650 to 1350), Yavadwipa (Java)(900 to 1350), and Janaggala and Kadri (1100 to 1360). Thereafter, Hindus stopped migrating to those places as Mohammedanism spread there from the 14th century onwards except on Bali island.

While these Vedic rulers of the Solar Dynasty were in Kambhoj (Cambodia), they built the city of Angkor in 680. From 802 to 1177 many kings of the same dynasty continued to rule over the area. This means that Cambodia had been part of the Vedic administration. As these rulers were lovers of the arts and culture, they constructed hundreds of big temples. The great temples of Angkor Wat (temples for Vishnu) and Angkorthom (Shiva's temples) were constructed in the eleventh and twelfth centuries. They contain thousands of sculptures and mural paintings of scenes from the *Ramayana, Mahabharata*, and *Harivamsha*.

"In 1160 A.D. anarchy spread in Cambodia when its ruler, Yasovarma, became a Buddhist monk and went away abandoning the throne. A leader by the name of Tribhavanaditya managed to re-establish peace and prosperity for about thirty years, but he was murdered when the neighboring ruler of Champa invaded Cambodia by sea with a naval army. In the ensuing confusion, the royal widow, Mara Ciuaco (Mama Ocollo or Asalu), with the princes and well-wishers, escaped in a ship and reached the western shore of South America. According to *Aryan Incas* the widow attributed the ruin which had befallen the land to the people's disobedience of the ancient Gods of the realm. She advised the young prince Rocca to establish a strong rule so that prosperous economic and social life might develop. With tears, she appealed to the prince to assume the throne relying upon Virococha and his own valor. [Viracocha refers to the Sanskrit Virabhadra, who is the manifestation of Lord Shiva's wrath, one of his guards.] In course of time, his successors, Ayar Manco Topa (Vedic--Aryamanasa Tapa), Uyssa Topa (Arya Ayusya Tapa), and Ayar Chaki Topa (Arya Shakti Tapa) established strong empires of Central and South America, including Mexico (pronounced in Sanskrit as Maghico, another name of Lord Indra), Yucatan (Yasastana), Guatemala (Guatamalaya), and Peru (Paru, or Prabhu, Surya, Land of the Sun).

"When the Spanish pirates discovered America, Montezuma (Sanskrit Mantrisuma, meaning learned flower) was the emperor of Mexico, and Atahuallpa (Atyalpa) that of Peru. The grandeur of these empires can be imagined even now seeing the hundreds of ruined palaces, temples, roads and aqueducts which are found there.

"The ruling dynasty of Mexico (Lord Magha, Magha in Sanskrit also means a sacred place) was known as Aztecs (Astikas), and that of Peru, the Incas (Angakas, or those belonging to Anga). The famous Shiva temple of Mexico was constructed by Ahuitzol (Avichala) between 1483 and 1490 A.D. by employing thousands of sculptors. For the opening ceremony of the temple, six million pilgrims and the princes of Tezuco (Taxaka) and Tlacopan (Trisopana) had arrived. Cuatemac (Gautamaha), successor of Avichala, was a great scholar. He had mastery in astronomy, law, administration, and warfare. He was acquainted with 1500 medicinal herbs and was a great patron of arts and learning. Montezuma (Mantrisuma) who succeeded him was the last Vedic ruler of Mexico. He was a most capable administrator and judge, and he had thirty assistant judges.

"The sun temple of Cuzco had the images of the discs of sun in gold and moon made of silver. They were surrounded with life-size golden images of 12 emperors and queens studded with jewels. The walls of the temple were covered with golden plates and surrounded by trees and shrubs of precious metals. The very first thing Pizarro started looting was the contents of the temples. This was similar to the destructive activities of Cortez and his followers in Mexico a decade before the murder of emperor Atahuallpa (Atyalpa).

"The emperors of Peru celebrated Ramotsava every year, and felt proud that they were the descendants of Sri Rama of the Solar Race [or dynasty]. They called their empire as the land of the sun, their Lord (Paru, or Prabhu, which became Peru). It extended from Chile to Equador and the Pacific Ocean to Cuzco (named after Kusha, the son of Sri Rama), the capital of Peru. The people practiced *varnashrama dharma* (the Vedic system of social arrangement) which helped them live peacefully with prosperity, no want of employment or essential articles, food, clothing or class conflicts.

"According to Bernard Diaz, the official historian of Cortez, the Aztec emperor of Mexico, Montezuma, had informed Cortez (the Spanish leader who betrayed him) that his ancestors had been conducted to Mexico by a ruler whose vassals they were. Once they had been established in a colony, the ruler returned to the land of the sun. Furthermore, in the *Myths of Pre-Columbian America*, the author, Sealer, quotes a Mexican hymn which states that their forefathers came in ships to the west coast of North America, and after surveying Pantla, Sierranevada, Popcate, and Guatemala, reached Tamoanchan before settling in Mexico."

Unfortunately, for nearly 150 years after the Spanish conquest of the Maya in 1542, the first Bishops of Mexico made a crusade to burn all the books of the American natives in their enthusiasm to bring all of them into the Christian fold. Around 1547, Juan de Zumarraga, the first archbishop of Mexico, in his campaign of destroying all traces of indigenous Indian culture, boasted of destroying 500 temples, 20,000 deities or images, and burning countless books while in office. He burned all of the records of the Texcoco Library in Tlateloco market square because he considered them to be works of the devil. Other bishops and priests followed suit, thus destroying in days what had been developed over centuries.

It was Fray Diego de Landa, the second bishop of Yucatan, who was fanatically convinced that his religious duty was to destroy as much of the Maya literature as possible, and, thus, irreparable damage to the study of the Maya culture. He wrote *A Narrative of the Things of Yucatan* in 1566. Therein he states, "We found a large number of their books of these letters, and because they did not have anything in which there was not superstition and falsehoods of the devil, we burned them all, which they felt very sorry for and which caused them grief." It was Landa that gave the orders for all the Mayas to bring all manuscripts to the public square in Mani to be burned. All of these books contained what would now be priceless information on astronomy, medicine, religion, and philosophy.

In spite of their mis-adventure, there are still innumerable stone-carvings in the hundreds of ruined temples and palaces of the pre-Spanish Indians. There are also three codices in Mayan script preserved in Madrid, Dresden, and Paris, as well as two Spanish transliterations of the Mayan books containing brief traditions of the Mexican Indians. One was said to have been written in the Quiche language by an Indian around 1550 and found by a Dominican monk, Father Francisco Zimenez, within the confines of a convent at Chichecastenango in the mountains of Guatemala, about 200 miles up the River Usamacinta from Palanque. Through translations this developed into what we now have as the *Popol Vuh*. Another Mayan book was compiled by Spaniards around the 16th century, entitled *Chilambalam*. What makes this more interesting is that "popol vuh" in Telugu means "a child's guesswork," and "chilambalam" is the mispronunciation of the Sanskrit word *chidambaram*, which means spiritual secret. These books describe in the symbolic language the origin of the world, creation of the living beings, as well as how the Astikas (Aztecs) became masters of Mexico from the thirteenth century onwards, up to the deceitful betrayal of its emperor Montezuma by Cortez. The *Chilambalam* deals with their religious beliefs.

It is known that both the Aztecs and Incas of Peru had 13 rulers each up to the

Spanish invasion of both Mexico and Peru by the Spanish pirates. In this regard, Dr. Gopalacharya goes on to explain: "Another interesting point is that the first Inca ruler of Peru was Ayarmancotopa (Arya Manasa Tapa). The stone inscription of his court depicting his counsel with the native chiefs of Guatemala with its title in both Kannada-Telugu and Mayan scripts has been discovered in Guatemala (Guatamalaya) in a place called 'Piedros Negros,' the Sanskrit form of which is *Priyadarsi Nagara*. In the Kannada inscription, 'Arya Manco Topa' is shown as 'Angaka Raja Sri Arya Manasa Tapa.' This makes it clear that the first ruler of Mexico was a vassal of Angakaraja Sri Arya Manasa Tapa, the first ruler of Peru (Land of Paru, the sun-god). The words Peru, Pampas, Cuzco, Inca, Andes, etc., of South America have a close relationship since they relate to the Solar Race of the Inca rulers. Peru is the corrupted form of Paru, or Prabhu Lord Sun. Pampas means the land of the sun in Sanskrit. The etymological meaning of this is the water drinker. In the Karnataka state, Hampi, the ancient capital of Vijayanagara, was so called because it is located in a hot place just as Pampas in Peru. Cuzco means Lord Kusha, son of Lord Rama. Inca is the adjective form of Angadesha. This has the same meaning as Angaka, one belonging to Anga and Karnataka.

"Toltecs are the Tantrikas or technicians. Takshakas, Nahushadala and Astikas of the Naga clans, subdued during the *Mahabharata* times, are the predecessors of the pre-Spanish American Indians, Nahuati, Tezuco and Zetecs, who migrated to America passing through the islands of the Indian and Pacific oceans.

"The words Aztec, Tezuco, and Nahuatl are the corrupted forms of Astika, Takshaka, Nahushadala, the Naga or snake tribes, meaning that they were worshipers of the Nagas or snakes, the spirit of navigation, since they were mostly navigators. The Mayans, Toltecs, and Nahuatl were related to the Mayas, Tantriks and Nahushadal of India who were expelled from India due to their practice of human sacrifices, according to the Indian tradition. [This would explain why some tribes in South and Central America practiced human sacrifice. They were forced out of India because their activities were contrary to Vedic principles.] All the pre-European American people, whether in North or South America, were known to the original European immigrants as Indians only [all lumped into one category without further distinctions]. Otherwise, they would not have been named thus.

"Is any more evidence needed to establish that pre-Spanish Central and South America were Indian colonies?"

The above is a most interesting description and also sheds light on how the area of Cambodia had been a part of the Vedic empire. More importantly, it shows how the Vedic culture came by ships from India, migrated through the islands of the South Pacific, and then sailed over the Pacific Ocean to the Americas. Then later on a second wave of Vedic people came from Cambodia to Mexico. This was a route that was known for many centuries by early Vedic Indian sailors. How else could there be ancient inscriptions in the Kannada and Telugu languages of India found in Peru? Or Vedic demigods found on the temples of the region? How else could the Aztec gods have names derived from the Telugu or Tamil languages from India? This shows how the Americas had long been a part of, and influenced by, the Vedic civilization, and that the Aztecs and Incas were but descendants from India. The Aztec and Inca gods, philosophy, architecture, and art are all remnants of that found in the ancient Vedic culture of India.

Another interesting piece of information that substantiates what we have been presenting, and shows how new evidence is continually being discovered, is found in the December, 1980 National Geographic Magazine. According to the article, while the Public Works department was digging for the Mexico City Metro System in 1967, an Aztec temple, The Great Temple of the Chacmool (or Sanskrit Sakraamula, described as Indra or Lord Vishnu), was discovered with figures of Talloc (Triloc) and Huitzilpochtli (Vitthalbhaktalu), the gods of rain and war at the top of the temple.

On page 770 of the magazine, it describes, "The myth of the battle between Huitzilpochtli and his sister Coyolxauhqui probably springs from an actual event. Nahuati literature recounts how Huitzilpochtli incited his people to have their Aztlan homeland under his leadership. A quarrel between two groups occurred at Caotpec, or Serpent Hill. One group was headed by Huitzilpochtli, the other by his many brothers, collectively called Huitznahua, pronounced Weetsnahwah, and his sister Coyolxauhqui. In the ensuing power struggle, Huitzilpochtli prevailed. It is significant that one of the barrios of the Aztec capital, Tenochtitlan, later bore the name of Huitsznahua. The myth took various forms. The grandson of Moctezuma, in one version, gave a description that the god, Chacmool, unearthed in the oldest structure, arrayed himself with painted face [in yellow color], and made circles around the eyes." [This is in reference to Sudradharana, decorating the face with sandalwood paste, a definite Vedic custom.]

Now, with information from Dr. Venu Gopalacharya's book, *World-Wide Hindu Culture* (p. 129), we can put a Vedic slant on this story. Huitzilpochtli (Witzil Poktli) is the Vedic Vitthal Bhaktalu. Vitthala is the presiding Deity in the famous Pandarpur temple and is worshiped by many thousands of Vaishnavas of Karnataka. Devotees decorate the Deity's face in the temple with sandal paste, and their own faces as well on occasion. Thus, Vitthala Bhaktalu means a devotee (Bhakta) of Lord Vitthala. So Huitzilpochtli was such a devotee.

The name of his sister, Coyolxauhqui, is the Tamil word Koyilvasi, which means a temple dweller, or a devotee. Huitznahua, pronounced (as the article says) weetsnahwah, is the perverted pronunciation of the word Vaishnava, a worshiper of Vishnu or Lord Krishna. Lord Vitthal is also Lord Krishna. Tenochtitlan, the barrio of the Aztec capital, is from the Sanskrit word Trinathatrana, which means the place of the Lord of the three worlds, or three planetary systems. Montezuma is from the Sanskrit word *matisuma* [or *mantrisuma*], which means scholar or learned flower. Chacmool means Sakramula, which is the originator of Sakra, the raingod's ancestor. Aztlan refers to Atalam, which is an island in the Pacific Ocean. So what all this means is that somehow there was a fight over power and land between a number of people who had come from India. Otherwise, how could there be so many references to Tamil and Sanskrit words and Vedic customs? This proves that the Aztecs originally belonged to South India. As more artifacts, temples, and places are found in South and Central America, more evidence will surface that will provide more proof of the connection between the people of this region and the Vedic Aryan culture of India.

MORE VEDIC LINKS IN THE INCA LANGUAGE

To help show the connections in language between the ancient American people and the Vedic Aryan culture of India, I have included a few samples given by Dr. Venu Gopalacharya in his book, *World-Wide Kannada, Tamil & Sanskrit Vocabulary*. In it there are many hundreds of words in various languages from around the world that are compared to Sanskrit, Kannada, and Tamil.

INCA	SANSKRIT/KANNADA	MEANING
Acqui	Kakki	Bird
Amaru	Amara	Name of a lake
Alwa	Aluva	To cry
Ala	Aala	Dig up
Ancu	Anju	Go off
Ankalu	Angattalu	Recline face downwards
Anuka	Aluku	Weaning
Asi	Haasya	Laugh
Atipa	Adippa	Beat
Apacita	Upaasita	Mountain shrine
Ayllu	Illu	Family
Chac	Sakra	Indra, demigod of rain
Chile	Chali	Cold land
Cicu	Sisu	Pregnant
Ciilu	Siilu	Thin haired
Copacaban	Taapasavana	Hermitage
Curya	Hiriya	Father
Cayaci	Kaayisu	To cook
Chakra	Chakra	Field or circular area
Cipi	Kapi	Monkey
Huaskar	Vasakara	Controller
Kalu	Kaalu	Corn
Kami	Kammi	Insult
Katakatata	Gadagada	Shivering

Kochipille	Kotipilla	Hanuman
Kuci	Sukhii	Happy
Kuta	Kuttu	Grind
Manaciku	Maanasika	Worry
Marca	Maarga	Way
Mayauel	Maayaaul	Magic
Mayan	Mayan	Engineer
Mlctalanteotl	Mrtrulinidevatlu	God of death
Pachacamac	Paasatamah	Controller
Pampas	Pampa	Land of sun
Paten	Pattana	City
Patara	Padara	Fold
Pataci	Pacchadi	A kind of soup
Pituka	Hiduko	Join hands
Pumapancu	Pampapanca	Five places
Qawa	Kaayuva	Watch
Quca	Kuupa	Well
Sumaq	Sumuka	Beautiful
Tambu	Tangu	Resting place
Teocalli	Devasaalai	Temple
Tlacopan	Trisoopaana	Three steps
Urubamba	Aarupampa	Sunriver
Viracocha	Viirasukha	Viirabhadra
Waasi	Waasa	House

I could supply more of the listed words, but I think this is enough to show how much of the language of the Incas is derived from the languages of India. This is certainly a very positive form of evidence for showing the connection between these two areas of the planet and the influence of the Vedic culture on the people of the Americas.

OTHER CULTURES THAT CAME TO AMERICA

There is also evidence that other cultures came to America and explored and settled here long before Columbus was ever born. As established in a previous chapter, Sumeria was a part or an outgrowth of the Vedic and Indus Valley cultures. So they knew of the major trade routes that the Indian Aryans used for reaching various continents and islands. Ur was a prominent Sumerian city around 2100 B.C. Evidence shows that Sumerians also had reached the Americas for trade. For example, in Columbia, petroglyphs have been found with Sumerian characters. Drawings at Chavin de Huantar and Tiwanaku show the Sumerian type of headgear and clothes. Inca mummies have also been found wearing ponchos with Sumerian designs. There are South American rivers with names that reflect the Eastern roots, such as Urubamba, Juruaf, Japura, Rurguay, or Parana, and Paraguay. There is also a tribe of Urus on the shores of Lake Titicaca. They explain that they were living on the lake before the Quechua or the Aymaraf, and had arrived in big ships from across the seas.

Evidence also shows that the early Phoenicians had sailed to America in the area of Brazil. Again, as discussed in a previous chapter, L. A. Waddell concluded that the Phoenicians were Aryans in race and speech, and, thus, also a part of the Vedic empire. In this case, they would have had access to the old trade routes and geography of the globe. Phoenicians called the east coast of South America Brazil, Land of Iron. And Brazil does have one of the largest reserves of iron in the world.

There are also records that indicate that the Scandinavian Vikings had voyaged to America. We have already provided evidence that the Vikings were in fact Vedic Aryan warriors who settled in Scandinavia as far back as before the *Mahabharata* war. In their tendency to explore the world, it is not unlikely that they continued on their way across the northern Atlantic to America. These routes across the Atlantic were known thousands of years ago. However, these routes became forgotten after many hundreds of years of not being used until they were only legends. An example of this can be explained as follows: After the Vikings again settled in Iceland from Norway in 880 A.D., the island soon became crowded with as many as 20,000 fierce Vikings. Eric the Red sailed west and discovered Greenland in 982. When he returned to Iceland, his stories aroused the curiosity of others, some of whom set sail and colonized the western and eastern coasts of Greenland. Then the Eskimos told them of legends of the big landmass to the southwest, and these new stories of mysterious lands aroused interest.

Leif Ericson, son of Eric the Red, set sail to search for the new land. He stopped at Helluland, the land of Flat Stones (Baffin Island); Markland, the Land of Woods (Labrador); and then to Vinland, or Newfoundland and on to the eastern coast of the United States. There they encountered American Indians, who they called Scraelings, and continued their explorations inland. In this way, these Vikings simply repeated the journeys of their ancestors, taking routes that had long been forgotten. All Viking settlements in Greenland slowly diminished until by 1410 they had disappeared. By then, those that had ventured west had already mixed with the American natives, the outcome of which was the White Indians, some of whom were noted for their blue eyes, descendants of the legendary Vikings. You can still find evidence of their explorations in Canada, such as Manitoba, Ontario, and Quebec, and in the United States in Minnesota (the Kensington Rune Stone), Ohio, the Mississippi Valley, as well as the coasts of the Carolinas and Virginia. Viking artifacts have also been discovered throughout the Canadian Arctic, Labrador, Newfoundland, Nova Scotia, and New England. Many words in the Algonquin language are also similar to the Old Norse language.

Another culture that seems to have made explorations to America back nearly 4000 years ago was the ancient Chinese. Chinese legends tell how ships from the area would sail northeast along the Chinese coast, always keeping it in view, and going over to Alaska, British Columbia, and on to Mexico and South America. The Japanese and Chinese knew of the current that could take them away from the mainland and on over to Mexico. This has happened to Japanese fishermen who were taken to Mexico by these same currents as recently as the nineteenth century.

One piece of positive evidence that indicates the ancient Chinese came to America is the *Shan Hai Ching* (Book of the Mountains and the Seas), which is said to be the most ancient geographical work the Chinese possess. Originally it was supposed to have been 32 books, but was reduced to 18 by the fifth century A.D. These books of maps were mentioned during the Shang dynasty.

How the *Shan Hai Ching* maps came to be is an interesting story. The Chinese explain that their first dynasties were those of the Five Monarchs, in which there were nine rulers who reigned consecutively from 2,852 to 2,206 B.C. Chinese legends tell of one of these rulers, Yao (2,357 B.C.), who brought harmony and prosperity to the land. Then there was a great flood so devastating that the people lost their direction. They could not tell which way was which. Yao assigned two men, an astronomer named Yu and prince Y, to help with the drainage of waters.

So Yu was the cultural hero credited with ridding China of its devastating flood. The legend is further elaborated in the Confucian works *The Classic History* and *Book of Mencius*. Therein it says that Yu's father had tried to control the flood by building dams but failed, and was executed by Emperor Yao, who then appointed Yu. Yu used natural methods and was made heir to the throne by Yao's successor, Shun. Yu is said to have been a great Chinese leader, a minister who founded the Hsia dynasty in 2205 B.C. and reigned until 2197 B.C. Thus, Yu is accepted as the legendary founder of the Hsia (or Chinese Xia) dynasty.

Modern scholars, however, do not accept the Hsia dynasty. There is no archeological or historical evidence to confirm the existence of it. It is based only on legends, which means the activities of Yu and the Yao legends could be more ancient than the above dates indicate. Scholars feel that the first accurately documented era of Chinese history began with the Shang dynasty (1766-1122 B.C.). However, we have already discussed the Vedic influence on China in a previous chapter. So in light of this Vedic influence, it may not be out of the ordinary to consider that the legend of Yu is connected with, or a carryover from, the Vedic legend of Manu. In Sanskrit, Yu means the one who unites. And Yu, being associated with the great flood, directs us to identify the name with Manu. The name Yu is probably the shortened Chinese version of the name Manu. Manu was one of the fathers of mankind after the last great flood, and the Vedic personality who united the world at that time. He also explained the science of Vedic knowledge to his disciple Iksvaku, who went on to be a great ruler. And the name of the Hsia dynasty, Chinese Xia, is related to the shortened version of the name Iksvaku. Leaving off the ending "ku" you have "Iksva," which is very similar to Xia. Iksvaku was also Manu's son who became a great king, which would explain the idea that Manu, or Yu, started the dynasty of Iksvaku, or Xia. Furthermore, the Vedic legend explains that after the global deluge when the waters receded, Manu ruled the world through his nine sons and successor monarchs. To do this, he sent many men throughout the world.

Similar to the legend of Manu, before Yu became emperor he was in charge of sending out men to explore the world. Chinese annals record that huge expeditions, complete with large ships, food, and horses, sailed out across the Indian Ocean, as well as across the Great Eastern Ocean, the Pacific.

These men visited all of the provinces, making maps and keeping records of everything they saw. They went on to visit many countries beyond the seas. From these adventures and records they composed what became the *Shan Hai Ching* maps. These are said to have been written in the periods of Yao and Shun, 2357-2205 B.C., over 4000 years ago. The maps give a detailed description of Fu Sang, the area that became the United States and Mexico. It correctly says that Fu Sang is 3300 miles from coast to coast, on the other side of which is another vast and immense ocean. The maps of America also recorded various rivers, mountains, and other characteristics of the land which, some feel, can still be identified today.

After a careful study of a set of such maps that he purchased, Hendon Mason Harris, a person greatly familiar with Chinese culture, wrote in an article, "Treasure Maps of Fu Sang" (recently published in a book called *Dragon Treasures*), "I will even venture to say that because the Chinese and Koreans refused to surrender the format of their old maps, we can now prove that the Chinese discovered America, were the ancestral fathers of several Indian tribes, and that the East Indians, the Chinese, the Japanese, and Koreans were the true builders of the Mexican, Central American, and Peruvian civilizations a thousand years before Columbus dreamed of the new world."

It is interesting that Mr. Harris saw the influence of the East on the Americas, but he got only part of it right. One fact that will counter his opinion is that the Maya and Olmecs had been there since 3100 B.C., as verified by the fact that they had already started their calendars at that time. This means that they must have been there for many years earlier to reach this level of development, or, as we mentioned previously, came as a pre-existing society from somewhere else. This was long before the Chinese ever entered the Americas. Furthermore, the people of Mexico and South America do not have any physical Chinese or Japanese traits. They resemble the East Indians far more than the Orientals. Plus, archeological evidence showing the presence of the Chinese and Japanese in the region is not very prominent.

Furthermore, though the maps seem to provide some hard evidence, not everyone believes in the authenticity of the maps of Mr. Harris. Professor Nakamura believes that the names on the world maps are mostly fictitious or merely legendary, especially in regard to the European area, which have been rather difficult to interpret. How much this may sway our opinion about the maps of America is relative. But from the information they supply, the maps do seem to indicate that the Chinese had visited the area, if not 4000 years ago, then at least previous to the Ling Dynasty of 502 A.D. or perhaps from the pre-Christian era.

Some evidence that does show the presence of the Chinese in the Americas is the similarities of the pottery of the Tajin culture of Veracruz and the late Chou decorative styles of China (700-200 B.C.). Another point is the recorded log notations during the Spanish explorations of 1544 in which it is stated that the Spanish found several large junks at anchor in the Gulf of California.

Evidence for the ancient Japanese having been in the Americas is the Japanese pottery found by archeologists from the Smithsonian at Ecuador dating to 2500 B.C. Thus, there may have been some trade going on between the two regions. However, there surely should be much more significant evidence than this if we are to be convinced that the Orientals played a prominent role in life in the ancient Americas. As it stands, there is little to bring us to conclude that the Chinese or Japanese had much influence on the people of the ancient Americas.

In any case, due to political fighting within China, by the year 1500 A.D. most sea trade had been stopped. The ruling party looked down on maritime trade with people they considered barbarians. The Chinese felt they were the most civilized of all cultures and trading with others was a disagreeable business. Thus, the Chinese junks spotted off the coast of California in 1544 may have been unauthorized traders or escapees from the trouble back home.

By the time Christopher Columbus sailed to America, knowledge of most of the old sailing routes had been forgotten. The Catholic dogma was that the earth was flat, and if you sailed too far out, you would fall off the edge, or even be devoured by huge sea monsters. This kept some sailors from going too far. Nonetheless, some of the Portugese sailors had reached India around the Cape of Good Hope. In 1500, Cabral was taken off course in West African waters and once again Brazil was discovered. Also, during the Renaissance, cartographers left out the Americas altogether and drew their maps to show Japan and China to be just on the other side of the Atlantic, which was much bigger than they thought it was. And Columbus came up with the idea of reaching Asia simply by crossing the Atlantic.

Failing to get any sponsors anywhere else, Columbus went to Spain. The Spanish royalty had become jealous over Portugal's success in African exploration. So, the Spanish listened to the ideas of Christopher Columbus. Thus, he was given facility to take his first voyage across the Atlantic in three ships: the Nina, Pinta, and the Santa Maria. Sailing from Cadiz, he followed the coast of Morocco south, picked up the Canary Current near the Canary Islands, and managed his way across the Atlantic. Finally, on October 12, 1942, they saw a low, flat island in the Bahamas which he called San Salvador. Thus, Columbus "re-discovered" the Americas and the new Indians.

CHAPTER FOURTEEN

Uncovering the Truth About India's History

As we have now investigated the rest of the world for remnants of the global Vedic culture, we must also focus our attention on India where it still thrives. However, now we will uncover some of India's real history. This will help us understand how much of its glory, beauty, art, music, architecture, and sciences have been falsely attributed to outsiders and foreigners. India has not been given credit where credit is due. India's skills in science, administration, art, architecture, and, of course, spiritual understanding, was once the highest in the world. However, because the emphasis on Vedic knowledge and culture has decreased, and in some cases been ignored, it has led to a weakened condition of the nation. This has allowed the commercial and military invasions into India, which has resulted in such plunder, impoverishment, and enslavement that India is a shadow of what it once was, and in some areas has become full of destitution, disease, and death. Furthermore, much of its real history has been pushed aside, distorted, perverted, and based on misinformation.

An example of this sort of invasion that has caused such a difference in Indian culture, history, and its status in the world is that of the British. The English attempted to divide and conquer India, to ruin the Vedic Aryan civilization, and to demean Indian culture, even to the point of trying to make its own people hate everything that is Indian. This is explained in *World-Wide Hindu Culture* (pp.165-6) by Dr. S. Venu Gopalacharya. He describes that on July 3, 1985, Lord Macaulay suggested that the only statesmanship of the Britishers to establish permanent imperialist sovereignty over their richest colony, India, was to make the Indians "Englishmen by Taste." This was to be accomplished through "English Education," similar to bringing under control hundreds of elephants by taming a couple of wild elephants. By 1854 when the whole of India came under British rule, Charles Woodraffe, the Director of the Education Department of the Government of India, in his minutes dated July 19, 1854, stated that it was the best opportunity to give effect to Lord Macaulay's suggestion. For getting grains for one year, sowing of corn is necessary; for getting fruits, trees are to be planted. Likewise, to get perennial or permanent service, human beings are to be sown. For erasing illiteracy, primary schools are to be opened. To get officials with less expenditure, secondary education is essential because importing Englishmen for that purpose is impossible. Colleges with English education is unavoidable to make the Indian educated class detest everything Indian, to make them look at it as nothing more than mean and illogical superstitions.

Macaulay's prophecy worked well, both to rule and impoverish the English educated class of Indians as well as their blind followers, the laymen of British India. The factory-made goods of the Britishers found a very good market, and one by one all the handicrafts and home industries lost their charm among the Indians. As the English factories were helped to get raw materials from India at the lowest rates and supply factory-made articles to the Indian consumers, all the home industries of the Indians became extinct within a couple of decades, not being able to compete with them. As English became the official language replacing Sanskrit, some of the educated class started to learn English to earn their living. All those who could not continue their hereditary occupations and learn English became jobless and miserably poor. Taking advantage of the changed situation, the missionaries tried to convert some of the weaker sections to Christianity by several inducements. However, seeing through this plan, some religious institutions of the Vedic followers, such as the Arya Samaj, Brahmasamaj, Ramakrishna Movement, Shivananda Movement, and others, fought against them.

With the freedom movements lead by Ranade, B. G. Tilak, V. D. Patel, Mahatma Gandhi and others, India finally got political freedom from the British. However, as time went on, the divide and rule policy of the British prospered by the post independent Indian secular rulers, even against Gandhi's and the people's wishes and appeals. The spiral of deterioration of Indian and Vedic culture has continued to this day. Thus, much of the misinformation that has been adopted as Indian history has yet to be corrected. We will look closer at this point shortly.

These are the kinds of invasions that have really affected India, but in the worst way. Another historical invasion that some talk about is the Aryan invasion, from which people think the glory of India began. However, as is becoming more and more apparent, and as we have shown in previous chapters, there has been no direct evidence for any Aryan invasion.

One primary basis for this theory about the Aryan invasion is that languages with Sanskrit affinities exist over a vast region, from Bali to the Baltic. Therefore, it is assumed that there must have been a pre-Sanskrit language that came close to Sanskrit, yet was something different. Whatever this Indo-European language was, it is argued that Lithuanian was the closest to it. Hence, those who spoke the original Indo-European language must have migrated into the region of India, and thence begot the Aryan culture and the Sanskrit language.

However, it would be a more valid conclusion to understand the Vedic culture as it was, and as it continues to profess: That it was a culture that shared its knowledge and spiritual understanding with the world rather than simply conquer areas and control them by force. It was this attitude that impelled them to push their explorations to the remotest lands to spread their knowledge and culture. Therefore, if European languages show a Sanskritic base, and if Sanskrit flourishes in its pristine glory only in India, the conclusion is obvious: It was enterprising Indians who migrated to all other continents. Later on, when links with India snapped over the course of centuries, the European languages retained only traces of Sanskrit while real Sanskrit still flourishes at its source: India.

As Mr. Oak explains in *Some Blunders of Indian Historical Research* (page 220), "It should be clearly understood that it was the Indians who migrated from their Indo-Gangetic, Punjab, Kashmir and Gandhar home to all parts of the world. The so-called Indo-European languages are all derived from the ancient-most language of India, namely Sanskrit. It is futile to regard Sanskrit as a collateral of languages like Persian and Latin and then try to find their common ancestor. These attempts all derive from the mistaken notion that there were a people called Aryans who lived somewhere in Europe and from there migrated to India. Since there were no such people, there was no fancied language of theirs. What then remains as the sole source of the world's ancient-most culture is not Indo-European, but only the *Indo* civilization and *Indo* language, which is Sanskrit."

In light of this, the belief of an "Aryan Race" coming from outside India is, indeed, a blunder of historical research. All references to the Aryans as a race who migrated to India should be deleted from history. There is no evidence that upholds this theory. In fact, the more research we do, the more evidence we find that counters this theory as we shall see as we proceed with this chapter.

One piece of evidence we can consider is that the *rishis* (sages) in the *Rig-veda* describe the Sarasvati as a mighty river that flowed directly into the sea. On the banks of this river, *rishis* performed penance and worship. The *Srimad-Bhagavatam* also describes how Srila Vyasadeva had his cottage on the banks of the Sarasvati and began compiling the *Bhagavatam* into a written format at that place. There are also geological researches that have testified to the finding that there has been a considerable length of time, possibly up to 500,000 years, since the Sarasvati River disappeared. Others feel it finally dried up no later than 1800 B.C. In either case, this would lead to the conclusion that the *Rig-veda*, far from being composed around 1200 B.C. or later as some think, is of immemorial antiquity as is rightly believed by present-day Vedic followers. It was part of a verbal tradition up until Srila Vyasadeva composed it into a written work about 5,000 years ago. The descriptions of the Sarasvati in the ancient Vedic texts help place the age and location of the Vedic culture at no later than 5,000 years ago.

The idea that the *Rig-veda* is only 3,000 years old or less has led to another blunder in estimating that Mohenjo-Dara, which existed 5,000 years ago, is pre-Vedic. We have already presented much evidence in the similarities between the Vedic science of city organization and what is found at Mohenjo-Dara in another chapter. However, the finding of a Shiva plaque, coins or seals with Vedic images, and names of the Vedic gods at Mohenjo-Dara have nullified the theory that it was a Dravidian, pre-Vedic civilization. The city was indeed connected with and part of the Vedic culture.

THE PLOT TO COVER VEDIC ARCHEOLOGY IN INDIA

We have to realize that there was a comprehensive strategy to overlook, cover, and falsify the real history of India. Not only did the invading Muslims try to do this over the centuries, but the British, while in India, also played a heavy hand in this. As pointed out by P. N. Oak in *Some Missing Chapters of World History* on page 16:

"Major General Alexander Cunningham, a retired army engineer was appointed in 1861 as the first archeological surveyor under the then British administration in India, not because he had any special knowhow or knowledge but because as early as September 15, 1842 when he was a mere Lt. A.D.C. to the Governor General Lord Auckland, Cunningham had suggested in a letter to Col. Sykes (a director of the British East India Company) a scheme for falsifying Indian archeology as an 'undertaking of vast importance to the Indian Government politically and to the British public religiously (so that) the establishment of the Christian religion in India must ultimately succeed.' In pursuance of that political objective Cunningham attributed a very large number of Hindu townships and buildings to Muslim authorship."

Max Mueller also expressed the same sentiment in a letter to the Duke of Argyll, who was then the Secretary of State for India: "India has been conquered once, but India must be conquered again and that second conquest should be a conquest by education." Thus, it seems that most high officials in the British administration were intent on using their own field of operation to subvert Hinduism and whatever was left of Vedic culture. Thus, the process of character assassination by the British, in cahoots with the Muslims, was on.

Here in we can see the motivation for perverting the real history of India. This is why the reading public has consistently been cheated for many years of the real glory and advanced nature of India and Vedic culture. Because of this, archeologists, historians, and architects, what to speak of scholars and tourists, have all along presumed the medieval monuments of India are all of Muslim origin. Or that without the Muslim invasions and their so-called artistic and architectural "contributions" India would never have had such wonderful monuments today. This idea that has gone on for the last six to eight centuries has created a monster which many antiquarians find difficult to shake off. We now must unlearn these false notions and histories and begin to associate such things as the dome, lime concrete, and the ornate carvings and art work as indigenous features of Indian architecture.

Prior to the founding of the British rule in India there was no archeological department. Incorrect and false archeological records started during the long alien

Muslim rule that preceded the British in India because of the Muslim practice of grabbing and misappropriating Hindu temples and palaces to become mosques and tombs. Thus, when the British came to power in India, all historic buildings were already under occupation and possession of Muslims. When the British first set up an archeological department, not only did they have their own reasons to falsify Indian history, but they also simply consulted the Muslims who occupied the buildings and recorded their bluff. Of course, if the Muslims told the truth about the Hindu origin of the buildings they occupied, they may have very well lost the right to the possession of such buildings. Such deceptions have gone on to become the basis of the archeological department of India.

Because of this, from the very first generation of European-trained Hindus up to the present day, a sizable section of Hindus have been wasting their time and energy discussing and even deploring all their own "faults" as pointed out by their detractors. Thus, they have fallen into playing the very game that their European Christian and Muslim critics have started.

We need to have a correct view of world, and especially Indian, history. In all honesty, it would be correct to say that at this point, Muslims and Christians should be deemed to be disqualified from writing on Hindu history not only because they have a record of hostility to Vedic culture, but also because their outlook on the world and their antiquity of history generally goes back no further than to a Mohammed or Jesus. They are unable to visualize any part of the world having a balanced or advanced society before Islam or Christianity came along to "save" everyone. To them anything that is pre-Christian has to have been heathen, barbaric, godless, or pagan, and traced back to Greece or Rome. Thus, their religious loyalties stunt their intellectual horizons. This is quite evident as viewed in the case when Mr. P. N. Oak wrote to Harvard University to a professor of the civilization of France asking for particular information about pre-Christian France. The single-line reply he received simply stated that they know nothing of pre-Christian France. This shows the appalling state of research that such noted universities as Harvard are content with. Thus, they have no interest in pre-Christian history.

Another example of the lack of real concern for the correct view of Indian history is explained in *World Vedic Heritage*, page 1127: "In addition to Cunningham's devilish plan delineated in the letter to Col. Sykes, we, luckily, have an unguarded testimony of a fellow Britisher, James Furgusson (see pp. 32-33 and 76-78, Indian Archeology, by J. Furgusson, 1884) that 'During the 14-years he has been employed in the Survey, he (Cunningham) has contributed almost literally nothing to our knowledge of archeology or architectural geography.' Naturally, because Cunningham looked upon archeology merely as a stick to beat the Hindus with.

"Consequently, once when Cunningham's assistant, J. D. Beglar expressed the view that the so-called Kutub Minar (in Delhi) was a Hindu tower, Cunningham haughtily overruled him to assert that it was a Muslim tower. This is on record." And thus, the Kutub Minar, which thousands of Indian and foreign tourists visit each year, is pronounced and recorded as a tower that was originally built by Muslims. Furthermore, Muslim inscriptions on such Indian buildings, mosques or tombs, should not necessarily be mistaken to signify the ORIGINAL builder, but only the captor, occupier, or usurper. Even Muslim chronicles may mention the building of such things as canals, giving themselves the credit, when actually the canals were already there.

It has been through this process that Hindus have been robbed not only of architectural credit, but also of anything else that is good and artistic, including music, poetry, literature, styles of painting, color decoration, gardens, fountains, pottery, porcelain, carvings, etc., even when found in India. Thus, the once global Vedic culture and India have been humiliated and made to appear small and despicable, while Hindus in general have been made to appear puny and insignificant by these same outside forces. Thus, it is time for people to realize the immense contribution that the Vedic culture and the ancient Hindus have given to the world.

THE TAJ MAHAL WAS A HINDU TEMPLE

One such example of how Indian history has been distorted is the Taj Mahal. There is evidence that shows the Taj Mahal is actually much older than Shahjahan, the person who has been given credit for building it, and is, in fact, a Vedic contribution to the world. As explained in *World Vedic Heritage* (p. 836):

"In a paper that professor Mills read in Chicago on November 4, 1983 at the 17th Annual Meeting of Middle East Studies Association of North America, based on his preliminary research endeavors involving an archaeometric analysis of the so-called Muslim buildings in ancient Spain, Mr. Mills observed, 'Two specific potentially fertile monuments for the application of archaeometry are the Taj Mahal and the (so-called) Mosque of Cordoba. Neither face Mecca. The (so-called) mosque that is part of the Taj complex faces due west whereas Mecca from Agra is 14 degrees 55 minutes south of west. It is oriented to the cardinal directions as would be typical of a Hindu temple in India.'

"Prof. Mills then describes how a wood sample he took from the rear, river-level doorway of the Taj and had it tested for carbon-14 dating by Dr. Evan Williams, Director of the Brooklyn College Radiocarbon Laboratory, provided that even the door was pre-Shahjahan. Similar samples taken from Fatehpur Sikri also proved that that township, usually attributed to the 3rd-generation Mogul emperor Akbar, is also much more ancient."

The Taj Mahal gets its name from its original name, Tej-Mahalaya, which is said to have been a resplendent shrine housing a Shiva-*linga*. So before it was converted into a Muslim mosque, it very well could have been a Hindu palace, part of which was a Shiva temple.

Further obvious evidence, most of which any tourist can witness for themselves, is explained in *Some Blunders of Indian Historical Research* on pages 304-5: "Its octagonal shape and the cupolas and four towers at the plinth corners are all Hindu features. [You can still see many temples in India, such as those at Khajarao, that are built on a platform with small temples or towers at each corner.] Havell, the English architect, has all along stressed that the Taj is entirely a Hindu structure in design and execution. Within its three floors--basement, ground and first floors--the marble structure has a nearly 25-room palace suite. The four towers used to sport multi-colored lights. The Taj precincts are a huge building complex encompassing over three hundred rooms. The locality was known as Jaisinghpur. It was surrounded by defensive structures like moats, hillocks and massive walls. Chronicles give the indication that Babar, the founder of the Moghul dynasty and his grandson Akbar, used to sojourn in the Taj. Babar even died there. But being a new-comer to India he had expressed a wish that he be buried in his native country. But for that fortuitous happening the Taj would have been known to posterity as Babar's (grand) mausoleum instead of Mumtaz's since all Muslim royal personages have been buried in conquered and occupied Hindu buildings.

"The ornate trellis work, entirely in the Hindu style, now encloses two tombs believed to be those of Mumtaz and Shahjahan. The network was stuffed with rare gems. Traditional accounts tell us that this enclosure had silver doors and gold railings to boot. Even Shahjahan's and Mumtaz's palaces never boasted of such fabulous fixtures when the pair was alive and kicking from the imperial throne. How come then that when Mumtaz died (1630 A.D.) all this wealth descended on earth all of a sudden. Far from that, this expensive and resplendent enclosure was made to house the dazzling Peacock Throne. That throne, wrongly credited to Shahjahan, came into his possession when he dispossessed the Taj Mahal's last Rajput owner, Jai Singh, of this fabulous ancient Hindu palace. So far from spending anything on the Taj Mahal, Shahjahan utilized the somber occasion of Mumtaz's death to enrich himself with Jai Singh's wealth."

Other evidence that the Taj Mahal was a Hindu temple is provided on page 1146 of *World Vedic Heritage*, in which it is described that Mr. P. N. Sharma, who lives in the Safdarjang Development Area (C-5/28) in New Delhi, had a peek inside a chamber underneath the marble basement of the Taj Mahal. With the help of a light he was able to see through a hole in the crumbling brick work with which Shahjahan or Cunningham sealed the chamber. This was in 1932 when he saw in the chamber a number of Vedic deities that had obviously been secretly dumped after having been dislodged from the various parts of the Taj Mahal.

This is not unlike the case in which an employee of the Archeological Survey of India, named E. R. Sathe, who wrote to Mr. Oak describing that around 1959 S. R. Rao, who was in charge of the Taj Mahal, noticed a big crack in a wall. To repair the wall, a number of bricks had to be removed. When this happened, out popped several images of Vedic goddesses known as Ashta Vasu. Rao referred the matter to Delhi to know whether he should probe other walls for other deities. The education minister, Abul Kalam Azad, and Prime Minister Jawaharlal Nehru simply told him to shut up the walls as well as his mouth. This shows that though Vedic images and Sanskrit inscriptions have been found from time to time at the Taj Mahal, everyone prefers to maintain silence rather than finding out the real truth of the matter.

Other points to consider include that there is a doorway in the Taj Mahal premises that is kept locked by the Archeological Survey of India. This door leads down a stately staircase to a massive, octagonal, seven-storied water well. The well is enclosed in the tower near the peripheral wall to the left as you stand below the marble platform facing the Taj. Surely for a mausoleum there is no such need for so much water. There are also several dry latrines in the well-house. This is all kept from the eyes of visitors and shows that the building was equipped for being more than a simple mausoleum, and more like a palatial Hindu palace and temple.

A great proof of Shahjahan's taking this building from another rather than building it himself is found in Shahjahan's own official chronicle, *Badshahnama* (Bibliotheca Indica series of the Asiatic Society of Bengal publication, page 403, Volume I). Therein he admits that the Taj Mahal is Raja Mansingh's mansion which, when taken over for Mumtaz's burial, was set amidst a majestic lush garden. This is an obvious proof that the current history of the Taj Mahal as we know it, that it was built by Shahjahan for his wife, is completely false.

In a letter written by prince Aurangzeb in 1652 to his ruling father, emperor Shahjahan, Aurangzeb reports doing an urgent repair to the cracked dome and leaking seven-storeyed complex. This is a blatant contradiction in the modern historical theory, especially considering how the archeological sign at the Taj asserts that it was first built in 1653.

Shahjahan left no records, receipts, building plans, or expense accounts regarding the building of the Taj Mahal. The Taj itself is built in the manner of a palatial palace, not as a tomb. Thus, it had to have been first a palace converted into a tomb.

Had Shahjahan really conceived and built the Taj himself, he never would have had to remind his paid court chronicler not to forget describing its construction in the official chronicle. Such an event would not have been forgotten by anyone. Furthermore, if a stupendous monument like the Taj is built for a consort, there certainly would be a burial date that would not go unrecorded. However, the burial date is not only unrecorded, but the date of the time in which Mumtaz must have been buried in the Taj varies from six months to nine years of her death. Mumtaz being a commoner never deserved a palatial monument. Even historically there is no record of any special out-of-the-ordinary attachment or romance between Shahjahan and Mumtaz during their life. Thus, the story is just a romantic concoction to justify the usurping of the Taj Mahal.

Furthermore, Shahjahan was no patron of the arts. The decorative patterns that cover the Taj are not only entirely of Indian flora but also of sacred Hindu motifs like the lotus. Such "infidel" characteristics, according to Muslim beliefs, would never allow any peace for the departed souls lying buried underneath.

Cunningham also played his part in destroying colossal Vedic evidence of its origin by destroying or displacing deities and Sanskrit inscriptions that once adorned the Taj. For example, a massive black basalt Stone with Sanskrit inscriptions was found at the Taj. It testified to the erection of the Taj as a "peerless, crystal-white Shiva Temple," but was misleadingly and deliberately branded by Cunningham as the Bateswar inscription. It was then taken away from the Taj to the attic of the distant Lucknow Museum, as can be inferred from noting Cunningham's own not-so-cunning assistant, Carlleyle. Carlleyle's report on Agra (pp. 124-5, Volume of 1871-72 A.D.) records, "the great square black basaltic pillar which was the base and capital of another similar pillar once stood in the garden of the Taj Mahal."

It is also apparent from Carlleyle that the original ancient Vedic documents and drawings of the Taj Mahal did exist. They passed into Mogul possession from Jai Singh when Shahjahan suddenly took the Taj Mahal with all its fabulous wealth for himself. Later, with the expulsion of the last Mogul, the Taj Mahal documents passed into the hands of the British Viceroy in India in 1858. Cunningham, having been chosen by the British administration to head the Archeological Society, took charge of the Taj Mahal papers along with those of many other monuments throughout India. He deliberately burned them all so he could have an open field to ascribe all historic towns, cities, towers, bridges, forts, canals and water tanks to Muslim authorship. More evidence of the way Cunningham credited the building of the Taj Mahal is found in a well-documented booklet recently published by an intrepid and courageous Hindu scholar, Mr. V. S. Godbole who resides in Bedford, England.

Another point that disclaims the idea that the Taj Mahal and buildings like it are of Islamic origin is that the arch and dome in architecture was pre-Muslim and Vedic in design. This is described in *Encyclopedia Britannica*, (14th edition, Vol. 15, page 651). It is related that, "When in a victorious advance the Arab followers of Mohammed subdued the old civilizations of Asia and Africa, Persians, Turks, Byzantines, Syrians and Copts, their own civilization was not yet much developed and in many respects dependent on those of neighboring countries. The architecture of the Mohammedan world, therefore, was created by members of those overthrown peoples who were clients of the Arabs and had themselves turned Muslim."

Furthermore, in Volume 12, page 221, it continues to describe, "As both arch and dome were known to the Sumerian builders in the 4th millennium B.C., there is nothing surprising in the fact that both appear in India long before the Mohammedan period and in fact from the Mauryan period onwards."

Another point is that Sumeru and Mount Meru are names that occur frequently in ancient Vedic literature. By understanding that Sumerians were Vedic people, as described in a previous chapter, it becomes obvious that the architecture that is most noted as Islamic in India actually contains elements in design that were known long before Islam ever came to India. They were Vedic in design, and used elements described in the Vedic *Shilpashastras*. Furthermore, the methods of construction were unknown to the invading Muslims. Thus, they were essentially incapable of building such structures anyway. So there is no way that such buildings can be given credit to the Islamic invaders.

The other most prominent building in Agra is the Red Fort, the twin to the Red Fort in Delhi. The name *Agra* itself is a Sanskrit name that indicates this was a flourishing Rajput city before the Muslims invaded. Thus, it had to have a fort. The fort itself is built in typical Rajput style. The architecture of the main halls bears a close resemblance to the main halls and interior apartments in the Amber Fort near Jaipur. Even it's gates bear Hindu names, such as Amar Singh Gate and Hathipol Gate. On the archways are also stone flower emblems, which display the usual ornamental style of Vedic temple *mandaps* (halls). Elephant images exist at the gateways of both forts. This is hardly what you will find on Muslim architecture since Islam frowns on such images. There is also no documented evidence that it was built by any Mogul emperor.

THE MISIDENTIFIED SO-CALLED MUSLIM BUILDINGS IN DELHI

Not only was the Taj Mahal a captured Vedic building, now labeled as Muslim, but many other buildings in the area, especially in Delhi, have also suffered the same fate. In fact, many of the buildings of Delhi and Agra are identical to the buildings of Amber, Bikaner, Jaisalmer, Jodhpur, and other places that are known to exist from pre-Muslim times. If such places did not exist before Muslim invasions, does that mean that Indian armies fought over vacant land? And where did they stay? In tents in the forests? If such is the case, then how do we explain names like Kot Kachwaha, Nagarkot, and Umarkot, since *kot* in Sanskrit means a fortified city. All cities in ancient times had fortifications.

Furthermore, there are no records, drawings, correspondence, or orders for the acquisition or commissioning of a site or construction of any building by a Saracen chief or ruler. Even names such as the Taj Mahal or Kutab Minar do not appear in any of the court papers of contemporary Muslim monarchs to whom they are credited. Yet thousands of books have been written in which the Taj Mahal is ascribed to Shahjahan. These are some of the inexcusable blunders of historians.

Some evidence provided by P. N. Oak on pages 64-5 in *Some Blunders of Indian Historical Research* indicates that the Red Forts in Delhi and Agra could have existed back in 370 A.D. This is long before the time of Islam, not to mention any Islamic invasions.

"Jahangir claims in his memoirs that he had installed a gold chain of justice in his palace at Agra Fort. The claim has been termed 'silly' by eminent British historians. The seemingly meticulous details provided by Emperor Jahangir about the chain have been discounted to be misleading and intended to impart veracity to his claim. It is also pointed out that Anangpal, the Tomar Hindu king of Delhi had, in fact, installed a chain of justice in his palace at Delhi. Since the Moguls and other Muslim rulers betrayed a singular weakness for grafting accounts of Rajput glories to their own reigns, Jahangir's reference to the gold chain of justice in Agra Fort is an incidental clue that the Red Fort at Delhi and Agra existed even in Anangpal's time, i.e. around 370 A.D.

"The architecture of the royal apartments at Amber closely resembles that of the Taj and the two Diwan halls in the Red Forts at Delhi and Agra. All the above considerations are proof enough that the Red Fort and the Taj Mahal of Agra are Rajput built monuments."

The area of the Red Fort in Delhi around Chandi Chowk is also inhabited almost exclusively by Hindus. If the Muslims had actually built the fort, it would be likely that there would be Turks, Afghans, Persians, and Arabs presently settled in the Chandi Chowk area.

More Vedic evidence about the Red Fort in Delhi that remains confidential is that there was a find of the footprints of Lord Shiva in the temple now known as Moti Mandic within the fort. The temple is now considered to be a mosque built by Aurangzeb. This has been hidden or kept secret from fear that this evidence would upset all historical and archeological assumptions about the Red Fort.

Similar evidence is given by Shri V. S. Bendre, a noted historian, in a paper called *Urgent Need for the Study of Literature on Science and Technology of Olden Times* (published in the Ruparel College Publications, Bombay) that he read at the Indian History Congress in 1955 at the Calcutta session. In it he observes that the *Akash Bhairav Kalpa*, a Sanskrit manuscript, gives detailed dimensions and qualities and strength of various kinds of fortifications, including walls, towers and doors. What is left of old forts including Delhi appear totally perfect with the descriptions in the Sanskrit text. Thus, they were built according to the Vedic principles of fort construction.

The Jama Masjid mosque is also said to have been built by Shahjahan. However, Tamerlain (Taimurlang), one of Shahjahan's ancestors 10 generations prior to him (about 230 years), gives his own testimony that the Jama Masjid mosque was previously a Hindu temple. He relates that in his memories entitled *Malfuzat-i-Timuri* wherein he describes the take over of Delhi and how many of the resisting Hindus assembled in the Masjid-i-Jami (meaning the Chief Temple) of Old Delhi preparing to defend themselves. Thus, the Jama Masjid had to have been a Vedic temple.

One story that gives proof of the Muslim tactics for acquiring such buildings, even in modern times, is told on page 45 in *Some Blunders of Indian Historical Research*. In 1985 in New Delhi, residents of the South Extension Part II were threatened by a Muslim mob who wanted to seize the historic monument known as the Masjid Moth and turn it into a fanatic Islamic pressure center. The worried Hindu residents approached Mr. Oak who toured the monument with their workers, along with an architect, a photographer, and a lawyer. Mr. Oak pointed out to them how every detail there proved the edifice to be a Hindu temple. A suit was later filed and an injunction was obtained restraining Muslims from offering prayers inside the building. Later a scrutiny of the relevant revenue records revealed that the name Masjid Moth was foisted on that monument in 1880. This was again obviously Cunningham's mischief.

Another point in this matter is that Hindus, historians, and tourists alike should be on guard to recognize such numerous signs as octagonal contours, filigree decoration, lotus emblems, ochre colored stone, zodiacal signs, images of mighty animals or dancers, or Koranic overwriting, and so many other architectural elements that reveal such buildings to be of Vedic origin. Thus, citizens can be learned enough to resist any fictitious claims on the originations.

THE KUTAB MINAR

Also in Delhi is the Kutab (Kutub or Qutab) Minar, the 238-foot tower which has a similarly vague history. Different people suggest a variety of theories about its origin. Such theories range from it being built by Kutubuddin Aibak, the Muslim slave ruler who ruled in Delhi from 1206 to 1210. Or it was built by his son-in-law and successor Iltmash. Or it may have been built or partly constructed by Allauddin Khilji. Or Feroz Shah may have helped build it.

P. N. Oak gives some hints to the background of this building on page 30 in his book *Some Blunders of Indian Historical Research*: "The township adjoining the Kutub Minar is known as Mehrauli. That is a Sanskrit word *Mihira-awali*. It signifies the township where the well known astronomer Mihira of Vikramaditya's court lived along with his helpers, mathematicians and technicians. They used the so-called Kutub tower as on observation post for astronomical study. Around the tower were pavilions dedicated to the 27 constellations of the Hindu Zodiac.

"Kutubuddin has left us an inscription that he destroyed these pavilions. But he has not said that he raised any tower. The ravaged temple was renamed as Kuwat-ul-Islam mosque.

"Stones dislodged from the so-called Kutub Minar have Hindu images on one side with Arabic lettering on the other. Those stones have now been removed to the Museum. They clearly show that Muslim invaders used to remove the stone-dressing of Hindu buildings, turn the stones inside out to hide the image facial and inscribe Arabic lettering on the new frontage."

On page 291 of the same book he goes on to explain that, "Even the Arabic term Kutub Minar signifies an astronomical tower. Kutub and Kutubuddin was a subsequent unwitting mix-up. Around the tower were 27 constellation temples which Kutubuddin's inscription vaunts to have destroyed. The tower too has 27 flutings. Near the first storey ceiling are 27 holes--one in each is likely. True to the significance of the term Kutub, this tower's entrance faces due north."

On page 538 of *World Vedic Heritage*, Mr. Oak describes a little about the way the temple used to be. He explains that underneath (the tower) lay a giant statue of Lord Vishnu reclining on Seshanaga. At the top of the tower on the seventh storey was an image of Lord Brahma sitting on a lotus flower seat. But the Muslims destroyed both of those images.

The mosque at the base of the Kutub Minar, the Quwat-ul-Islam, is also said to be the very first mosque in India, built with the remains of numerous destroyed Hindu temples. However, the ornately carved columns provide proof that this was once a Hindu temple. Besides, if the tower was a Hindu observatory, it is in line with tradition that there would be a Hindu temple nearby and other shrines for the nine planets.

This is confirmed by Sir Sayyas Ahmad, father of the Muslim League and a founder of the Akigarh Muslim University. He has said, "The current tradition which ascribes the Minar and the adjoining temple to the Hindu period appears to be correct."

OTHER BUILDINGS AROUND DELHI

There is also evidence that the building known as Humayun's Tomb is none other than a captured Lakshmi Temple. The style of the building, with the bastions, numerous gateways, surrounding annexes, guest houses, guard rooms and walls all point to a typical Vedic temple structure. There is even a Shakti Chakra, overlapping triangles, that adorn its top facade. Humayun is not even buried there. Abul Fazal says Humayun is buried in Sirhind while Farishta says he is buried in Agra. There is only a couple side rooms which have a few cenotaphs. And for that the whole structure is designated as a Muslim tomb.

Furthermore, French writer G. Le Bon has published in his book, *The World of Ancient India*, a photo of marble footprints found in the building. He describes them as the footprints of Lord Vishnu. This is also very typical of a Vedic temple, to have the footprints of the main Divinity of the shrine. In this case it is the husband of Lakshmi, Vishnu.

Sikandra, the so-called tomb of Akbar, is located about six miles north of Agra. It is called Sikandra after Sikandar Lodi lived in it. He was a Pathan (Muslim) ruler. It is wrongly believed that Akbar died in the Agra fort, but no funeral procession was ever seen to take place from the fort, even though Muslim chronicles say the body was removed through a specially blasted hole in the wall and taken the six miles away. In his chronicle, Akbar's son Jahangir falsely claims to have built this for his father. Dishonest historians supplement that falsehood with another myth that Akbar started building his tomb before he died. It is such myths that are piled up to cover inconvenient and contradicting evidence which makes up the Muslim history of India. That is why the celebrated historian Sir H. M. Elliot calls it an "impudent and interested fraud" in the preface to his

18-volume critical study of Mediaeval Muslim chronicles. The design of the building is again one of typical Vedic style with its multi-storeyed mansion and geometrically patterned garden, along with interlocking triangles as an esoteric sign which has no place in Islamic theology or design. Manuchi, an East India Company officer, has recorded that the sepulchral mound in this building does not contain Akbar's remains. Actually, it could be a fake, which Muslims would do to set up a somber religious tone over usurped Hindu buildings to prevent recapture and resist revived claims.

Another building for which there is evidence that it is a Muslim captured structure is Safdarjang's tomb. Once again any visitor can see the typical Vedic design of the four towers, one in each corner of the complex, inlaid with marble, with a shrine in the middle. If the evidence regarding this place is true, then the grave is a fake and it is originally a Hindu building. The point to consider is that there are two mounds of loose red-brick powder which gets blown away and which the archeology department needs to keep replacing fraudulently to maintain the pretense of the burial. The other mound is supposed to be Safdarjang's wife, but which wife is hard to say since he had a full harem. There are two mounds in the basement but only one unlabeled cenotaph on the first floor. It is known that Safdarjang was buried at Paparghat in Uttar Pradesh. Therefore, the tomb in the building at Delhi has to be a hoax.

The Nizamuddin is also Vedic in design. The saffron colored tall archway under the tree at the left hand top is one proof of the Vedic origin of the site. The whole area, under Muslim occupation for the last few centuries, has a magnificent spacious stepped well which is a Hindu feature. The so-called Amir Khusro tomb with a white dome is part of that great Vedic temple complex. The lotus-petal border of the terrace and the lotus cap above the dome are strictly Vedic features.
The Nizamuddin complex contains Muslim graves because the area, being a Vedic temple complex, came under repeated Muslim attacks with carnage every time. Muslims would station themselves in captured Vedic ruins and lay claim to it by burying their dead leaders in such buildings and say it was Muslim property or Muslim constructed. Since Islam existed only since 622 A.D., most Muslims in the area are the descendants of Hindu ancestors who were captured and forcibly converted to Islam.

There is evidence that Fatehpur Sikri, the fort city an hour's ride west of Agra, was built many years before Akbar, who is credited with having built the city. Numerous points in this regard are listed on pages 57-63 in P. N. Oak's *Some Blunders of Indian Historical Research*. For example, Muslim chronicles pertaining to the reigns of rulers preceding Akbar list the city as Fathpore, or Sikri, or even Fathpore Sikri. The book titled *Akbar* by Justice J. M. Shelat (published by The Bharatiya Vidya Bhavan, Bombay) carries a painting on page

82 captioned "Humayun's troops entering Fathpore." Humayun was Akbar's father. So how could Akbar build Fatehpur Sikri before his father's time?

Akbar lived in the township but it had already been attacked and damaged by the battle between Rana Sanga and Babar, Akbar's grandfather. Babar's troops were killing innocent civilians and ravaging the county-side, forcing Rana Sanga out of the city to do battle. This is also when the water supply of Anup Lake was poisoned. Thus, Fatehpur Sikri had been conquered by Babar two generations before Akbar.

The typical history of this place is that Jala-ud-Din Akbar began building thjis town in 1571 and completed it in 1585. It is often said, and any tourist will hear this story, that Akbar left the city several years after completing the construction because the water supply went bad. However, the water supply already had been poisoned before that. The gaping holes in the surrounding walls are proof of the battle and attack by Babar's troops. The name of the lake itself, Anup, is Sanskrit which also indicates that it was built by Rajputs in pre-Muslim times. The lake being old and neglected, finally burst in 1583 which made Akbar permanently leave Fatehpur Sikri. If it had been newly constructed as a water-reservoir, it should not have burst.

Further evidence is that an Englishman, Ralph Fitch, visited Fatehpur Sikri in September of 1583. In his notes he considered the city to be very old, comparing it to ancient Agra. Therefore, it was not a new township as Muslim chronicles try to indicate. Even the Muslim chronicles are not in agreement with the start of the city's construction, mentioning dates from 1564, 1569, 1570, or even 1571. The date of 1583 is recorded as when the city was completed. However, why would Akbar have left only a few years later in 1585 if the city was in good shape. He should have stayed and simply made a few repairs. But no, he left because he did not have the skilled men who knew such construction repair.

Furthermore, there is not one piece of paper that provides any evidence that this city was built, commissioned, or designed. Nor are there any to show that materials were ordered or transported, or that any laborers were paid in order to build this city. Contemporary Jesuits at Akbar's court have recorded that not one stone-cutter's chisel was ever heard or any building materials ever seen during the time when the city was supposed to have been built. Therefore, either the city had already been built years ago, or it was constructed overnight. And the idea that such a city could be built overnight without any building supplies scattered about, or any records of construction, is typical of the sentimental nonsense used to manipulate historical truths.

The townships intricately ornamental workmanship is in the traditional Rajput style. While the two huge Rajput style stone elephants flanking the Hathpol gate bear the marks of Muslim defacing since their heads have been chiseled away. The elephant has always been a symbol of royal and divine might in Hindu iconography. The so-called tomb of Salim Chisti within Fatehpur Sikri is actually an ancient Hindu temple that was for the family deity. It shows the delicate and ornate stone work, as well as a per ambulatory passage for circling the deity, common in all Vedic temples, which would serve no function in a tomb. On page 321 of *Akbar the Great Mogul* by Vincent Smith, he says, "It is surprising to find unmistakable Hindu features in the architecture of the tomb of a most zealous Musalman saint, but the whole structure suggests Hindu feeling, and nobody can mistake the Hindu origin of the columns and struts of the porch."

The one verandah that is designated as a mosque has many Hindu features in its intricate workmanship, as noted by the western historian E. W. Smith. Even in front of the Panch Mahal building is a huge Chaupat (Backgammon) board on the paved redstone floor. The tourists are told that Akbar would play the game using girls as the life-size game pieces. However, this is an exclusively Hindu game of ancient origin, very popular in mediaeval times, which is not played in Muslim households.

Another point is that the name "Sikri" is of Sanskrit origin, which comes from the Sanskrit word *Sakata*, which means sand. From this a native principality in Rajasthan is known as Sikar. The diminutive feminine form of Sikar is "Sikri." This lends credence that the original founders of Fatehpur Sikri were a clan of Rajputs, probably from Sikar. The suffix "Pur" also indicates a township in Sanskrit. The prefix "Fateh" signifies a captured township. Thus, the name makes it obvious that it was an earlier Rajput township captured by invading Muslims.

AHMEDABAD

The capture and conversion of Hindu temples into mosques in Ahmedabad is a particulary important case in point of how Rajput monuments have been ascribed to Muslim rulers. Mr. Oak provides much insight into this on pages 69-71 in *Some Blunders of Indian Historical Research.*

"Before being named after Ahmed Shah I, Ahmedabad was known as Rajnagar, Karnavati and Ashaval. Its history extends to a very remote past. Ahmad Shah was a very fanatic and tyrannical ruler. As was the practice with Muslim invaders, Ahmad Shah used captured Rajput temples and palaces as mosques and tombs. A glimpse of his intolerant depredations can be had from Mr. Ashok Kumar Majumdar's article titled *Three Saints*, which was published in the special Gujarat number of the *Caravan Magazine* (Delhi) of August 1959.

"In that he observes, 'In 1414 A. D. Sultan Ahmad Shah of Gujarat appointed an officer to destroy all Hindu temples of his kingdom, and the task was executed with great diligence. Next year the Sultan himself went to Siddhapur and broke the famous Rudramahalaya temple of Siddharaj and converted it into a mosque. . . The reign of the notorious bigot Muhammad Bagda (1459 to 1511) was yet to come.' The word "destroy" here obviously signifies that only Hindu worship was destroyed and the same buildings were occupied and used as mosques.

"The thickly populated area of the ancient walled town of Ahmedabad is still known as 'Bhadra.' That is a Sanskrit word meaning 'auspicious.' It was given that name because it teemed with temples. All those temples have now been turned into mosques. Ahmedabad is full of mosques more than any other comparable town. At almost every few hundred yards there is a tomb or a mosque. What is more, they are all in the ornate Rajput style.

"In Ahmad Shah's time the Muslim population of Ahmedabad was infinitesimal. As such it was impossible that the ruler constructed mosques galore all over town for such a small section of his subjects. Neither could he have got the mosques and tombs done in the Hindu temple style. One who would have had abiding love for Hindu architecture would not destroy temples, convert them into mosques and loot and massacre the people as Ahmad Shah did. . .

"The main mosque of Ahmedabad known as Jama Masjid was the ancient Bhadrakali temple. That was the presiding deity of the city. From its portico to the innermost sanctuary its highly ornate architecture is glaring proof of its earlier role as a Hindu temple. The aisle of the sanctuary has over a hundred closely set pillars as are common in Hindu goddess temples. Genuine Muslim mosques do not have even a single pillar since they hamper mass prayers.

"In the niches of the sanctuary are fixed stone-flower emblems as the Muslims were wont to do in the case of all captured and converted monuments. A part of this huge temple has been used as a graveyard.

"The carvings reveal many Hindu symbols like flowers, chains, bells and niches. The upper portion of one of the twin spires of the shrine has been chopped off as could happen in the first flush of victory and consequent iconoclastic fury.

"Ornamental stones which fell off the stormed temples can be seen scattered in the vicinity. One such ornamental slab is used as a filling in a wall of the public lavatory opposite the mosque on the main thoroughfare known as Mahatma Gandhi Marg."

Undeniable proof that the Ahmedabad Jama Masjid mosque is indeed a Hindu temple was supplied when its claim of being a mosque was successfully challenged in a local court of law. The story is very interesting. Around 1963-4 an article by P. N. Oak appeared in some Gujarati papers that claimed all of Ahmedabad's 1000 mosques were actually captured Hindu temples, and that the main Bhadrakali temple was being used by Muslims as their Jama Masjid. Shortly thereafter, a rich hosiery firm (M/s K. C. Bros) demolished its decades old building and built a large mansion.

The Muslim trustees of the Jama Masjid filed a suit in a local court demanding that the hosiery firm demolish its mansion. The claim was that the mansion dwarfed the mosque, so it was an insult to Allah. The K. C. Bros were worried. When the owner sought advice, some of his friends had read the article by Mr. Oak and learned his address. The owner wrote of his distress and requested Mr. Oak to help him. Mr. Oak wrote back saying that he was itching to prove his finding in a court of law, that no historic edifice or township throughout the world is of Muslim origin. He requested the owner not to worry about the Muslim bluff since he was there to help him see to it that the building would not be demolished.

On Mr. Oak's advice, the firm's lawyer drafted the defendants' rejoinder that the plaintiff Muslims had no right to file the suit since the building which they claimed to be a mosque was a captured Bhadrakali temple and, therefore, should be given back to the Hindus. Never before had the Muslims received such a stunning retort. After holding agitated consultations with mullahs, archeologists and historians, they were all convinced that it was indeed a captured Hindu temple. This was in spite of the marble plaque that had been placed in the ochre stone wall by wily Cunningham declaring in English that the Jama Masjid was built in 1414 A.D. by Ahmad Shah I. Thus, the Muslims realized that Cunningham was a liar. So, ultimately, in great frustration the Muslims in Ahmedabad beat a hasty retreat and precipitously withdrew their suit thereby conceding that they were in fact conducting Islamic rites in a Hindu temple. Unfortunately, this does not perturb them because this has been the Muslim practice throughout history. They force captured people or intimidate them to become Muslim and then usurp their buildings to be used as mosques. More than simply understanding their foolishness, the Muslims withdrew their case because they were afraid that far from being able to demolish K. C. Bros's mansion, they might also have to surrender the temple they were misusing as a mosque when during the hearing it would turn out to be a captured Hindu temple.

From this story we can also realize that Muslims should be more willing to trace out their own Hindu lineage. This goes for Indian Christians as well. Their ancestors were Hindu and they should not be ashamed to look at this fact, nor see their real spiritual heritage. Rather than looking for ways to quarrel with their brethren in their own mother country, India, Bharat Varsha, they should be more willing to embrace their brothers. And Hindus should welcome them. However, those who do not show such courage and close their eyes to their own history will naturally ignore the truth and patronize a special concoction of world history as has been manufactured by a people and religion who try to usurp the land for themselves and for their own purposes.

BIJAPUR

Another city that is known for being a great Muslim town is Bijapur. Of course, once again we can see that Bijapur is a Sanskrit name. *Pur* is Sanskrit for city or township, and *Bija* is also Sanskrit meaning "seed" or "essence."

Bijapur was captured and ruled over by the Muslim Adil Shahi dynasty. The Gol Gumbaz, the great and ancient domed building, is now known as the tomb of Adil Shah and some of his relatives. Most of the buildings in Bijapur are credited with Muslim construction. However, again we can ask ourselves why they built no palaces for themselves while they were alive, and we find only mosques and tombs, all of which show a strong resemblance to the Vedic styles of architecture.

The Gol Gumbaz was the ancient Shiva temple of the Lingayats who were the local Shaivite community, worshipers of Lord Shiva. Around the shrine has been found many Vedic images, often buried in the ground. A few of them have been collected in a nearby building. The dome is known for echoing the slightest sound 11 times. When the tourists and kids visit, the noise can be a loud and never-ending din. So you need to visit early in the day while it is quiet. The dome was meant to produce what is called the *Nada-Brahma*, or phonetic ecstasy, especially during the great Shivaratri festival. This would recall Lord Shiva's dance of destruction, the Tandava Nritya, which is accompanied by a great ecstatic roar of *mridanga* drums, cymbals, bells, and other instruments. Once they all get going with each sound being echoed 11 times, it is just a steady pitch of noise. So, for this building to have been built as a tomb for the peace of the departed souls, to be observed with quiet reverence and a somber mood by the visitors, then this is the wrong place. Having personally visited this place I can honestly say they obviously do not get much peace in this building. Everybody likes to try the echo, and when visitors are there noise is a constant.

Historically speaking, Mr. G. G. Joshi, an architect from Nagpur, has also written to Mr. Oak stating that after visiting the Gol Gumbaz, he agrees that it is a pre-Muslim building, built to the specifications of the Vedic *Shilpashastra*. As S. Padmaraj has observed in his book, *The Intelligent Tourist's Guide to the Glory that is Bijapur*, there is no evidence of any foreign influence in the buildings at Bijapur. On the contrary, there is strong evidence of the Hindu tradition, "adopting itself to the Muslim requirements. There is not a detail in the splendid buildings at Bijapur that cannot be explained as the logical sequence of India's living building craft. To understand the buildings of the Muslim Bijapur, the student must first turn to the Hindu Vijayanagar (the famous capital of the mediaeval Hindu empire)."

So if the so-called Muslim architecture at Bijapur so closely resembles that of Vijayanagar, this is further proof that the Muslim invaders actually used earlier indigenous buildings as tombs and mosques and then made the false claim to have built them themselves. Such is the case at Bijapur, whose buildings were already existing long before the Muslims ever arrived.

MISIDENTIFIED HINDU BUILDINGS IN OTHER AREAS

There are also many other Hindu forts and temples that have been misidentified as being of Muslim origin. Take the Allahabad Fort, which is ascribed to Akbar again. When you consider the intricate design and the ornamental pattern of the windows overlooking the confluence of the Yamuna and Ganges rivers, the intricate carvings in some of the inner chambers, the existence of the Ashok Pillar, the Pataleshwar temple, and the Akshayya Wat (immortal banyan tree) inside the fort, this is adequate proof that the fort was built long before the Muslims arrived. Certainly if it was of Muslim origin there would not have been any temples in the fort, and there would have been no regard for the banyan tree and Ashok Pillar. This is a typical instance of how Indian history has become distorted by the slippery guesswork of some blundering authors. Therefore, the fort was not built by Akbar, but he only occupied it in 1584. In fact, as many as 48 Hindu temples were destroyed by Shahjahan in Allahabad, as he claims in his Memoirs. Thus, his pride was toward destroying what the Hindus had built.

Other places that have experienced great Vedic temples being turned into mosques include Mathura at Krishna's birth place where Aurangzeb destroyed the temple and built a mosque in its place. The same thing happened at Banaras (Varanasi) where Aurangzeb destroyed the original Vishwanatha Shiva Temple as well as the Bindu Madhava Krishna Temple. Both important temples were destroyed and mosques were put in their places. Smaller Vedic temples had to be rebuilt in those places again. In Ayodhya, the Babri Masjid mosque was built 500 years ago where a Rama temple once stood. This had been greatly debated, but recent archeological evidence shows that a beautiful Vishnu temple did once stand there. In Pune, the former Punyeshwar and Narayaneshwar temples are now known as Sheikh Salla Dargahs. The so-called Ganesh Peth in Pune is a captured Dattatreya temple. For the past few years it has been reluctantly admitted that the Kamalmaula mosque at Dhar in Central India is the ancient Saraswati Kanthabharana. The falling of the camouflaging plaster has revealed the stone panels with Sanskrit dramas inscribed on them. These are just a few of the places, besides the ones already mentioned, that are scattered across India where there has been the attempt to destroy Vedic culture.

One question we could ask: If there are so many historic buildings in Delhi, Agra, Ajmer, Ahmedabad, Bijapur, Gulbarga, Bidar, Mysore, Bangalore, Srirangapatnam, Aurangabad, and so many other places that are ascribed to Muslim invaders, then what is left to be claimed by the millions of Hindus who have lived here for thousands of years? Should we think that they were simply content to live in tents amidst forests, fields and wild beasts? Just by a short study of the ancient Vedic texts and the depth of knowledge and spiritual understanding that they have, we can understand that such would never be the case. Thus, we must conclude that much of what was once a part of Vedic culture has been hidden, or attempted to be kept secret, by the deliberate manipulation of the true history of India. It is time to uncover that history as we have tried to do in presenting the above information.

HINDUS CONSTRUCTED, MUSLIMS DESTROYED

The fact is that Hindus had constructed buildings while the invading Muslims merely destroyed or captured them. Most tombs, forts, mosques, canals, etc., that are ascribed to various sultans or Mogul rulers are merely usurped Hindu constructions put to Muslim use. And it does not take long for any traveler in India to see how many of the remaining temples in India were defaced or dismantled by the fanatic Muslim invaders. Some of the most beautiful temples you can see have much of their ornate stone carvings disfigured by those marauders who had no appreciation for the art of the "infidels."

In fact, the Islamic way of life never put much emphasis on the arts. However, dancing and music was always held in high regard in the Vedic lifestyle. So when people point out the number of Muslim artists or musicians in India as being the Islamic contribution to the arts, they need to remember that most of the tunes and melodies that are used are of immemorial Vedic origin. Secondly, many of the Muslim musicians are either converts or descendants of Hindu artists. Thirdly, many musicians and dancers lead saintly lives in India, and were very often involved in the religious festivals. That is quite the contrary in the Islamic tradition, wherein such artists were often considered unnecessary.

The Koran forbids all decoration, so art can hardly thrive in such an environment. The way most art was made on Islamic structures in the Middle East was due to the fact that invaders into India brought back Indian craftsmen. Only with the help of such Indian architects, engineers and workmen, do the west Asian or Middle-Eastern monuments have a close resemblance to those of India. The telltale sign is to analyze the structures to see how they have been built according to the principles provided in the Vedic text of the *Shilpashastra*.

In fact, as Mr. Oak explains on page 132 of *Some Blunders of Indian Historical Research,* "Accounts of Mohammad Ghazni's and Taimurlang's invasions confess as much when they state that taken aback by the beauty and grandeur of Indian palaces, temples and river ghats, the otherwise barbaric invaders used to spare skilled workmen and technicians from mass massacres only to drive them at sword point to West Asian lands to have tombs and mosques built comparable to Indian monuments."

On page 70 and 71 of *Some Missing Chapters of World History,* Mr. Oak continues, "The great Islamic invader Tamerlain who plundered and burned Delhi confesses in his Memoirs that Mediaeval Muslims were so utterly devoid of any building skill that they were forced to spare the lives of the Hindus whom they deeply hated, so that they could be marched away to distant Islamic lands just to design and build buildings as grand and beautiful as the Hindu buildings in India. Tamerlain observes that before ordering a general massacre of Hindus taken prisoner 'I ordered that all the artisans and clever mechanics, who were masters of their respective crafts, should be picked out from among them and set aside, and accordingly some thousands of craftsmen were selected to await my command. All these I distributed among the princes and amirs who were present, or who were engaged officially in other parts of my dominions. I had determined to build a Masjid-i-Jami in Samarkand, the seat of my empire, which should be without a rival in any country; so I ordered that all builders and stone masons should be set apart for my own special service,' (page 447, Vol. III, Elliot and Dowson's translation of *Malfuzat-i-Timuri*).

E. B. Havell, the great British scholar, supplies the following quotes from the opening part of his book, *Indian Architecture--Its Psychology, Structure and History from the First Mohammedan Invasion to the Present Day*. These give evidence at the admiration the Muslims had for Indian architecture. "Albiruni, the Arab historian, expressed his astonishment at and admiration for the works of Hindu builders. 'Our people,' he said, 'when they see them, wonder at them and are unable to describe them, much less to construct anything like them.'

"Abdul Fazal (wrote), 'It passes our conception of things; few indeed in the whole world can compare with them.'

"Such admissions of Tamerlain, Abul Fazal, Albiruni and Mahmud Ghanzi quoted above indicate the validity of Mr. Havell's observation that there is no such thing as Saracenic art in any part of the world, much less in India. Even as far as Samarkand, Baghdad, Mecca and Alexandria all ancient and mediaeval buildings were built according to the architectural styles, techniques and skills developed by the Hindus."

Another point is that it often takes highly developed skills carefully nurtured and practiced over a number of generations. The invading hordes of West Asian Muslims were mostly uncultured and illiterate desperados unskilled in any human art except fighting. So how could such people come to India and suddenly begin building the fantastic monuments that they claimed to have built? If such was the case, then why do so many of such monuments show the disfiguring of the carvings by the very Muslims said to have built them? Another point is that the invaders were so engaged in the turmoil of defensive and offensive military activity, when and how did they have time to build such monuments? Furthermore, although India has had a very clear science of architecture, as set down by the *Shilpashastra*, the ancient Muslim world has nothing to correspond to it. Any community claiming architectural skill must have basic treatises describing structural forms, designs, and material used in construction. Ancient and mediaeval India had these, while the invading Muslims had none.

The fact is that there are many Vedic texts, from varying time periods, that provide a code of architectural procedures and information. Texts such as the *Mayamata, Samarangana-sutradhara* (dating to the 11th century A.D.), and the *Vishnudharmottara* (450-650 A.D.) elaborately deals with the science of architecture. The *Munasara* (dating to the 11th to 15th century in its present form) also mentions a 12-storeyed palace for a monarch. So sky-scrapers were also not unknown at the time. Furthermore, the *Arthashastra* (2.3,4) includes information on the building of ramparts, tower gates, *gopurams*, palaces, temples for Deities, and residential quarters for different kinds of people.

The *Shilpashastra* is also a Vedic classic on architecture, house construction, and town planning. More of the latter is also found in the *Vastu Vidya*. Some of the information in the *Vastu Vidya* is in the *Jataka* stories and Buddhist Pali cannons. This similarity confirms that the *Vastu Vidya* existed during the time and after the death of Lord Buddha, from 500 B.C. to 100 A.D. Thus, the technical aspects of the *Vastushastra* were fully developed no later than the time of Buddha, which is long before any Muslims ever existed. Furthermore, when we consider the descriptions of the opulent buildings and the town planning of Dwaraka city in the Tenth Canto of the *Bhagavata Purana*, we can understand that such knowledge had already been established and utilized several thousand years ago.

The *Vastushastra*, along with references in the Vedic epics, the *Arthashastra*, and *Jatakas* also make mention of building materials and that different sizes of bricks and stones were used for the building of pillars, lintels, and the construction of dome roofs. This also helps verify that the dome design was a pre-Islamic invention in India long before Muslims arrived. Thus, Muslims were not the inventors of the dome, which had already existed in some of the ancient buildings of India and the Middle East from many years prior. If anything, they were impressed with Indian architecture, such as the dome, and increasingly used it in their own buildings, or even captured Indian craftsmen to take back to their countries to build them. Even the many canals that are credited to Muslim construction does not hold up when specific Vedic texts, such as the *Vrikshayarveda* portion of the *Agni Purana*, discuss forms of irrigation by means of canals. This shows that the technical rules and procedures for all kinds of construction were fully developed in India before the time the Muslims began to invade the country, and that any idea of a Muslim contribution to the architecture of India is indeed a production of misinformation.

Another question we should ask is why did the invading Muslims build so many tombs, if that is what they did, rather than building large palaces for themselves? Usually the ruling monarch will build many large palaces for himself and his children before he will concern himself with building a large tomb, or one for a dead ancestor. Furthermore, many of the ruling monarchs at the time were also at war with each other. Why would they allow a large tomb for a rival instead of taking it for themselves? Both of these considerations should convince us that there are so many more tombs than corresponding palaces because the Muslim monarchs built neither tombs nor palaces. They merely usurped the already standing Hindu buildings and used it for themselves.

Many stories are presently told about the glories of Shahjahan and the love he had for Mumtaz, who was only one of many wives. However, there are other stories that tell of how he had illicit relations with the wives of his own kin, like brother-in-law Shaista Khan and wives of courtiers like Khaliullah Khan, and, as some suspect, even with his own eldest daughter Jahanara.

Shahjahan's reign of just over 29 years was full of 48 campaigns. He demolished many Hindu temples and murdered many of his rivals. He never engaged in the construction of any buildings. He merely took over the Taj Mahal for himself and made sure that it was recorded that he built it. Shahjahan's own court chronicle, the *Badahahnama*, records that he had ordered that not even one Hindu temple must be allowed to stand in his realm. In the district of Allahabad alone 76 temples were destroyed, 48 of which he mentions in his memoirs. It is also known that Shahjahan used to threaten captured Hindus and Christians alike to become Muslims under pain of torturous death.

Thus, after considering all of the information in this chapter, we need to ask: What was the real "Muslim contribution" to Indian culture? It is based mostly on the invasion and rule over India by a host of aliens like Arabs, Turks, Iranians, Iraqis, Kazaks, and Uzbeks during a period of nearly 1,235 years, from Mohammad-bin-Kasim to Bahadurshah Zafar. After all, if a gang of dacoits invade a peaceful village and loot all the people's wealth, torture and kill the males, or sell them into slavery, rape the women, abduct the girls into harems, and massacre all others, can that be considered a contribution to society? It would be clear to any sensible person that such invaders were never wanted by the Indian people. The invaders also had no respect for India or the people and culture. They only wanted to exploit it to the maximum. They tried to dominate India in every way and reduced it to a land of slums and abject poverty, taking what they could for themselves and leaving the rest in ruins. Al Biruni, a Muslim chronicler who accompanied the invader Mohammad Ghazni, has himself said that Mohammad Ghazni ground to dust the life of the Hindus and scattered it to the winds.

Wherever Islam invaded, the first priority was to force the local people to forget and hate their ancient culture. This was accomplished by destroying old monuments, past historical records, and changing history by writing new records. Thus, Arabian history begins with the words that Arabia was a land lost in turmoil before the appearance of Islam. Throughout the Middle-East, those people who have been forcibly converted to Islam can hardly remember what their previous culture was, and assert that before Islam the whole world was dark. Can a system which has thrived on conversions through torture and terror lay any claim to the word "culture"?

Testimony to the cruelty of the Muslim tyranny is found in Paper Two, in the *Papers Relating to East India Affairs*, House of Commons, London, dated June 3, 1813. In there is recorded a letter by J. D. Patterson, posted as a judge in Dacca by the erstwhile British East India Company, addressed to the president of the Police Committee in Calcutta, dated August 30, 1799. By this time Islam had completed its 1087-year rule in India. Patterson wrote:

"To give the Board a true account of the Police of this district, it is necessary, in the first place, to make them acquainted with the manners and morals of the people, especially the lower sort.

As a picture of human degradation and depravity can only give pain to a reflecting mind, I shall be as brief as possible.

Under the Hindu dominion, the ranks and professions of men were classed into 36 castes, and the individuals of each were obliged to learn and follow the profession of his ancestors. By this establishment, each individual of a caste had the means of support in his profession. These castes were under the direction of their Pundits and the Punchayats, or General Assembly of the caste, and used to examine the conduct of the member of their society, and the consequence of their censure, was sometimes a total exclusion of the guilty individual from the community.

No Brahmin was supported by the public who was unlearned or who did not contribute his assistance informing the minds of the lower classes, and teach them morality, and the duties enjoined by laws. Under such an establishment for the instruction of the lower classes, it was not difficult to form an efficient Police. But the cruel reverse, which the invasion of the unprincipled and bigoted Musalmans [Muslims] introduced, may account for the wide torrent of corruption that has overflowed this country.

They considered the conquered Hindus as infidels, and treated them with unrelenting persecution and cruelty. They thought that every insult and injury upon them were acts pleasing to God and the Prophet. Their destructive bigotry attacked the books and learning of the Hindus, and the Brahmins, persecuted with incessant atrocities, ceased to exercise their functions. The spirit of despotism completed the corruption of morals, and in process of time, the human mind in this country was completely revolutionized. In this manner for some centuries, under the Pathan Government, they continued, from want of the ancient discipline, to fall from degradation to degradation.

Many of the lower ranks became converts to the Mohammedan faith, without conviction of its being more rational than what they professed before, because it sheltered them from the persecuting bigotry they had suffered, but the mind experienced no rise. The stern despotism of their rules still kept it down.

Unprotected, however, and unsupported by the authority of the Government, the Brahmins themselves sinking under centuries of oppression, were too much involved in the general wreck to think of renewing the ancient discipline. Their learning fell into neglect, and in course of time the Brahmins came to want that instruction themselves which it was their duty to afford to others. Missing in all the selfish squabble of common life, they gradually lost, by their own example, in the eyes of the Hindus, that respect which was so necessary to give force and energy to instruction."

Herein we can clearly see by the eye-witness account of Judge Patterson how society plummeted into a shambles from what once was the Vedic form of administration. Therefore, according to Judge Patterson, Islam is responsible for the social chaos, corruption, and moral breakdown that occurred.

TIME TO PLAN THE SURVIVAL OF VEDIC CULTURE

From the above information that has been provided, we can fairly safely say that since Islam existed only from 622 A.D., the majority of Muslims in India and Bangladesh today are descendants of captured, mistreated, or distressed Hindus. A blatant example of this is the story of one Nazir Ali, which appeared in a Letter to the Editor in the *Weekly Organizer* (New Delhi, July 13, 1997). Nazir Ali was a Muslim man who had settled in the United States. He and his family had been away from India for a long time and invited his grandfather from Mehrauli (New Delhi) to come to America to get acquainted with his grandchildren. After the grandfather's arrival, the children would gather around him in the evening for a nostalgic chat. On one such occasion Nazir Ali asked his grandfather as to why the male elders in their family always wore *dhotis* (the traditional Indian Hindu dress) though they were Muslims. Thereupon, to Nazir Ali's great consternation and distress, the old man broke into uncontrollable sobs and tears, and stuttered out the words, "Beta, how should I tell you? Ours was a Brahmin family owning a Hanuman temple in Merauli. But 400 years ago as victims of an invading Muslim army some of our ancestors were slain while some others with sword points pressed on their throats agreed willy-nilly to survive only as Muslims. But to keep alive the memory of our Hindu ancestry, our elders made it a rule that all males should invariably stick to the *dhoti*."

Hearing the heart-rending account, Nazir Ali was in a great fix. Like Nazir Ali's ancestors, a number of so-called Muslims continue to tenaciously stick to tender tokens of their Hindu ancestry, such as imprinting Ganesh on their wedding invitations, retaining a tiny *Bhagavad-gita* inside the Koran, calling in a Hindu priest to apply a *bindi* to a bride, and lisping the name of Lord Rama while doing the Namaz (Muslim prayers). Thus, Muslims in India are descendants of Hindus, some of whom still hold dear to their hearts their ancient Vedic heritage. In this same line of thought, we can also point out that most historic buildings and townships credited to Muslims are captured properties that were once Hindu. In this way, it is time to recognize the glory of Vedic India and work to preserve it and keep it the home of Vedic culture.

We must realize, however, there is much that is working against this from happening. The deterioration of Indian Vedic culture is rapidly taking place. One thing that is very prominent in causing the disintegration of Vedic culture is the so-called "secular" nature of the Indian government leaders over the past several decades. Secular should mean democratic, in which every religion is protected. However, for the sake of getting votes and approval, many politicians have pandered to the demands of Muslims, promoting Islamic interests in India at the expense of the Hindus, Sikhs, Jains, and others. They have carved up Malabar district just to create the Muslim majority district of Malappuram. There are states in which the whole school gets half-a-day off on Fridays to offer Namaz, even if only two students in a class are Muslim. Yet, for the real progress of Muslims, which depends on education and modernization, they have done nothing.

Other ways that Vedic principles are being eroded away can be recognized in the following example: Article 48 of the Indian Constitution states that, "The state shall take steps for preserving and improving the breeds, and prohibiting the slaughter of cows and calves and other milch and drought cattle." This should mean a complete ban on the slaughter of cows, bulls, and calves. Protecting and preserving cows is definitely a Vedic principle. However, the courts have interpreted this article to mean that aged and disabled bulls can be slaughtered. Taking advantage of this loophole, cattle are maimed and "certified" as disabled and then slaughtered. In the years from 1976 to 1992, beef sale has gone up from 70,000 tons to over 1,100,000 tons. This not only goes against the principles of India and Vedic culture, but it makes cows more scarce and milk expensive.

Article 44 of the Indian Constitution says: "The state shall endeavor to secure for the citizens a uniform civil code throughout the territory of India." This would include a uniform ban on polygamy, but the Muslims want to be free, and have been, from following such a law. Thus, Muslim men can easily have several wives. Such implementation of the law would provide a greater security for Muslim womanhood, and also prevent irresponsible Hindu males from converting to Islam simply to have more than one wife.

To show even further how Congress-trained politicians, though Hindus themselves, have been following the suicidal policy of curbing Hindu rights and pampering all kinds of minorities by conferring on them special privileges can be seen in a special report. This was written by Dr. Edmund Weber and presented at the fifth International Hindu Conference in Germany in 1992. Some of the findings are: "The religious minority of 100,000 Ladakhi Buddhists are officially marked as Hindus and they, in contrast to the over 100,000,000 Indian Muslims, have no right to follow their traditional marriage law."

"The pseudo-secularism of India is not even today ready to fulfill the demands of the Hindu democrats to introduce the same civil code for all their citizens. This mentality has only the mind to maintain privileges of powerful groups.

"The pseudo-secularism discriminates particularly the Hindus in the educational area. The education bills are valid only for them, while the minorities constituted by the state are over privileged, e.g. they are exempted from all those rules.

"The Tamilnadu Education Acts do show in a special way (that a) Hindu institution must get permission before starting a school. Prior permission is not required in the case of minority [Muslim or Christian] schools.

"Hindu institutions must adopt communal representation for appointing teachers, i.e. Muslims, Christians, etc., but a Minority school need not (follow) that rule." This means that Muslim or Christian schools do not have to provide any Hindu teachers, although the community may be primarily Hindu. This is how the Vedic culture is disappearing. The most efficient way to take over a country or change the viewpoint of a population is to take over all forms of communication and the educational systems. This is the legal right that has been given by the politicians to the minority groups in India.

The report goes on: "While every Hindu school must have a school committee including teachers, Minority schools need not have such committees.

"The most dangerous kind of blockade against the renewal of Hinduism is that the great monasteries and temples in India were forced to have temple committees. . . while pseudo secularism, out of political opportunism, grants non-Hindu religions full autonomy (over) their holy buildings and places; e.g. in Kerala a non-Hindu was deliberately (made a) member of the Guruvayoor temple committee. The nomination was canceled only after a vehement protest and the non-Hindu member was replaced by a Harijan [Hindu].

"Those so-called secular governments who do not dare to interfere in any manner in the management of churches, maqbaras, mazars and mosques [of the minority groups] make unjustified and most objectionable and unethical evil attempts to take over control of Hindu Mutts and Mandirs [temples]."

This is further explained by Dr. Gopalacharya in his book, *World-Wide Hindu Culture* (p.v), "The anti-Brahmin movement started by the cunning policy of the Britishers was followed by the post independent Indian secular Governments, which made laws to uproot (general Hindu society) by the tenancy acts enabling the Government to make the temples, *maths,* and religious educational institutions lose their lands and other resources for their maintenance. For want of resources, the above institutions became defunct. The greatest tragedy was that these laws were not imposed on non-Hindu religious institutions. As their properties of the religious institutions were given special facilities, instead to get lump votes, *the urgent need of the majority community is to get all the unjust laws repealed and choose only those which do justice to all the communities without partiality."*

This is very important, otherwise many of these problems that we have mentioned will only increase. You find these problems today as when you have colleges run by the Catholic church in India who penalize you with a fine if you speak your native tongue on their campus. They want English only because the vernacular languages are associated with heathen deities. Bible and Christian prayers are mandatory at the start of class is such schools, yet secular government ministers are known to have objected to including Indianized moral and spiritual education in regular Indian schools. The Bible can be taught in Christian schools, but to impart moral codes based on the *Upanishads* or *Puranas* in regular Indian schools becomes highly objectionable.

The same thing goes on with the Muslim schools, only Urdu is spoken, not native local languages. Thus, such students grow up knowing Urdu, which assists in directing them to become Muslim converts, if they are not already Muslim. By also encouraging Muslim principles throughout India, like allowing Muslim men to have four wives and easy divorces, and have the government pick up the tab for maintaining them, is a way to break down Vedic society in India and make it an extension of Pakistan.

This same bias is viewed in other ways as well. Taxes are collected from Hindu charities but none from Muslim or Christian religious properties, which are tax-free. Even in West Bengal, the Communist-run government admits being anti-Hindu and recently pulled down a Shiva temple. Other government ministers have halted Vedic *yajnas*, fire rituals, because they considered it a waste of using ghee. Yet, in order to show their secular tendency, the same ministers participate in the Muslim Bakrid festival when many milk-producing cows are slaughtered in the name of religious tenets. Does this make sense? This is outrageous.

Though Christian churches and Islamic mosques cannot be touched, Vedic temples are often taken over to be managed by the government. Then they often appoint members to the board who may be atheists, Communists, or of different faiths who care little for the well-being of the Vedic temple. What is worse, they may simply run the temple down, or steal funds meant for maintaining the temple, or take land and jewels of the Deity that were lovingly donated by devotees over many centuries. It is in this way that secularism in India works for upholding Christianity and Islam at the expense of Hinduism.

Even now the wealthy classes in India often prefer to send their children to schools where English is taught. Unfortunately, many of the English schools are operated by Christians, in which Christian tenets are expounded and any regard for Vedic culture and history is ignored. Thus, Indian children of the wealthy and influential classes grow up with little regard for their own culture. Meanwhile, children of Muslim countries and schools are taught strong respect for the Koran and Islamic principles. Thus, Vedic culture is being lost even willingly in India.

All Hindus and followers of the Vedic culture had better understand the meaning of the above information and begin to demand changes in their government in India. They must remove from power all who talk of secularism at the expense of, or to kill, Hinduism. Annie Besant once said that India and Hinduism are always connected: One cannot be without the other. India is India only with the presence of the Vedic culture. If that is not maintained, then the Vedic motherland of India will no longer be the motherland. And then Hindus may wake up one day to find that they no longer have a home.

Although it will take much time to recover from the great degradations and deterioration that have occurred in Indian society from the time of the Vedic reign, and it may never fully recover, nonetheless it is time to bring back the united, peaceful, purposeful, and pious Vedic culture. The first thing to do is for Hindus to arm themselves with knowledge about their great World Vedic Heritage. India should make sure that it is a place where the practicality of Vedic culture is permanently preserved. This culture, properly called "*Sanatana-Dharma*," which is the everlasting social order based on the eternal nature of the soul, refers to the righteous, enlightened order meant for the impartial and affectionate upliftment of every individual.

In order for this to take place, the 85% Hindu population of India must no longer be a timid people who are afraid to give up their neutralist stand, avoidance of proselytizing, or defending themselves. It is time to recognize the elements that are working to stifle and push down Vedic culture. To keep itself from certain death, Hinduism, *Sanatana-Dharma*, those of the Vedic culture, must once again enter a phase of self-assertion and subdue the various forms of intimidation and discrimination in order to assure that India remains the home of Vedic society.

In India, such governmental discrimination should be stopped, and everyone should follow one set of laws, not that minorities have the liberty to set their own laws at the disadvantage of the majority of Hindus. India has already been broken into parts, such as Bangladesh and Pakistan, for the sake of separatists. How much more does it need to be broken up, or broken down, in order to satisfy or calm the minority non-Hindus in India who refuse to change their ways? It is time to draw the limits and set the standard if we are intent on the survival of Vedic culture.

AN ACTION PLAN FOR THE SURVIVAL OF
VEDIC CULTURE IN INDIA AND ELSEWHERE

It is obvious that in many areas Vedic culture, and other cultures, too, such as Tibetan Buddhism, are under attack. Every genuine religion should have the right to exist to assist its followers in developing and improving themselves spiritually. And Vedic culture is one of the foremost and oldest of all spiritual paths. Furthermore, from the evidence we have provided in this book, we can see that it has been one of the most expansive of any religion and civilization in history. It is and always has been a great and noble path. Unfortunately, when viewed by those who have closed minds because of their prejudice and bias, it can be misunderstood. And often when those who belong to other religions want to help Hindus who may be in need of support materially, they quite often do so when they see an opportunity to make converts. Thus, we find more than a few missionaries who go among those who live in poverty do so with offers of free clothes, food, medicine, education, etc., in exchange for conversion or in an attempt to try and show some kind of superiority in their religion. In this way, their assistance is not offered as real help, but merely as an covert bribe to convert.

However, we should ask, "What is the Hindu being converted from?" They are expected to convert from one of the greatest traditions in the world, and one of the most profound and lofty philosophies found anywhere. Thus, Vedic tradition must be allowed to have expression and has much to offer if people can be receptive.

So how can there be changes in the Hindu communities to assure the future of Vedic culture? Internally, Hindu communities often suffer from being fragmented by language and regional distinctions and loyalties, as well as by being under-developed materially, financially, and organizationally. To counter this:

(1) Community and temple leaders must become more trained both in Vedic knowledge and organizational skills. They must provide programs that go beyond regional distinctions, and bring people together in a way that focuses on their unity

in their Vedic heritage. (2) Hindus and devotees must also have programs that will provide them with exposure to the depths of Vedic philosophy and connect them with what is actually God-centered. This will also counter the western religions and missionaries who are trying to make converts by emphasizing material comforts and the glitter of the more modern way of life, while putting the focus on God as secondary. This will actually attract anyone who is really searching for the means to perceive their spiritual identity. (3) Another point is that Hindus need to make sure they participate in the Vedic *samskara* ceremonies. These provide the purificatory rituals that mark the various stages of life in connection with the Vedic purpose of making spiritual progress.

(4) Parents also must be educated in the importance of Vedic knowledge in order to be able to pass this along to their children, especially in the home in the West, or wherever regular schools provide no such emphasis. Parents must make sure their children are properly trained in Indian history and culture, and Vedic traditions and principles. And parents can only be properly educated with the assistance of the temple pandits and genuine spiritual leaders. Doing this in conjunction with the programs or functions at the local temple will benefit the children, and create lasting memories of the joy in associating with other children while learning the great Vedic epics, legends, and principles of life, as well as participating in the worship of the Supreme.

(5) Not only local pandits, but also the wealthy and all educated and knowledgeable Hindus and devotees should take responsibility to protect their culture, as is often seen in other religions. (6) They all need to become Vedic ambassadors, which means they need to be ready to show anyone and everyone the importance of past and present contributions and achievements of Vedic culture.

(7) Also, by providing spiritual festivals, pandal tent celebrations and feasts, people will continue to be entertained, and socially and spiritually rejuvenated and enlivened. The Vedic culture has to be taken outside the temples to the people and congregation. As people participate in these joyous activities of the Vedic path, and also contribute to each other's spiritual and material well-being, everyone will naturally feel a higher sense of self-esteem. They will feel proud of their Vedic heritage. In this way, the community will assure itself of its future by attending to the needs of its members. Otherwise, someone else will likely come along to do it.

(8) In this regard, when there is only focus on the temple activities to define one's relation to Vedic culture, many other needs of the Hindu community may be left out and ignored. This is what is picked up by outside religions and missionaries. These needs include visiting the sick, attending to medical problems, family problems, assisting those in poverty, providing food and clothing, education, and much more. These needs have to be attended. Temples should have or develop outreach programs to facilitate the people of the community who have such needs. Thus, they will not need to go to others, but will be able to stay within their own community for assistance.

(9) Modern facilities must be used to unite and advance the Hindu

community, to assist with its needs, and to push forward the Vedic way of life. Hindus must become more well organized, more well funded. Money is crucial to the success of the spiritual programs which are necessary to bring Vedic *Dharma* back to its rightful place, and in the center of the devotee's life. Strong finances are one of the cornerstones of any successful religion. Hindus who are able must provide a fixed percentage of their income as a tithe to their favorite temple, preaching project, or outreach program. This not only helps maintain what is there, but also helps defend and spread the culture.

(10) They must also consistently use information by making and distributing literature and plans for activities in which people can participate. Hindus and Vedic followers must also use the various means of communication to unite their community, such as radio stations, television, newspapers, etc. Without modern means of communications, they simply become more fragmented from each other and cut off from their own culture.

Vedic or Hindu organizations must work to provide the means for Vedic education among all people, and help establish the necessary means to ensure this. This would include, (1) Hindu schools must be staffed with proper teachers. (2) They should also begin writing and manufacturing their own school books that maintain Vedic values. (3) Financing preaching programs, *satsanghs*, to take the Vedic message to all people is also necessary. (4) There is also a need to produce more pamphlets, books (such as this one), tapes, videos, etc., that help show the significance of the Vedic way of life. Distributing such literature, and establishing more traveling preaching programs and festivals, is practically more important than establishing more temples. Some people live too far away to regularly attend temple programs. But books, pamphlets, tapes, and photographs they can keep with them always, wherever they are. However, for those temples that are established, providing the programs which will bring all people, young and old, to participate and be involved in their cultural heritage is of vital importance.

(5) All educated Hindus and devotees on the Vedic path should be encouraged to do their part to help, such as in their local temples with management, teaching congregational members, distribution of Vedic literature, food (*prasadam*) distribution, and looking after others in the community in various ways. Organizing projects that can focus on and take care of the needs of the people, such as solving the problems of family violence, alcoholism, the poor, the sick, the aged, etc., will help and is necessary. (6) Also, organizations should form committees to monitor and defend against local attacks on Hinduism in the media, and promote the accomplishments and advantages of the Vedic way of life, and what achievements local Vedic communities and individuals have attained.

On an individual basis, (1) one should realize that he or she should first seek the proper knowledge and means of enlightenment to try and attain liberation from material existence after death and return to the spiritual realm through devotion to God. One should understand that everything in material life is temporary, and that the basis of the Vedic path is to reach that realm which is eternal, beyond the illusory nature in which we so often must focus in our daily lives. Such knowledge should be attained from authorized Vedic books, spiritual authorities, associating with like-minded devotees, and other means. (2) A person should also live a life defined by Vedic values in all situations, whether at home, at work, or while traveling. This would include avoiding the consumption of meat, intoxicants, and gambling and illicit sex. (3) This should also include regular daily reading of scripture, such as *Bhagavad-gita*, as well as performing spiritual activities, worship, and chanting prayers such as the Hare Krishna *mantra*. Otherwise, one gradually loses sight of the purpose of life and the reasons for the Vedic standards. (4) One should also respect other religions, but should not feel you must compromise your own values or traditions to do so. And do not argue with those of other faiths who lack respect for your own. Better to keep your own values and reasoning without giving them over to the contradiction of foolish men. After all, everyone knows that a fool talks all nonsense. There is no need in wasting one's valuable time with such a person.

(5) Furthermore, if one has been blessed with wealth, talents, or a position of influence, you must realize it is a blessing from God. Therefore, you should also show your gratefulness for such blessings by taking time to contribute to the well-being of others and local temples and causes to help preserve your Vedic heritage. You must set an example, knowing that whatever a great man or woman does, others will follow.

(6) Finally, any individual can help monitor and petition the media to increase positive coverage of Hindu occurrences, and protest biased reporting. Simply acquire the address or phone numbers of the local paper, radio or television station to write a letter of concern or protest when something is published that is prejudicial in its view of something that is Hindu. Don't be afraid of speaking out. And connect with those who have similar concerns. The media listens the more people speak out.

These are all points that can help promote the continuation of Vedic culture, and arrange for its survival under the attacks that are likely to increase in the future. Such attacks are not only from those of other religions who would like to see the demise of the Vedic way of life, but also from the lack of sincerity and the complacency of those who consider themselves followers of the Vedic path but are not serious about it.

One last thing that the global Vedic community should consider is to be more flexible and accommodating to those who are from outside Vedic culture who wish to join and participate in its ways. I personally have traveled all over India and have visited more holy places than most Indians. And it is not uncommon for temples to post signs stating, "No non-Hindus allowed." This exclusiveness is usually based on race more than one's faith, and I have often been excluded from such temples. However, being dressed in traditional clothes, such as a *dhoti*, and being a devotee of Krishna has helped me enter temples that may otherwise exclude me. Of course, I can understand the idea that cynical people who visit temples can simply cause problems or contaminate the atmosphere. However, there are many people from outside India, or who were born of non-Indian parents, who sincerely want to be a part of, or who already practice, the Vedic path. And some of them are following higher spiritual standards than many Indians by being completely vegetarian, abstaining from illicit sex, intoxicants, and so on. In my travels through India, for example, I have personally met and seen Indian Brahmins who ate eggs or smoked cigarettes, which is completely non-brahminical. And they are nonetheless allowed in all temples. So why not the Westerners? Fortunately, there are also many temples and ashramas in India who do allow Westerners in, and they are not the worse off for it. And, of course, Vedic temples in America do not exclude anyone.

The point I am getting at is that as Christianity, Buddhism, Islam, and other paths have an open door policy that allow anyone to enter the churches and temples and most mosques, and participate and join, these religions receive much support from their new members. Just as so many Indians have joined Christianity or converted to Islam and are now supporting their new religion in terms of giving donations of money, time, energy, and ideas, many Westerners would also like to participate in Vedic culture in the same way. And the Vedic communities could certainly use more of that support. The larger a group is, the more influence and support it has to offer, if used appropriately. Even though Hinduism has opened many of its doors that were once closed to outsiders, Hinduism has to be more willing to give and share its knowledge with others, and to open itself in allowing others to participate and be part of it. Many people have been and are inspired by the Vedic path of India. After all, there have already been Western people who were very influential supporters of the Vedic path and its wisdom. This could only expand if more Hindus gave up their attitude of exclusivity.

The Vedic Aryan spiritual path is *Sanatana-Dharma*, which is the eternal nature of the soul, which is everybody. So this knowledge belongs to everybody, and everyone can use it to better understand themselves and the purpose of this life. It does not simply belong to one class of people. Therefore, the Hindu or Vedic community has to be willing to open itself up and give and share its knowledge and culture with others, especially in India. Thus, everyone can better understand it and benefit from it. Otherwise, as other religions and institutions continue to expand, if the Hindu or Vedic community does not adopt the proposals as outlined above, then they will witness or cause its own instability, or even its own slow demise.

In this way, by helping protect and restore Vedic culture, we are saving what is left of the original seed from which all social advancements, scientific observations, religious customs, and spiritual philosophy can be traced. Indeed, it still offers the loftiest and most complete spiritual understanding found anywhere, and is the oldest living culture, rich in tradition, without which the world would lose its connection to its earliest roots.

Conclusion

The purpose of supplying all of this information and evidence is to show what is our common cultural and spiritual heritage. It is to show the actual history of the planet and our real roots. It is to look beyond the facade and veil of manipulated history and forged legends and stories. It shows that beyond our recently developed allegiance to a particular religion, country or culture, we have all got something in common. That common factor is that we are all descendants of the one great community and way of life, which is the Vedic culture. This Vedic culture, as evidence shows, was once a global civilization, and still is an influence in our lives today in every part of the world. It is the Vedic culture which promotes peace, a balanced life, justice, and the material and spiritual progress for one and all. It is that culture of which we now see only remnants in the various fragmented religions and traditions today. Even India, the center of Vedic culture today, has still been invaded and conquered and ruled over so many times that it is now only a dim reflection of the great empire and country it once was. What else can be expected when it also has begun to forget the high standards of consciousness and spiritual principles that the Vedic way of life promoted and held so dear?

Nonetheless, we have provided plenty of evidence in this volume to show that humanity was far more advanced thousands of years ago than most people think. How much farther we may have come if the world could have kept advancing along the Vedic path before it was divided into so many factions and regional or localized religions and cultures? This certainly could have been a much more united, peaceful, and cooperative world.

As is clearly shown in this book, no matter whether we presently consider ourselves to be Christians, Muslims, Jews, Buddhists, or French, English, Chinese Arabs, or Americans, our ancient forefathers were once members of a global Vedic brotherhood. People have forgotten this common heritage, a heritage that means we are all spiritually and materially related. Thus, the divisions of the world presently divided by language, scripture, customs, and nations, often times one against the other, is a great tragedy. It is only due to a lack of historical understanding, a forgetfulness of our true heritage, and an absence of genuine spiritual awareness, that keeps us from being a more united, harmonious, and global society. Certainly the whole world would benefit if we simply tried to awaken these characteristics in everyone. This book is a step in pointing the way and reminding us of what our real roots are and from where we have all come. As Max Muller wrote when he was nearing the end of his life in his book, *India-- What Can It Teach Us?*, "We all come from the East--all that we value most has come to us from the East, and in going to the East. . . everybody ought to feel that he is going to his 'old home,' full of memories, if only he can read them."

APPENDIX ONE

More Information About Vimanas

In supplying information about the advancements of Vedic science, the subject of Vedic airplanes, *vimanas*, is almost in a classification of its own. Some of this information is so amazing that for some people it may border science fiction. Nonetheless, as we uncover and explain it, it provides serious food for thought.

First of all we need to understand that the Vedic conception of universal time is divided into different periods. For example, a period called one day of Brahma is equivalent to 4,320,000,000 of our years on earth. Brahma's night is equally as long and there are 360 of such days and nights in one year of Brahma. Each day of Brahma is divided into one thousand cycles of four *yugas*, namely Satya-yuga, Treta-yuga, Dvapara-yuga, and finally the Kali-yuga, which is the *yuga* we are presently experiencing. Satya-yuga lasts 1,728,000 years, and is an age of purity when all residents live very long lives and can be fully developed in spiritual understanding and mystical abilities and remarkable powers. Some of these abilities, or mystic *siddhis*, include changing one's shape, becoming very large or microscopically small, becoming very heavy or even weightless, securing any desirable thing, becoming free of all desires, or even flying through the sky to wherever one wanted to go on one's own volition. So at that time, the need for mechanical flying machines was not necessary.

As the *yugas* continued, the purity of the people, along with their mystical abilities, decreased by 25% in each age. The age of Treta-yuga lasts 1,296,000 years. During that age, the minds of humanity became more dense, and the ability for understanding the higher spiritual principles of the Vedic path was also more difficult. Naturally, the ability to fly through the sky by one's own power was lost. After Treta-yuga, Dvapara-yuga lasts 864,000 years, and Kali-yuga lasts 432,000 years, of which 5,000 have now already passed. At the end of Kali-yuga, the age of Satya-yuga starts again and the *yugas* continue through another cycle. One thousand such cycles is one day of Brahma. Now that we are in Kali-yuga, almost all spiritual understanding disappears, and whatever mystical abilities that remain are almost insignificant.

It is explained that it was not until the beginning of Treta-yuga that the

303

development of *vimanas* took place. In fact, Lord Brahma, the chief demigod and engineer of the universe, is said to have developed several *vimanas* for some of the other demigods. These were in various natural shapes that incorporated the use of wings, such as peacocks, eagles, swans, etc. Other *vimanas* were developed for the wiser human beings by great seers of Vedic knowledge.

In the course of time, there were three basic types of *vimanas*. In Treta-yuga, men were adept in *mantras* or potent hymns. Thus, the *vimanas* of that age were powered by means of knowledge of *mantras*. In Dvapara-yuga, men had developed considerable knowledge of *tantra*, or ritual. Thus, the *vimanas* of Dvapara-yuga were powered by the use of tantric knowledge. In Kali-yuga, knowledge of both *mantra* and *tantra* are deficient. Thus, the *vimanas* of this age are known as *kritaka*, artificial or mechanical. In this way, there are three main types of *vimanas*, Vedic airplanes, according to the characteristics of each *yuga*.

Of these three types, there is listed 25 variations of the *mantrika vimanas*, 56 variations of the *tantrica vimanas*, and 25 varieties of the *kritakaah vimanas* as we find today in Kali-yuga. However, in regard to the shape and construction, there is no difference between any of these *vimanas*, but only in how they were powered or propelled, which would be by *mantras*, *tantras*, or mechanical engines. Ancient Vedic texts, such as the *Vimaanika Shastra* of Maharshi Bharadwaja, give detailed descriptions of how these various machines are put together. Some of them are described as being several floors tall and quite large. Others are small and only for a few persons.

The *Vimaanika Shastra* also describes in detail the construction of what is called the mercury vortex engine. This is no doubt of the same nature as the Vedic Ion engine that is propelled by the use of mercury. Such an engine was built by Shivkar Bapuji Talpade, based on descriptions in the *Rig-veda*, which he demonstrated in Mumbai (Bombay), India in 1895. I more fully explained this in Chapter Three of this volume. Additional information on the mercury engines used in the *vimanas* can be found in the ancient Vedic text called the *Samarangana Sutradhara*. This text also devotes 230 verses to the use of these machines in peace and war. We will not provide the whole description of the mercury vortex engine here, but we will include a short part of William Clendenon's translation of the *Samarangana Sutradhara* from his 1990 book, *Mercury, UFO Messenger of the Gods*:

"Inside the circular air frame, place the mercury-engine with its electric/ultrasonic mercury boiler at the bottom center. By means of the power latent in the mercury which sets the driving whirlwind in motion, a man sitting inside may travel a great distance in the sky in a most marvelous manner. Four strong mercury containers must be built into the interior structure. When those have been heated by controlled fire from iron containers, the *vimana* develops thunder-power through the mercury. At once it becomes like a pearl in the sky."

This provides a most simplistic idea of the potential of the mercury engines. This is one kind of a propulsion mechanism that the *vimanas* of Kali-yuga may use. Other variations are also described. Not only do these texts contain directions on how to make such engines, but they also have been found to contain flight manuals, aerial routes, procedures for normal and forced landings, instructions regarding the condition of the pilots, clothes to wear while flying, the food to bring and eat, spare parts to have, metals of which the craft needs to be made, power supplies, and so on. Other texts also provide instructions on avoiding enemy craft, how to see and hear what occupants are saying in enemy craft, how to become invisible, and even what tactics to use in case of collisions with birds. Some of these *vimanas* not only fly in the sky, but can also maneuver on land and fly into the sea and travel under water.

There are many ancient Vedic texts that describe or contain references to these *vimanas*, including the *Ramayana*, *Mahabharata*, *Rig-veda*, *Yajur-veda*, *Atharva-veda*, the *Yuktilkalpataru of Bhoja* (12th century A.D.), the *Mayamatam* (attributed to the architect Maya), plus other classic Vedic texts like the *Satapathya Brahmana*, *Markandeya Purana*, *Vishnu Purana*, *Bhagavata Purana*, the *Harivamsa*, the *Uttararamcarita*, the *Harsacarita*, the Tamil text *Jivakacintamani*, and others. The *Vymaanika Shastra* also refers to as many as 97 past works and authorities of these flying machines, all of which now seem to be extinct. Thus, scholars have dated this text from at least the fourth century B.C. Furthermore, the text refers to some 36 authorities of different technical sciences, all of which date to at least the eighth century B.C. or earlier. From the various descriptions in these writings, we find *vimanas* in many different shapes, including that of long cigars, blimp-like, saucer-shapes, triangular, and even double-decked with portholes and a dome on top of a circular craft. Some are silent, some belch fire and make noise, some have a humming noise, and some disappear completely.

These various descriptions are not unlike the reports of UFOs that are seen today. In fact, David Childress, in his book *Vimana Aircraft of Ancient India & Atlantis*, provides many reports, both recent and from the last few hundred years, that describe eye witness accounts of encounters with UFOs that are no different in size and shape than those described in these ancient Vedic texts. Plus, when the pilots are seen close up, either fixing their craft or stepping outside to look around, they are human-like, sometimes with a Oriental appearance, in clothes that are relatively modern in style. In other reports, we have read where the craft may have alien type beings on board along with ordinary humans navigating the craft.

Does this mean that these are ancient *vimanas* that still exist today? Are they stored in some underground caverns somewhere? Or are they simply modern-built, using the ancient designs as described in the Vedic texts? The UFOs that have been seen around the world may not be from some distant galaxy, but may be from a secret human society, or even military installation. However, many of the Vedic texts do describe interplanetary travel. So even if these space machines are from some other planet, they may be using the same principles of propulsion that have already been described in the universal Vedic literature. The answer awaits us.

APPENDIX TWO

Reestablishing the Date of Lord Buddha

Most of us are taught that Buddha was born around 560 to 550 B.C. However, once we start doing some research, we find evidence that this date may be too late. Buddha may have been born much earlier.

For example, in *Some Blunders of Indian Historical Research* (p. 189), P. N. Oak explains that the *Puranas* provide a chronology of the Magadha rulers. During the time of the *Mahabharata* war, Somadhi (Marjari) was the ruler. He started a dynasty that included 22 kings that spread over 1006 years. They were followed by five rulers of the Pradyota dynasty that lasted over 138 years. Then for the next 360 years was the 10 rulers of the Shishunag family. Kshemajit (who ruled from 1892 to 1852 B.C.) was the fourth in the Shishunag dynasty, and was a contemporary of Lord Buddha's father, Shuddhodana. It was during this period in which Buddha was born. It was during the reign of Bimbisara, the fifth Shishunag ruler (1852-1814 B.C.), when Prince Siddhartha became the enlightened Buddha. Then it was during the reign of King Ajatashatru (1814-1787 B.C.) when Buddha left this world. Thus, he was born in 1887 B.C., renounced the world in 1858 B.C., and died in 1807 B.C.

Further evidence that helps corroborate this is provided in *The Age of Buddha, Milinda and King Amtiyoka and Yuga Purana*, by Pandit Kota Venkatachalam. He also describes that it is from the *Puranas*, especially the *Bhagavat Purana* and the *Kaliyurajavruttanta*, that need to be consulted for the description of the Magadha royal dynasties to determine the date of Lord Buddha. Buddha was the 23rd in the Ikshvaku lineage, and was a contemporary of Kshemajita, Bimbisara, and Ajatashatru, as described above. Buddha was 72 years old in 1814 B.C. when the coronation of Ajatashatru took place. Thus, the date of Buddha's birth must have been near 1887 B.C., and his death in 1807 B.C. if he lived for 80 years.

Professor K. Srinivasaraghavan also relates in his book, *Chronology of Ancient Bharat* (Part Four, Chapter Two), that the time of Buddha should be about 2259 years after the *Mahabharata* war, which should make it around 1880 B.C. if the war was in 3138 B.C. Furthermore, astronomical calculations by astronomer Swami Sakhyananda indicates that the time of the Buddha was in the Kruttika period, between 2621-1661 B.C. More evidence besides this could be presented to establish that the Buddha lived much earlier than what modern history teaches us.

Therefore, the fact that Buddha lived much earlier has a number of ramifications. First, the time of the Buddha's existence is underestimated by about 1300 years. Secondly, this means that Buddhism was in existence in the second millennium B.C. Thirdly, we also know Buddha preached against the misused Vedic rituals of sacrifice. Such misuse can only happen after a long period of prominence. Therefore, this pushes the Vedic period farther back from the time of Buddha than originally figured. And lastly, everything else we have figured according to the time frame of the appearance of Buddha now has to be re-calculated. Again we find that history has to be adjusted away from the speculations of modern researchers, and that many of the advancements in society and philosophy had taken place earlier than many people want to admit.

REFERENCES

Ancient Indian Technologies as Seen by Maya, The Great Asura, by Ravindranath Ramchandra Karnik, Published by the organizers of The Second International Seminar on Mayonic Science and Technology, Thiruvanathapuram, Keral India, 1997

Annals and Antiquities of Rajasthan, Col. James Tod

Aryatarangini, Asia Publishing House, Bombay, 1969

A History of India, Hermann Kulke and Dietmar Rothermund, Dorset Press, New York, 1986

The Aryan Invasion Theory: A Reappraisal, by Shrikant G. Talageri. Published by Pradeep Kumar Goel for Aditya Prakashan, F-14/65, Model Town II, Delhi 110 009. 1993

The Aryans, V. Gordon Childe, Dorset Press, New York, 1987

Atharvaveda, translation by Devi Chand M.A., Munshiram Manoharlal Publishers, New Delhi, 1980

Bhagavad-gita As It Is, translated by A. C. Bhaktivedanta Swami, Bhaktivedanta Book Trust, New York/Los Angeles, 1972

Bhakti-yoga and Islam, by Airavata Dasa, Turkish Society for Philosophical and Social Science, Istanbul, 1996

Bharat (India) As Seen and Known by Foreigners, By G. K. Deshpende, Swadhyaya--Mandal, Killa Pardi, District Surat, 1950

Bhavisya Purana

Bible, New York International Bible Society, 1981

Bible Myths and Their Parallels in Other Religions, by T. W. Doane, reprinted by Health Research, P. O. Box 70, Mokelumne Hill, CA 95245, 1985

Book of Jasher, Published by The Rosicrucian Order, San Jose, California, 1934

Book of Morman, The Church of Jesus Christ of Latter-day Saints, Salt Lake City, Utah, 1976

Breakthrough, Clifford G. Hospital, Orbis Books, Maryknoll, New York, 1985

Buddhist and Christian Gospels, Albert J. Edmonds, Yukwan Publishing House, Tokyo, 1905

Caesar's Commentaries on the Gallic War, translated by T. Rice Holmes, Macmillan & Co. Ltd., St. Martins Street, London, 1908

Caitanya-caritamrta, translated by A. C. Bhaktivedanta Swami, Bhaktivedanta Book Trust, Los Angeles, 1974

Chips From a German Workshop, Max Mueller

Collectania De Rebus Hibernicus, Lt. Gen. Charles Vallancy, Craisberry and
Campbell, 10 Back Lane, Dublin, 1804

Dictionary of Philosophy and Religion, Reese, Humanities Press, Atlantic
Highlands, New Jersey, 1980

Dragon Treasures, Donald Cyr, Stonehedge Viewpoint, Santa Barbara, CA
1989

Egyptian Civilization, L. A. Waddell, Christian Book Club, Hawthorne, CA

Elements of Hindu Iconography, by T. A. Gopinatha Rao, Motilal Banarsidass,
Delhi, 1985

Encyclodaedia Judaica, Heter Publishing Co., Jerusalem

Hindu Influence on Greek Philosophy, Timothy J. Lomperis, Minerva
Associates (Publications) PVT. LTD., Calcutta, 1984

Hymns of the Rig-veda, tr. by Griffith, Motilal Banarsidass, Delhi, 1973

The Indo-Sumerian Seals Deciphered, L. A. Waddell, Omni Publications,
Hawthorne, California, 1980

Inner Reaches of Outer Space, Joseph Campbell, Harper & Row, New York,
1986

In Search of the Cradle of Civilization, Georg Feuerstein, Subash Kak, &
David Frawley, Quest Books, Wheaton, Illinois, 1995

In Search of the Indo-Europeans, J.P.Mallory, Thames & Hudson, New York,
1989

India in Greece, by Edward Pococke

India's Past, A. A. Macdonell

India--What Can It Teach Us, Max Mueller

Indian Architecture--Its Psychology, Structure and History, E. B. Havell

*Indian Wisdom; or Examples of the Religious, Philosophical, and Ethnical
Doctrines of the Hindoos*, by Monier Williams, M.A., Professor of Sanskrit
in the University of Oxford, London, W. H. Allen, 1875.

Islam, Alfred Guillaume, Penguin Books Ltd., Hammomnds Worth, Middlesex,
UK, 1954

Jesus Lived in India, Kersten, Element Book Ltd., Dorset England, 1986

The Jesus Mystery, Bock, Aura Books, Los Angeles, 1980

Jesus the Magician, Smith, Harper & Row, San Francisco, 1978

Journal of the Discovery of the Source of the Nile, Colonel John Speke

Mahabharata, Kamala Subramaniam, Bharatiya Vidya Bhavan, Bombay, 1982

Mahabharata: Myth and Reality–Differing Views, edited by S. P. Gupta and K.
S. Ramachandran, Agam Prakashan, Delhi, 1976

The Makers of Civilization, L. A. Waddell, Hollywood, CA. 1929

Matter, Myth and Spirit, or Keltic and Hindu Links, by Dorothea Chaplin, Scot
Rider & Co., Paternoster Row, London, 1935.

Millennia of Discoveries, Alexander Adams, Vantage Press, New York, 1994

Memoirs of India, R. G. Wallace, 1824

Monumental Christianity, or the Art and Symbolism of the Primitive Church as

Witness and Teachers of the One Catholic faith and Practice, by John P. Lundy, Presbyter, New York: J. W. Bouton, 1876.

Namaz: The Yoga of Islam, by Ashraf F. Nizami, Nizami Compound, Pratapnagar Road, Baroda

Narrative of a Journey Overland From England to India, Mrs. Colonel Elwood, published by Henry Calhoun, London, 1830

Oriental Mythology, Joseph Campbell, Penguin Books, New York, 1962

Origines, by Sir W. Drummond, printed by A. G. Valpy, Red Lion Court, Fleet Street, London

Ramayana of Valmiki, tr. by Makhan Lal Sen, Oriental Publishing Co., Calcutta

Readings From World Religions, Selwyn Champion, Dorothy Short, Fawcett World Library, New York, New York, 1951

Revisiting Indus-Sarasvati Age and Ancient India, Editors Bhu Dev Sharma and Nabarun Ghose. Published by World Association for Vedic Studies, c/o Dr. Deen B. Chandora, 4117 Menloway, Atlanta, GA. 30340. 1998

Primitive Mythology, Joseph Campbell, Penguin Books, New York, 1959

Puranic Encyclopaedia, Vettam Mani, Motilal Banarsidass, Delhi, 1964

Sanskrit and Its Kindred Literatures--Studies in Comparative Mythology, Laura Elizabeth Poor, C. Kegan Paul & Co., Paternoster Square, London, 1881

Science and Technology in Ancient India, Edited by Dr. Manabendu Banerjee and Dr. Bijoya Goswami, Published by Snaskrit Pustak Bhandar, Calcutta, 1994

Some Blunders of Indian Historical Research, and by Purushottam Nagesh Oak, published by P. N. Oak, 10, Good Will Society, Aundh, Pune, India, 411007

Some Missing Chapters of World History, by Purushottam Nagesh Oak,

Sri Isopanisad, translated by A. C. Bhaktivedanta Swami, Bhaktivedanta Book Trust, New York/Los Angeles, 1969

Srimad-Bhagavatam, translated by A. C. Bhaktivedanta Swami, Bhaktivedanta Book trust, New York/Los Angeles, 1972

Srimad Valmiki-Ramayana, Gita Press, Gorakhpur, India, 1969

Story of Civilization, by William Durant

Surya Siddhanta: A Textbook of Hindu Astronomy, translated by Rev. Ebenezer Burgess, Motilal Banarsidass, Delhi, (latest edition) 1989

The Celtic Druids, Godfrey Higgins, Rowland Hunter, St. Paul's Churchyard, Hurst & Chance, St. Paul's, Churchgate & Radgway & Sons, Picadilly, 1929

The Chosen People, John M. Allegro, Granada Publishing Ltd., Park Street, St. Albans, Herts, England, 1973

The Diegesis: Being a Discovery of the Origin, Evidences, and Early History of Christianity, by Reverend Robert Taylor, J. P. Mendum, London edition, 1873

The Holy Quran, 'Abdullah Yusaf 'Ali, Amana Corporation, Brentwood, Maryland, 1989

The Law of Manu, [Manu-samhita], translated by Georg Buhlerg, Motilal Banarsidass, Delhi, 1970

The Mystical Life of Jesus, H. Spencer Lewis, published by Supreme Grand Lodge of AMORC, San Jose, CA., 1953

The Origins of the Aryans, by Sir Isaac Tailor

The Pentateuch and Book of Joshua Critically Examined, by the Right Reverend John William Colenso, D. D., Bishop of Natal. Longmans, Green & Co., London, 1863

The Problem of Aryan Origins (From the Indian Point of View), K. D. Sethna. Published by Rakesh Goel for Aditya Prakashan, 4829/1 Prahlad Lane, 24 Ansari Road, New Delhi. 1992

The Secret Teachings of All Ages, Manly P. Hall, The Philosophical Research Society, Inc., Los Angeles, California, 1962

The Secret Doctrine of Jesus, H. Spencer Lewis, published by Supreme Grand Lodge of AMORC, San Jose, CA., 1953

The Sphinx Speaks or The Story of Prehistoric Nations by Jwala Prasad Singhal, M.A., LL.B., Ph. D., Published by Sadgyan Sadan, 7A, Pandara Road, New Delhi, India, 1963

The Story of Indian Music and its Instruments, Ethel Rosenthal

The Sumerians, C. Leonard Woolley, W. W. Norton & Co., New York, 1965

The Teachings of the Vedas, Reverend Morris Philip

The Theogony of the Hindus, Count Biornsttierna

The Wanderings of a Pilgrim in Search of the Picturesque, by Fanny Parks, Oxford University Press, London, 1975

The Wonder That Was India, A. L. Basham, Fontana, London, 1971

Travels in Arabia, by John Lewis, published by Henry Calhoun, London, 1829

Tibetan Buddhism, L. A. Waddell, Dover, New York, 1972

Twelve Essential Upanishads, Tridandi Sri Bhakti Prajnan Yati, Sree Gaudiya Math, Madras, 1982. Includes the Isha, Kena, Katha, Prashna, Mundaka, Mandukya, Taittiriya, Aitareya, Chandogya, Brihadaranyaka, Svetasvatara, and Gopalatapani Upanishad of the Pippalada section of the Atharva-veda.

Vedanta-Sutras of Badarayana with Commentary of Baladeva Vidyabhusana, translated by Rai Bahadur Srisa Chandra Vasu, Munshiram Manoharlal, New Delhi, 1979

Vedic Aryans and The Origins of Civilization, by Navaratna S. Rajaram and David Frawley. Published by World Heritage press, Quebec, Canada, and Voice of India, 2/18, Ansari Road, New Delhi 110 002, 1995, 1997

Vimana Aircraft of Ancient India & Atlantis, David Childress, Adventures Unlimited Press, Stelle, IL 60946, 1991. (Contains a translation of *The Vimaakia Shastra* of Maharshi Bharadvaja.)

Vimana in Ancient India, Dileep Kumar Kanjilal, Sanskrit Pustak Bhandar, 38, Bidhan Sarani, Calcutta, India, 1985

Vishnu Purana, translated by H. H. Wilson, Nag Publishers, Delhi. 1980

What the Great Religions Teach, Health Research, Mokelumne Hill, California, 1958

Who Wrote the Bible?, Richard Elliott Friedman, Harper SanFrancisco, a division of Harper Collins Publishers, New York, 1989

Who Wrote the New Testament?, Burton L. Mack, Harper SanFrancisco, a division of Harper Collins Publishers, New York, 1995

With Lawrence of Arabia, Lowell Thomas

World Religions, From Ancient History to the Present, Parrinder, Facts on File Publications, New York, 1971

World Vedic Heritage, by Purushottam Nagesh Oak, published by P. N. Oak, 10, Good Will Society, Aundh, Pune, India, 411 007

World-Wide Hindu Culture and Vaisnava Bhakti, Dr. S. Venu Gopalacharya, 1471-D, Jains' Colony, Ashoka Nagar, Mandya, 571 401, India, 1997

World-Wide Kannada-Tamil & Sanskrit Vocabulary, Dr. S. Venu Gopalacharya, 1471-D, Jains' Colony, Ashoka Nagar, Mandya, 571 401, India, 1989

Yajurveda, translation by Devi Chand M.A., Munshiram Manoharlal Publishers, New Delhi, 1980

Glossary

Acarya or *Acharya*--the spiritual master who sets the proper standard by his own example.

Agni--fire, or Agni the demigod of fire.

Agnihotra--the Vedic sacrifice in which offerings were made to the fire, such as ghee, milk, sesame seeds, grains, etc. The demigod Agni would deliver the offerings to the demigods that were referred to in the ritual.

Akasha--the ether or etheric plane; a subtle material element in which sound travels.

Ananda--spiritual bliss.

Aranyaka--sacred writings that are supposed to frame the essence of the *Upanishads.*

Arati--the ceremony of worship when incense and ghee lamps are offered to the Deities.

Arca-vigraha--the worshipable Deity form of the Lord made of stone, wood, etc.

Aryan--a noble person, one who is on the path of spiritual advancement.

Asana--postures for meditation, or exercises for developing the body into a fit instrument for spiritual advancement.

Asat--that which is temporary.

Ashrama--one of the four orders of spiritual life, such as *brahmacari* (celibate student), *grihastha* (married householder), *vanaprastha* (retired stage), and *sannyasa* (renunciate); or the abode of a spiritual teacher or *sadhu.*

Asura--one who is ungodly or a demon.

Atma--the self or soul. Sometimes means the body, mind, and senses.

Atman--usually referred to as the Supreme Self.

Avatara--an incarnation of the Lord who descends from the spiritual world.

Aum--om or *pranava*

Ayodhya--the town of Lord Rama in East India.

Ayurveda--the original holistic form of medicine as described in the Vedic literature.

B

Bhagavan--one who possesses all opulences, God.

Bhajan--song of worship.

Bhakta--a devotee of the Lord who is engaged in *bhakti-yoga.*

Bhakti--love and devotion for God.

Bhakti-yoga--the path of offering pure devotional service to the Supreme.

Brahma--the demigod of creation who was born from Lord Vishnu, the first
    created living being and the engineer of the secondary stage of creation
    of the universe when all the living entities were manifested.

Brahmacari--a celebate student who is trained by the spiritual master. One of the
    four divisions or ashramas of spiritual life.

Brahman--the spiritual energy; the all-pervading impersonal aspect of the Lord;
    or the Supreme Lord Himself.

Brahmana or brahmin--one of the four orders of society; the intellectual class of
    men who have been trained in the knowledge of the *Vedas* and initiated
    by a spiritual master.

Brahmana--the supplemental books of the four primary *Vedas*. They usually
    contained instructions for performing Vedic *agnihotras*, chanting the
    mantras, the purpose of the rituals, etc. The *Aitareya* and *Kaushitaki*
    Brahmanas belong to the *Rig-veda*, the *Satapatha Brahmana* belongs to
    the *White Yajur-veda*, and the *Taittiriya Brahmana* belongs to the *Black*
    Yajur-veda. The *Praudha* and *Shadvinsa Brahmanas* are two of the eight
    Brahmanas belonging to the *Atharva-veda*.

Brahmastra--a nuclear weapon that is produced and controlled by *mantra*.

Brahminical--to be clean and upstanding, both outwardly and inwardly, like a
    brahmana should be.

Buddha--Lord Buddha or a learned man.

C

Caitanya Mahaprabhu--the most recent incarnation of the Lord who appeared
    in the 15th century in Bengal and who originally started the *sankirtana*
    movement, based on congregational chanting of the holy names.

Chakra--a wheel, disk, or psychic energy center situated along the spinal column
    in the subtle body of the physical shell.

Causal Ocean or Karana Ocean--is the corner of the spiritual sky where Maha-
    Vishnu lies down to create the material manifestation.

Cit--eternal knowledge.

D

Deity--the *arca-vigraha*, or worshipful form of the Supreme in the temple, or
    deity as the worshipful image of the demigod. A capital D is used in
    refering to Krishna or one of His expansions, while a small d is used
    when refering to a demigod or lesser personality.

Devas--demigods or heavenly beings from higher levels of material existence,
    or a godly person.

Devaloka--the higher planets or planes of existence of the devas.

Devaki--the devotee who acted as Lord Krishna's mother.
Dham--a holy place.
Dharma--the essential nature or duty of the living being.
Dvapara-yuga--the third age which lasts 864,000 years.

E

Ekadasi--a fast day on the eleventh day of the waxing and waning moon.

G

Gandharvas--the celestial angel-like beings who have beautiful forms and voices,
      and are expert in dance and music, capable of becoming invisible and
      can help souls on the earthly plane.
Ganesh--a son of Shiva, said to destroy obstacles (as Vinayaka) and offer good
      luck to those who petition him.
Ganges--the sacred and spiritual river which, according to the *Vedas*, runs
      throughout the universe, a portion of which is seen in India. The reason
      the river is considered holy is that it is said to be a drop of the Karana
      Ocean that leaked in when Lord Vishnu, in His incarnation as
      Vamanadeva, kicked a small hole in the universal shell with His toe.
      Thus, the water is spiritual as well as being purified by the touch of
      Lord Vishnu.
Garbhodakasayi Vishnu--the expansion of Lord Vishnu who enters into each
      universe.
Gayatri--the spiritual vibration or *mantra* from which the other *Vedas* were
      expanded and which is chanted by those who are initiated as *brahmanas*
      and given the spiritual understanding of Vedic philosophy.
Gosvami--one who is master of the senses.
Govinda--a name of Krishna which means one who gives pleasure to the cows
      and senses.

H

Harinam--refers to the name of the Lord, Hari.
Hatha-yoga--a part of the yoga system which stresses various sitting postures and
      exercises.

I

Incarnation--the taking on of a body or form.
Indra--the King of heaven and controller of rain, who by his great power
      conquers the forces of darkness.

K

Kali--the demigoddess who is the fierce form of the wife of Lord Shiva. The word *kali* comes from *kala*, the Sanskrit word for time: the power that dissolves or destroys everything.

Kali-yuga--the fourth and present age, the age of quarrel and confusion, which lasts 432,000 years and began 5,000 years ago.

Kalpa--a day in the life of Lord Brahma which lasts a thousand cycles of the four *yugas*.

Karanodakasayi Vishnu (Maha-Vishnu)--the expansion of Lord Krishna who created all the material universes.

Karma--material actions performed in regard to developing one's position or for future results which produce *karmic* reactions. It is also the reactions one endures from such fruitive activities.

Karma-yoga--the system of yoga for dovetailing one's activities for spiritual advancement.

Kirtana--chanting or singing the glories of the Lord.

Krishna--the name of the original Supreme Personality of Godhead which means the most attractive and greatest pleasure. He is the source of all other incarnations, such as Vishnu, Rama, Narasimha, Narayana, Buddha, Parashurama, Vamanadeva, Kalki at the end of Kali-yuga, etc.

Krishnaloka--the spiritual planet where Lord Krishna resides.

Kshatriya--the second class of *varna* of society, or occupation of administrative or protective service, such as warrior or military personel.

Ksirodakasayi Vishnu--the Supersoul expansion of the Lord who enters into each atom and the heart of each individual.

Kuruksetra--the place of battle 5,000 years ago between the Pandavas and the Kauravas ninety miles north of New Delhi, where Krishna spoke the *Bhagavad-gita*.

L

Lakshmi--the goddess of fortune and wife of Lord Vishnu.

Linga--the phallic symbol of Lord Shiva which means universal energy.

M

Mahabharata--the great epic of the Pandavas, which includes the *Bhagavad-gita*, by Vyasadeva.

Maha-mantra--the best *mantra* for self-realization in this age, called the Hare Krishna *mantra*.

Maha-Vishnu or Karanodakasayi Vishnu--the Vishnu expansion of Lord Krishna from whom all the material universes emanate.

Mandir--a temple.

Mantra--a sound vibration which prepares the mind for spiritual realization and delivers the mind from material inclinations. In some cases a *mantra* is chanted for specific material benefits.

Maya--illusion, or anything that appears to not be connected with the eternal Absolute Truth.

Mitra--the deity controlling the sun, and who gives life to earth.

Mleccha--a derogatory name for an untouchable person, a meat eater.

Moksha--liberation from material existence.

Murti--a Deity of the Lord or spiritual master that is worshiped.

Murugan--means the divine child, the Tamil name for Subramaniya, one of the sons of Shiva and Parvati, especially worshiped in South India.

N

Narayana--the four-handed form of the Supreme Lord.

Nirvana--the state of no material miseries, usually the goal of the Buddhists or voidists.

O

Om or *Omkara*--*pranava*, the transcendental *om mantra*, name of the Supreme.

P

Paramatma--the Supersoul, or localized expansion of the Lord.

Pradhana--the total material energy in its unmanifest state.

Prana--the life air or cosmic energy.

Pranayama--control of the breathing process as in *astanga* or *raja-yoga*.

R

Raja-yoga--the eightfold yoga system.

Rajo-guna--the material mode of passion.

Ramachandra--an incarnation of Krishna as He appeared as the greatest of kings.

Ramayana--the great epic of the incarnation of Lord Ramachandra.

Rishi--saintly person who knows the Vedic knowledge.

S

Sacrifice--in this book it in no way pertains to human sacrifice, as many people tend to think when this word is used. But it means to engage in an austerity of some kind for a higher, spiritual purpose.

Shabda-brahma--the original spiritual vibration or energy of which the *Vedas* are composed.

Sac-cid-ananda-vigraha--the transcendental form of the Lord or of the living entity which is eternal, full of knowledge and bliss.

Sadhana--a specific practice or discipline for attaining God realization.

Sadhu--Indian holy man or devotee.

Sanatana-dharma--the eternal nature of the living being, to love and render service to the supreme lovable object, the Lord.

Sankirtana-yajna--the prescribed sacrifice for this age: congregational chanting of the holy names of God.

Sannyasa--the renounced order of life, the highest of the four *ashramas* on the spiritual path.

Sarasvati--the goddess of knowledge and intelligence.

Sattva-guna--the material mode of goodness.

Satya-yuga--the first of the four ages which lasts 1,728,000 years.

Shaivites--worshipers of Lord Shiva.

Shakti--energy, potency or power, the active principle in creation. Also the active power or wife of a deity, such as Shiva/Shakti.

Shastra--the authentic revealed scripture.

Shiva--the benevolent one, the demigod who is in charge of the material mode of ignorance and the destruction of the universe. Part of the triad of Brahma, Vishnu, and Shiva who continually create, maintain, and destroy the universe. He is known as Rudra when displaying his destructive aspect.

Srimad-Bhagavatam--the most ripened fruit of the tree of Vedic knowledge compiled by Vyasadeva.

Sruti--scriptures that were received directly from God and transmitted orally by *brahmanas* or *rishis* down through succeeding generations. Traditionally, it is considered the four primary *Vedas*.

Sudra--the working class of society, the fourth of the *varnas*.

Svami--one who can control his mind and senses.

T

Tilok--the clay markings that signify a person's body as a temple, and the sect or school of thought of the person.

Tirtha--a holy place of pilgrimage.

Treta-yuga--the second of the four ages which lasts 1,296,000 years.

U

Upanishads--the portions of the *Vedas* which primarily explain philosophically the Absolute Truth. It is knowledge of Brahman which releases one from the world and allows one to attain self-realization when received from a qualified teacher. Except for the *Isa Upanishad*, which is the 40th chapter of the *Vajasaneyi Samhita* of the *Sukla (White) Yajur-veda*, the *Upanishads* are connected to the four primary *Vedas*, generally found in the *Brahmanas*.

V

Vaikunthas--the planets located in the spiritual sky.

Vaishnava--a worshiper of the Supreme Lord Vishnu or Krishna and His expansions or incarnations.

Vaisya--the third class of society engaged in business or farming.

Vanaprastha--the third of the four *ashramas* of spiritual life in which one retires from family life in preparation for the renounced order.

Varna--sometimes referred to as caste, a division of society, such as *brahmana* (a priestly intellectual), a *kshatriya* (ruler or manager), *vaisya* (a merchant, banker, or farmer), and *sudra* (common laborer).

Varnashrama--the system of four divisions of society and four orders of spiritual life.

Vedanta-sutras--the philosophical conclusion of the four *Vedas*.

Vedas--generally means the four primary *samhitas;* the *Rig, Yajur, Sama,* and *Atharva.*

Vimana--the Vedic airplanes.

Vishnu--the expansion of Lord Krishna who enters into the material energy to create and maintain the cosmic world.

Vyasadeva--the incarnation of God who appeared as the greatest philosopher who compiled all the *Vedas* into written form.

Y

Yajna--a ritual or austerity that is done as a sacrifice for spiritual merit, or ritual worship of a demigod for good *karmic* reactions.

Index

ABOUT THE AUTHOR

Stephen Knapp grew up in a Christian family, during which time he seriously studied the Bible to understand its teachings. In his late teenage years, however, he sought answers to questions not easily explained in Christian theology. So he began to search through other religions and philosophies from around the world and started to find the answers for which he was looking. He also studied a variety of occult sciences, ancient mythology, mysticism, yoga, and the spiritual teachings of the East. After his first reading of the *Bhagavad-gita*, he felt he had found the last piece of the puzzle he had been putting together through all of his research. Therefore, he continued to study all of the major Vedic texts of India to gain a better understanding of the Vedic science.

It is known amongst all Eastern mystics that anyone, regardless of qualifications, academic or otherwise, who does not engage in the spiritual practices described in the Vedic texts, cannot actually enter into understanding the depths of the Vedic spiritual science, nor acquire the realizations that should accompany it. So, rather than pursuing his research in an academic atmosphere at a university, Stephen directly engaged in the spiritual disciplines that have been recommended for hundreds of years. He continued his study of Vedic knowledge and spiritual practice under the guidance of a spiritual master. Through this process, and with the sanction of His Divine Grace A. C. Bhaktivedanta Swami Prabhupada, he became initiated into the genuine and authorized spiritual line of the Brahma-Madhava-Gaudiya *sampradaya*, which is a disciplic succession that descends back through Sri Caitanya Mahaprabhu and Sri Vyasadeva, the compiler of Vedic literature, and further back to Sri Krishna. Besides being *brahminically* initiated, Stephen has also been to India several times and traveled extensively throughout the country, visiting most of the major holy places and gaining a wide variety of spiritual experiences that only such places can give.

Stephen has been writing *The Eastern Answers to the Mysteries of Life* series, which so far includes *The Secret Teachings of the Vedas*, *The Universal Path to Enlightenment*, *The Vedic Prophecies: A New Look into the Future*, and *How the Universe was Created and Our Purpose In It*. Other books he has written include *Toward World Peace: Seeing the Unity Between Us All*, as well as *Facing Death: Welcoming the Afterlife*. He has also written *Destined for Infinity*, for those who prefer lighter reading, or learning spiritual knowledge in the context of an exciting spiritual adventure. Stephen has put the culmination of over twenty-five years of continuous research and travel experience into his books in an effort to share it with those who are also looking for higher levels of spiritual understanding.

If you have enjoyed this book, or are serious about finding higher levels of spiritual Truth, you will also want to get Volume One of this series:

The Secret Teachings of the Vedas

This book presents the essence of the ancient Eastern philosophy and summarizes some of the most elevated and important of all spiritual knowledge. This enlightening information is explained in a clear and concise way and is essential for all who want to increase their spiritual understanding, regardless of what their religious background may be. If you are looking for a book to give you an in-depth introduction to the Vedic spiritual knowledge, and to get you started in real spiritual understanding, this is the book!

The topics include: What is your real spiritual identity; the Vedic explanation of the soul; scientific evidence that consciousness is separate from but interacts with the body; the real unity between us all; how to attain the highest happiness and freedom from the cause of suffering; the law of karma and reincarnation; the karma of a nation; where you are really going in life; the real process of progressive evolution; life after death--heaven, hell, or beyond; a description of the spiritual realm; the nature of the Absolute Truth--personal God or impersonal force; recognizing the existence of the Supreme; the reason why we exist at all; and much more. This book provides the answers to questions not found in other religions or philosophies, and condenses information from a wide variety of sources that would take a person years to assemble. It also contains many quotations from the Vedic texts to let the texts speak for themselves, and to show the knowledge the Vedas have held for thousands of years. It also explains the history and origins of the Vedic literature. This book has been called one of the best reviews of Eastern philosophy available.

There is also a special section on traveling to the major historical holy sites of South India with over 75 photographs of art work, sculptures, deities, architecture, and some of the most amazing temples you will see anywhere. This section elaborates on the many ancient legends connected with these important places and what it is like to travel and see them today.

To get your copy, order it from your local bookstore (ISBN:0-9617410-1-5), or simply send $14.95, plus $2.50 for postage and handling ($7.50 for overseas orders) to:

The World Relief Network, P. O. Box 15082, Detroit, Michigan, 48215-0082, U. S. A.

Much rare information is also found in Volume Two:

The Universal Path to Enlightenment

Although all religions and spiritual processes are meant to lead you toward enlightenment, they are not all the same in regard to the methods they teach, nor in the level of philosophical understanding they offer. So an intelligent person will make comparisons between them to understand the aims and distinctions of each religion, and which is the most elevating. This book presents a most interesting and revealing survey of the major spiritual paths of the world and describes their origins, histories, philosophical basis, and goals. This book will help you decide which path may be the best to give you the highest levels of spiritual understanding, and see the similarities of all religions and spiritual paths.

You Will Discover

--the essential similarities of all religions that all people of any culture can practice, which would bring about a united world religion, or "THE UNIVERSAL PATH TO ENLIGHTENMENT."

--how Christianity and Judaism were greatly influenced by the early "pagan" religions and adopted many of their legends, holidays, and rituals that are still practiced today.

--about evidence that shows Jesus may have traveled to the East and learned spiritual knowledge, and then made bhakti-yoga the essence of his teachings.

--who were the real Vedic Aryans, the founders of the earliest of religions and organized cultures, and how widespread and influential their civilization was to other cultures, such as Egyptian, Greek, Oriental, etc., and how their Vedic teachings are still found in Christianity and other traditions today, which makes them the source of the world's spiritual heritage.

--the philosophical basis and origin of Christianity, Judaism, Islam, Hinduism, Buddhism, Zoroastrianism, Jainism, Sikhism, and many others.

--about the different yoga systems, such as raja-yoga, hatha-yoga, bhakti-yoga, mantra-yoga, etc., what their goals are, and how practical they are in this age.

--about the different mystic powers and experiences attained through yoga.

--what the qualifications are of a genuine spiritual teacher.

--the bliss and results of attaining spiritual enlightenment.

--and, most importantly, what is the real purpose of a spiritual path, and how to practice the path that is especially recommended as the easiest and most effective for the people of this age to attain real spiritual enlightenment.

There is also a special section on seeing spiritual India with a tour of the famous temples and holy places of Eastern India, with almost 100 photographs of a variety of sacred temples and towns where several of the major religions originated, and holy sites, art, sculptures, and people engaged in all aspects of life in India and Nepal.

To get your copy, see your local book store to order it (ISBN 0-9617410-2-3), or simply send $14.95, plus $2.50 for postage and handling ($7.50 for overseas orders) to: The World Relief Network, P. O. Box 15082, Detroit, Michigan, 48215-0082, U. S. A.

The Vedic Prophecies:
A New Look into the Future

The Vedic prophecies take you to the end of time! This is the first book ever to present the unique predictions found in the ancient Vedic texts of India. These prophecies are like no others and will provide you with a very different view of the future and how things fit together in the plan for the universe.

Now you can discover the amazing secrets that are hidden in the oldest spiritual writings on the planet. Find out what they say about the distant future, and what the seers of long ago saw in their visions of the destiny of the world.

This book will reveal predictions of deteriorating social changes and how to avoid them; future droughts and famines; low-class rulers and evil governments; whether there will be another appearance (second coming) of God; and predictions of a new spiritual awareness and how it will spread around the world. You will also learn the answers to such questions as:

- Does the future get worse or better?
- Will there be future world wars or global disasters?
- What lies beyond the predictions of Nostradamus, the Mayan prophecies, or the Biblical apocalypse?
- Are we in the end times? How to recognize them if we are.
- Does the world come to an end? If so, when and how?

Now you can find out what the future holds. The Vedic Prophecies carry an important message and warning for all humanity, which needs to be understood now!

There is also a special section on seeing spiritual India. This takes you through the famous temples and holy places of Western India, from Jaipur in Central India all the way to Bangalore in the South. Now you can tour them through their histories, legends, and miraculous stories, along with over 65 photographs of temples, holy sites, art, sculptures, sages and people of India. A wonderful addition!

To get your copy, order it from your bookstore (ISBN:0-9617410-4-X) or simply send $14.95 plus $2.50 for postage and handling ($3.50 for Canada, or $7.50 for overseas orders) to: The World Relief Network, P.O.Box 15082, Detroit, Michigan, 48215-0082, U.S.A.

How the Universe was Created And Our Purpose In It

This book provides answers and details about the process of creation that are not available in any other traditions, religions, or areas of science. It offers the oldest rendition of the creation and presents insights into the spiritual purpose of it and what we are really meant to do here.

Every culture in the world and most religions have their own descriptions of the creation, and ideas about from where we came and what we should do. Unfortunately, these are often short and generalized versions that lack details. Thus, they are often given no better regard than myths. However, there are descriptions that give more elaborate explanations of how the cosmic creation fully manifested which are found in the ancient Vedic *Puranas* of India, some of the oldest spiritual writings on the planet. These descriptions provide the details and answers that other versions leave out. Furthermore, these Vedic descriptions often agree, and sometimes disagree, with the modern scientific theories of creation, and offer some factors that science has yet to consider.

Now, with this book, we can get a clearer understanding of how this universe appears, what is its real purpose, from where we really came, how we fit into the plan for the universe, and if there is a way out. Some of the many topics included are:

- Comparisons between other creation legends.
- Detailed descriptions of the dawn of creation and how the material energy developed and caused the formation of the cosmos.
- What is the primary source of the material and spiritual elements.
- Insights into the primal questions of, "Who am I? Why am I here? Where have I come from? What is the purpose of this universe and my life?"
- An alternative description of the evolutionary development of the various forms of life.
- Seeing beyond the temporary nature of the material worlds, and more.

This book will provide some of the most profound insights into these questions and topics. It will also give any theist more information and understanding about how the universe is indeed a creation of God.

To add a little more adventure, there is also a special travel section to the holy places of northern India as we venture into the Himalayas and elsewhere to some of the locations that are directly connected to the Vedic legends of the universal creation and ancient history. With this tour is included rare descriptions and over 70 photographs of temples and Deities, ancient holy sites, the Himalayas, as well as sages and people of the region.

Order your copy now! Published by The World Relief Network, P. O. Box 15082, Detroit, MI. 48215. Retail price, $14.95, plus $2.50 postage ($7.50 overseas surface mail). Or from your bookstore, ISBN: 0-9617410-8-2. 312 pages, 6"x 9."

Toward World Peace:
Seeing the Unity Between Us All

This book points out the essential reasons why peace in the world and cooperation amongst people, communities, and nations have been so difficult to establish. It also advises the only way real peace and harmony amongst humanity can be achieved.

In order for peace and unity to exist we must first realize what barriers and divisions keep us apart. Only then can we break through those barriers to see the unity that naturally exists between us all. Then, rather than focusing on our differences, it is easier to recognize our similarities and common goals. With a common goal established, all of humanity can work together to help each other reach that destiny.

This book is short and to the point. It is a thought provoking book and will provide inspiration for anyone. It is especially useful for those working in politics, religion, interfaith, race relations, the media, the United Nations, teaching, or who have a position of leadership in any capacity. It is also for those of us who simply want to spread the insights needed for bringing greater levels of peace, acceptance, unity, and equality between friends, neighbors, and communities. Such insights include:

- The factors that keep us apart.
- Breaking down cultural distinctions.
- Breaking down the religious differences.
- Seeing through bodily distinctions.
- We are all working to attain the same things.
- Our real identity: The basis for common ground.
- Seeing the Divinity within each of us.
- What we can do now to bring unity between everyone we meet.

This book carries an important message and plan of action that we must incorporate into our lives and plans for the future if we intend to ever bring peace and unity between us.

To get your copy, order it from your bookstore (ISBN:0-9617410-5-8), or send $5.95 plus $2.00 for postage and handling ($3.00 for Canada, $5.00 for overseas orders) to: The World Relief Network, P.O.Box 15082, Detroit, Michigan, 48215-0082, U.S.A.

Facing Death
Welcoming the Afterlife

Many people are afraid of death, or do not know how to prepare for it nor what to expect. So this book is provided to relieve anyone of the fear that often accompanies the thought of death, and to supply a means to more clearly understand the purpose of it and how we can use it to our advantage. It will also help the survivors of the departed souls to better understand what has happened and how to cope with it. Furthermore, it shows that death is not a tragedy, but a natural course of events meant to help us reach our destiny.

This book is easy to read, with soothing and comforting wisdom, along with stories of people who have been with departing souls and what they have experienced. It is written especially for those who have given death little thought beforehand, but now would like to have some preparedness for what may need to be done regarding the many levels of the experience and what might take place during this transition.

To assist you in preparing for your own death, or that of a loved one, you will find guidelines for making one's final days as peaceful and as smooth as possible, both physically and spiritually. Preparing for death, no matter what stage of life you are in, can transform your whole outlook in a positive way, if understood properly. This will make things clearer in regard to what matters most in this life, especially when you know the remainder of your life may be short. It is like looking into the Truth of yourself, and taking a pilgrimage to the edge of the spiritual dimension. Some of the topics in the book include:

- The fear of death and learning to let go.
- The opportunity of death: The portal into the next life.
- This earth and this body are no one's real home, so death is natural.
- Being practical and dealing with the final responsibilities.
- Forgiving yourself and others before you go.
- Being the assistant of one leaving this life.
- Connecting with the person inside the disease.
- Surviving the death of a loved one.
- Stories of being with dying, and an amazing near-death-experience.
- Connecting to the spiritual side of death.
- What happens while leaving the body.
- What difference the consciousness makes during death, and how to attain the best level of awareness to carry you through it.

So no matter whether you are afraid of death or concerned about surviving the death of a loved one, or are worried about those that you will leave behind if you depart, or what death will be like and how to prepare for it, this book will help you.

Order your copy today! Published by: The World Relief Network, P. O. Box 15082, Detroit, Michigan 48215-0082, or available through your local bookstore. ISBN: 0-9617410-7-4, trim size 5 ½" x 8 ½", 110 pages. Retail price: $6.95, plus $1.50 shipping ($5.50 for overseas surface mail).